EFFECTIVE COMMUNICATION
in the Business World

DAVINA CLARKE

Florida International University

Kendall Hunt

publishing company

Cover image © Shutterstock, Inc.

Kendall Hunt
p u b l i s h i n g   c o m p a n y

www.kendallhunt.com
Send all inquiries to:
4050 Westmark Drive
Dubuque, IA 52004-1840

CONTENTS

ABOUT THE AUTHOR

Dr. Davina Clarke is the course director for the Business courses at Florida International University. She teaches several business courses, including Advanced Communication for Business, Speech and Writing for Business, and Business and Professional Communication.

Dr. Clarke is a published author in *International Journal of Humanities and Social Sciences*. She appeared as a guest speaker in her local communities, and served as a chairperson for an undergraduate symposium. Her interests include Nonverbal Communication, Intercultural/Interracial Communication, and Conflict Management.

SECTION I

FOUNDATIONS OF BUSINESS COMMUNICATIONS

INTRODUCTION TO BUSINESS COMMUNICATION

1

LEARNING OUTCOMES

After reading this chapter, you should be able to:

1. Understand the importance of communication skills.

2. Identify the principles of communication.

3. Describe the elements in the model of communication.

4. Discuss communication in professional networks.

5. Provide reasons communication may fail.

6. Identify the characteristics of successful communicators.

© ImageFlow/Shutterstock.com

SELECT KEY TERMS

Communication skills
Culture
Verbal communication
Nonverbal communication

Listening
Formal network
Informal network

IMPORTANCE OF COMMUNICATION SKILLS

© REUTERS/Alamy Stock Photo

Most people may not be familiar with Howard Schultz, but just about everyone is familiar with Starbucks. Schultz has led Starbucks to the successful company it is today, and he has attributed his leadership success to **communication skills** he acquired at Northern Michigan University.[1] As Schultz remarked, "We're not in the coffee business serving people, but in the people business serving coffee."[2] The more you focus on the clients, the more likely you will tailor to their needs, and continue to grow as a business. As Schultz mentioned, businesses should be people-oriented.

Communication is vital to the success of any business.[3] In one study, "people skills" such as communication and **listening** were the important determinants in the longevity of up to 75% of businesses.[4] This may be attributed to the fact that we spend up to 90% of our day communicating with others.[5] Without effective communication skills, business can lose millions of dollars every single day in the form of wasted time, decline in customer loyalty, and lost business.[6] In 2009, one specific mid-size company spent 17 hours per week clarifying its communication, which costs $524,569 annually.[7] Effective communication is so important that a national survey of organizations show that inadequate oral/written skills would hinder prospective applicants from entering into the workplace.[8]

Jack Welch, former chairman of General Electric, said that he looked for people who were comfortable conversing with anyone in the world.[9] A survey from the National Association of Colleges and Employers (NACE) shows that employers rated the ability to work on a team, and written communications skills, and oral communication as some of the top qualities they look for in job candidates.[10] Another study showed that managers and executives valued oral communications, teamwork/collaboration, and professionalism/work ethic as very important job skills.[11] These communication skills are very important, especially during challenging economic times.[12]

ZOOM COMMUNICATION

© ymphotos/Shutterstock.com

We know all too well about challenging times since the upsurge of COVID-19 in 2020. It has changed the way we lived our lives, including the way we conduct business. In a matter of days many businesses allowed employees to work from home, and unfortunately, some employees were furloughed and some were laid off. It was quite a dramatic shift, but in light of all these changes, effective communication is still needed. Many organizations rely on the virtual meetings such as Zoom, and other similar sites to carry out work functions. Workers has to learn how to engage in effective communication skills such as managing one's appearance on camera, being mindful of background interferences, and adjusting the settings for optimal communication.

There are several benefits of effective communication skills in the workplace, including good employee relations, good customer–client relations, and generating income. Due to the extensive benefits of effective communication, it is important to have an understanding of the principles of communication, examine the communication model, and explore how to improve its processes in professional settings.

PRINCIPLES OF COMMUNICATION

COMMUNICATION IS GOVERNED BY RULES

Communication has both implicit and explicit rules. Implicit rules are guided by the context, and are not expressed overtly; whereas explicit rules are clearly articulated. If you notice that people motion to speak before stating their opinion during a meeting, then you will start putting this implicit rule into practice. However, if your supervisor tells you that your break time is 30 minutes, then an explicit rule was stated.

COMMUNICATION IS NECESSARY

We use communication to help us to meet our *relational needs*. We would not be able to meet our personal and professional relationship without communication.[13] Even if you are unable to hear the verbal message, you can still communicate nonverbally to meet those needs. Communication also allows us to meet our *identity needs* as we are able to choose how we want to present ourselves to others.[14] This may mean dressing formally and using formal language to convey our professionalism on the job, or using informal language to express our relaxed nature when meeting after lunch. We also use communication to fulfill our *informational needs* as we get and share information with others.[15]

COMMUNICATION IS BOTH VERBAL AND NONVERBAL

Verbal communication means using words to send messages, which includes spoken words, written words, and sign language. **Nonverbal communication** includes communication without the use of words, including gestures, body movement, facial expression, how we dress, use time and space, and so on. The way your work station is set up communicates status, and your style.

COMMUNICATION HAS CONTENT AND RELATIONAL DIMENSIONS

The content is the actual information that is communicated. For example, if your supervisor says, "I need this report by tomorrow," then the statement reveals the content. *How* the message is communicated gives insight into the relationship that exists between the speaker and listener. If the message is communicated in a stern voice, then it shows that the supervisor is exerting his [or her] authority.

PEOPLE GIVE COMMUNICATION ITS MEANING

Words and gestures do not have meaning unless people assign meaning to them. A word may have one meaning in one cultural context, but has a completely different meaning in a different **culture**. For example, elevators are called "lifts" in England. Meanings in nonverbal communication may also vary from one cultural context to another. For example, the "okay" gesture in the United States, means "you're worth nothing" in some areas in France.

MODEL OF BUSINESS COMMUNICATION

Communication can occur using both verbal and nonverbal communication. Verbal communication involves using language, which is a set of symbols and rules that allows us to understand each other. Nonverbal communication includes facial expression, gestures, body movement, attire, use of space, and use of time. In order to have a better understanding of what communication entails, let's explore its core elements: context, speaker, channel, message, noise, listener, and feedback.

MODEL OF COMMUNICATION

Image © VLADGRIN/Shutterstock.com

CONTEXT

Communication occurs in a context. It is the setting where communication takes place, and includes the physical context, chronological context, cultural context, and social context. The physical context is the actual place where communication occurs, such as the boardroom, office, hallway, and conference room. The chronological context refers to the time/date when communication takes place, for example, after lunch, or during downturn of business cycle. The cultural context refers to the ethnic or organizational background of the individuals in the communication process. Finally, the social context refers to the history of the interpersonal connection between the employees. This includes whether there are age differences or similarities, personality conflicts or harmonies, or out-of-office relationships. All four contexts affect the tone and the type of message that should be delivered. For example, communication in the boardroom will take on a different tone from communication by the water cooler.

SPEAKER

Communication begins with the speaker, who is the source of the message. The process of creating the message is called encoding. In order for the speaker to be effective, she or he needs to anticipate the needs of the listeners and understand their socio/cultural backgrounds. Individuals from different sociocultural backgrounds may interpret messages differently from what the speaker intended. For this reason, it is more effective to use words that are easily understood. For example, instead of saying, "This is just off the top of my head" say, "Here's a quick idea." Instead of saying, "Don't let him get to you" say, "Don't let him upset you." Non-English speaker may misinterpret the message if it is not expressed clearly.

CHANNEL

The channel is the means through which we communicate a message, for example, face-to-face, email, and so on. Synchronous communication means that the communication is occurring in real time, for example, face-to-face interaction, online chat sessions, video conferencing, and phone calls. Asynchronous communication means that the communication is not occurring in real time, which means there may be a delay in the feedback. Letters, memos, emails, and faxes are examples of asynchronous communication.

CHOOSING THE RIGHT CHANNEL

© PopTika/Shutterstock.com

How do you know whether you should email, meet face-to-face, or use another form of channel? The answer depends on the purpose of communication. Draft and Lengel proposed the media-richness theory, which places communication channels on a continuum from rich to lean. The more the media engages more sensory stimulation, the richer the medium. For example, face-to-face is richer than an email. Media-rich channels allows instant feedback, and more personal approach.

If your message is important to others, may be misunderstood, or has highly sensitive information, then face-to-face communication is best. On the other hand, if your communication is routine, simple, noncontroversial, or directed toward a mass audience, then sending an email or other media-lean channel is acceptable.

Consider the following scenarios. Which channel is best for each situation:
- Solving a problem as a team.
- Reminder about weekly staff meeting.
- Resolving a conflict between two coworkers.
- Distribute meeting minutes.

MESSAGE

The message is the information that is transmitted by the sender, and may consist of both verbal and nonverbal communication, or it may be solely nonverbal. There are two aspects of a message: the first is the content and the second is the relational dimension. The content refers to the *what* of a message, whereas the relational dimension refers to *how* the message is transmitted. The *what* communicates information, whereas the *how* communicates emotions, power differences, and attitudes between the communicators. For example, someone may say "I am glad to see you," but if there is no inflection in the person's voice and the facial expression is dull, then the other person may interpret that the message is not sincere. Nonverbal communication plays a significant role in the interpretation of the message.

LISTENER

The listener is the recipient of the message, whether or not they were the speaker's intended target. The process of interpreting or assigning meaning to the message is called decoding. When a message is received by someone else besides the intended recipient, this may be problematic, particularly if a breach of information is involved. Examples include if papers with confidential information is left on the copy machine, email is addressed to the wrong recipient, or hackers target information.

FEEDBACK

The response provided from the listener is called feedback. The more specific the feedback is, the more likely the speaker can confirm that the message was understood as intended. In the event that the message was misunderstood, the speaker can try to express the information differently, or offer examples. For example, if an employee asked a colleague for a copy of the report, the colleague may ask a question to ensure that the correct report will be copied.

NOISE

Communication is never as simple as sending and receiving messages as oftentimes there are barriers to effective communication. Anything that interferes with the processing of the message is referred to as noise. There are different types of noise: internal and external. External noise are distracting sounds in the physical environment, for example, a ringing phone, another conversation, or fax machine. Internal noise occurs within the individual and may include psychological noise such as bias and prejudice, or it may include physiological noise such as a headache. Psychological noise interferes with our ability to process the message based on how we think, whereas physiological noise affects the way we process the message based on the physical state of our body. Noise may occur at any time during the communication process. Regardless of the form that noise takes, it often prevents us from processing the message the way the speaker intended.

COMMUNICATION IN PROFESSIONAL NETWORKS

In the business environment, there are both formal and informal networks. In the **formal network**, information flows in four directions. Downward communication flows from top management to middle management to frontline workers as information, upward communication flows in the opposite direction, from frontline workers, to middle management, then to top management. In horizontal/lateral communication, information is given among peers or colleagues with equal positions in the organization, and diagonal communication crosses departmental lines while moving up or down.

The degree of formality is based on the size of the organization, its culture, and the relationships established within the organization. The more formal the structure, the more protocols, rules, and politeness is involved. Communication with external stakeholders and upper management tends to be more formal than communication within the organization, and among peers. As familiarity increases, formality typically decreases.

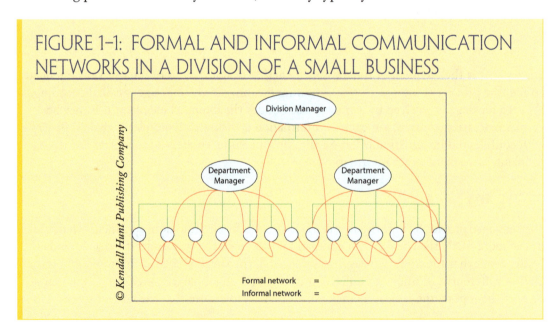

FIGURE 1-1: FORMAL AND INFORMAL COMMUNICATION NETWORKS IN A DIVISION OF A SMALL BUSINESS

© Kendall Hunt Publishing Company

Division Manager

Department Manager

Department Manager

Formal network   =   ⎯⎯⎯
Informal network   =   ∿∿∿

In **informal networks**, connections are voluntary, such as the relationships established with coworkers. These networks form a complex set of relationship of smaller networks of certain group members, with no typical structure or set pattern. These networks are often referred to as the *grapevine*. Information can be quickly moved along, including gossip and rumors. It is best to be careful about what you share so that you do not hurt your professional image. These types of relationships may also be useful for informal mentoring and training.

REASONS COMMUNICATION MAY FAIL

As you communicate with others in these professional networks, it is important to manage the impressions you form. One way to do this is to avoid ineffective communication. Let's look at some of the reasons communication may fail:

POOR TIMING

Timing is key. If business reports are sent too late, or if a meeting is poorly timed, then the information loses value as the necessary changes cannot be implemented. This can result in the loss of profits or loss of other opportunities.

INSUFFICIENT INFORMATION

In some cases, employers withhold information from the employees to avoid information overload. However, the omission of information may prevent the employees from working to their best potential.

INFORMATION OVERLOAD

On the other hand, sometimes too much information is disclosed. When managers are not sure about the information that should be provided, some may provide too much information and overwhelm the employees.

POOR-QUALITY INFORMATION

When information is ambiguous, disorganized, outdated, or erroneous the message cannot be interpreted correctly. In addition, the credibility of the individual and the organization is negatively affected.

LACK OF FEEDBACK

Feedback is a very important part of the communication process as it confirms that the message was received as intended, or it gives the speaker the opportunity to clarify the message. When no feedback is given, miscommunication can easily occur.

INAPPROPRIATE CHANNELS

Conveying a group message to individuals waste company's time and resources as the information could be conveyed by an email or during a meeting. On the other hand, highly personal and sensitive information should only be given privately in a face-to-face meeting, for example, dismissing someone from the job.

THE PROFESSIONAL COMMUNICATOR

© Pressmaster/Shutterstock.com

We know what professionals look like, and what is expected from them. Here are some characteristics of business professionals:

- Are mindful of their behavior.
- Listens and thinks before responding to others.
- Do not lose their temper.
- Answers messages efficiently and appropriately.
- Go above the call of duty.
- Observe cell phone etiquette when in meetings.

What other behaviors do you expect professionals to display?

CHARACTERISTICS OF SUCCESSFUL COMMUNICATORS

Communication is not simply sending and receiving messages; rather, it is when shared meaning has occurred that communication takes place. Meanings are in people, not in words.[16] People's backgrounds, experiences, and roles influence how a message is created and interpreted. This means that the successful communicator must be mindful of the context, and any other factor that may shape the meaning of the message.

BE INTENTIONAL ABOUT COMMUNICATING

Successful communicators are aware of the messages they send in social situations. They must mindful about what they say and how they say it, rather than carelessly say something they might later regret. In addition, they monitor their nonverbal responses as these are powerful indicators of their emotions. If someone is experiencing negative emotions, for example, anger or sadness, they should be especially mindful of their actions during that emotional state as irrational behavior could lower their credibility.

Being intentional also requires that speakers be aware of who their listeners are, and tailor the message to them. Communicating to senior executives will take a different approach from communicating to entry-level employees. It important to also be aware of your own thoughts, assumptions, and behaviors. Choose words carefully, and use nonverbal communication to complement the message you are sending.

When people are mindful of their actions and what they communicate based on the context, they are high self-monitors. On the other hand, low self-monitors do not think about the impressions they make, nor do they try to adapt their behaviors.

THE COMPETENT COMMUNICATOR

Take the assessment at the following link and add up your score once done.

https://mypages.valdosta.edu/mwhatley/7670/activity/sm.htm

High Score: 15–22

Intermediate Score: 9–14

Low Score: 0–8

USE EFFECTIVE LISTENING SKILLS

Active listening is needed in order to accurately interpret messages. This means that speakers should listen for the main ideas, and use nonverbal cues to help to understand the message. In additional to listening intentionally, paraphrasing is an important skill to use to check understanding. Paraphrase means that the speaker should restate the listener's ideas in his or her own words to verify that the message is understood.

RESPOND APPROPRIATELY

Understanding the expectations and rules when you are in a professional environment will help you to know how to respond appropriately. Successful communicators also strive to respond ethically to any situation encountered. Ethics is referred to as the moral code that guides our actions.

Addressing situations in a timely fashion, showing sensitivity, and managing conflicts are some of the responsibilities of a successful communicator. It is important to be mindful of expectations in other cultures as customs that may be acceptable in one culture, may be unacceptable in another.

OVERVIEW OF TEXTBOOK

This textbook is designed to enhance the written and spoken communication skills in the professional environment. The first section of the book focuses on the interpersonal aspect of communication in professional environments, and includes business etiquette, verbal and nonverbal communication, interpersonal communication skills, and team communication. These aspects of communication provide the foundation of business communication.

The second section of the book covers business communication technology including social media. The third section focuses on business writing. This includes the preparation of memos, which are typically used for internal communication and letters, which are typically used for external communication. In addition to chapter covers writing business reports and proposals. While the previous section focused on written communication skills, section four focuses on business presentations, including how to develop, deliver, and integrate visual aid effectively.

As we live in a global economy, it is imperative to have an understanding of culture in business communication. Each chapter is written with this perspective in mind to help to prepare the readers to be able to adapt to any communication environment.

Notes

1. Schultz, H. (1997). *Pour Your Heart into It*. New York, NY: Hyperion.

2. Read, C. We're in the People Business. Retrieved from https://readthinkact.com/were-in-the-people-business/

3. Robles, M. M. (2012). Executive perceptions of the top 10 soft skills needed in today's workplace. *Business Communication Quarterly, 75*, 453–465.

4. Klas, P. (2010). Communication breakdown. *California Job Journal, 28*, 1–9.

5. Emanuel, R., Adams, J., Baker, K., Daufin, E. K., Ellington, C., Fitts, E., . . . Okeowo, D. (2008). How college students spend their time communicating. *International Journal of Listening, 22*, 12–28.

6. Maggiani, R. (2014). The costs of poor communication. Retrieved from http://www.solari.net/documents/position-papers/Solari-Costs-of-Poor-Communication.pdf

7. SIS International Research. (2015, February 1). SMB communications pain study white paper: Uncovering the hidden cost of communications barriers and latency. Retrieved from https://www.sisinternational.com/smb-communications-pain-study-white-paper-uncovering-the-hidden-cost-of-communications-barriers-and-latency/

8. Casner-Lotto & Barrington. (2006, October). Are they really ready to work? Employers' perspectives on the basic knowledge and applied skills of new entrants to the 21st century U.S. workforce. *The Conference Board, Partnership for 21st Century Skills, Corporate Voices for Working Families, and Society for Human Resource Management*. Retrieved from http://wwww.conference-board.org/publications/describe.cfm?id=1218

9. Granville, N. T. (2010). *The new articulate executive: Look, act, and sound like a leader* (p. 3). New York, NY: McGraw-Hill.

10. National Association of College and Employers. (2015, November 18). Job Outlook 2016: Attributes employers want to see on new college graduates' resumes. *NACE*. Retrieved from http://www.naceweb.org/s11182015/employers-look-for-in-new-hires.aspx

11. The Conference Board, Corporate Voices for Working Families, the Partnership for 21st Century Skills, and the Society for Human Resource Management, "Are they ready to work? Employers' perspectives on the basic knowledge and applied skills of new entrants into the 21st century workforce," October 2, 2006, p. 21. Retrieved from http://www.p21.org/storage/documents/FINAL_REPORT_PDF09-29-06.pdf

12. Braud, G. (2009, March-April). Ready for the worst. *Communication World*, 48.

13. Hall, J. A., & Davis, D. C. (2017). Proposing the Communicate Bond Belong theory: Evolutionary intersections with episodic interpersonal communication. *Communication Theory, 27*, 21–47.

14. Sinigaglia, C., & Rizzolatti, G. (2011). Through the looking glass: Self and others. *Consciousness and Cognition, 20*, 64–74.

15. Kashian, N., & Walther, J. B. (2016). Does uncertainty reduction facilitate the perceptual disconfirmation of negative expectancies in computer-mediated communication? *Journal of Media Psychology, 30*, 139–149.

16. Beebe, S., & Mottet, T. (2010). *Business and professional communication: Principles and skills for leadership* (p. 4). Boston, MA: Pearson.

FIRST IMPRESSIONS AND BUSINESS ETIQUETTE

2

LEARNING OUTCOMES

After reading this chapter, you should be able to:

1. Describe the four major benefits of adhering to the rules and rituals of business etiquette.

2. Explain the difference between business etiquette and social etiquette.

3. Discuss the guiding principles of business etiquette.

4. Discuss the role of company culture on business etiquette.

5. Describe appropriate dress in today's business place.

6. Describe networking protocol.

© Keith Bell/Shutterstock.com

SELECT KEY TERMS

INTRODUCTION

Business etiquette refers to sets of suggested rules that guide how we interact with each other in the business place. Such rules vary somewhat among organizations as well as globally. Some of the benefits of adhering to business etiquette rules include improved employee morale, improved workplace quality of life, a sharper company image, and higher profits. With the popularity and proliferation of Internet-based electronic communication within organizations, netiquette, including social media etiquette, are increasingly important. Respect for others and courtesy, for obvious reasons, are central to good business etiquette.

The intent of this chapter is to impress upon you how employees are expected to act in the business place. This goal is realized through discussions regarding the impact of business etiquette, business etiquette in the office, and business etiquette when conducting business outside of the office.

THE IMPACT OF BUSINESS ETIQUETTE

Business etiquette is defined as "a set of rules that guide how we interact with each other in the business place. Such rules make is possible for us to communicate and interact in a civilized manner."[1] Without rules of civil conduct, work teams can become dysfunctional, business relationships can become strained, office morale can diminish, and productivity can decrease.[2]

> **business etiquette**
> Sets of proposed rules guiding how we interact with each other in the business place.

The ability to communicate effectively and interact in a appropriate manner in today's diverse workplace is essential. Bad behavior in the professional workplace, in turn, can easily result in lawsuits and loss of business. Burgeoning litigation is one result of a workforce that is continuously adjusting to major changes in its composition.

One initiative that the business community is taking to avoid these hazards is to push for the return of etiquette and manners to the workplace. Many businesses have hired etiquette trainers to teach workshops on etiquette to their employees. Training in business etiquette is really behavioral training on consideration for others.[3] These businesses see considerable benefits in adhering to the rules and rituals of business etiquette. These benefits range from improved employee morale and lower employee turnover to higher productivity and improved public relations.

Knowing global business etiquette can also save you from many embarrassing situations when conducting business internationally. Besides, it provides a wonderful opportunity to learn about what others value and, in turn, show respect for your international business partners. Figure 2-1 contains some helpful global business etiquette reminders.

FIGURE 2–1: SAMPLE GLOBAL BUSINESS ETIQUETTE REMINDERS

While businesspeople around the world are similar in regard to some of their preferences, be careful not to assume they share all of your preferences. Here are some examples of some of our similarities and differences. Additional examples will be mentioned throughout the chapter.

- **Greetings.** Greetings are certainly commonplace. In many countries this involves a handshake. For example, in the United States a handshake is part of a standard greeting. The same is true in Guatemala when greeting a male. However, shaking hands with a Guatemalan woman is done only at her discretion.
- **Gift Giving.** While gift giving may be thought to be a simple process, there is plenty of room for offending your international business partner if you do not learn ahead of time what is acceptable and what is not. For example, recommended gifts for Hungarian business partners include alcohol and flowers. In contrast, you would not want to give your Malaysian counterpart alcohol as a gift since it is prohibited to practicing Muslims.
- **Punctuality.** Being punctual for all appointments, including meetings, is common in most countries. This is especially true in Germany and New Zealand. In contrast, punctuality is not strictly observed in Nicaragua. It is admired, however.
- **Dress.** While conservative, formal business dress (e.g., suit, tie, jacket, skirt, conservative dress) is the expectation in most countries, there are exceptions. For example, in Italy business attire should be elegant and fashionable. Furthermore, in Middle Eastern countries such as Kuwait, where modesty is highly valued, choose clothing that covers most of your body.

Practicing good business etiquette is a mainstay of professionalism. Some people believe that once they earn a college degree they are a professional. What determines if a person is a professional, instead, is how he or she conducts him or herself in professional working settings—not a college degree in hand. Thus, if we want to truly call ourselves professionals, we must walk the walk which involves being courteous, respectful, and civil with others in the workplace.

FIGURE 2-2: HAS SAYING THANK YOU BECOME A CLICHÉ?

This may sound like a silly question, but it is a question worth exploring. Saying thank you is a sign of courtesy, which is certainly an element of good business etiquette. However, there are many instances when these two simple words—thank you—go unmentioned. In such cases, others often form poor perceptions of us. They can easily perceive us as being ungrateful, rude, inconsiderate, entitled, unprofessional, etc. Such perceptions can, in turn, negatively influence a host of important decisions in the professional business place ranging from bonus and pay raise decisions to promotion decisions. Even though extending a thank you is such a logical thing to do, some people simply don't. For example, have you ever held a door for someone else behind you as you entered a building or room only to have them march through without saying thank you? Possibly this same thing has happened to you when you extended the common courtesy of holding an elevator door for another person to board only to be ignored. Or, someone e-mailed you asking you to do something for him or her which you then did but a thank you did not follow in any form be it an e-mail reply, a phone call, or a text message.

© karen roach/Shutterstock.com

Then, there is the matter of those who either believe they, and the rest of us for that matter, are too busy today to take the time to extend a thank you and/or believe "thank you" is cliché. Fortunately, I have not met a lot of people who share these viewpoints, but have met enough of them to get my attention. Where do you stand on such viewpoints? Hopefully you still believe in the need for and power of saying thank you. In the professional business world job stability and career growth are dependent, in large part, on good interpersonal skills (people skills), and your willingness to extend the two simple words "thank you" can go a long way in helping you achieve both.

This chapter covers the dos and don'ts of acceptable behavior in the workplace. First we will explore business etiquette in the office and then move on to business etiquette outside the office.

SUMMARY: SECTION 1— THE IMPACT OF BUSINESS ETIQUETTE

- Business etiquette is defined as a set of rules that allow us to communicate and interact in a civilized manner.
- Rudeness is on the rise, including in the workplace.
- Bad behavior in the workplace often results in lawsuits and loss of business.
- Some benefits of adhering to the rules and rituals of business etiquette include an increase in employee morale, an improved quality of life in the workplace, a sharper company image, and higher profits.
- Business etiquette expectations vary extensively around the globe. It is both necessary and respectful to learn and practice what your global business partners' value.

BUSINESS ETIQUETTE AT THE OFFICE

Business etiquette basics are simple, according to Hilka Klinkenberg, director of Etiquette International. The first general principle is the differences between business etiquette and social etiquette. Social etiquette is based on chivalry, a code based on the dated notion that women need protection. In contrast, business etiquette has its origins in the military code of etiquette, which is based on hierarchy and power. Business etiquette, then, is based on rank, or the pecking order, not on gender.

Business etiquette's first guiding principle is to treat people according to rank rather than gender. Men and women are peers in the workplace. If you are a man, you should hold open a door for a woman if you would hold it open for a man in the same circumstance.[4] The general rule is: Whoever reaches the door first, opens it. Whether you are a man or a woman, doors are held open for superiors, clients, and those who have their arms full of folders and packages. If it's a revolving door, you enter first to get it moving and then wait on the other side as your group files through.

FIGURE 2–3: HOLDING THE DOOR

Here are three general rules for holding doors:

1. Junior ranking people should open and hold doors for senior ranking people.
2. Doors should be opened and held for customers and clients.
3. Assistance should be offered to persons with a disability.[5]

Another instance of deciding who goes first is when exiting an elevator. Unless a woman happens to be your CEO or your client, whoever is closest to the door exits first, regardless of gender. A man who treats a woman in a chivalrous manner may be perceived as condescending. This perception can create a workplace climate of hostility. Many women believe that they cannot be perceived as equal if they are treated chivalrously.[6]

Professionals with disabilities should be treated with the same courtesy that you would afford any other business professional. When in doubt about how or whether to accommodate someone's physical needs, ask the person what he or she prefers rather than evade the situation. The main thing is to be yourself, and act as you would around anyone else.[7]

The second guiding principle of business etiquette is to always treat people with consideration and respect. This seems simple enough, but basic consideration of others seems to be lacking in today's workplace. The return of the Golden Rule to business means that you should treat everyone as you would like to be treated.[8]

MASTERING THE FINE ART OF INTRODUCTIONS

Introductions are a given in our business lives. The most important rule when making business introductions is to make them—even if you do not remember all the rules or all the names involved. The second most important rule is that business introductions are based on rank rather than gender. Therefore, you should always introduce the person of lesser rank to the person of greater rank, stating the name of the person of greater rank first, like this: "Ms. or Mr. Person of Greater Rank, I would like to introduce you to Ms. or Mr. Person of Lesser Rank."[9] Remember to look at each person as you say his or her name.

Remember that the person who outranks every person in your organization is the client. If a client is involved, always introduce the client first, even if the client holds a lesser position than the top executive in your firm.[10] Most executives prefer that the client be given the position of greatest importance in introductions.[11]

The best way to introduce two people is to make eye contact with the person who needs the information, not with the person whose name you are saying.[12] That way each person clearly hears the name of the other person.

One final tip when making introductions: Introduce people with thoughtful details, like this: "Ms. or Ms. Person of Greater Rank, meet Mr. or Ms. Person of Lesser Rank. Ms. Greater Rank is our executive vice president in charge of accounts. Mr. Lesser Rank is my colleague and works in the art department." By revealing a few details about each person, you will have helped to spark a short conversation between the two people when you leave them.

> **introductions** How people greet each other in the business place.

SHAKING HANDS

The basic component of the introduction is the handshake. Handshakes communicate friendliness and respect for the other person. In the business world, men and women in the United States should shake hands, rather than kiss or hug, as in some other countries.

Shaking hands may seem elementary, but since you are judged by the quality of your handshake, the following list presents a few pointers to help you achieve that perfect "handshake."

© Rawpixel.com/Shutterstock.com

- Keep fingers together and meet the web of your hand—the skin between the thumb and forefinger—with the web of the hand of other person.
- Shake hands firmly but without crushing the other person's hand. Usually a handshake lasts about three seconds and may be pumped once or twice from the elbow with a combined upward/downward movement of approximately 12 inches.
- Make eye contact with the other person throughout the introduction.
- Release after the handshake, even if the introduction continues.
- When someone extends a left hand—perhaps because the right is impaired—shake hands as best you can, maybe from the side of the hand.[13]
- Stand and shake hands when being introduced, no matter what the status of the person.
- Shake hands when meeting someone for the first time, when greeting someone you know, and for all good-byes.
- At cocktail parties, if you are drinking, keep your drink in your left hand to avoid a wet handshake.[14]

When being introduced to another person, remember to make eye contact with that person, shake hands, and repeat the person's name: "Hello, Ms. X" or "Nice to meet you, Ms. X." Repeating the person's name (1) helps you remember it and (2) gives the other person a chance to correct you if you are mispronouncing his or her name. In addition, never assume that you can use someone's first name. Always use their title—Mr./Ms./Dr./etc.—before their last name. If people want you to use their first name, they will tell you: "Please, call me Charles."[15] Your politeness and respect by using their last name will be appreciated. Once you have been introduced, say a few words, like, "It was nice to meet you," before walking away.

If you join a group of people who know each other well, no one may make the effort to introduce you. In a situation like this, wait for a pause in the conversation and introduce yourself.[16] If you are seated next to someone at a table and no one introduces you, introduce yourself briefly and make a comment. The person then may or may not choose to have a conversation with you.[17]

MAKING GROUP INTRODUCTIONS

When you must introduce one or more people to a group of five or more, state the name of the new person(s), and then ask the people in the group to introduce themselves. On the other hand, if you are dining at a restaurant and a group of people stops by your table to say hello, you do not need to introduce them to everyone at your table unless they stay for a while.

REMEMBERING NAMES

We have all forgotten someone's name during an introduction at one time or another. The embarrassment of forgetting a name can be so great that we paralyze our memories, which makes recalling the name almost impossible. If this happens to you, try one of the following techniques before you admit that you have gone totally blank.

Shake hands and introduce yourself to the other person, even if you believe the person remembers you: "Hello, I'm Jan Huff from PWC" or "Hello, I'm Jan Huff. Remember, I met you last year at the graphic artists' convention in San Francisco."[18] If this works, the person will respond with his or her full name. Giving your name first will spare him or her the embarrassment of not remembering your name. You would not want to prolong some-one's embarrassment by making a joke of it, like "Ha, I knew you didn't remember me. I'll give you a hint: My name begins with S."

If you cannot remember the person's name, admit that you cannot remember by saying something self-deprecating like, "I cannot even remember my own name today; what was yours again?" or "I'm terrible with names. Could you please tell me yours again?" As long as you do not make it sound as though it is their fault for your forgetfulness—"You must not have made a very big impression on me because …"—then you will not offend anyone by asking. We have all been in that situation and know how it feels. To help improve your memory for names, look over the tips provided in Figure 2-4. You might find just the thing to help you remember.

FIGURE 2-4: SOME TRICKS FOR REMEMBERING NAMES

Use these hints to help you improve your memory for names:
- As you are introduced, concentrate on the name and the person rather than on yourself and what you will say next.
- Repeat the person's name when you say hello to them then keep repeating it in your mind.
- Imagine virtually writing the name on the person's forehead.
- Associate the name with something about the person's appearance or with a word that you associate with the name. For example, Ms. Green could remind you of green leaves or grass.
- Identify one or two standout features of the person such as their smile.

If you forget a person's name, go on with the introduction and admit that you have a terrible memory for names. Apologize but always perform the courtesy of making introductions.[19]

If you are introducing people and you go blank, say something like "I'm terrible with names. Would you all mind introducing yourselves?" Although this is not the best option for making introductions, it is definitely better than not making them at all.[20] The following list contains the most common mistakes in making introductions.
- Failing to introduce people.
- Remaining seated when meeting someone. Exceptions include when the other person is seated or when you are in a position that makes standing difficult. In that case, making an effort to rise is acceptable.
- Offering your fingers to someone rather than your hand.
- Failing to offer your hand in a business situation.[21]

LEARNING YOUR COMPANY'S CULTURE

Every company and organization has its culture. You have to be there to see, experience, and absorb it, but the faster you do, the greater your success will be.[22] The guiding rule for all employees in any workplace, no matter what their rank, is the Golden Rule: Always treat everyone with the same consideration and respect that you expect. In other words, remember to be polite and kind at all times. The following examples of polite behavior will improve your chances of successfully adapting to nearly any company culture.

- Make liberal use of words and phrases such as "Please," "Thank you," "I appreciate that," and "Excuse me."
- Make it a priority to always greet coworkers in the morning and say good bye when leaving for the evening.
- Smile, even when you do not feel like it.

These basic rules of consideration for others should be observed no matter what the level of formality at your workplace.

ADDRESSING OTHERS

Company culture dictates when you should use courtesy titles when addressing all other employees, regardless of rank. However, even if you work in an informal office where all employees, up and down the corporate ladder, call each other by their first names, when introducing your boss, peers, or subordinates to outsiders, use their full name or their title and last name as a courtesy. For example, if you were introducing your office receptionist to your client, you would say, "Meet Mr. Mahoney" or "Meet Mike Mahoney," not "Meet Mike." Of course, calling assistants "your boy" or "your girl" is definitely inappropriate.

INTERACTING WITH PEERS

Offices are made up of all types of people, people with whom you will spend more time than with your own family. While you do not want to be overly familiar with peers, you will soon find that it is hard to avoid getting pulled into the latest office gossip or argument. As you meet your coworkers, you will find that some people thrive on creating upset and contention, while others keep completely to themselves. Both extremes are dangerous. Learning to negotiate the thorny world of office politics is part of being successful in the workplace.

First, mastering the art of small talk is essential and an important part of building business relationships.[23] Whether you are waiting to use the copier, getting a cup of coffee, or waiting for a meeting to begin, chatting with coworkers is how you get to see their personalities and how they get to see yours. Being easy to talk to is something that is to your advantage in the workplace. Here are a few tips on making small talk.

- Avoid inflammatory, indiscreet, malicious, or derogatory topics.
- Be aware of the other person's receptiveness when you are initiating small talk. If the other person seems distracted or does not respond, take the hint and leave the chat for another time.[24]
- Whatever the subject, avoid dominating the conversation. Ask questions to get others involved. Listen carefully when others are talking, and respond with comments that show you are listening and that you have a genuine interest in others' opinions. Remember to ask people about themselves.
- When you are having a conversation, try not to let it drag on. Small talk should not get in the way of business.
- If you are talking in a hallway, move to the side to let others pass by. Also, be aware of the volume of your conversation and what effect it is having on those around you. If coworkers appear bothered or distracted by your conversation, move the conversation elsewhere.

- Keep up with what's going on in the outside world. This gives you more to talk about than the latest copy machine breakdown. On the other hand, avoid touchy subjects like religion or politics—if you know your coworker gets really heated about the subject—and personal issues such as people's weight, the state of marriage, and sexual topics.
- Be agreeable; be a good listener.
- To end small talk, leave on a positive note and only after you have made a closing statement. A comment like "Well, great talking to you, but I've got to get to that report now," makes a smooth transition back to work.
- If a coworker interrupts you at a bad time, make it clear that you're busy but that you'll touch base later. If you interrupt someone at a bad time, do not be offended if the person cannot stop to talk. Talk later when your coworker is available.

Second, be ready to deal with disagreements. Disagreements, even over minor details like keeping the coffee pot full, can balloon into full-fledged hostilities that divide offices, pitting coworkers against each other and forcing weaker coworkers to take sides. Needless to say, this kind of open hostility can taint the atmosphere of any office, making it uncomfortable to go to work each day. How should you handle this kind of situation when it happens to you?

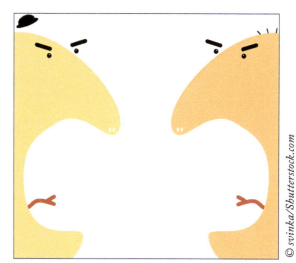

© svinka/Shutterstock.com

If the situation is not integral to the work process, like keeping the coffee pot full or the printer loaded with paper, handle squabbles in private. Usually, you will find that a problem peer—the gossip, the victim, or the backstabber (see below for a discussion of these personality types)—is behind the hostilities and divisiveness. In these situations, try to be the mediator: Ferret out the facts that underlie the argument, be objective, and get to the heart of the problem. Listen carefully to all sides, then confront the parties involved with a compromise or solution. Others will quickly identify you as a truthful and trustworthy person who can cut through others' anger, petty jealousies, and frustrations. Your coworkers will open up and be truthful with you. If you do this a couple of times, you will quickly adopt the role of office mediator, a star employee in any office.

On the other hand, if the disagreement is integral to the work process—you favor one solution but someone else favors another—do not avoid confrontation; but avoid making it personal. Focus on the pros and cons of the argument. State your side calmly and objectively, and back it up with facts and figures. Avoid getting into a shouting match or name calling. If hostilities reach this level, it is best to call a truce and meet at another time after both parties have cooled off. If you win the argument, avoid gloating over it; if you lose, be gracious, rather than spiteful. For example, "John really knows his stuff" is more gracious than "John really knows his stuff, but he is still a jerk."

Another common office problem is gossip. Gossip is rampant in all offices. Whether it's called the grapevine, the dish, or the buzz, gossip happens wherever people spend lots of time together. Natural subjects for gossip include work-related topics, such as what is going to happen at the next meeting, who is being promoted and why, who is being fired, and in what direction management will choose to go next. Personal gossip is often malignant, whether intentional or not. Handling gossip and rumors, when they are directed toward you, is another matter.[25]

Anything you reveal about yourself, whether public or private, can make you the subject of office gossip. Refusing to reply to gossip or giving vague answers can be fodder for the gossip mill. When you believe you have become the subject of a potentially destructive rumor, try to uncover the source. Usually a close friend will name the source if you promise confidentiality. Then, in private, confront the person who started the rumor. Be concerned, not angry or confrontational: "Michael, I hear you told a couple of people that I'm looking for a new job and that I've been meeting with a headhunter. The truth is that I had lunch last week with my old college roommate, and he happens to work for an employment firm. But I am not looking for a job, and that story could really cause me a lot of trouble here."[26] Even if the gossiper denies everything, she or he will be stung by your direct approach and think twice before gossiping about you again.[27]

Gossiping cuts both ways. If you sit and listen to gossip and add a comment now and then, you are as much to blame as anyone. Gossiping can hurt your professional reputation. You never know who is friendly with whom, so remember that participating in gossip can backfire on you. Most important, remember that anything you reveal about your personal life, even in the strictest confidence, can and probably will make its way to someone else. Do not be surprised if your supervisor finds out about something that you thought you revealed strictly on the quiet and asks you about it, especially if for some reason the supervisor senses your work has lately been below par. The best way to handle gossip is to leave the room when people begin to gossip about someone else. You do not have to jump up and stalk out, simply say you have loads of work waiting and leave. You never know when one of your coworkers will end up being your supervisor, so it's best to treat everyone in a friendly, polite way and avoid gossiping as much as possible.

Every office has certain coworkers whom you should watch out for. These people are not usually innately hateful; however, they can make your life miserable if you do not know how to handle them.

<table>
<tr><td valign="top">

backstabber
  Someone who will turn on coworkers if it is to his or her benefit.

tattletale
  Someone who willingly divulges something that should be held in confidence to another.

victim
  Someone who is a pessimist and a chronic complainer.

</td><td valign="top">

- **The Backstabber.** The professional backstabbers are difficult to detect. They know their game well and always cover their tracks. These people may well be the most genuinely charming people you know; however, their charm masks a lack of human feeling. Backstabbers will turn on a coworker in an instant if it is to their benefit. The best way to deal with the backstabbers is to be friendly, watch your back, and scrupulously document all your office activities.
- **The Tattletale.** The tattletale is a less malicious version of the backstabber. This person loves a good story and will happily divulge any confidence to a willing listener. If you trace a rumor to its source, that source is often a tattletale. This person is not to be confused with the whistleblower, however, who reports genuine problems.[28]
- **The Victim.** The victim is the classic doomsayer and chronic complainer. This person blames management for his or her lack of advancement and trashes coworkers who have moved ahead. If the victim is a female, she may be quick to interpret innocent displays of friendliness from male coworkers as less than honorable.[29] The victim believes that management conspires against workers at all levels and disaster for all will occur any minute. The victim at his or her worst can taint the atmosphere of the entire office with groundless suspicions, accusations, and fears. The best way to combat the victim's statements is to counter them with provable facts that show these statements to be groundless.[30]

</td></tr>
</table>

- **The Sycophant.** This person flatters anyone who can advance his or her career, especially the boss for whom this person cannot seem to do enough. In addition, agreeing with everything the boss says is this person's forte, at least whenever the boss is within hearing distance. While this person may be annoying, the sycophant's maneuvers are blatantly obvious and usually become the butt of office jokes rather than posing a threat to anyone.

sycophant
Someone who flatters anyone who can advance his or her career.

In most instances, coworkers want as much as you do to make the office a comfortable, pleasant place to work. Figure 2-5 contains several tips on how to be a star coworker as opposed to a problem one.

FIGURE 2–5: RULES TO WORK BY

Here are six rules to follow to be a model coworker.

1. Be friendly and helpful to newcomers and temps. Coworkers who are new to the office, especially temporary workers, often feel on the outside. Offering them a helping hand, showing them where supplies are kept or where the coffee is can ease their transitions and make them feel at home.
2. Remember to give credit where credit is due and to not hog all the credit, especially for team efforts.
3. Try not to be a know-it-all, especially around the boss.
4. Keep personal problems private unless you want to the entire office, including your supervisor, to know about them.
5. Accept responsibility. If it is your fault or partially your fault when something goes wrong, say so. Don't point fingers at others and blame them instead.
6. Stay away from gossip, and do not spread gossip yourself.
7. Being a top employee who moves easily up the corporate ladder means being an ethical employee. The tips in Figure 2-6 offer advice on taking workplace ethics seriously.

INTERACTING WITH SUBORDINATES

When dealing with employees in subordinate positions, avoid abusing your rank. If company culture dictates, use courtesy titles—Mr., Ms., or Mrs.—even if everyone calls everyone else by first names. If you are introducing an employee in a subordinate position to someone from outside your office, use the employee's courtesy title rather than his or her first name. Also, if your assistant is much older than you are, you should use a courtesy title to show respect until the person tells you that using his or her first name is fine. Remember to say, "Thank you," often and with sincerity.

Do your best to avoid pulling rank. Some employees pull rank on subordinates to get them to do work that they themselves should have done but did not. These rank pullers quickly become known as slackers. For instance, if the receptionist has the photocopying machine in his or her office and is in charge of keeping it running smoothly, do not assume that he or she must also be available to do your photocopying. In most offices, each person does his or her own copying. If you have a large job and are up against a deadline, politely asking for help from coworkers who are not busy at the moment is not out of line. However, when you habitually impose on subordinates to help you out, you are quickly labeled as an office shirker and someone to be avoided.

© Jiang Dao Hua/Shutterstock.com

Often you will find yourself in the position of needing last-minute help with a project. If you have freely given help to others in a pinch, if they can, they will usually help you out. When you are willing to help, others will be willing to return the favor.

INTERACTING WITH SUPERVISORS

Whatever name they go by (boss, supervisor, manager, executive), bosses have bosses, too; even the CEO must report to the board of directors, and entrepreneurs must report to lenders and to their market. Bosses are responsible for their performance to everyone above them in the hierarchy, and they are also responsible for your performance.[32] They, like everyone else in business, have ambitions and fears, hopes and insecurities; in short, they are human, too.[33]

Here are two simple rules to follow when dealing with your boss:

1. Accept that the boss is in charge. Show your respect for your boss's decisions by not grumbling or groveling when taking and carrying out orders.
2. Do your job, and do it on time. Before you begin to take on extra tasks to please your boss, master your job and do it well.[34] Doing your job well is important in building a good relationship with your boss. Remember that your boss's job is to get the work done in the most productive and profitable manner.[35] When you do your job well and complete it on time, you look good and you make your boss look good.

GETTING THE MOST OUT OF YOUR RELATIONSHIP WITH YOUR BOSS

Whether you like it or not, your boss is your superior. In that role, he or she deserves your respect, and it is your responsibility to get along with this person. Some people do not like to be in a subordinate role. They react either with extreme obsequiousness or masked hostility. Neither emotion will win you any points. Bosses do not want yes-types, nor do they want someone who will argue with their every decision or badmouth them behind their backs. In general, showing respect means "respecting the boss's intelligence and experience" while offering up your own ideas when needed.[36] Here are some tips on how to establish and keep a good relationship with your boss:

- **Respect rank.** Respecting your boss's rank means to use your boss's preferred courtesy title—Mr., Ms., Mrs., Dr.—until he or she tells you to do otherwise, and to respect your boss's privacy. If you need to meet with your boss, call ahead to set up a convenient time, and knock before you enter his or her office. Then wait a moment so that he or she can tell you to sit down if you're going to need more than a minute or so of his or her time. Avoid barging in without first knocking.
- **Offer ideas when appropriate.** Most bosses appreciate fresh ideas from the people they supervise.[37]
- **Do your homework.** Be prepared with your supporting documents before you meet with the boss. Have copies made ahead of time to show you are organized. Be clear and concise when presenting your ideas.
- **Be on the lookout for problems you can solve.** Supervisors like employees who show initiative.
- **Ask for help.** When you need help, do not hesitate to ask for it. It shows that you recognize the boss's knowledge and experience.
- **When you do not know, it is ok to say so.** Trying to make up answers, or answer questions about which you know nothing can get you in trouble and label you as untrustworthy. Instead, offer to find out, and make sure you get the answers in a timely manner.[38]

- **Be a team player.** Bosses like people who are part of a cohesive group and who are ultimately more productive than superstar individualists.[39]
- **Accept your boss's decisions.** Even when contrary to your ideas, graciously accept your boss's final decisions.
- **Accept criticism without hostility.** Learning to take criticism without taking it personally is difficult for many young people who have never been subjected to criticism. All supervisors will make both positive and negative judgments on your work, so it is best to develop a thick skin to profit from criticism. Rather than hear and react to criticism, listen and think.[40] This will enable you to learn and improve from it, rather than to look for hidden meanings: "Jeez, the boss hates me and my work. She thinks I'm stupid."
- **Be loyal.** Company politics can be brutal—reorganizations, mergers, layoffs—and your boss may be caught in the crossfire. Most etiquette manuals advise you to remain loyal to the person above you whatever the outcome, even if your boss gets fired or laid off. Loyalty is a scarce commodity in today's cutthroat workplace, and your willingness to support your boss in the face of company upsets will be noted by others.[41]

Finally, many of us forget that when we are having a one-on-one meeting with our supervisor, our body language reveals volumes about how we are feeling and how we are reacting. To become more aware of what your body language says about you and how to control it, especially around supervisors and managers, see Figure 2-7 for a crash course in body language basics.

FIGURE 2-7: BODY LANGUAGE BASICS

When dealing with coworkers and supervisors, be particularly mindful of what your body language says to them. Try not to send the following ambiguous signals:
- Folding your arms across your chest usually shows that you are either defensive or that you disagree. Sometimes people simply stand like this. If you typically cross your arms, try to be more aware of it, and keep your arms at your sides or rest them on the table at a meeting.
- The way you sit says a lot about you. Slouching may be interpreted as laziness or tiredness, leg crossing can be seen as defensive, and knee jiggling can show apprehension or insecurity.[42]
- Scratching the back of the neck or shrugging the shoulders may denote uncertainty.
- Covering one's mouth with the hand can say to some that you not being entirely truthful.
- Holding your boss's eyes a little too long may be interpreted as a sign of disrespect or as a challenge to authority. Staring at someone can look threatening or just plain strange.
- Fidgeting too much during a meeting—drumming your fingers, cracking your knuckles, rocking your leg back and forth—makes you look uninterested if not downright bored.
- Nodding is good—it can look like you are being attentive—unless you overdo it, in which case you can look like a brown-noser, especially if the nods are directed at your boss's every word.[43]

DEALING WITH DIFFICULT BOSSES

Difficult bosses are simply difficult people who have risen to a supervisory level. Difficult bosses are not tough bosses, the ones who have the ability to drive you to perform beyond your wildest expectations. Difficult bosses, in contrast, make life at the office a nightmare worthy of the best horror films. These bosses range from non-communicators to abusers. They may be control freaks, tantrum throwers, blamers, bigots, or abusers, but whatever they do, they are difficult and oblivious to the way their behavior affects their employees.[44] Beneath the surface, the difficult boss is simply an incompetent manager of people.

© PathDoc/Shutterstock.com

A non-confrontational meeting might help if you can both be specific about your complaints, and you can show that the problem is widespread and affects productivity.[45] If you can offer to help rather than blame your boss as being the root cause of the office's problems, you might be able to defuse your boss's immediate defensive reaction and even garner a willingness to adjust the nonproductive behavior in the future.[46] You could also go over or around your difficult boss to his or her supervisor or to human resources. However, if you take this route, keep the boss informed of your actions; do not do it behind his or her back. Emphasize that you are trying for positive change for everyone, including the boss.[47] Other than these tactics, you can try the following suggestions for dealing with a difficult boss.

- **The tantrum thrower.** This boss is out of control and erupts into screaming fits of rage for seemingly no reason. After these fits, he or she may feel genuinely sorry, but real abusers enjoy humiliating their employees when they least expect it, whether in private or in public. Three things may help you in dealing with the tantrum thrower: (1) document every detail of your boss's fits of rage; (2) set up a time for you and your coworkers to meet with your boss and confront the situation; and (3) if you have no other option, remember that you are not responsible for the boss's bad behavior, which is clearly out of control. Do not blame yourself.[48]

- **The blamer.** The blamer is difficult to spot because, unlike the tantrum thrower, he or she does not rant. Instead, he goes behind your back to assign blame to you when you are not present. The blamer acts from a defensive posture. He or she never accepts responsibility for his or her failures, blaming others instead. Low-level employees are particularly vulnerable to this kind of abuse as they are defenseless. Since the blamer always believes his or her own interpretation of events, the blamer cannot see your point of view. If you document your work and results carefully, performance reviews may present a chance for you to reveal his or her fabrications, since a solid paper trail and the testimony of others can refute a bad evaluation. If you can wait long enough, blamers will finally trap themselves in their lies and fabrications, or their superiors may finally grow tired of their constant refusal to accept responsibility.[49]

- **The bigot.** The bigot is a boss who makes demeaning remarks about people of different ethnicities, religions, nationalities, or sexual orientation. The bigot is detrimental to individuals in these groups because he or she often assigns them the less important work assignments, thereby granting him- or herself permission to pass over them

tantrum thrower
Someone who erupts into fits of rage for seemingly no reason.

blamer
Someone who goes behind another's back to assign blame to him or her when he or she is not present.

bigot
Someone who makes demeaning remarks about people of a different ethnicity, religion, nationality, gender, or sexual orientation.

when making promotion and merit raise decisions.[50] Bigots use their position to draw otherwise decent employees into silently supporting their unfair behaviors. Since federal and state laws forbid discrimination, the bigot is easy to foil these days. If employees document the bigot's words and actions, he or she will quickly be scrutinized by upper management. Today, companies are aware of their liability for their employees' words and actions. Employees with bigoted bosses should notify the boss's superiors immediately.[51]

TELEPHONE ETIQUETTE

Do not underestimate the power of the telephone as a vehicle to improve the public's perception of your organization. The way any employee, from entry level to the CEO, answers the phone, leaves voicemail messages, or engages in phone conversations reflects on the efficiency and client orientation of any business. Observe these essentials of impeccable **telephone etiquette**.

telephone etiquette
Guidelines for placing and answering telephone calls in the business place.

PLACING AND ANSWERING CALLS

Placing a phone call is second nature to most people. We just pick up the phone and place the call, right? It's not that simple if you are placing a business call. When placing a business call, get your thoughts in order before you place the call. Prepare for your call by having the information you need or want to impart in front of you on paper or screen. In addition, have your paper or electronic calendar nearby in case you need to look up dates. Finally, have a pen and notepad in front of you and be ready to take notes so you can refer to them later.[52] Avoid relying on your memory for facts, figures, and decisions that are mentioned during the phone conversation.

Keep in mind that unless you have a scheduled appointment to speak with the other person on the telephone, you are intruding into his or her day. When you begin your conversation, immediately ask if he or she is available for a short conversation or let the person know that you intend to make it quick.[53]

Remember that you may be the first contact a caller has had with your organization, so make a good impression. Be pleasant, polite, and efficient; inject interest in your tone; speak slowly and clearly; and show genuine enthusiasm without sounding ingenuous.

The polite greeting is usually some form of the following: "Good morning/afternoon. This is David Moyer at Handley Corporation. How may I help you?"[54] If you have caller ID, open by greeting the caller by name: "Hello, Mr. Moyer." Use the caller's courtesy title if you are unfamiliar with him or her; otherwise, use his or her first name. If the caller asks for you before you identify yourself, say, "This is he" or "This is David."[55]

If you are the receptionist, after you have identified the company, ask, "How can I direct your call?" Smile when you are speaking. A smile actually improves your tone of voice because when people are smiling, they typically sound alert and enthusiastic.[56]

When answering the phone avoid sounding abrupt or rude, mumbling, speaking in a disinterested monotone, failing to give your name or your company's name, or speaking so quickly that your name is garbled. Customers might hang up if they are put off by an inappropriate tone of voice or by an abrupt or rude reply to their questions.

SCREENING CALLS

If your calls are screened or if you screen calls for someone else, the tone and content of your explanation are important when establishing a good business relationship with the caller. The worst scenario is the caller who is asked, "What does your call concern?" then hears the ubiquitous you-are-now-on-hold music only to be told shortly that the person you wanted to speak with is unavailable. This caller feels as if he or she is being snubbed and that their call must not be important enough to warrant someone's attention. The question "What does your call concern?" if asked brusquely can also annoy the caller, who may resent having an assistant determine the worth of his or her call. While any language in this situation might provoke an annoyed reaction in the caller, a polite "May I ask what this call is in reference to?" or "Ms. Stein is in a meeting at the moment. May I have your name and company, and she'll return your call as soon as possible," or "Ms. Stein is unavailable at the moment. May I direct you to her voicemail?" may allay a caller's irritation at not getting through.

PLACING CALLERS ON HOLD

When you place a phone call, do you like to be placed on hold? I didn't think so. No one likes to be placed on hold. So, if at all possible, don't place callers on hold.

If you are forced to place callers on hold, however, do not say to them "May I place you on hold?" and then immediately switch them to hold before they have time to respond. Wait instead for callers to respond.

If the caller indicates that he or she is ok with being placed on hold, give an approximate length of time this will be. Even then, avoid leaving him or her holding for more than 20 seconds without giving him or her a progress update such as "I am sorry. Mr. Jackson is still on the other line." In addition, play some generally acceptable background music so the caller isn't left wondering if the call has been dropped. Don't substitute continuous-loop advertisements praising your company's exceptional products and customer service for background music. Such advertisements become very annoying for most!

A caller may instead prefer that you take a message, transfer him or her to voicemail, or call back later.[57] So ask him or her if he or she would prefer you take a message or transfer him or her to voicemail instead of continuing to hold. A basic courtesy such as making sure the caller's wishes are met shows that your company cares, and that can affect the way outsiders perceive your organization.[58]

Finally, avoid expressions such *"Please continue to hold. Your business is important to us"* which can easily be perceived as being hypocritical. After all, if a business truly values callers' business, they will extend the common courtesy of not placing them on hold.

LEAVING A VOICEMAIL MESSAGE

When you leave a voicemail message, be sure to include sufficient information (e.g., your name, date, time of day, where you can be reached, and a brief statement of the reason for your call). Speak clearly and more slowly than usual, especially when sharing your phone number and e-mail address. Phone numbers stated too quickly are often difficult for people to decipher and retain. Always try to respond to your phone messages within 24 hours. Doing so shows you are a courteous person.

TAKING A MESSAGE

When you take a message for someone, ask for the caller's complete name and the name of his or her company. Ask for the spelling of either or both if you are unsure, and read back the phone number and e-mail address to the caller.[59] The caller may give you a summary of the subject of the call. If so, get to the essence of the message so the message recipient will have an easy time following up. In addition, jot down the time and date of the call and add your initials to the written message to show who took the message in case the person wants to know more about who called.

WHILE YOU ARE TALKING

Remember that, while you are talking on the phone, the caller is registering the tone of your voice and word choice. Therefore, make an effort to sound both professional and personable.[60] As far as the tone of the conversation goes, take your lead from the other person on the call. If the person wants to talk business, do so. If person is chatty, go ahead and briefly discuss nonbusiness matters. This may lead to the discovery of common interests, which will help you develop a bond that will make your business relationship run more smoothly.[61]

If you are interrupted by another call and it is important that you speak to this caller, take the call but explain that you are in the middle of another conversation and will call back shortly. In any event, never leave your original caller on hold for more than 30 seconds. Generally speaking, it is rude to leave your original caller for another, so be sure the incoming call is urgent enough to do so. If you do, either ask your original caller to briefly hold or politely ask if you could call back shortly. Apologize and explain the reason for attending to the urgent interruption.[62] Otherwise, let the second call go to voicemail.

FIGURE 2-8: PHONE CALL GAFFES

Avoid the following telephone errors. They can make the person at the other end doubt your credibility.

- While on the phone, avoid doing other things at your desk such as texting, e-mailing, tweeting, or shuffling papers. If your phone partner suspects you are doing other things, he or she might think you are uninterested in the conversation.
- Do not chew gum or eat during phone conversations.
- Do not sneeze, cough, or blow your nose near the receiver. Excuse yourself and turn away.
- Always ask the caller's permission before putting him or her on the speakerphone.
- Always ask the caller's permission before putting him or her on hold.
- Do not answer calls while in meetings, training sessions, presentations, job interviews, conversing with others face-to-face or via a videoconference.
- Do not answer or place calls while on elevators.
- Do not answer or place phone calls while in restrooms.

ENDING THE CONVERSATION

Ending a business conversation can be tricky if you are dealing with a long-winded person. Wrap up the conversation with some indication of what you will do next. For example, "I'll get that report to you by Monday" or "I'll summarize the conclusions we reached in a memo and e-mail it to you tomorrow." Other things you can do to end a phone call include mentioning that you have an important meeting coming up or that you have pressing work. Of course, state your case politely, and end with a courteous, "Thank you for calling" or "I look forward to talking with you soon."[63]

CONFERENCE CALL ETIQUETTE

Conference calls are a fact of life in the workplace. The basics of conference call etiquette are simple. The person who sets up the call should set the agenda and be sure that everyone on the call receives a copy in advance of the call. This person should also make sure that everyone is connected before the business of the conference call begins and that everyone can be heard.

Other suggestions include making sure that you are in place when the call comes through, briefly saying "hello" to everyone when you are connected, speaking clearly and loudly enough so everyone can hear you, not interrupting while another person is speaking, refraining from making jokes in the background while someone is speaking, and signing off with a polite "Thanks everyone; it was good to talk to you" or something similar.[64] The person placing the call might also summarize what was accomplished and assign tasks if appropriate before signing off.

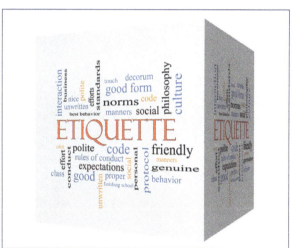

Etiquette that provides guidelines for acceptable behavior when communicating electronically is referred to as netiquette. Figure 2-9 contains a number of practical netiquette suggestions.

FIGURE 2–9: ELECTRONIC DEVICES ETIQUETTE SUGGESTIONS

Avoid these errors when using electronic communication devices such as smartphones, cell phones, tablets, netbooks, and laptops.

- Smartphone and cell phone users should adhere to the following rule: Do not let your phone ring where it will disturb others, whether in meetings, theaters, restaurants, or any number of other settings. If you must take a call during a business meal or meeting, explain ahead of time to your guests or coworkers, put your phone on vibrate, and politely excuse yourself before you take the call outside.
- Be aware of the people around you when you are on a plane, train, bus, etc. If you talk business in close quarters, others around you cannot help but hear what you are saying. In addition, people nearby will be irritated with being subjected to your chatter. Keep business conversations private by making them in private locations.

FIGURE 2-9: ELECTRONIC DEVICES ETIQUETTE SUGGESTIONS

- If you are making calls from a car, know the hazards of doing so. Inform the caller if others are in the car and will be privy to the conversation.[65]
- Do not allow your phone to ring during meetings, presentations, training sessions, etc.
- Do not request a pay raise or promotion via e-mail. Doing so is bad form.
- Do not resign from a job via e-mail or voicemail. Doing so is bad form.
- Do not reprimand employees via e-mail or voicemail.
- Do not participate in the following activities during meetings, presentations, training sessions, etc.: e-mailing, instant messaging, texting, blogging, tweeting.
- Do not check your voicemail messages during business conversations.[66]

SOCIAL MEDIA ETIQUETTE

The Remote Worker's Guide to Office Etiquette http://lifehacker.com/ the-remote-worker- s-guide-to-office- etiquette-1707166009

Nancy Flynn, author of the *Social Media Handbook*, sums up social media etiquette as follows. Adhere to the rules of social media etiquette. Be polite, polished, and professional. Write, post, and publish content that is 100 percent appropriate, civil, and compliant.[67] Figure 2-10 contains additional social media etiquette advice.

FIGURE 2-10: BE PROFESSIONAL

- Do not mix your business profile with your personal profile.
- Represent your company well. Think about the screen name you are using and information you are posting.
- Offer valuable information.
- Remember to proofread.

© 13_Pbunkod/Shutterstock.com

ELEVATOR ETIQUETTE

Using elevators is a fact of life in many office and apartment buildings. There are many elevator-related etiquette suggestions to keep in mind, ranging from allowing others to board first to holding the elevator doors open for others while you are exiting. When using elevators, there are plenty of opportunities to be courteous and helpful and, if you are not careful, plenty of opportunities to be rude and annoying.

While some people are comfortable using elevators, others are not. Some individuals avoid elevators altogether for a variety of reasons ranging from claustrophobia and sharing germs in close quarters to concerns about cables breaking and getting stuck in a malfunctioning elevator for an extended period of time. Whether a fellow passenger is mildly anxious about the ride or downright frightened, courteous behavior on your part will be appreciated. Here are some examples of good elevator etiquette that is typically appreciated by elevator passengers.

- Hold elevator doors open for others as they board.
- Offer to push the button for their desired floor.
- Wear a pleasant facial expression.
- Avoid staring at fellow passengers.
- If possible, keep out of fellow passengers' comfort zone (arm's length).
- Hold elevator doors open for others as you exit so the doors do not slam shut on them.
- Do not talk to others in elevators unless you know each other.

A little common sense, combined with basic respect for others, will go a long way toward reducing the anxiety some of your fellow passengers experience when riding on elevators. Unfortunately, everyone does not act accordingly. A CareerBuilder study of 3,800 workers nationwide provides us with a list of bad elevator-riding habits. These are listed in Figure 2-11 in rank order, starting with the most annoying behavior.

FIGURE 2–11: BAD ELEVATOR-RIDING HABITS

1. Talking on a cell phone.
2. Not holding the door open when others are running to get the elevator.
3. Standing too close to others when there is plenty of room in the elevator.
4. Squeezing into an already-crowded elevator.
5. Not stepping off the elevator to let others exit.
6. Holding the elevator doors open for an extended time while waiting for someone to get on.
7. Cutting in line to get on the elevator when other people have been waiting longer.
8. Taking the elevator to go up one or two floors instead of taking the stairs.
9. Pushing the wrong button, so the elevator stops at more floors.
10. Facing away from the elevator door, instead of toward the door like everyone else.

Source: From The Ups and Downs of Office Elevator Behavior by Susan Ricker. Copyright © 2012 by Career-Builder. Reprinted by permission.

On a related note, business employees are often judged on their interpersonal skills. With this in mind, in the world of elevator travel you can easily see plenty of opportunities to practice good interpersonal skills.

DRESS

Business dress is typically dictated by your profession and your corporate culture. Dress for men can range from the classic navy, black, or gray suits in conservative organizations to khakis, sports jackets, jeans, and golf-shirts in less formal organizations. Women have a wider range of clothing and styles from which to choose, but they should also observe the dress rules of their work environment. A general rule, men and women should dress conservatively during the first few weeks of a new job until they have had a chance to see and adapt to the office standard. Listed here are a few tips for dressing for success at the office. These should help keep you from making a major sartorial mistake.

- Although the navy, black, or gray suit is not as indispensable for men as it once was, you should have at least one well-tailored suit. You may find yourself wearing it for major presentations and meeting important clients. Be sure the weight of the fabric fits the season: cotton or gabardine for spring and summer; worsted wool for fall and winter.[68]
- For men, the tie is still the most important fashion accessory. While some believe in expressing their individuality with loud colors or wild designs, many fashion experts advise against quirky ties that may offend clients or customers.[69] As a compromise, keep a conservative tie in your office for a quick change if the situation dictates.
- If they work for a conservative organization, women should wear closed-toed pumps with no more than 1½-inch heels.
- Women should wear understated clothes. Your clothes should make you look authoritative and competent. Low-cut blouses, short skirts, or tight pants might be construed as alluring; an image you definitely do not want to project at work.

Any clothes that veer too far from the company standard could be considered as flippant or as showing contempt for standards. Neither will aid your career growth goals and could be cause for dismissal.

"I assume my reasons for abolishing Casual Fridays are clear to everyone in this room."

GROOMING

Men and women should pay careful attention to their grooming. Hair and fingernails should be clean and neat looking. For men, keep nose and ear hair clipped. Keep your breath fresh with a quick toothbrush touch-up after lunch and breath mints. Keep your shoes shined. Heels should not look worn down. Wear clothes that are clean and freshly pressed. Keep a spot remover in your desk for those unexpected accidents, and keep a lint removal brush nearby; especially if you have pets at home.

CUBICLE ETIQUETTE

Cubicles are small employee workspaces that are commonplace in offices. Unlike offices with solid walls, a ceiling, and a door, cubicles have moveable partitions 4–5 feet high for walls, a ceiling too high to block out sounds, and no door. Furthermore, your cubicle may be bordered on three sides by other cubicles. Given the openness and closeness of cubicles, some cubicle etiquette suggestions are in order. These are presented in Figure 2-12.

As you can see, cubicle etiquette is grounded in respect for your coworkers. It really comes down to treating others as you would like to be treated. You will get along fine with your cubicle neighbors if you let your common sense and these suggestions guide your actions.

© totallyPic.com/Shutterstock.com

FIGURE 2–12: CUBICLE ETIQUETTE

- Do not stop by a coworker's cubicle uninvited. E-mail, text, or call him or her and arrange a time to visit.
- In your quest to personalize your cubicle, be sure it remains professional looking. Items such as small, framed pictures, desk accessories such as pen and business card holders, and small plants are advised.
- When speaking to others face-to-face or over the phone, keep your volume down for obvious reasons.
- Do not place calls on speaker phone.
- Do not eat noisy foods (e.g., chips, pretzels) in your cubicle. Doing so can easily distract fellow workers nearby.
- If you listen to music or the radio, use headphones.
- Do not subject your coworkers in neighboring cubicles to personal conversations.
- Be sensitive to the fact that coworkers can be distracted or harmed by (in the case of allergies) some smells (e.g., certain foods, hairspray, perfume).
- Do not make a habit of looking into coworkers' cubicles. Doing so is an invasion of their space. It is fine to smile and say hi as you walk by if the occupant is looking your way.

Source: Mindy Lockard, "Cubicle Etiquette: Sights, Sounds, and Smells."
http://www.forbes.com/sites/work-in-progress/2011/06/16/cubicle-etiquette-sights-sounds-and-smells/

RESTROOM ETIQUETTE

I suspect you are already familiar with what I will say about restroom etiquette. Hopefully, I will not insult your intelligence or offend you by sharing my thoughts. However, some basic reminders will not hurt.

As a general rule, when using the facilities, do not strike up conversations with people you do not know. Others often find that being drawn into such conversations is uncomfortable and awkward. Most of us visit restrooms for purposes other than conversation and prefer to get on with our business.

Do not participate in phone calls in restrooms. Doing so is considered to be in poor taste and unprofessional, speaks to a lack of modesty, and is discourteous to others using the facilities.

An age-old expression is "there is a time and a place for everything." Well, good etiquette suggests that when using the restroom, it is neither the time nor the place for conversations.

OFFICE PARTIES

A scene in the movie *Bridget Jones's Diary* captured the essence of an office holiday party gone bad. Bridget, complete with tinsel reindeer horns and a drink in her hand, slurs out a karaoke song at the office holiday party just as the boss walks in. According to etiquette gurus Peter and Peggy Post, such office parties are "virtually over and gone."[70] Today's office parties have grown up and are geared more toward building morale and providing employees a chance to form friendships rather than seeing who can drink the most alcohol. Even then, watch out for these office party pitfalls.

- Since drinking too much at work-related social functions can result in behaving in an unruly manner, limit your alcohol intake or do not drink alcoholic beverages at all. Otherwise, you may cause serious damage your reputation, credibility, and career hopes. An extreme drinking-related example resulted in tragedy at a holiday office party when an inebriated employee threw himself against a 22nd-floor, outer-glass wall to prove it was shatterproof. Unfortunately, it was not, and he fell to his death.
- As a concerned coworker or host, be a good colleague and watch out for fellow employees who are overindulging. Try to steer them away from the alcohol and, instead, toward the coffee pot. At least offer to drive them home (if you have not been drinking) or call a cab for them.[71]

When the party has ended, keep others' transportation needs in mind. If someone faces a commute with no designated driver, suggest a cab if no one can give the person a ride home.

SUMMARY: SECTION 2— BUSINESS ETIQUETTE AT THE OFFICE

- Business etiquette differs from social etiquette.
- One of the guiding principles of etiquette is to always treat people with consideration and respect.
- Be sure to make business introductions.
- Shaking hands is the standard greeting in the U.S. workplace.
- Adapting to company culture involves liberal use of "please," "thank you," and "excuse me"; greeting coworkers in the morning and saying good-bye when leaving in the evening; and smiling, even when you do not feel like it.
- Master the art of small talk.
- Learn how to handle backstabbers, tattletales, victims, and sycophants.
- When interacting with a subordinate, do not abuse your rank. When interacting with a supervisor, accept that he or she is in charge, treat him or her with respect, do your job well, and do it on time.
- Learn how to deal with tantrum throwers, blamers, and bigots.
- Understand the role telephone etiquette has on others' perceptions of your organization.
- Practice courteous, helpful elevator etiquette.
- Dress conservatively the first few weeks at a new job until you have had a chance to see and adapt to the office standard.
- Understand proper cubicle etiquette.
- Conduct yourself as expected during restroom visits.
- Office parties build morale and provide employees with a chance to form real friendships.

BUSINESS ETIQUETTE OUTSIDE THE OFFICE

Whenever you conduct business outside the office, everything you do or say reflects not only on your professionalism and character, but also on the image and credibility of the organization you represent. The focus in this section is on interaction with clients and customers outside the office in areas ranging from networking and business card protocol to **dining etiquette**.

NETWORKING

Networking is about making business contacts. However, not all contacts are created equal. Hilka Klinkenberg, director of Etiquette International, recommends ways to make the most out of networking at industry and association events. These include mastering the art of the networking conversation and handing out business cards.

dining etiquette
Guidelines for conducting ourselves during business meals.

networking
Building a network of professional contacts for business purposes.

NETWORK
VECTOR ILLUSTRATION

The key to successful networking is active networking, even when you are not looking for a job. If you are always networking and making connections, then when the time comes it will be more natural to mention that you are looking for a job. To maintain an active network, keep in touch with your connections, and help others out when you can. In addition to your natural network, take advantage of specific networking events.[72]

Employing the art of making conversation work for you at networking events begins with one simple rule: Never make a sales pitch at a networking function.[73] Doing so makes you appear pushy, desperate, and inexperienced, and it instantly turns the object of your pitch—the corporate client—against you. In fact, corporate members of organizations often complain of being so over hustled by consultants at industry events that the executives stay away to avoid the annoyance and stress of being barraged with unwanted solicitations.[74]

Rather than appear pushy, try the following ways to make the best of your networking time at any function.

- Spend only 5–7 minutes with any one person, and never stretch it past 10. Once you have reached your goal with that contact or have reached a dead end, excuse yourself politely and move on. This gives the people with whom you talk a chance to meet other people.
- Listen more than you talk: Take the focus off yourself at networking functions by listening rather than doing all the talking. If you keep quiet and give the people you meet the opportunity to talk about themselves, they will appreciate your giving them that opportunity. Plus, you will have learned enough about that person to help you form a working relationship with that prospect in the future.[75]
- As you close a conversation with someone who you believe could be a quality contact, arrange to meet at a later date to discuss ideas you have that could be mutually beneficial.

BUSINESS CARD PROTOCOL

Your business card serves many purposes: (1) it invites a new acquaintance to get in touch with you; (2) it defines your position and responsibilities; and (3) it provides at least four ways for someone to reach you: your mailing address, your e-mail address, your phone number, and your fax number.[76] In addition, your business card can easily route others to additional information via a Quick Response Code (QR code). With the swipe of their smartphone over a QR code (optical label) on your business card, they will be able to digitally access information of your choosing that extends far beyond the basic contact information customarily included on business cards.

As a savvy businessperson, you should always have a few clean, unwrinkled business cards with you because you never know when you'll need them: at the baseball park, at dinner, or at a party. To keep them in pristine condition, buy a business-card holder at any office supply, department, or stationery store.[77]

Passing out business cards willy-nilly to anyone and everyone is not the approach to take unless you want them to wind up in the nearest dumpster or unless you want to hear from the person from whom you would least like to hear. One cardinal rule of offering your business card or asking for one is the rule of rank: If the person clearly outranks you, he or she should be the one to request your business card. Otherwise, be reasonably sure that you

FIGURE 2–13: CAPTURING BUSINESS CARD INFORMATION DIGITALLY

Imagine a scenario in which you get together in person for the first time with another businessperson. Early in this meeting you will likely decide to exchange business cards. This is a typical scenario in the business world. However, instead of cluttering your pockets, wallet, or top desk drawer with card-stock business cards, you decide to capture your business partner's business card information digitally. You can do this using a business card reader app such as *CamCard*. With *CamCard*, and similar apps, you simply snap a picture of your business partner's business card. From there, you can digitally store his or her business-card information.

© KPG_Payless/Shutterstock.com

This all sounds very practical. However, you are advised to consider varying cultural expectations pertaining to exchanging business cards. For example, Japanese businesspeople prefer exchanging traditional card-stock business cards. When a Japanese businessperson receives your business card, he or she will typically hold it with both hands while studying it and just might prefer you do the same. In contrast, simply snapping a photo of your Japanese business partner's business card may be perceived as being disrespectful and unprofessional. Furthermore, in several cultures the expectation is that the same information will be on both sides of the business card—in the business partner's native language on one side and in your language on the other side. In these cultures, you would hand the business card to your business partner with his or her native language facing up. Will such business card handling expectations fade away with the advent of business card reader apps such as *CamCard*? If so, it is doubtful it will happen soon. In the meantime, carry some card-stock business cards with you and be considerate of others' expectations pertaining to them.

If you do collect business cards the traditional way but want to store them digitally, you can do so easily with a business card scanner. Among the more highly rated of these are *WorldCard Pro* and *DSmobile*.

will be contacting a person in the future before you ask for his or her card and give yours in exchange. Remember that when you're given a card, you should take a moment to study it and perhaps even compliment the design before putting it into your wallet or datebook.[78] Finally, when you are attending a social event, offering your card privately to someone is fine; however, refrain from holding a business conversation at that time.[79]

BUSINESS DINING ETIQUETTE

© issay-studio/Shutterstock.com

Mealtimes have become one of the essentials of conducting business in a rapidly expanding global economy.[80] The business meal is one of the few places where all your social graces are on display, including your conversational abilities, your self-confidence, and your table manners.[81] How you use your knife and fork, put food in your mouth, and use your napkin are big parts of your professional and social image.[82] A lack of table manners is interpreted by others as a lack of polish and people skills, both essential in today's fast-paced and competitive business world. Luckily the rules of dining are not difficult to master, and knowing what to do and when to do it will relieve your nervousness and put you at ease in the most formal of business dining settings.

PROTOCOL FOR THE HOST

The host is an indispensable part of the business dinner. He or she is the person who makes every decision from where to have the meal and who to invite to paying the check and leaving the tip. One of the most important jobs of the host is to make everyone feel comfortable. This includes watching to make sure that all the guests are introduced to the other guests and that no one feels left out. Guests will fondly remember a host who pays careful attention to the smallest details and who is considerate of everyone.

The host picks the location of the meal and sets the time. The location should be convenient for the guests and should be a place where the host knows the guests will feel comfortable. Invitations are also the job of the host, who sets the time and contacts each guest to extend the invitation.[83]

Making reservations and picking a table that is out of the way and conducive to business are also the host's responsibilities. If you are the host, reconfirm your reservation the day before to make sure everything is set, and call the guests to confirm the date, time, and location. On the day of the meeting, as host, arrive at least 15 minutes early to check out the table and make arrangements to pay the check. Seat the other guests as they arrive, but refrain from ordering until the guest of honor arrives. If for some reason the guest of honor is more than 30 minutes late, you can either go ahead and order or leave a tip (for holding the table) and depart.[84]

SEATING ARRANGEMENTS

Seating arrangements are determined by rank and status. At formal affairs, place cards indicate where everyone is to sit. Tradition says that the guest of honor or a person of rank is seated to the host's right. Those lower in the business hierarchy are seated further down the table, reflecting where they fall in the pecking order.[85]

AT THE TABLE

Once seated, guests should wait for the host to unfold his or her napkin. Men should unfold the napkin and place it over one knee with the fold facing toward the knees. Women should also place the fold toward their knees, but they should put the napkin across their lap.[86] When you need to wipe your mouth, do so with the one edge of the folded napkin, dab the corners of your mouth, and then replace the napkin. Any food or stain will then be on the outer side of the napkin so that it will not soil your dress or pants.[87] If you need to leave the table, place your napkin either on the seat of your chair or to the left of your plate.[88]

TALKING BUSINESS

Guests should wait for the host to bring up business issues. For most formal dinners, only one or two business topics should be discussed. Save the serious negotiations for the office.

DECIPHERING THE FORMAL TABLE SETTING

A formal place setting can be daunting. However, every piece is set for a particular purpose and has a practical use. The silverware is placed in a logical progression from the outside in, and each piece corresponds to a particular food course. Sometimes the servers bring the necessary silverware as they serve the next course.[89] Usually, the forks are on left of the plate, and the knives and spoons on the right. The only fork you may find on the right is the seafood fork with its tiny tines.[90]

The only change in the fork arrangement occurs when you are eating in Europe or in a place that serves continental style with the salad coming after the entrée rather than before. In that case, the salad fork is the closest one to the plate.

The dessert fork and spoon usually appear above the dinner plate or on either side of the dessert plate, adjacent to it.[91] If there are also two forks to the left of your plate, the fork to the far left is for salad and the other for the entrée. If you are unsure what utensil to use next, watch the host. If you use the wrong utensil by mistake, do not panic, simply ask the server for another one before the next course.[92]

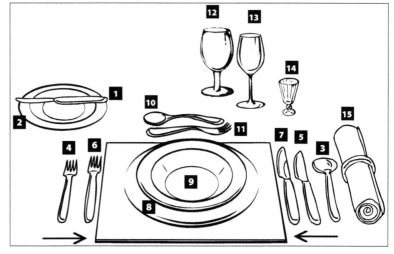

© Liza Dmitrieva/Shutterstock.com

GLASSES AND CUPS

Glasses and cups are always on the right and are arranged in the order they will be used. They are placed above the knife and the soup spoon with the water glass directly above the tip of the knife. Begin with the glass farthest to the right. Each glass is removed along with the course to which it was assigned.[93]

PLATES

The bread and butter plate is placed at the top of the setting to the left. Place your bread and the butter knife across the top of the bread and butter plate when you are not using it. You can use your bread and butter plate for bread and butter as well as for small pieces of paper, like empty packets of sweetener. Before you are served the entrée, you will often find a service plate in front of you. It serves as a place to put the various courses that arrive before the entrée. As the pre-entrée courses are brought to the table, they are placed on the service plate. It is removed when the entrée comes.[94]

ETIQUETTE BY COURSE

After the host directs guests to their seats, move to the right side of your chair and then sit down.[95] Once seated, unfold and place your napkin on your knee or across your lap. After receiving the meal, pause a minute to give the guest of honor the opportunity to pray or to bow silently for a moment.

Bread. If you are the person sitting directly in front of the bread/roll basket or plate, the correct way to pass bread is to one's right, but not before first extending the bread to the person on one's left as a gesture of courtesy.[96]

Soup. Hold the soup spoon like a pencil, and dip the soup away from you in a horizontal movement. Move the bottom of the spoon across the back of the bowl to remove excess that might drip. When you sip from the side of the spoon, do not make noises.[97] Always rest your soup spoon on the plate beneath your bowl, never in the bowl. If you accidentally hit the handle, it could go flying!

Fish Course. Use the fish fork to flake the fish before eating it. The tines of the fish fork are for lifting the skeleton of the fish if it is served with bones.[98] To signal that you are finished with a course, rest the knife and fork side by side in the 10 and 4 o'clock position diagonally on your plate. Always place the cutting edge of the knife toward the center of the plate and the tines of the fork facing down. The handles should extend toward the lower right side of the plate.[99] Place your silverware in the resting position to indicate you are pausing to sip water or take a break.

Sorbet Course. This follows the fish course and is used to cleanse your palate. This course is always served immediately before the entrée.

Entrée. When cutting the entrée, always cut off only one or two bites at a time.

Dessert. As for the dessert course, hold the spoon in your right hand and the fork in your left to secure a difficult dessert, like frozen pie, while you spoon into it. Pie or cake should be eaten only with the dessert fork, while pudding or ice cream should be eaten with the dessert spoon.

FIGURE 2-14: THE 10 MOST COMMON BUSINESS DINING TABOOS

1. Chewing with your mouth open, or speaking with food in your mouth.
2. Putting used cutlery back on the table.
3. Holding the knife like a dagger and the fork overhanded like you are bowing a cello.
4. Ordering indecisively and finishing the meal well before or after everyone else.
5. Using a cell phone during the meal.
6. Putting keys, gloves, a purse, or similar object on the table.
7. Picking or poking at your teeth.
8. Flapping the napkin and putting it on the table before the end of the meal.
9. Slouching, squirming in, or tilting the chair.
10. Leaving lipstick smears.

Source: Mary Mitchell, The Complete Idiot's Guide to Business Etiquette (Indianapolis: Alpha Books, 2000).

DRINKING ALCOHOLIC BEVERAGES AT A BUSINESS DINNER

First, do not feel you have to drink alcoholic beverages because others are. You should feel comfortable sipping on a glass of ice tea, soda, or water if that is your wish. If you do decide to drink an alcoholic beverage, know your tolerance and do not overdo it. However, if you are dining in an international venue, you may find yourself having to break with this strict limit to appear sociable.

For tips on dining etiquette when you are overseas, see Figure 2-15.

FIGURE 2-15: INTERNATIONAL DINING TIPS

- Accept what is on your plate with thanks. It indicates your acceptance of the host, country, and company.
- Whether you are offered sheep's eyes in Saudi Arabia or bear's paw soup in China, take at least a few bites. It is often better not to ask what you are eating.
- In Italy, Spain, and Latin America, lunch is the biggest meal of the day and can often go to seven courses. Of course, you are expected to work afterward. To avoid being overstuffed and overtired for those afternoon meetings, eat only a small serving of everything.
- Except for Islamic and some other cultures, many hosts try to get visitors tipsy as a sign of their hospitality. Usually, saying you do not drink will not get you off the hook. A few sips must be taken, especially when the toasts begin, to avoid offending your hosts.

TOASTS

The host may choose to make a toast before the appetizer or before the dessert. For this, the host stands while the guest remains seated. He or she may hold a glass but should not drink to him- or herself. The guest may then rise to propose another toast. When a toast is proposed, sipping water is fine or raising an empty glass is acceptable if you do not drink.

When the meal is completed, the host places his or her napkin to the left of the plate. The guests should then follow suit. Never refold a napkin or place it on a plate or in a used glass.

TEXTING DURING A BUSINESS DINNER

Texting during a business dinner is considered to be an ill-mannered behavior. Family and friends may tolerate such behavior when out to dinner at a restaurant, but texting during business dinners is strongly discouraged.

LEAVING THE TABLE DURING A BUSINESS DINNER

If you must leave the table during a business dinner, for example to use the restroom, simply say "Excuse me" and then leave. Keep in mind, however, that it is really bad manners to leave the dinner table to place a call.[100]

THANK-YOU NOTES

A thank you addressed to the host thanking him or her for the dinner should be handwritten on fine stationery or an appropriate card and mailed to the host within 24 hours of the dinner. This not only shows that you are considerate but also affirms that you enjoyed the meal. It seals the business relationship.

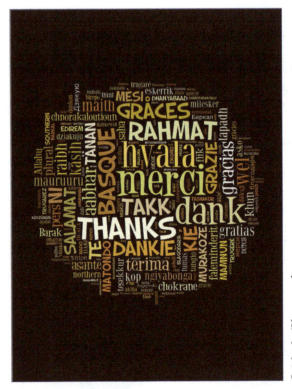

© jobarbu/Shutterstock.com

SUMMARY: SECTION 3— BUSINESS ETIQUETTE OUTSIDE THE OFFICE

- Your conduct outside the office reflects on both your professionalism and the credibility of the organization for which you work.
- Master the art of networking conversation and handing out business cards.
- When you are given a business card, take a second to look at it and perhaps to compliment the design before putting it in your wallet or datebook.
- Business meals are commonplace, and a lack of table manners is interpreted by others as a lack of polish and people skills, both of which are essential in today's fast-paced, competitive business world.
- Dinner hosts should not only make the dinner arrangements but also be the one to initiate conversation regarding business issues.
- While the number of alcoholic beverages you drink at international business dinners may vary significantly, the general rule in the United States is to limit yourself to three drinks—one before dinner, one during dinner, and one after dinner if you choose to drink alcoholic beverages.

Business Etiquette Tips
http://www.business-managementdaily.com/glp/28411/Business-Etiquette.html

Notes

1. June Hines Moore, *The Etiquette Advantage* (Nashville: Broadman & Holman, 1998), 1.

2. Ibid., 11.

3. Ibid., 3.

4. Hilka Klinkenberg, "Manners Mom Never Taught You." accessed June 23, 2002, http://www.etiquetteinternational.com/Articles/MannersMomNeverTaughtYou.aspx

5. Ibid.

6. Peggy Post and Peter Post, *The Etiquette Advantage in Business* (New York: Harper Resource, 1999), 71.

7. Klinkenberg, "Manners," 1.

8. Ibid., "Manners," 2.

9. Moore, *Etiquette Advantage*, 104–05.

10. Ibid., 106.

11. Ibid.

12. Ibid., 105.

13. Hilka Klinkenberg, "Cocktail Party Panache," http://www.etiquetteinternational.com/Articles/CocktailPartyPanache.aspx.

14. Moore, *Etiquette Advantage*, 112.

15. Ibid., 109.

16. Ibid., 110.

17. Ibid.

18. Ibid., 111.

19. Ibid., 119.

20. Post and Post, *Etiquette Advantage*, 53.

21. Ibid., 54.

22. Ibid.

23. Ibid., 61.

24. Ibid., 63.

25. Ibid.

26. Ibid., 71.

27. Ibid., 65.

28. Ibid.

29. Ibid.

30. Ibid.

31. Ibid., 105.

32. Ibid., 106.

33. Ibid.

34. Ibid., 107.

35. Ibid., 108.

36. Ibid., 115.

37. Ibid., 107.

38. Per Haldbo, *Gold Nuggets Galore—How to Behave in Business* (Copenhagen: Copenhagen Business School Press, 2005), 63.

39. Post and Post, *Etiquette Advantage*, 117.

40. Ibid., 118.

41. Ibid.

42. Peggy Post and Peter Post, *Emily Post's The Etiquette Advantage in Business*, 2nd ed. (New York: Harper Resource, 2006), 216.

43. Ibid., 118.

44. Ibid., 116.

45. Ibid., 117.

46. Ibid., 119.

47. Ibid.

48. Ibid., 288.

49. Ibid., 289.

50. Moore, *Etiquette Advantage*, 46.

51. Ibid., 49.

52. Ibid., 48.

53. Beverly Langford, *The Etiquette Edge: The Unspoken Rules for Business Success*, (New York: AMACOM Books, 2005), 91.

54. Moore, *Etiquette Advantage*, 51.

55. Post and Post, 292.

56. Ibid., 294.

57. Ibid.

58. Ibid., 294.

59. Ibid., 294–95.

60. Ibid., 297.

61. Moore, *Etiquette Advantage*, 60.

62. Ibid., 61.

63. Post and Post, 150–51.

64. Post and Post, 75.

65. Hilka Klinkenberg, "Networking No-No's," http://www.etiquetteinternational.com/Articles/NetworkingNoNos.aspx.

66. Ibid., 2.

67. Nancy Flynn, *The Social Media Handbook: Policies and Best Practices to Effectively Manage Your Organization's Social Media Presence, Posts, and Potential Risks* (San Francisco: Pfeiffer, 2012), 327.

68. Klinkenberg, 2.

69. Post and Post, 226.

70. Ibid., 226.

71. Ibid., 227.

72. Ibid., 314.

73. Ibid., 122.

74. Moore, *Etiquette Advantage*, 122.

75. Post and Post, 391; Moore, 122.

76. Moore, *Etiquette Advantage*, 122.

77. Ibid., 125.

78. Ibid., 127.

79. Post and Post, 434.

80. Moore, *Etiquette Advantage*, 136.

81. Ibid.

82. Ibid., 133.

83. Ibid.

84. Ibid., 134.

85. Ibid.

86. Ibid.

87. Ibid.

88. Ibid., 135.

89. Ibid., 141.

90. Ibid., 143.

91. Ibid., 144.

92. Ibid., 147.

93. Ibid.

94. Ibid., 148.

95. Ibid., 19.

96. Eddy Wang, "Business Dinners: Meal etiquette still matters," *The Dallas Morning News*, July 26, 2015, 2D.

97. Moore, 136.

98. Ibid.

99. Post and Post, 185.

100. Eddy Wang, "Business Dinners: Meal etiquette still matters," *The Dallas Morning News*, July 26, 2015, 2D.

VERBAL AND NONVERBAL COMMUNICATION

3

LEARNING OUTCOMES

After reading this chapter you will be able to:

1. Differentiate between verbal and nonverbal communication

2. Describe how verbal and nonverbal communication function in the communication process

3. Explain techniques for successful verbal communication

4. Describe characteristics of nonverbal communication

5. Define sexual harassment

6. Describe the process of hearing, listening, and the creation of meaning

7. List the steps in the process to improve your listening skills

8. Describe the distinction between active and passive listening

© Ivanko80/Shutterstock.com

From *Competent Communication at Work: Communication, Technology and Professional Practices, Fourth Edition*, by Hopkins et al. Copyright © 2020 by Kendall Hunt Publishing Company. Reprinted by permission.

SELECT KEY TERMS

Verbal communication

Ambiguous word

Concrete meaning

Slang

Jargon

Tag question

Hedges and qualifiers

Vocal filler

Polite language

Articulation

Pronunciation

Nonverbal communication

Vocalics

Paralanguage

Kinesics

Gestures

Adaptor

Emblem

Regulator

Illustrator

Proxemics

Chronemics

Hearing

Listening

Passive listening

Active listening

INTRODUCTION

Rahima Martin, a senior at a large university on the East Coast, is enrolled in her required communication class. She has put the class off as long as possible, not because class times don't fit into her schedule, but because she is afraid of standing up and speaking in front of her peers. She feels fine about her conversational skills with her friends, but whenever she has spoken to a group, her grade has been low. Comments from teachers include, "We have trouble hearing and understanding what you say," and "Be specific in your remarks. Talk to your audience," and, "Slow down. You talk too fast." Rahima can't understand why she seems successful in communication with her family and friends and unsuccessful when communicating with peers, supervisors, professors, and strangers. Now, her confidence about her communication skills is low, and she dreads the semester to come. But her business degree requires the class, and she has too much time and money invested to change majors now.

Rahima doesn't comprehend the importance of verbal and nonverbal communication skills. She is comfortable talking and texting with friends and colleagues because she sees these as informal activities—part of her everyday life. But, when she has to speak solo in front of a group, or even when she speaks as part of a group in front of others, she lets her fear take over. She forgets that her mission is to communicate her message to her specific audience, whether that is six people or 600.

Rahima fears public communication. She is not alone. Many people—just like you, perhaps—dread taking any class that involves public speaking in college. Many professionals won't take a job if public speaking is a requirement of that job. Some professionals do accept jobs where public speaking is required, but they don't do that part of the job well. The book *I'd Rather Die Than Give a Speech*[1] states that many executives called on to make presentations before such groups as boards of directors, analysts, stockholders, regulators, employees, or franchisees experience some form of apprehension, or some form of concern.

Most people fear speaking in public or speaking to or in front of their supervisors, colleagues, and peers because they don't want to look foolish or to fail. What they might not realize is that excellent verbal and nonverbal communication skills are essential to success as a communicator in various settings—interviews, group presentations, sales proposals, meetings, and speeches. Once you realize the importance of both your verbal and nonverbal communication, you can then work to improve these areas and create messages that assist your audiences in listening to and understanding your messages.

Consider this scenario for a moment: you are sitting in your required Business and Professional Communication or Public Speaking class on the first day of the semester. The professor hands out the syllabus, which contains the assignments for the semester. You scan it quickly, noting a group project, an interview project, a sales speech assignment, and an informative speech assignment. Your first thought is, "Help. I can't do this. I'll just drop this class and take it another time." But, what if you see those assignments and feel fully confident that you can successfully complete them all? What if you are confident in your verbal and nonverbal communication skills? These hypothetical questions become real very quickly. Both verbal and nonverbal communication skills are crucial to your success as a communicator in today's workplace.

By understanding what makes communication successful, you can change your outlook and change your effectiveness as a communicator.

© GaudiLab/Shutterstock.com

VERBAL COMMUNICATION

**Verbal
communication**
What you say or
the message that
you send.

Verbal communication refers to *what* you say, or the message that you send. Do you speak clearly? Is your *intended* message always the message that is received?

Della Manchella, a speaker and trainer for companies who want to ensure the successful performance of their employees, says that when we speak, only approximately 10% of the words we use get through to others. If we want our message to be understood, we must be careful of the words we use. Boaz Keysar and Anne S. Henly[2] researched whether speakers overestimate their own effectiveness. They concluded that speakers expect their audiences to understand their intentions more than is warranted. Speakers perceive their own utterances as more transparent than they really are. The concern here is that if speakers believe their listeners understand them, they might be less likely to verify that the listener did indeed arrive at the intended meaning.

When you are writing down your thoughts and remarks for a verbal presentation, make sure you remember to write for the ear, and not for the eye. You are writing words that a person or a group of people are going to hear. They will not have your remarks in front of them. They will only have their ears, and they will only get one chance to hear and understand you.

If you are reading a textbook, your email, or a text and are interrupted, you can reread the material or even flip back to another page to remind yourself what you were reading before the interruption. You can also read one passage several times for clarification. If you read a word, and you don't know its definition, you can leave the passage, look up the definition, come back, and continue to read. When you are listening to someone speak, you only have one shot to understand what they say. You can't rewind a DVD or ask them to do it over. If you don't understand what someone is saying, then you might stop listening.

When you speak to people whom you know well on an informal basis, you might take it for granted that you communicate clearly. Your conversation might contain run-on sentences, incomplete thoughts, jargon, slang, ambiguous words, and vocal fillers. Still, your message has a good chance of being communicated successfully for several reasons: (a) Your listeners know you well; (b) your listeners are familiar with your speaking style; (c) your listeners have similar interests and hobbies; and (d) your listeners can ask questions to clarify what they hear.

If you take that same style of speaking and use it when asking the boss for a raise or a promotion, or with a new client with whom you are trying to make a sale, or even as you address your coworkers in a meeting, your communication might be unsuccessful. If people have to work hard at trying to understand what you are saying, they probably will not put forth the effort.[3] You need to write or compose your thoughts differently for an audience of listeners than you do for an audience of readers. You need to write down your thoughts and then read them out loud, editing as you read to ensure that your meaning is clear.

TIPS FOR SUCCESSFUL COMMUNICATION

The tips in the following sections will help you produce successful verbal communication.

Clarity Be clear. Misunderstandings and miscommunications cost a business time and money. If your boss needs a committee report to be completed *before* the staff meeting at the end of the month, and you understand that it isn't due until *after* the staff meeting, then no one involved with your project can move forward on time. When *you* are the recipient of verbal communication, clarify, paraphrase, or ask questions about the message. Make certain you understand exactly what is expected of you. If your boss gives you verbal directions, take notes, paraphrase, and repeat it back, asking if you understand the directions clearly. Paraphrase what your boss tells you, repeat it back to her, and ask if you understand the directions clearly. If you initiate the communication, check your message for any ambiguities. An **ambiguous word** leaves receivers uncertain of its meaning; **concrete meaning**, on the other hand, is specific.

Ambiguous word
Leaves receivers uncertain as to its meaning.

Concrete meaning
Specific; leaves no uncertainty in its meaning.

© Pormezz/Shutterstock.com

DO YOUR WORDS MATCH YOUR MEANING?

TOOLS OF THE TRADE
SLANG, JARGON, AND BUZZ WORDS

Examples of ambiguous statements:

1. I need that committee report soon. (When exactly do you need that?)
2. I'll be there in a little while. (When will you actually arrive?)
3. You did pretty well. (How exactly did I do?)

Example of concrete meaning or specific statements:

1. That report needs to be 2 pages long, double-spaced, using 12-point font.
2. I'll be there in 25 minutes.
3. Your report was well organized with a clear beginning, middle, and end, but I would like to see more specific examples of your sales figures.

Slang
Informal language typically used or shared by groups.

Jargon
Words known only by those people in your area of specialty.

Be careful with slang and jargon. **Slang** and jargon are both "shortcut" talk, and their use is fine when you're talking to family, friends, and colleagues. But in a more formal group or speaking situation, this "shortcut" talk becomes a distraction. You might be asked to present research to supervisors, colleagues, and laypersons in hopes of gaining necessary funding to continue to research and publish your results. If you supplement your speech with **jargon**—or words only known by those people in your area of specialty—then you will confuse and lose the attention of the laypeople unfamiliar with the language you use. They will not write a check if they don't understand what you need it for. Always remember who is in your audience, whether it's two people or 200 people, and tailor your message to each specific audience. Jargon and slang are only clear to those people who know what they mean. People who don't know the meaning will feel left out, and so they will tune you out.

Most career fields have their own jargon or buzzwords. Some jargon has become well-known. For example, you are probably familiar with military terms like AWOL, MIA,

HAVE YOU EVER BEEN CONFUSED BY A DOCTOR USING MEDICAL JARGON?

© Syda Productions/Shutterstock.com

Jeep, and SNAFU. If you've seen the movie *Saving Private Ryan* or the Ken Burns PBS documentary *The War*, you are also familiar with the term FUBAR. From the medical field, you probably recognize STAT, upper GI, and preemie.

In the financial world, investment brokers might refer to the "dead cat bounce" when talking about a stock that's been sold off a lot, makes a short, sharp rebound, but then continues its decline. Brokers also use the term *bull market* to refer to a good market, *bear market* to refer to a market that is down, and *short sale* to refer to selling a stock you don't own. They might use the term *naked call* when they are talking about selling a call on a stock you don't own. If the stock is called away, you have to then buy it and sell it, leaving you exposed or naked.

Texting slang includes the following:[4]

LOL	laughing out loud
OMG	Oh, my God
IDK	I don't know
UOK?	You Okay?
BBIAS	Be back in a second

Powerful and Powerless Language Use It's not only important to use language that is clear and free of slang and jargon, but also to examine our speech in terms of powerful and powerless language. Of course, the language you use should reflect the context or situation you are in, so being a competent communicator relies on how flexible you are in adapting your language to fit different situations. Powerful language is thought to be more direct and task-related while powerless language is thought to be indirect or hesitant.

Powerless speech includes the use of tag questions, hedges, qualifiers, verbal fillers, and polite forms. **Tag questions** are statements that end with a question. The question seems to seek confirmation or verification from others, therefore lessening the strength of the primary statement. **Hedges and qualifiers** are words and phrases which make statements sound more tentative. These tentative statements serve to weaken the primary statement by making a person sound unsure. The end effect is that the statement is self-defeating; in other words, the speaker discredits the thought they are about to share. Intensifiers are another form of powerless language demonstrating an effort to make the subject of a sentence seem more important. We often use words such as "very" or "so" to emphasize the importance of something. These types of words are not very creative and add little color to our speech. **Vocal fillers** are words or utterances used to fill the gaps in our language when we should allow a pause in order to articulate a specific word. Examples of vocal fillers include the words "like," "uhm," and "okay." Finally, while being polite and courteous is important in the business world, being excessively so serves to weaken your language. Overly **polite language** includes unneeded apologies or excessive expressions of thanks.

Tag Questions:	"We need to double our quota for next quarter . . . *don't you think*?"
Hedges/Qualifiers:	"*This might not be a good time to ask this question*, but . . . "
	"*You might have already thought about this*, but . . . "

Tag question
A statement that ends with a question which serves to seek agreement or confirmation from others.

Hedges and qualifiers
Words and phrases which make statements sound more tentative.

Vocal filler
Words or utterances used to fill the gaps in our language instead of using a silent pause.

Polite language
Overly polite statements which include unneeded apologies or excessive expressions of thanks.

Intensifiers:	"We are *very* glad to have you as a new customer . . . "
	"This account is so complex and so time-consuming."
Vocal Fillers:	Using like, uhm, okay
	"Uhm, the layout of this ad is like, so busy."
	"I, uhm, wonder if I could, like, take a vacation day next week?"
Polite Language:	"I'm sorry the copy machine broke on you."
	"Thanks for allowing me to take a vacation day next week. I'm sorry I gave such short notice."

These powerless forms of speech are conversational and mostly intended to provide support and express understanding to other parties; however, excessive use of them or using them in the wrong context can lessen your credibility. According to Deborah Tannen,[5] a leading researcher in the area of gender and discourse, women are more likely to use these powerless forms of speech in business settings in an effort to establish and maintain relationships, while men are more likely to engage in report-talk or task-oriented, direct communication. Many professionals have figured out the key to success is to be flexible and adjust their communication according to the organizational culture and the situation. A mix of both "powerful" and "powerless" language or "task" and "relational" communication can go a long way toward establishing your credibility.

Articulation and Pronunciation Be clear in your articulation and pronunciation. Do you speak clearly? Do other people frequently ask you to repeat yourself? **Articulation** refers to pronouncing the individual speech sounds. For example, the word *asks* has the consonant blend *sks*. When some people say this word, it sounds like *aks*. This is an articulation error. Another example is the word *going*. The *ing* on the end needs to be clearly pronounced. Instead, many people will say *goin*. The words *want to* can often sound like *wanna*. Some people run these words together. Your verbal communication needs to be clear and clean. Make sure you say each sound correctly.

Articulation
Pronouncing the individual speech sounds.

MANY PROFESSIONALS HAVE CONCLUDED THAT THE KEY TO SUCCESS IS TO BE FLEXIBLE IN YOUR COMMUNICATION STYLE.

© Photographee.eu/Shutterstock.com

Pronunciation refers to the way you put the sounds together to form a word. It also includes knowing which syllable of the word is emphasized. Here are some examples of words that are commonly mispronounced:

Athlete is not *ath uh lete*. You don't want to add a syllable.

Library does have an *r*. It is not *li bar y*.

Probably is *pro ba bly*. Some people say *prob ly*.

Subtle is *sut-ul*. The *b* is silent.

Candidate is *can-di-date*. The error here is usually *can uh date*.

Barbed wire is not *bob wire*.

Et cetera leaves out the *x* sound.

Regardless is a word. *Irregardless* is not.

We can use tongue twisters to help with our articulation and our pronunciation. Tongue twisters are words, phrases, or sentences that are put together in a way that makes your mouth work hard to say all the sounds correctly. You are probably familiar with the tongue-twister "Peter Piper picked a peck of pickled peppers." For more practice, try saying these sentences out loud, clearly:

She sends sappy soliloquies southward.

Mary mopes much in March.

Seth searches silently, sending signals surreptitiously.

Westward wanders William, while Waylon weighs wood.

> **Pronunciation**
> The way you put the sounds together to form a word.

SKILL BUILDER

Practice your articulation and pronunciation with these tough tongue twisters:

1. If I assist a sister-assistant, will the sister's sister-assistant assist me?
2. Alice asks for axes (say this one three times).
3. A big bug bit a bold bald bear and the bold bald bear bled blood badly.
4. Blake the baker bakes black bread.
5. The brave bloke blocked the broken back bank door.
6. Clean clams crammed in clean cans.
7. A canner exceedingly canny, one morning remarked to his granny, "A canner can can anything that he can, but a canner can't can a can, can he?"
8. A chapped chap chopped chips.
9. Cuthbert's cufflinks (say this one three times).
10. The fish-and-chip shop's chips are soft chips.
11. Does this shop stock cheap checkers?
12. Crisp crust crackles (say this one three times).
13. Few free fruit flies fly from flames.
14. She sells Swiss sweets.
15. Strange strategic statistics.[6]

SKILL BUILDER

USING WORDS CORRECTLY

In addition to articulating and pronouncing words correctly, it is also important to use them accurately. Sometimes people get words mixed up and use the wrong word when they speak. *The English Composition and Grammar* textbook lists words that are often confused:[7, 8]

Advice is a noun that means to give counsel. (He gave me some excellent advice.)
Advise is a verb that means to give advice. (She advised me to finish high school.)

Affect is a verb that means to influence. (What he said did not affect my final decision.)
Effect is a verb that means to accomplish or a noun that means a consequence will result. (The mayor has effected many changes during her administration. The effect of these changes has been most beneficial.)

All ready is a pronoun plus an adjective that means everyone is ready. (When he arrived, we were all ready to go.)
Already is an adverb that means previously. (Sharon has already gone.)

Capital is a noun that means a city or money used by a business. It can also be an adjective meaning punishable by death or of major importance or excellent. (Raleigh is the capital of North Carolina. Mrs. Dawson will need more capital to modernize her equipment. Killing a police officer is a capital crime.)
Capitol is a noun meaning building or statehouse. (In Raleigh, the capitol is located on Fayetteville Street.)

Choose means to select and is used for present and future tense. (You may choose your own partner.)
Chose is used with past tense and rhymes with hose. (They chose pizza for lunch.)

Formally means properly, according to strict rules. (Should he be formally introduced?)
Formerly means previously, in the past. (The new counsel was formerly a senator.)

Its is the possessive of it. (The bird stopped its singing.)
It's means it is. (It's an easy problem.)

Passed is a verb, and it is the past tense of pass. (He passed us on the highway.)
Past is a noun, and it means the history of a person. It can also be an adjective meaning former, or a preposition meaning farther on. (I didn't inquire about his past. Her past experience got her the job. I went past the house.)

Than is a conjunction used for comparisons. (Jimmy enjoys swimming more than golfing.)
Then is an adverb or conjunction indicating at that time or next. (Did you know Barbara then? I ate my lunch, and then I went for a walk.)

NONVERBAL COMMUNICATION

Our verbal communication, specifically our language use, is incredibly important for establishing credibility, but our nonverbal communication is equally important. Many people think of nonverbal communication as body language. And it is. But that's only part of what makes up this aspect of communication. **Nonverbal communication** refers to the unspoken messages that we send.

Read the following paragraphs and see if you can determine the role and nature of nonverbal communication:

1. You have scheduled a lunch meeting with your boss to run through some ideas for a new product line. In the restaurant, there are several large-screen television sets scattered about, all tuned to sports channels. One is in back of you, but clearly visible to your boss. As you carry on the conversation, you find that your boss continually looks at the screen instead of you. You wonder if she's even listening to you. Eventually, you stop talking.

2. Your colleague catches you in the hall as you leave for a meeting upstairs. He begins a conversation about a ball game on television the evening before. You want to be cordial to your colleague, but you also want to be on time for the meeting because you have a short presentation to deliver. You glance at your phone several times and turn away slightly from your colleague. Your colleague wraps up the conversation and you make it to the meeting on time.

3. You have been asked to deliver a brief presentation at the weekly staff meeting. Your team is leading the sales department, and the boss has asked you to share your successful techniques. You are nervous about speaking, but carefully write out a brief outline to help you stay on track. As you begin to speak, you notice that many people are nodding their heads and giving you great eye contact. You begin to feel good about what you are saying. Then you notice one or two people who have their arms folded and their eyes closed. They don't seem to be paying attention, and you begin to panic. You must be boring them! You lose your confidence and begin to stumble over your words as you rush to finish. After your presentation, one of the people who had her eyes closed congratulates you on your great sales figures, paraphrasing your presentation in a brief statement.

Nonverbal communication The unspoken messages that we send.

© Antonio Guillem/Shutterstock.com

SOME NONVERBAL SYMBOLS SPEAK LOUDER THAN WORDS.

These are three examples of nonverbal communication in action. Lack of eye contact, use of subtle regulators to control the flow of conversation, and even misperceptions play a part in our nonverbal communication.

SOME THINGS TO KNOW ABOUT NONVERBAL COMMUNICATION

Contradict, Complement, or Regulate Nonverbal communication can contradict or reinforce or regulate verbal messages. If you are having a good day, you usually will have a smile on your face, your posture will be upright, and you will walk and move in a confident manner. If you have received bad news or if you are having a frustrating day at work, you may move more slowly, your shoulders may stay hunched, and you may have a frown on your face instead of a smile. These nonverbals match or complement the mood of the communicator, but sometimes nonverbals contradict our verbal messages. If someone approaches you and asks if you're having a bad day (due to the frown on your face and your hunched shoulders) and you say, "No, I'm good," this serves to contradict the nonverbal message. In business and professional settings, we may use contradictory messages in an attempt to hide how we truly feel, but sometimes our nonverbals communicate more than we intend.

WHAT IS THE ROLE OF CONTEXT IN DETERMINING THE APPROPRIATENESS AND EFFECTIVENESS OF APPEARANCE?

© wavebreakmedia/Shutterstock.com

Involuntary or Unintentional Nonverbal communication can be involuntary or unintentional. Nonverbal communication includes those behaviors that are mutually recognized and socially shared codes and patterns with a focus on message meaning. For example, an unintended frown when reading a text or email may function as a message because most people regard it as a sign of displeasure. You may not be aware that you are frowning, but it will be interpreted negatively by someone else.

We also use nonverbal communication to regulate other people's communication with us. If a coworker stops in your office or cubicle to gab and you have a deadline, after a courtesy chat you might glance at your smartphone, read something on your computer, or shift in your seat. These nonverbal behaviors are your way of regulating the conversation or of trying to signal that you need to get back to work.

Powerful Nonverbal communication is powerful. People pay a lot of attention to nonverbal behaviors and are more likely to trust nonverbals over verbal messages. Sometimes we dislike a neighbor or a coworker, and we're not sure why because their verbal communication has always been quite pleasant. Something about them, though, just bothers us. Usually, you are picking up on some nonverbal behavior that they exhibit. You may not be aware of what it is, but you know that something is not right. Because competency judgments are strongly impacted by nonverbals, business communicators must be aware of their appearance, body language, and eye contact. You might not hire someone because of a nonverbal behavior, and you might not get a particular job because of your own nonverbal behavior.

Tied to Culture Nonverbal communication is tied to culture. Did you know that the popular American "thumbs-up" sign is considered to be an obscene gesture in Australia? It's important to be familiar with other cultures' views on nonverbal communication. If you plan to travel or do business in other countries, remember that culture plays a huge role in nonverbal communication. Before you can even say a word, your posture, gestures, and eye contact convey a message to your audience. Crossing your legs in the United States is completely natural: sitting in the same position in Kuwait may be impolite.[9]

Here are some tips on nonverbal communication in other countries:

- **Germany:** It is considered rude to leave your hands in your pockets while doing business. People in Germany may not smile to indicate that they are pleased about something.
- **Hong Kong:** A bow is an appropriate greeting when meeting a business contact. Punctuality is important. You should maintain a two-arms'-length distance from your contact. Touching and patting are considered taboo. Men should not cross their legs when sitting. You should present your business card and gifts with both hands.
- **Indonesia:** You should eat with your right hand, not your left. It is considered good manners to take a second helping of food. Hugging and kissing in public is considered inappropriate. In a private home, remove your shoes and point them toward the door you entered.
- **Japan:** Be prompt. This culture is time-sensitive. The American "okay" sign means "money" in Japan. Be aware that, similar to other Asian cultures, extended direct eye contact is considered disrespectful.
- **Singapore:** Gesture with your entire hand. Pointing with one or two fingers is considered rude.
- **Korea:** Cover your mouth when laughing in public. Loud laughter is considered rude. Nose blowing should be done in private. Lower your eyes to show respect for elders.
- **United Kingdom:** The victory sign with the palm facing inward is considered to be an obscene gesture. Make sure your palms face outward. Point with your head rather than with your fingers.[10]

Ambiguous at Times Nonverbal communication can be ambiguous. Much of our understanding of nonverbal communication is not learned in school. We learn from past experience, and we learn as we face new situations. Body language conveys important but

© LightField Studios/Shutterstock.com

unreliable clues about the intent of the communicator.[11] The more information you can get about the clues you are trying to decode, the more likely you will be to decode them correctly.[11] If you are presenting a plan to your team to increase sales in your division, and some team members look away, yawn, and glance at their phones or laptops, you might interpret these nonverbal cues to mean that your audience is bored. You might hurry to finish your presentation and leave out important facts. The reality might be that they are listening to you, but several of them had late nights, two are hungry and check the time to see how close lunch is, and one is shy and has a hard time meeting your eyes. Although many nonverbals are universal, they can be difficult to interpret.

Examples of our inability to interpret ambiguous nonverbals is seen in the research on deceptive communication. University of San Francisco psychology professor Maureen O'Sullivan studies how well people detect deception by relying on nonverbal cues from others. Given a video of subjects to review in controlled studies, most laypeople detect lying about 60% of the time—barely above a flip of the coin. "Most people are pretty terrible at discerning whether other people are lying," O'Sullivan says. "But if you ask them, 'Is the person you're watching uncomfortable?' most will be able to determine that the liar is less comfortable than the nonliar, but they won't go to the next step of calling them a liar."[12]

TYPES OF NONVERBAL COMMUNICATION

We use nonverbal communication to help represent who we are through our appearance, our posture, our facial expressions, gestures, use of time and space, use of our voices, use of touch, and even the arrangement of furniture in our home and our office.

Keep in mind nonverbal messages are shaped by three primary factors: the culture, the relationship, and the situation.[13]

TOOLS OF THE TRADE
VOCALICS: THE VOICE

The term **paralanguage** refers to vocal characteristics, which include the following:

- **Volume:** loudness or softness
- **Rate:** the speed at which you speak
- **Pitch:** high or low
- **Inflection:** change in pitch or loudness (usually done for emphasis)
- **Vocal fillers:** um, ah, er, like, you know
- **Resonance:** richness or thinness of the voice
- **Pauses:** silences; used for emphasis.

Vocalics
The voice.

Paralanguage
Vocal characteristics, including volume, rate, pitch, inflection, vocal fillers, resonance, and pauses.

Good communicators are aware of vocal characteristics and use them appropriately when speaking to add variety to their words and delivery. Breathing from the abdomen instead of shallow breathing (where your shoulders go up and down) will help steady your pitch. When you are nervous, your pitch will be higher, making you sound less confident. Practice breathing from your diaphragm. You'll know when you are doing this correctly because your abdomen will move in and out instead of your shoulders moving up and down. Another problem with shallow breathing is that you will run out of air before the end of a sentence, making your communication choppy and breathless sounding. Stand up whenever you are asked to speak. It will allow you to straighten up, and that will make breathing from your diaphragm much easier. You will have more volume, and you will sound more confident. You will also be more comfortable physically because you won't feel as breathless.

Don't be afraid to pause for emphasis. The pause is one of the most underutilized vocal techniques that you have at your disposal. A pause of a few seconds at a strategic place in your communication will allow your listeners to catch their breath and wonder, "What's next?" Many speakers avoid the pause because they are afraid of the silence, or they think that the audience will wonder if they've lost their place. Use the pause. It will demonstrate confidence to your listener.

Before you speak, look over your notes. Say the words out loud to practice. Which words need to be emphasized? Which words need to be spoken a little slower? Where do you need to get louder or softer?

For example, look at this sentence: *This is what I believe*. Say it out loud, placing the emphasis on the word *this*. It changes the meaning of the sentence. Now try it with the emphasis on the word *I*. The meaning changes again.

Be especially aware of eliminating vocal fillers from your communication. Nothing is worse than hearing someone fill their sentences with the words *like* or *you know*, or *um*. These are distracting, and they interrupt the communication process. If you aren't sure if you overuse these fillers, tape yourself having a normal conversation for about 5 minutes. Play it back and see if these words crop up. These fillers become a distraction and even an annoyance to your listener, so you want to work hard to eliminate them from your communication.

© Gorodenkoff/Shutterstock.com

Appearance Appearance is another important nonverbal because it's often the first thing your audience will notice. This includes your clothes, hairstyle, makeup, cologne, perfume, fragrance from other products, use of jewelry, tattoos, piercings, and posture. People will judge you by your appearance. In a perfect world, you should be able to dress as you please, have multiple piercings, dye your hair any color you wish, and have many visible tattoos. But people will make judgments about you as soon as they see you, so be aware of what is appropriate for different contexts or situations.

Remember that you *can* smell too good. The only thing worse than being near someone who smells bad because of lack of personal hygiene is being near someone who smells too good from using too many fragrances. Be careful when you splash or spritz on perfume, cologne, or aftershave. Also be aware of hair styling products, shower gels, and moisturizers with a strong smell.

How do you know what is appropriate dress for work? The easiest thing to do is to ask someone during the interview or observe those who interview you. As you walk through the building, look at other people who will be working alongside you. Some organizations have a written dress code. For women, that may include wearing closed-toe shoes instead of sandals, and a restriction on ear piercings and other jewelry. For men, it can require wearing a jacket and tie every day. It may dictate the color of your belt or your shoes or the length of your hair. Many organizations don't have a dress code, but they expect you to dress professionally. If you meet clients every day, you will be expected to dress more conservatively than if you don't. Get familiar with terms like "business casual" and "professional business attire." If you don't know, ask someone who works in a position similar to yours. If you do business across the country, you'll need to do some research. "Business casual" in Boston might be different than "business casual" in the Midwest or even on the West Coast.

The book *Business Etiquette*[10] states that you will be judged by your personal appearance, and this is never more apparent than on "dress-down" days when what you wear can say more about you than any business suit ever could. When dressing in "business casual" clothes, recognize that the real definition of business casual is to dress just one notch down from what you would normally wear on "business professional" attire days. Avoid jeans;

worn, wrinkled polo shirts; sneakers; scuffed shoes; halter tops; and revealing blouses. For men, try wearing any pair of pants and a button shirt with long or short sleeves that has more color or texture in the fabric. For women, wear skirts or tailored pants with blouses, blazers, and accessories that mean business yet convey a more casual look than your standard business attire. Avoid wearing clothes that reveal too much or leave little to the imagination. Remember, there are boundaries between your career and your social life. You should dress one way for play and another way when you mean business. Always ask yourself where you're going and how other people will be dressed when you get there. When in doubt, always err on the side of dressing slightly more conservatively than the situation demands. Remember, you can always remove a jacket, but you can't put one on if you didn't think to take it with you![10]

You also need to learn to be flexible. William Herman Jones is an investment broker who wears a suit or jacket and tie to work at a bank every day. He has several clients who farm for a living, and during the planting season, those farmers can't always take time to come to the bank to do their business. So, William Herman Jones changes into khakis, a collared shirt, and work boots and meets his clients in their fields. Business is done over the back of the client's truck in casual attire to be more equal to the client. It also just makes sense.

Body Language Body language, or **kinesics**, is the study of human body motions and movements. This includes facial expressions, gestures, eye contact, and posture. How comfortable are you with eye contact? Most people are uncomfortable with prolonged eye contact—lasting more than a few seconds. But, we are also uncomfortable if someone never looks us in the eye. When you are communicating, eye contact will help you establish a relationship with your listener. Looking at the ceiling, at your listener's ear or nose, or past his or her head will be quite apparent. It is perfectly acceptable to look at your listener for several seconds and then glance away. You can also regulate other people's conversation with your eye contact. If you are having a conversation with two people, and a third person approaches your group, you all may not give them immediate eye contact, preferring to finish your thoughts before visually "inviting" them into the group.

> **Kinesics**
> The study of the human body's motions and movements.

DO YOUR GESTURES BECOME DISTRACTING WHEN YOU'RE NERVOUS?

Smiles are nice. A smile usually lets your listener know that you are confident and comfortable. It also can indicate friendliness or approachability. People do smile for all sorts of reasons. Whatever their origin or motivation, smiles have a powerful effect on us humans. As Daniel McNeill points out, "Though courtroom judges are equally likely to find smilers and nonsmilers guilty, they give smilers lighter penalties, a phenomenon called the 'smile-leniency effect.'"[11] Keep in mind that a smile can also have multiple meanings, so be careful about assigning meaning to this nonverbal message.

Posture is also important. Standing up straight will allow you to breathe from your diaphragm, which will help your voice sound stronger. It also indicates confidence.

Gestures are also part of nonverbal communication. We all talk with our hands to some extent. If you get nervous, you may use more gestures and not realize it. These can become distracting. If you do have to speak in front of other people or deliver a speech, you might try recording yourself to check your gestures. You can hold note cards or papers in your hand, not just as your notes, but also to keep yourself from fidgeting. Don't hold a pen, ruler, or anything else that you can tap or click or make noise with. When you get nervous, you're not always aware of your own fidgeting. Gestures should be used for emphasis. This is another reason to practice a presentation before you deliver it in front of other people.

People can also use gestures to supplement or to take the place of verbal communication. Several examples include the following:

1. **Adaptors:** Touching your hair, your face, or your body or adjusting your glasses or your clothes. These are comforting gestures that help us calm down or reassure ourselves. They can become distracting, however.
2. **Emblem:** Takes the place of a word or phrase. The classic example is when a hitch-hiker sticks his thumb out, indicating that a ride is needed. Another example is the extension of the middle finger, the V for victory sign, the peace sign, or the thumbs-up sign.
3. **Regulators:** These help control the flow of conversation. Students might start packing up their books before class is actually over. They want to make sure the professor is aware that class time is ending. If we are trapped by a chatty coworker, we might glance at our cell phone for the time, or turn slightly away as if we need to leave. If a colleague we don't know that well gets a little too close, we might cross our arms or move back.
4. **Illustrators:** Hand gestures that help explain or illustrate what we are talking about. When giving directions, we might point down the street. When describing someone, we might indicate with our hands how tall they are.

Proxemics Proxemics is the use of personal space. We all have our own personal space. Anthropologist Edward Hall categorizes four distance zones: *intimate space*, which ranges from physical contact to about 18 inches (arm's length); *casual-personal*, which ranges from 18 inches to about 4 feet; *social distance*, which is from 4 feet up to 12 feet; and *public*, which is 12 feet and beyond.[14] We usually allow family, very good friends, a partner, spouse, or significant other into our personal space. We get uncomfortable when other people get too close. If you're standing in the checkout line at the grocery store, you might feel crowded when the person next in line gets too close behind you, especially if you are using a credit or debit card. It's an unwritten rule at the ATM machine that the next person in line stands a certain distance away from you. In business situations, you usually move into the intimate space zone for a handshake and then move back to the casual distance that is acceptable. In a meeting, you might sit closer than the 18 inches to 4 feet dictated by social

---

Gestures
Nonverbal communication, such as talking with your hands, that can supplement or take the place of verbal communication.

Adaptor
Comforting gestures such as touching your hair, your face, or your body or adjusting your clothes or glasses.

Emblem
Takes the place of a word or phrase, such as the peace sign or thumbs-up sign.

Regulator
Helps control the flow of conversation, such as glancing at your watch to show that you need to leave.

Illustrator
Hand gestures that help explain what we're talking about, such as pointing when giving directions.

Proxemics
Use of personal space.

distance, but you are usually side by side or sitting in front or behind someone, and not face-to-face. In a college classroom, you might be crowded together, but you are usually in rows, so that you are facing the back of someone. In this situation, your personal space does not seem violated. This shows that proxemics differ based on different contextual rules.

> How do you feel about your personal space? Who do you let in your personal space?

Chronemics Chronemics refers to the use of time: Are you always late wherever you go? Do you always arrive at your destination early? Do you love to be on time? Your use of time is part of your nonverbal communication. If you are late to class, the professor may not let you in, or you may be docked points for tardiness. If you are late for a job interview, you can knock that job off your list of possible job opportunities. If you are consistently late to work, you will probably be reprimanded, and if it continues, you might be fired. Lateness to important events is usually a sign that you had other, more important things to do. That might not be true, but it is the perception that other people will have. People who hold more power in organizations have greater control over their use of time; however, how they use their time is often scrutinized by other employees, especially subordinates.

<aside>
Chronemics
Use of time.
</aside>

SEXUAL HARASSMENT

Sexual harassment is real, and you might encounter it in the workplace. It may be expressed through verbal or nonverbal communication. It might be blatant—your supervisor tells you that you will get a job promotion or an increase in salary if you grant him or her certain sexual favors (*quid pro quo*). It might also be less obvious because a supervisor or coworker can create an atmosphere that makes you feel uncomfortable (hostile work environment). This could include allowing questionable pictures to be displayed, allowing offensive jokes and remarks to be part of the workday, and tolerating personal space violations. Clearly, sexual harassment involves inappropriate verbal and nonverbal elements.

> Here is a website that will tell you more about sexual harassment: www.eeoc.gov/facts/fs-sex.html

Sexual harassment is a form of sex discrimination that violates Title VII of the Civil Rights Act of 1964. Title VII covers all private employers, state and local governments, and education institutions that employ 15 or more individuals. These laws also cover private and public employment agencies, labor organizations, and joint labor management committees controlling apprenticeship in training. Unwelcome sexual advances, requests for sexual favors, and other verbal or physical conduct of a sexual nature constitutes sexual harassment when submission to or a rejection of this conduct explicitly or implicitly affects an individual's employment, unreasonably interferes with an individual's work performance, or creates an intimidating, hostile, or offensive work environment.

- The victim or the harasser may be a woman or a man.
- The victim does not have to be of the opposite sex.
- The victim does not have to be the person harassed but could be anyone affected by the offensive conduct.

© YAKOBCHUK VLACHESLAV/Shutterstock.com

- The harasser can be the victim of a supervisor, an agent of the employer, a supervisor in another area, a coworker, or a nonemployee.
- The harasser's conduct must be unwelcome.[15]

You do want to do a reality check to make sure that you didn't misinterpret the intended communication. Words and behavior can be misinterpreted. If you feel that you are the victim of sexual abuse, document the incident or incidents. You can then approach the harasser personally, take your complaint to your supervisor or the personnel office, or even pursue legal action.

CONCLUSION

Rahima Martin, the college senior from the beginning of this chapter, enrolled in her Business and Professional Communication class with fear and anxiety. She didn't understand the importance of verbal and nonverbal communication, and she dreaded the group and individual speaking assignments, but she knew her senior year at college meant lots of interviews for career opportunities, and she wanted to do well. She also wanted to feel confident when asked to present information to her professors, colleagues, and peers, so she stayed in the class. By the end of the semester, she successfully completed one group presentation, one professional interview at the Career Center, and two individual presentations. She didn't perform perfectly, but she felt confident in her newfound knowledge and eager to sharpen her skills. Rahima strengthened her verbal communication by working to create clear, formal, and powerful messages free of slang and jargon. She also paid closer attention to her use of nonverbals and was able to overcome her nervousness, project her voice, and express enthusiasm and confidence. When conducting research for her projects, she engaged in active listening through interviews with experts and learned the importance of gauging her audience's reactions to her messages in a way that allowed her to develop more sensitive messages.

After reading this chapter, you should now understand the difference between verbal and nonverbal communication. You should also understand how verbal and nonverbal communication function in the communication process as meaning is co-constructed.

Notes

1. Klepper, M. M. (with Gunther, R.). (1994). *I'd rather die than give a speech*. Irwin.

2. Keysan, B., & Henly, A. S. (2002). Speakers' overestimation of their effectiveness. *Psychological Science, 13*(3), 207–213.

3. Menechella, D. (2001). *How to master the art of verbal communication*. Personal Peak Performance Unlimited.

4. NoSlang.com. (2005–2008). *25 Internet slang terms all parents should know*. noslang.com/top20.php

5. Tannen, D. (1994). *Talking from 9 to 5: Women and men in the workplace: Language, sex, and power*. William Morrow.

6. Rosenbloom, J. (1986). *World's toughest tongue twisters*. Sterling.

7. Warriner, J. E. (1988). *English composition and grammar*. Harcourt Brace Jovanovich.

8. Hacker, D. (2009). Commonly misused words and phrases. In *A writer's reference* (6th ed.). Bedford/St. Martin's.

9. Naguib, R. (2005, October). International audiences. *Toastmaster*.

10. Sabath, A. M. (1998). *Business etiquette: 101 ways to conduct business with charm and savvy*. Career Press.

11. Morgan, N. (2002). The truth behind the smile and other myths. *Harvard Management Communication Letter, 5*(8), 3–4.

12. Zielinski, D. (2007, September). Body language myths. *Toastmaster*, p. 27.

13. Ciccia, A. H., Step, M., & Turkstra, L. (2003). Show me what you mean: Nonverbal communication theory and clinical application. *The ASHA Leader, 8*(22), 4–34.

14. Adler, R. B., & Elmhorst, J. M. (2008). *Communicating at work*. McGraw-Hill.

15. U.S. Equal Opportunity Commission. (2002). *Facts about sexual harassment*. http://www.eeoc.gov/facts/fs-sex.html

INTERPERSONAL COMMUNICATION SKILLS

4

LEARNING OUTCOMES

After reading this chapter you will be able to:

1. Understand the role of interpersonal communication in the workplace

2. Describe the types and functions of relationships

3. Identify different approaches to conflict

4. Determine how certain conflict styles work in different situations

5. Analyze and apply negotiation strategies that meet different objectives

6. Provide and evaluate constructive feedback

7. Identify and apply Gibb's framework for building positive climates

8. Understand the role of technology in maintaining strong organizational relationships

© pathdoc/Shutterstock.com

SELECT KEY TERMS

Interpersonal communication

Interdependence

Uniqueness

Mixed-status relationship

Leader-member exchange
theory (LMX)

In-group

Out-group

Same-status relationship

Informational peer

Collegial peer

Special peer

Border crossers

Conflict

Avoiding

Accommodating

Compete

Compromise

Collaborate

Negotiation

Constructive feedback

Organizational climate

Descriptive message

Problem-focused message

Spontaneous communication

Empathetic message

Message of equality

Provisional message

INTRODUCTION

Cora Sims has worked at Kelpin Publishers as a project manager for 5 years. In this role she works with many different members of the organization to facilitate the publication of elementary school reading materials. From graphics to technology to accounting, she has developed relationships with many different departments. She reports directly to the senior publishing partner, Mack Lewis. Although she feels that she has a strong relationship with Mack, she sometimes feels disappointed that he does not consult with her on big decisions. This is especially upsetting because she sees her coworker Sue having lunches and meetings with Mack where she gets to share her opinion and provide input. Many times, she'll filter messages for Mack through Sue because she feels as though he is more likely to listen to ideas coming from her. Sue encourages Cora to make more of an effort to work with Mack and to not be afraid of telling him when he's leaning toward making the wrong decision. Even though Cora feels that her relationship with Mack could be stronger, she is more confident in the relationships she has developed with others in the organization. She considers Sue one of her best friends, and they even carpool daily where they talk about work and their families. She plays on the company softball team which provides a fun way to interact with people from the departments she relies on for meeting publication deadlines. Although her relationships are strong, she has some fear about what the future might bring. Mack informed her that a massive, corporate-wide budget cut is in the works. He's holding the project managers directly responsible for decreasing expenses and plans to monitor costs associated with advertising, instructional technology, and graphics. She contemplates how she might handle the tough times ahead knowing that she'll have to be assertive in meeting the new budget goals.

Cora's situation demonstrates the interconnectedness of workplace relationships and the importance of competent interpersonal communication. She relies on coworkers for social and professional support and she networks with people from different departments. That said, she feels challenged by her relationship with her supervisor and wonders how she might communicate more openly with him. The following sections describe different

© G-Stock Studio/Shutterstock.com

HOW DOES OUR ABILITY TO COMPETENTLY COMMUNICATE AT WORK AFFECT OUR JOB SATISFACTION?

Interpersonal communication
Communication of a relational nature between two or more people marked by interdependence, uniqueness, and quality.

Interdependence
A characteristic of interpersonal relationships describing how people rely on each other equally for both personal and professional support.

Uniqueness
A characteristic of interpersonal communication signifying the special quality of the communication between individuals.

Mixed-status relationship
The relationship an employee has with people above or below his/her own position in the organization.

Leader-member exchange theory (LMX)
A theory explaining how leaders have groups of employees who emerge as part of their in-group, middle-group, and out-group.

aspects of interpersonal communication at work including strategies for negotiating with others and building supportive communication climates. As you read, consider how the relationships and climate at Kelpin Publishers are critical for dealing with major organizational change.

DEFINING INTERPERSONAL COMMUNICATION

Interpersonal communication is critical to the basic functioning of any organization. **Interpersonal communication** is defined as communication of a relational nature between two or more people. These relationships are marked by **interdependence**, where people rely on each other equally for both personal and professional support, and **uniqueness**, which signifies the special quality of the communication between individuals. Relationships form between many individuals in the workplace and are marked by communication that is *task oriented* (focused on completing projects and duties) and *relationship oriented* (focused on supporting others or sharing personal information). We form relationships with coworkers, supervisors, and clients or customers. Our ability to communicate competently with people at work affects our job satisfaction, feeling of belongingness in an organization, and ability to complete tasks and projects successfully and in functional and rewarding ways. Many of the chapters in this book deal with issues of interpersonal communication, including nonverbal communication, language use, multiculturalism, diversity, and working with others in small groups. This chapter focuses on the different types of relationships you are likely to encounter, how to develop effective relationships through understanding the communication patterns of others, and learning how to manage relationships through negotiation, constructive feedback, and strategies for enhancing relational climates.

TYPES OF WORKPLACE RELATIONSHIPS

You are likely to form many types of relationships at work as much more happens during a work shift than merely accomplishing tasks. Through completion of duties we come to know and interact with many different organizational members and form friendships. These relationships are often classified as same status or mixed status. These terms signify whether you work on the same organizational level or whether one person holds higher status or power, such as a supervisor. Let's begin by examining mixed-status relationships.

MIXED-STATUS RELATIONSHIPS

Mixed-status relationships refer to relationships employees have with people above or below their own position in the organization. Mixed-status relationships often are referred to as supervisor–subordinate or leader–member relationships. The nature of these relationships can vary significantly, depending on individuals and organizational structures. One theory that describes outcomes of the quality of these types of relationships is **leader–member exchange theory (LMX)**.[1] The basic premise of this theory explains how leaders typically have groups of employees who emerge as part of their in-group, middle-group,

© Mr.Music/Shutterstock.com

and out-group. Being in the **in-group** signifies a higher level of liking and higher-quality communication, which results in more support, resources, and even responsibility. **Out-group** membership means that an employee is not in the supervisor's inner circle and has lower-quality communication exchanges, resulting in less support, resources, and responsibilities. Quite a bit of research on this topic shows that members of the in-group often receive greater benefits than those of the out-group. Scholars recommend that managers work to include all their employees in the in-group and to promote equality among employees to reduce the perception that they show favoritism in distributing resources. The stronger, more positive the superior–subordinate relationship, the higher the performance and innovation levels among employees. Additionally, these relationships likely motivate employees to go above and beyond their role responsibilities for the organization.[2]

SAME-STATUS RELATIONSHIPS

Same-status relationships include a wide variety of people in the organization, specifically at the same level of power and authority within or outside an employee's department or work group. These types of relationships provide a wide range of support, ranging from what Kram and Isabella describe as informational, collegial, and special peers.[3] **Informational peers** are coworkers with whom we primarily share information about work, whereas **collegial peers** are coworkers with whom we discuss work-related topics as well as family and personal issues. Finally, **special peers** are considered the most intimate peers with whom we share personal information and from whom we receive emotional and social support. Smooth working relationships with coworkers provide us many benefits, including an ability to complete our work efficiently and at higher quality levels. They also provide us with social support to cope with burnout and workplace stressors. Friendship enhances our interest and motivation at work and can help us to identify more with our organizations. After all, organizations are made up of people, so forming meaningful relationships can translate into meaningful work. A study by Bridge and Baxter[4] found that

In-group
Being a member of a leader's inner circle, which signifies a higher level of liking and quality communication.

Out-group
Employees who are not in the supervisor's inner circle marked by lower-quality communication exchanges.

Same-status relationship
Includes a wide variety of people in the organization, specifically at the same level of power and authority within or outside an employee's department or work group.

Informational peer
Coworker with whom we primarily share information about work.

Collegial peer
Coworker with whom we discuss work-related topics as well as family and personal issues.

Special peer
Coworker who is considered the most intimate peer with whom we share personal information and from whom we receive emotional and social support.

© New Africa/Shutterstock.com

workplace friends decrease tension and increase cohesion, especially when employees face role conflicts. Of course, not all same-status relationships are classified as friendships, but cultivating strong same-status ties is important for organizational satisfaction, productivity, and commitment.

© racorn/Shutterstock.com

⌐INTERGENERATIONAL RELATIONSHIPS

If you've been out of school and working for a while, you may notice that the new generation of workers seems a bit different from your own generation. You may worry that their expectations are too high, they demand too much too soon, and they want everyone in the workplace to abandon paper and rely exclusively on technology. If you are new to the corporate life, you may be bewildered at the norms and rules established by the older generations of workers. You may wonder why they are so slow to innovate, why they rarely take vacation time, and why they work so hard for such little return.

Much has been written in the popular literature about Generation Y (also known as the Millennials, the Net Generation, and the Echo Boomers), who were born between approximately 1977 and 1994. Like other generations (such as the baby boomers and the Gen Xers), Gen Yers are heavily influenced by the events, music, politics, technology, and pop culture of their time. Certainly, no generation of workers is more educated or more technologically savvy than the Millennials. Growing up with smartphones, laptops, the Internet, texting, e-mail, Google Docs, instant messaging, Twitter, Snapchat, YouTube, instant news, phablets or tablets, and hundreds of TV channels, Gen Yers rely extensively on electronic media for news, entertainment, study, consumer purchase, and social networking. And technology use is likely to continue increasing. Gen Z is reporting to work soon! According to a Kaiser Family Foundation 2010 report, children between age 8 and 18 were consuming an average of 7 hours and 38 minutes of media per day, or more than 53 hours per week.[5] In other words, in 2010, children spent as much time using media as most adults spend at work. Consider these statistics:

- 66% of these kids owned cell phones.
- Besides using cell phones to talk, children used cell phones 49 minutes per day to access TV, music, and games.
- 76% of them owned iPods or MP3 players.
- TV viewing was down, with children watching 3–4 hours per day, but Internet usage was up.
- 74% of high school students had a social profile online, and they spent 22 minutes per day visiting social Internet sites.

These somewhat dated 2010 statistics revealed that the Internet accounted for only about 18% of daily usage of media; in 2016 the Internet accounts for closer to 30% of daily media use. iPods and MP3 players are obsolete or redundant, replaced by smartphones and streaming music services, such as Jango, Amazon Prime, Pandora, and Spotify. Moreover, hardcopy magazines and newspapers have been virtually replaced with e-versions of both. In the last ten years, we've seen American adults' usage of social media increase from a mere 7% in 2005 to 65% in 2015.[6] With smartphones penetrating the United States at a near saturation rate of 80%, today smartphone apps account for half of all digital media consumption.[7] A distinguishing characteristic of Millennials may very well be their reliance on mobile-only devices, rather than desktop platforms and televisions.

Reliance on technology is not the only difference between Gen Y and Z (the generation following Y that will enter the workforce in the next 5–10 years), and generations before them. Researchers have found that over the years, workers have changed gradually in ways that influence how they view work and how they interact with others.[8] More emphasis on leisure time and a balance between work and family life, increased self-esteem and narcissism, greater anxiety and depression, and more concern for wealth, looks, status, and autonomy—all these changes are likely to affect how the Millennials behave and respond to others at work.

So how do coworkers from different generations get past these differences and communicate effectively with one another? Critical to effective communication between generations is the ability to accommodate what you say and how you say it. Interestingly, older people are often perceived as *underaccommodative* in their encounters with younger people, whereas younger people are perceived as *overaccommodative* with their elders.[9] Either way, the potential for intergenerational miscommunication is high.

For instance, older people are perceived to hold and express negative stereotypes about the younger generation; they do not seem to appreciate the younger generation's needs and wants, and they tend to brag about "the good old days." So you might expect younger people to find conversation with older people difficult and disagreeable. Yet research reveals that these kinds of underaccommodative comments by older people are not intended to demean younger people, but to assert the elders' continued vibrancy and relevance. On the other hand, younger people are often perceived to be talking down to their elders, evidenced by slowing their speech, smiling excessively, nodding their head, and other apparently condescending behaviors. In reality, these overaccommodative attempts are likely born out of the younger peoples' desire to nurture or to be attentive than to patronize, denigrate, or demean.[10]

© Rido/Shutterstock.com

Communicating effectively between generations requires that younger and older people work to better accommodate one another and to translate or seek to understand when the other over- or underaccommodates. As it turns out, generational differences are often perceived to be much greater than they actually are. Looking beyond the popular literature, researchers have documented similarities among the generations in the workplace, noting that many perceived differences in values, for instance, are more likely a function of age, status, and longevity in the organization.[11]

In addition to accommodating our speech to them, we should make a point of interacting more often with people outside our generational group, moving beyond our comfort zone. Discovering similarities, or what you have in common with one another, will often override assumptions about differences. Perhaps most important to effective intergenerational communication is seeking each other's advice and help. For older workers, reaching out to Gen Yers for help designing an effective Twitter campaign for a project, or for advice on new innovations recommended by younger workers; or just informally talking about useful apps that younger coworkers might be using makes good communication and work sense. For younger workers, asking more experienced coworkers to explain the origins of current policies as well as the more informal rules and asking for mentoring can only make their work more productive.

GENDER RELATIONSHIPS

Not until the late 1800s did women find their way into the workplace outside the family home. Today women make up 58.6% of the labor force in the United States, with projections of even greater representation in the future.[12] Obviously, it's in everyone's best interest for men and women coworkers to relate effectively. Knowing how to accommodate each other can make working together easier and more productive. In order to be able to accommodate the other gender appropriately, you need to reflect first on how women and men communicate.

No innate, or biological, differences account for how women and men communicate differently. But how children are socialized influences how they relate and, more important, how they perceive others to communicate. Women and men are a product of their socialization. Throughout their lives, they learn to view the world differently and to think and behave in particular ways. Growing up male implies being part of a masculine culture, and growing up female means being a member of a feminine culture. When men and women don't behave in the expected ways, they often encounter negative reactions.

As a member of a female culture, a woman is often expected to place a high priority on personal relationships and to provide support, show compassion, and nurture others. To achieve symmetry or equality, women often "match experiences"[13] to show others they have felt the same way or the same thing happened to them. Because women value being polite, showing respect, and acting courteously, they "avoid criticizing, outdoing, or putting others down."[14] In contrast, men, as members of a male culture, are expected to give high priority to individual success and achievements, appreciate competition, assert themselves and challenge others, and control or dominate interactions.

How might these gender differences influence how women and men communicate with each other at work? Given the demands of the workplace, men may fail to appreciate women who they perceive as weak and unsure of themselves, and women may respond negatively to men who they perceive as attempting to dominate or self-promote. Recognizing differences in their values or priorities is one way for men and women to begin accommodating one another. Men may need to appreciate that women give support ("I like how you handled that situation"), communicate a sense of equality when working on tasks ("Let's try to analyze this problem *together*. How should *we* begin?"), and share the success of joint achievements ("We did a really good job on this project. I couldn't have done it without you"). Women may need to assert themselves while affirming their male coworkers' abilities ("I know that you already know how to do this. Let me give it a shot this time"), promote their own successes ("I feel really good about the work I did on this project"),

and engage in more powerful talk by using fewer qualifiers (*maybe* and *perhaps*), tag questions ("don't you agree?" or "isn't that so?"), and intensifiers ("very, very happy").[15] Women and men respect each other more when they try to accommodate each other's communication styles.

The failure to accommodate often leads to miscommunication and misunderstandings. At the extreme, it can lead to sexual harassment. In recent years, the U.S. Supreme Court has identified behaviors that might be perceived as hostile or victimizing, including telling off-color jokes, discussing explicit sexual conduct, using demeaning or inappropriate terms ("honey" or "babe"), or using crude or offensive language.[16] Perhaps no other kind of work relationship requires greater efforts to accommodate than the one between genders. The consequences of not doing so can be damaging to the organization—and potentially illegal.

© XiXinXing/Shutterstock.com

ROMANTIC RELATIONSHIPS

Most organizations today discourage romantic relationships between coworkers, with an increasing number of organizations (about 42%) having policies prohibiting them.[17] Many companies frown on office romances because they want to avoid allegations of sexual harassment and acts of retaliation after bitter breakups. Both employers and employees strongly agree that romances between supervisors and their subordinates are unhealthy. However, relationships between colleagues of equal status are perceived more positively.[18]

Regardless of company policy, coworker romances are likely for several reasons. For example, with work hours steadily increasing over the last two decades, we are spending more time together at work, so we may have less time to find potential mates in other settings. Finding one at work is somewhat natural. In addition, proximity, shared interests, and similar work values are predictors of attraction.[19] It's no wonder, then, that about 40% of employees today report involvement in a workplace romance at some point during their career.[20]

The consequences of workplace romances can include marriage, divorce, sexual harassment, decreased morale and productivity, stalking, and even workplace violence. Coworkers may gossip about the romantic couple, complain of favoritism, attribute questionable motives, and exhibit signs of jealousy.[21] Whether you are involved with someone at work or you work with couples who are involved, steps should be taken to manage these relationships so that they do not adversely affect the workplace morale.

Work–family border theory provides a contemporary view of the workplace environment that does not separate the work domain from one's personal life. This theory views work and life as two separate domains with permeable borders that individuals move in and out of throughout any given day.[22] People become **border crossers** as they move from work to home and back again. These domains overlap considerably for workplace romances, making the distinctions between work life and personal life arbitrary and less meaningful. Accommodating coworkers in a romantic relationship requires rethinking an older paradigm that views romance and work as two separate and distinct entities. We can no longer prohibit office romance, nor do we seem to want to these days.[23] People are more tolerant of personal relationships at work, particularly when so many experience work romances themselves. In general, human resource professionals agree that when they learn about an office romance, they should simply keep an eye on the situation. Both employees and managers suggest that they should be on the lookout for potential problematic behavior and, when necessary, "talk to the employees involved" and "monitor conflict" and "productivity." In addition, a number of employees argue that romantic relationships should be supported, for example, by offering common vacation time.[24]

Two authors of this book, Dr. Plax and Dr. Kearney, are married to each other and work together at the same university. As married people who have been border crossing for thirty years, they have worked out a series of rules for how they want to relate to each other at work. Perhaps these simple rules will help you as you manage your own workplace romance.

- **Rule 1:** Treat each other the way you would treat any other professional colleague at work—with respect and professionalism.
- **Rule 2:** Avoid using terms of endearment or making nonverbal contact that might make others feel awkward or embarrassed.
- **Rule 3:** Disclose the nature of the relationship. Attempts to hide or keep secret the relationship only invites distrust.
- **Rule 4:** Keep personal conflicts at home. Sharing marital conflicts only makes colleagues feel uncomfortable.
- **Rule 5:** Retain your own separate professional identity. Insist that others respond to you as individuals, not as a unit. Ensure that phone and e-mail correspondence remains separate. Invitations, promotions, praise, pay raises, and assignments should be given to the deserving individual, not to the couple.

While it's easy to think of organizations as being primarily task-focused, organizing in and of itself is relational. Relationships make up the social fabric of organizations which are living networks. Being able to create and maintain relationships is critical to your organizational success, and you need specific tools for managing potentially difficult situations. Learning specific skills such as how to negotiate conflict and offer constructive feedback are important ways to build positive working relationships with employees of higher or equal status. The following sections focus on these skills and ways you can frame your messages to maximize success.

RESEARCH NOTE

WORKPLACE BULLYING: DYSFUNCTIONAL RELATIONSHIPS AT WORK

"Adult bullying at work is a shocking, terrifying, and at times shattering experience. What's more, bullying appears to be quite common, as one in ten U.S. workers report feeling bullied at work, and one in four report working in extremely hostile environments. Workplace bullying is repetitive, enduring abuse that escalates over time and results in serious harm to those targeted, to witnessing coworkers, and to the organizations that allow it to persist. Bullying runs the gamut of hostile communication and behavior and can consist of excluding and ignoring certain workers, throwing things and destroying work, public humiliation and embarrassment, screaming and swearing, and occasionally even physical assault. What makes workplace bullying so harmful is its persistent nature. Exposed workers report that bullying goes on and on, lasting for months and—in many cases—even years."[25]

Dr. Pamela Lutgen-Sandvik describes the prevalence and harmful nature of workplace bullying. For a full transcript of the story go to: http://www.communicationcurrents.com/index.asp?bid=15&issuepage=8.

Have you ever witnessed or been the target of workplace bullying? How do you think this behavior affected the communication climate of the workplace? What were the direct personal affects for you and others who witnessed the treatment? What options did you have for addressing the situation?

© fizkes/Shutterstock.com

DEALING WITH CONFLICT

Conflict is an inevitable part of life, especially worklife, so learning how to deal with difficult people and situations is critical to maintaining relationships and being successful. In organizations, conflicts arise over many different issues, including personal differences, budgets, resources, office space, methods, procedures, and policies. At the root of most conflict is the idea that we have differing goals and often different styles and values from other people. Learning your own tendencies in dealing with conflict and knowing the style of others is critical to managing situations. This next section reviews the basic conflict management styles with a focus on the pros and cons to each style.

Conflict

The verbalized tension occurring between two or more people with differing goals or wants.

Conflict, broadly defined, describes the verbalized tension that occurs between two or more people with differing goals or wants. Conflict is often characterized in terms of wins and losses, but you should examine these styles beyond the terms of a scoreboard because what might appear as a win or a loss in reality might not be successful or unsuccessful, depending on different situations. Five conflict styles are used based on different situations: avoiding, accommodating, competing, compromising, and collaborating. These styles were developed by Killman and Thomas,[26] who categorized a person's orientation to conflict based on their concern for people and their concern for task.

AVOIDING

Avoiding

Withdrawing from conflict resulting in neither party gaining what they want.

The **avoiding** strategy is often referred to as the withdrawing style, because instead of dealing with conflict directly, a person will avoid it altogether. The outcome of avoiding or withdrawing is that neither person gets what they want. The person who engages in an avoidance strategy either gives up their desires or they meet their desires by failing to engage in the conflict to begin with. Avoidance can be a sufficient strategy if the issue is not important or if engaging in the conflict would be detrimental to the relationship or if we could hurt someone by pursuing the conflict. The downside of overreliance on this strategy is that the person using avoidance will not have their needs met and the conflict may never be resolved. This can wear on a relationship over time. Many times people engage in rather bizarre behavior when avoiding conflict, such as reducing eye contact, ignoring phone calls, or going out of their way when walking to avoid crossing paths with someone. As you can see, these tactics do not facilitate solutions and more than likely postpone them.

ACCOMMODATING

When we have a strong preference about something such as a policy or proposal, but instead decide to let the other person have their way, we are **accommodating**. In this situation, we don't withdraw from the conflict altogether, but we work at smoothing things over to allow the other person to get what they want. Smoothing is another term used to describe this conflict approach. Accommodating is a skillful tool when the other party is really passionate about a specific course of action and you do not feel as strongly. However, accommodating can be detrimental when you always use this specific strategy. In the workplace people may perceive you as lacking initiative, especially if you continually give up your power to persuade by always allowing someone else to get their way. Always being accommodating can also make you feel like a doormat.

> **Accommodating**
> Smoothing over conflict by allowing the other person to get what they want.

COMPETING

The word *competition* evokes a sense of winning and championship over another person, and that is exactly what this conflict strategy describes. When we **compete** with others in conflict, we seek to persuade others that our courses of action or desires are supported over another person's or another group's. When one person "wins" a conflict, then the other party loses. There are times in organizations where this is a highly valued skill, especially when negotiating for new business. Sometimes, organizations themselves set individuals and groups up to compete for resources, which is not always the best course of action for promoting strong interpersonal relationships. Losers may come out disappointed and hurt, which affects morale. If your primary style is to compete, you need to analyze each situation to see if the outcome is really worth potentially damaging relationships.

> **Compete**
> When one person "wins" a conflict, and the other party loses.

COMPROMISE

Compromise is a useful tool because it allows both parties to gain a solution by each sacrificing a part of what they want. Although something must be given up, a reasonable solution can be arranged that makes both parties happy. Compromise is probably one of the more common ways of negotiating conflict. In the workplace, overreliance on this conflict strategy can promote more strategic bargaining from both parties. Situations can be manipulated in that if you know going in that you will have to give something up, you may fight to include something that's not all that important so that you can show a good faith effort at compromising by giving up this item later. It can result in a much more strategic conflict resolution than necessary. On the other hand, there are positive outcomes of compromise because everyone gets a little bit of what they want.

> **Compromise**
> A conflict strategy that allows both parties to gain a solution by each sacrificing a part of what they want.
>
> **Collaborate**
> When two parties work together to develop a joint solution that meets all the needs, goals, or demands of the situation.

COLLABORATION

Ideally, when parties **collaborate**, they both come out with all their goals met. Perhaps their goals are not met in the way they initially intended, but as two opposing groups or people collaborate, they can actually come up with joint solutions that meet all the needs, goals, or demands of the situation. Although collaboration is thought to be one of the healthiest conflict management approaches, it is not always possible or optimal in all situations, depending on money, relationships, and time pressure. Collaboration is more time-consuming than other conflict approaches because it requires consensus and careful negotiation.

NEGOTIATION

Regardless of the status of the other person, specific interpersonal skills are critical to smooth interpersonal relations. First, we must understand how to negotiate and deal with potential conflict. As a student of communication, you should take the time to assess the motivations and the communication styles of others, as this tells you a lot about which communication strategies will be most effective in dealing with others and in making sure both parties are able to have their goals and needs met. **Negotiation** is a means to reach mutual agreement through communication.[27]

WHY IS COLLABORATION A USEFUL TOOL IN CONFLICT?

© George Rudy/Shutterstock.com

According to Teresa Smith, business professor at the University of South Carolina, Sumpter, and organizational consultant, most organizational members make six common mistakes when negotiating.[28] They negotiate emotionally, take it personally, fail to ask for what they want, accept "no" too quickly, and lack knowledge and flexibility. To avoid these pitfalls, she recommends the following strategies:

1. Decide what you want.
2. Understand the other side's bargaining style.
3. Analyze the situation.
4. Structure the situation to your advantage.
5. Display confidence.

Any time you go into a negotiation, you need to have a goal in mind and know what you are willing to accept as an outcome. Typically, this means you should prepare to ask for something more than you are willing to settle for and then offer compromise solutions that move you closer to your desired goal. You also have to go into the situation knowing whom you're dealing with. Knowing a person's basic approach to conflict and negotiation helps you to plan your communication strategies accordingly. For example, if you know that your supervisor or another department manager hates small talk and likes to cut to the chase, then be prepared for that scenario. Sometimes the person will allow you to make your case, but other times they will want to begin by asking questions. Knowing what to anticipate from the other person helps you to construct the most persuasive arguments. This also suggests that you must be able to demonstrate your knowledge of the issue and to address different perspectives. Communicating in an informed, assertive way builds your competence and confidence and makes a positive outcome more likely. Arguing for your position takes persuasive skill, which requires practice. This does not come naturally for very many people, so it is a great idea to practice the negotiation with a colleague or family member.

Research suggests that when relationships are a priority in negotiation, higher relational capital can be an end result, even if the most economically feasible solution is not reached.[29] Communication researchers also find that when employees perceive an open, task-oriented relationship with supervisors, they feel more confident in their ability to negotiate their work roles, resulting in higher job satisfaction and a reduction in role conflict.[30]

Negotiating is often affiliated with the concept of interpersonal persuasion or your ability to persuade others to hold a certain belief or take a specific action. Gaining compliance from others is an important skill. Another form of compliance gaining through the use of interpersonal persuasion is offering constructive feedback in an effort to get coworkers or supervisors to comply with your requests. More than likely, negotiating with supervisors and coworkers will involve constructive feedback. Employees need to determine specific ways to offer and receive constructive and sometimes not so constructive criticism as a natural part of work life, whether it is in negotiating, working in groups, or going through the performance appraisal process. The following section provides important advice for competently communicating constructive feedback.

GIVING AND RECEIVING CONSTRUCTIVE FEEDBACK

Although frequently termed constructive *criticism*, **constructive feedback** constitutes communication intended to motivate others to change a process, procedure, or even a belief. Constructive feedback need not be critical in a negative sense, but can focus specifically on helping others grow in their organizational roles or correct a process or procedure that is not leading to success for the individual or the organization. The ability to provide constructive feedback is an important skill in organizations.

Dealing with conflict or providing constructive criticism is tricky business. It is easy to offend someone or to escalate the conflict by using the wrong words or language. You can assert yourself and/or use effective communication by using "I" language instead of "You" language. "You" language places the blame on someone else. In fact, many people interpret "You" language as accusatory and then they become defensive in response.

Constructive feedback Communication intended to motivate others to change a process, procedure, or even a belief.

NEGOTIATING WITH SUPERVISORS AND COWORKERS USUALLY INVOLVES CONSTRUCTIVE FEEDBACK.

Some examples of "You" language are:

- "You need to adjust your schedule so that you aren't always late for meetings."
- "Your report is missing important data, so you'll need to revise it."
- "Your remarks in the meeting today were confusing and created anxiety for the other departments."

Can you see that these three statements are not examples of effective communication? Each statement is direct, but offers no constructive criticism or helpful advice, and places the blame on the other person.

"I" language is also descriptive language. "I" language focuses on the speaker instead of on the other person. See these two examples of "I" language:

- "I need to emphasize that our weekly meetings begin promptly at 8:00 a.m. Everyone needs to be here on time."
- "I feel that your report contains some errors that will keep it from being taken seriously. Let's go over it together and edit it for mistakes."

Start out simply. Instead of saying to someone, "You are wrong about that issue," say instead, "I don't agree with your views on that issue." The other person still holds the same view, and you still disagree, but you are not accusing that person of being wrong. It is fine to disagree. You each are left with your own opinion and your self-worth.

Developing constructive messages takes care, planning, and empathy. Many situational factors come into play such as the nature of the problem as well as the personalities involved, but the following guidelines can be used in a variety of circumstances.

- **Prepare a structure for your approach.** If you are engaging in a formal feedback session such as a performance appraisal, make sure you prepare a structured approach for the process. This might involve forms that you and the other person prepare, as well as outlets for responding, especially in the case of a disagreement.

- **Be specific in describing the problem or behavior, including consequences.** When communicating with someone about a specific issue such as a mistake in a procedure or a personnel issue such as tardiness, be direct in delivering the message and be sure to provide examples of the behavior as well as the impact it has on other people or the business in general. Avoid directing the critique at the person, and instead describe the behavior. You can still promote a strong interpersonal relationship while also being direct. A study by Asmub[31] found that when supervisors avoid presenting constructive feedback as socially problematic, they are better able to communicate the issues directly and allow for more positive interaction with the other person.
- **Allow for two-way communication.** Competently and carefully resolving conflict involves two-way communication in which both parties are able to discuss the issue openly. How the recipient receives the feedback is often connected to how the supervisor feels about the social implications of delivering criticism. According to Asmub[31] an "interview preparation form can be designed in a way that helps the supervisor produce negative feedback in an unproblematic way" (p. 425). This can be done by allowing both the supervisor and the employee to write down criticism prior to meeting.
- **Focus on solutions.** Another important element of providing constructive feedback is to work with the other employee on solutions for the problem. Many times feedback takes the form of growth feedback, in other words, a discussion of specific mechanisms or procedures can be developed to assist the employee and the organization to grow and improve. This also allows for two-way communication and becomes a negotiation of sorts geared toward growth, not necessarily correction. By focusing on solutions, all parties will feel empowered to resolve the issues and goodwill results.
- **Be concrete about expectations and goals.** Once solutions are developed, consider setting goals, time frames, and expectations about when the issue will be revisited. Formal performance interviews allow for scheduled follow-ups, but there are less formal strategies such as adding deadlines to joint calendars or planning to touch base with someone via email.

Successfully delivering feedback is an important skill that requires a high degree of consideration in terms of how to construct the best messages to gain compliance. Strong interpersonal relationships and negotiation skills go a long way toward facilitating growth. Employees and supervisors should be vigilant at constructing supportive messages that help to create a positive work climate where all individuals strive to do their best work for the organization and for one another. The next section of this chapter provides specific types of messages you can use to create positive relational climates.

© fizkes/Shutterstock.com

SUPPORTIVE MESSAGES CREATE A POSITIVE WORK ENVIRONMENT WHERE EVERYONE STRIVES TO DO THEIR BEST.

TOOLS OF THE TRADE

In a blogpost on *Fast Company*, Courtney Seiter[32] describes the importance of giving and receiving constructive feedback. Seiter emphasizes the importance of using positive forms of communication and recommends using the "Criticism Sandwich" popularized by Mary Kay Ash which describes ways to inject positivity into feedback. Can you think of a time when you were given constructive feedback with this type of message strategy? How did you feel after receiving the message? Did it reduce negative feelings or feelings of threat?

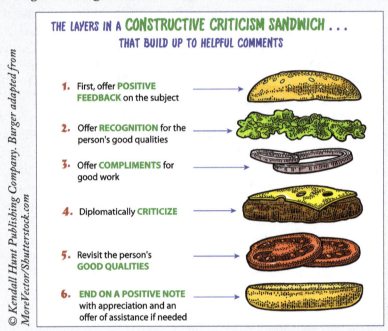

© Kendall Hunt Publishing Company. Burger adapted from MoreVector/Shutterstock.com

THE LAYERS IN A **CONSTRUCTIVE CRITICISM SANDWICH ...**
THAT BUILD UP TO HELPFUL COMMENTS

1. First, offer **POSITIVE FEEDBACK** on the subject

2. Offer **RECOGNITION** for the person's good qualities

3. Offer **COMPLIMENTS** for good work

4. Diplomatically **CRITICIZE**

5. Revisit the person's **GOOD QUALITIES**

6. **END ON A POSITIVE NOTE** with appreciation and an offer of assistance if needed

In addition to skillfully providing constructive feedback, we also need to be able to receive constructive feedback. Supervisors can assist with this by practicing the strategies described above and by developing a set structure in meetings to allow for feedback. This structure provides an opportunity for give-and-take that is expected and less threatening. When feedback is not a regular way of communicating with coworkers and supervisors or when we only receive critical feedback during performance appraisals then it becomes more psychologically threatening. When threatened, our basic instinct is to become defensive or maybe even to withdraw. That said, we should avoid having a negative reaction and be open to the opportunity for growth. A *Forbes* magazine contributor[33] provides the following tips for receiving feedback: (1) Stop your first reaction (defensiveness and negativity); (2) Remember the benefit of getting feedback (think of it as an opportunity for growth); (3) Listen for understanding (keeping in mind that the person giving the feedback might be nervous); (4) Say thank you for the feedback; (5) Ask questions to clarify the concern and gain advice on improving; and (6) Ask for a time to follow up on the feedback so that you can check on your improvements and address any concerns. Creating feedback loops that present opportunities for open dialogue with teammates and supervisors is critical to building open and honest communication climates.

DEVELOPING SUPPORTIVE COMMUNICATION CLIMATES

Organizational climate
Describes the way the communication environment feels in an organization.

Being a savvy negotiator and a skilled giver and receiver of constructive feedback are key elements in maintaining positive communication climates. Whereas an **organizational climate** is made up of many factors, it is simply the way things *feel* in an organization. Is your workplace welcoming and friendly, or formal and strict, or hostile and paranoid? Climate quite literally relates to the temperature and feel of a workplace, and it is said to be a shared perception by most people in the organization. In addition to organizational climates, each relationship also has a climate that can be positive or negative. The positive and negative nature of a climate is determined by the types of messages exchanged. In 1961, Gibb developed categories describing supportive and defensive organizational communication climates.[34]

Supportive climates are marked by descriptive, problem-focused, spontaneous, empathetic, equal, and provisional types of messages. On the other side of the spectrum, *defensive climates* are marked by messages that are evaluative, controlling, strategic, neutral, superior, and certain. Read the following descriptions for examples of each.

Economic Security

Supervisor Task Support

Climate of Respect and Trust

Effective Workplace

Work-Life Fit

Autonomy

Job Challenge and Learning

© arka38/Shutterstock.com

DESCRIPTIVE MESSAGES

Descriptive message
Message that focuses on describing issues that have occurred, as opposed to stating an evaluation.

Descriptive messages focus on describing issues that have occurred as opposed to stating an evaluation. Consider how this might fit within the relationship of a student and teacher. A teacher who uses descriptive communication when grading a paper will offer a student specific, constructive feedback on problems identified, whereas a teacher who uses evaluative communication might simply state, "This is poor work" or "Wrong answer." Clearly, describing the problem is more helpful for communicating areas for improvement.

Supportive Messages	Defensive Messages
Descriptive Consider making this report more formal by adding titles and section headings.	**Evaluative** This report reflects badly on you. You need to work on being more professional in your writing.
Problem Focused The deadline for this report has just been moved up to the end of the workday today. Would you mind clearing your schedule to assist me?	**Controlling** Clear your schedule today, we have a new deadline that you need to meet.

Supportive Messages	Defensive Messages
Spontaneous We are sponsoring a table at the health fair this Saturday. Are you available to staff the table for a couple of hours?	**Strategic** Are you busy on Saturday?
Empathetic I understand why you feel frustrated when Sheila constantly complains about how much work she's doing, as if you have nothing to do.	**Neutral** Oh well, some people are more attention starved than others. That's life.
Equality You have great ideas for the marketing plan. Do you mind sharing them with the committee?	**Superior** Don't bother making suggestions for the marketing plan, the committee has a lot of training and it's really their project to be concerned with.
Provisional When we worked on this project 3 years ago, the vice president never approved our final draft.	**Certain** The vice president did not approve of our revision to the project.

Problem-focused message
Message that poses a request by focusing on how to solve problems together, as opposed to a message that communicates control over another person.

PROBLEM-FOCUSED MESSAGES

Second, positive communication climates are marked by **problem-focused messages**, as opposed to control-focused ones. Posing requests in a problem-focused way makes it clear to the other person that there is an issue that needs a resolution. Control messages serve to command others to act. If a supervisor needs assistance with a project, it is much more competent to say, "I have a deadline coming up on the expansion proposal, could you assist

WHY SHOULD YOU USE A DESCRIPTIVE MESSAGE RATHER THAN AN EVALUATION OF THE PROBLEM?

© fizkes/Shutterstock.com

me?" as opposed to "You will help with this project, ASAP." Or, when a manager develops and distributes a new policy, it is more problem-focused to provide a rationale and explain the problems it addresses. A control message would stipulate that the new policy must be followed, no questions asked.

SPONTANEOUS MESSAGES

Another interesting quality of supportive messages includes **spontaneous communication** as opposed to strategic communication. When we communicate spontaneously we seek to convey our thoughts and messages in a way that indicates sincerity and objectivity. When we plan messages in advance in an effort to manipulate others or when we carry hidden agendas, we speak in a way that intends to hide our motive. Many times, others will become suspicious of these messages and react negatively. You may experience this bluntly when a telemarketer calls you and asks, "How are you doing today?" when you know that there is another reason for the call. Another example is when a coworker asks if you will attend a meeting in his/her place, knowing that the meeting will be long and boring. Once you have experienced the true intention of the other person, you are likely to mistrust future requests. This is considered a very indirect form of communication.

> **Spontaneous communication** Communicating our thoughts and motivations in a way that indicates sincerity and objectivity and does not hide agendas.

EMPATHETIC MESSAGES

The fourth dimension of climate is communicating empathy as opposed to being neutral. **Empathy** is a very powerful skill that involves identifying with others on an emotional level. It is a way that we express caring for others and is a sign of our ability to see issues and events from other people's perspectives. When we remain neutral to certain topics or individuals, we are sending a message that we are indifferent to the needs of the other person. Consider the response you get from a coworker when you express frustration about having to work late for 3 days in a row. An empathetic response might sound something like this, "I know it's really difficult for you and your family when you have to work overtime" as opposed to a more neutral response such as, "Today's organizations expect employees to do what it takes. You win some, you lose some." Clearly, empathetic responses recognize the emotion and difficulty of a person's situation, whereas the neutral response does not tailor the message to the concerns of the coworker.

> **Empathetic message** Communicating in a way that identifies with others on an emotional level.

MESSAGES OF EQUALITY

Gibb's next dimension is that of **equality** versus superiority. Treating others with equality is evidenced in the messages you receive from others. Speaking to others as equals involves recognizing the needs and rights of others. Speaking with an air of superiority sends the message that you are better than or more powerful than others. Even when employees do have more positional power and authority than others in the organization, it is not a license to treat others as such. Imagine that your boss is offering a critique of your work saying, "I know you thought your proposal was on track, but I've been here a lot longer than you, and it is not up to par." This type of message conveys a sense that one person is superior to another. A different way to frame this message in a way that communicates equality might sound like, "Your proposal is a great start, but there are a few suggestions I have that would appeal to the board; would you like to meet to work on this together?" This message conveys the value and worth of the other person while being direct in explaining that improvements could be made.

> **Message of equality** Message that recognizes the needs and rights of others.

PROVISIONAL MESSAGES

Provisional message
Message that acts as a provision or statement indicating that there are multiple meanings or that our assessment of a situation may not always be correct.

Gibb's final category for supportive and defensive messages includes speaking **provisionally** as opposed to with certainty. So many topics in life and business are uncertain, so it makes sense that we would communicate messages in a way that is provisional, or that allows for alternative meanings. When we speak provisionally, we add on a provision or statement that says our opinion may not always be correct. Provisional tags we place on statements include, "As I recall" or "Last year" or "When we last spoke." When people speak with absolute certainty, they essentially claim to know all things, even when they are making an educated guess or an assumption. Phrases that communicate certainty send the message that you are right while others are wrong. For example, if a coworker says, "Jack is not in favor of your proposal," they sound absolutely certain of Jack's position. However, knowing another person's position is not always an easy thing to ascertain. A more appropriate provisional statement might sound like this, "The last time I spoke with Jack about your proposal he raised several concerns" or "Jack may not like some of your options, but he's been known to change his mind."

By focusing on supportive messages, employees and managers work together in creating a positive climate. Positive climates focus not only on achieving goals but also on preserving relationships and making the workplace a meaningful place to spend your time. That said, many employees telecommute on a regular or full-time basis and do not physically "spend time" at the office. These arrangements can pose a challenge for relationship development and maintenance, as communication technology becomes the main channel through which we give and receive information and feedback. The next section addresses the role of ICT and interpersonal relationships at work.

GIVE SUGGESTIONS THAT CONVEY THE VALUE AND WORTH OF THE OTHER PERSON WHILE EXPLAINING IMPROVEMENTS THAT COULD BE MADE.

© fizkes/Shutterstock.com

ICT AND INTERPERSONAL COMMUNICATION AT WORK

Communication technology is an important part of maintaining workplace relationships. Not only do we use technology tools such as email and instant messaging to ask questions, distribute information, and touch base with workmates, but we also use technology for more interpersonal goals such as offering support, connecting with friends at work, and even resolving conflicts. That said, there are mixed findings with regard to technology.[35]

While it is critical for maintaining relationships, research also shows that telecommuters may often feel disconnected and isolated from their organizations and their supervisors. Even with geographically dispersed teams, it is important to schedule some face-to-face meetings and to integrate visual teleconferencing into meetings. This helps employees to connect socially, develop new relationships, and provides the social capital needed to persuade others, resolve conflict, and provide constructive feedback.

Given the importance of technology for developing organizational relationships it is important to avoid hiding behind technology, especially when the need to address serious conflict calls for more face-to-face contact.[36] Instead of simply calling someone or stopping by their office, we use the convenience of email to draft the "perfect" message that will strengthen our position. Overreliance on technology tools can lead to further misunderstandings as the tone of our message may be misinterpreted. Without nonverbals accompanying sensitive messages, important meanings could be lost. Leaders are finding that part of managing organizational culture is actively engaging employees interpersonally where the values of the organization are enacted, discussed, and negotiated.

The following tips are important considerations for technology use and workplace relationships:

1. If possible, avoid using technology for sensitive messages that would be better delivered by phone or face-to-face.
2. Be considerate of how text-based messages lack important nonverbal elements that help receivers interpret messages. The closer the relationship between coworkers, the better they may be able to interpret your messages based on past behavior, but be careful of using dry humor or sarcasm with coworkers with whom you are not close.
3. Consider ways to gather geographically dispersed teams in a physical location on a quarterly basis so that coworkers can connect interpersonally.
4. Provide a comfortable space for telecommuters to work when they come to the office for meetings/work. This helps to decrease feelings of discomfort which can cancel out the benefits of working onsite.
5. When possible, find creative ways to use video technology to communicate with coworkers including video texts and integrating video conferencing for meetings.

CONCLUSION

This chapter focuses on a variety of interpersonal communication issues ranging from the types of relationships we have at work to specific ways we can navigate the interpersonal terrain through competent conflict negotiation, skillful constructive feedback, genuine supportive messages, and thoughtful use of information communication technologies. As discussed at the beginning of this chapter, Cora Sims has some food for thought as she debates how to develop a stronger relationship with her manager, while also maintaining strong relationships with her coworkers as they face severe budget cuts. Based on LMX theory, Cora needs to find ways to improve her communication and connections with her boss so that she can emerge as a member of his in-group. Asking for feedback and requesting face-to-face meetings as opposed to over relying on email could go a long way toward helping her deal with upcoming challenges. Furthermore, she has fostered strong relationships with her coworkers as informational, collegial, and special peers due in large part to the supportive communication climates she has developed through work projects but also through social events like the company softball team. All this provides her with more negotiating power when it comes to budget cuts. By knowing the personalities of different

TOOLS OF THE TRADE
EMAIL

Email is still the most widely-used information communication technology tool used by employees, so skillful messaging with this medium is extremely important for developing and maintaining relationships. Christy-Dale Sims from the University of Denver[37] offers the following tips to her students on the art of email netiquette.

P's and Q's of Professional Emailing:

- **Personalized:** The message is clearly not a form email. There is a personal element in the opening, closing, and body.
- **Prepared:** Offers the information needed using detailed language. Information is complete before the email is sent.
- **Precise:** The subject line clearly states what the reason is for sending this email.
- **Polite:** The email is written in proper language, is appropriately friendly, and includes the use of such phrases as "please" and "thank you."
- **Proofread:** Be sure to review carefully, paying attention to spelling and grammar, as well as the accuracy and formatting of the email.
- **Queries:** The email addresses any questions and makes clear requests for information.

people in the organization and having perspective on the challenges, wants, and needs of different groups, Cora can develop specific strategies that can lead to more collaborative outcomes. The importance of interpersonal relationships at work cannot be overlooked by employees or managers.

Notes

1. Graen, G. B., & Uhl-Bien, M. (1995). Relationship-based approach to leadership. Development of leader-member exchange (LMX) theory of leadership over 25 years: Applying a multi-level multi-domain perspective. *Leadership Quarterly, 6,* 219–247. https://doi.org/10.1016/1048-9843(95)90036-5

2. Sias, P. M. (2009). *Organizing relationships: Traditional and emerging perspectives on workplace relationships.* Sage.

3. Kram, K. K., & Isabella, L. A. (1985). Mentoring alternatives: The role of peer relationships in career development. *Academy of Management Journal, 28,* 110–132. https://doi.org/10.5465/256064

4. Bridge, K., & Baxter, L. A. (1992). Blended relationships: Friends as work associates. *Western Journal of Communication, 56*(3), 200–225. https://doi.org/10.1080/10570319209374414

5. Long, M. (2010, January 20). Survey finds children's media use jumps in five years. *Top Tech News.* Retrieved from http://www.toptechnews.com/story.xhtml?story_id=11000CHGZ8SE&page=2

6. Social media usage (2015, October 8). *Pew Research Center.* Retrieved from http://www.pewinternet.org/2015/10/08/social-networking-usage-2005-2015/

7. Sullivan, W. (2016, April 26). Trends on Tuesday: Smartphone ownership reaching saturation, fueling media consumption. Retrieved from http://www.digitalgov.gov/2016/04/26/trends-on-tuesday-smartphone-ownership-reaching-saturation-fueling-media-consumption/

8. Twenge, J., & Campbell, S. (2013). Generation me and the changing world of work. In P. A. Linley, S. Harrington, & N. Garcea (Eds.), *Oxford handbook of positive psychology and work* (pp. 25–35). New York, NY: Oxford University Press.

9. Giles, H. (2008). Accommodating translational research. *Journal of Applied Communication Research, 36*(2), 121–127. doi:10.1080/00909880801922870

10. Giles, Accommodating translational research.

11. Cennamo, L., & Gardner, D. (2008). Generational differences in work values, outcomes and person-organisation values fit. *Journal of Managerial Psychology, 23*(8), 891–906. Retrieved from ABI/INFORM Global. (Document ID: 1591442681).

12. Women in the labor force in 2010. *U.S. Department of Labor.* Retrieved from https://www.dol.gov/wb/factsheets/qf-laborforce-10.htm

13. Wood, J. T. (1994). *Gendered lives: Communication, gender, and culture* (p. 141). Belmont, CA: Wadsworth.

14. Wood, J. T. (1994). *Gendered lives: Communication, gender, and culture* (p. 141). Belmont, CA: Wadsworth.

15. Kearney, P., & Plax, T. G. (2006). *Public speaking in a diverse society* (3rd ed.). Mason, OH: Thomson.

16. Kadue, D. (2001). Preventing sexual harassment: A fact sheet for employees. Retrieved from http://www.dotcr.ost.dot.gov/Documents/complaint/Preventing_Sexual_Harassment.htm

17. Workplace romance. (2013, September 24). *Society for Human Resource Management.* Retrieved from https://www.shrm.org/research/surveyfindings/articles/pages/shrm-workplace-romance-findings.aspx

18. Horan, S., & Chory, R. (2009). When work and love mix: Perceptions of peers in workplace romances. *Western Journal of Communication, 73,* 349–369. See also Brown, T. J., & Allgeier, E. R. (1996). The impact of participant characteristics, perceived motives, and job behaviors on co-workers' evaluations of workplace romances. *Journal of Applied Social Psychology, 26,* 577–595.

19. Fatal attractions: The (mis)management of workplace romance. (2007, July 1). *International Journal of Business Management.* Retrieved from http://goliath.ecnext.com/coms2/gi_0198-475353/Fatal-attractions-the-mis-management.html

20. Workplace romance. (2013, September 24). *Society for Human Resource Management.* Retrieved from https://www.shrm.org/research/surveyfindings/articles/pages/shrm-workplace-romance-findings.aspx

21. Sias, P. M. (2009). *Organizing relationships: Traditional and emerging perspectives on workplace relationships.* Los Angeles, CA: Sage.

22. Clark, S. C. (2000). Work/family border theory: A new theory of work/family balance. *Human Relations, 53,* 747–770. Document ID: 54990585. For more current research relying on this theory, see: Horan, S. M., & Chory, R. M. (2011). Understanding work/life blending: Credibility implications for those who date at work. *Communication Studies, 62*(5), 563–580. doi:10.1080/10510974.2011.582663

23. Parks, M., *2006 workplace romance poll findings.* Alexandria, VA: Society for Human Resource Management. Retrieved from http://www.shrm.org/research/surveyfindings/documents/2006%20Workplace%20Romance%20Poll%20Fi ndings.pdf

24. Parks, M., *2006 workplace romance poll findings.* Alexandria, VA: Society for Human Resource Management. Retrieved from http://www.shrm.org/research/surveyfindings/documents/2006%20Workplace%20Romance%20Poll%20Fi ndings.pdf

25. Lutgen-Sandvik, P. (2007). How employees fight back against workplace bullying. *Communication Currents.* http://www.communicationcurrents.com/index.asp?bid=15&issuepage=8

26. Killman, R., & Thomas, K. (1975). Interpersonal conflict handling behavior as reflections of Jungian personality dimensions. *Psychological Reports, 37,* 971–980. https://doi.org/10.2466/pr0.1975.37.3.971

27. Downs, L. J. (2008). *Negotiation skills training.* ASTD/Versa Press.

28. Smith, T. L. (2007, October–December). Let's make a deal: A guide to successful workplace negotiations. *Business & Economic Review,* 11–14.

29. Curhan, J. R., Neale, M. A., Ross, L., & Rosencranz-Engelmann, J. (2008). Relational accommodation in negotiation: Effects of egalitarianism and gender on economic efficiency and relational capital. *Organizational Behavior & Human Decision Processes, 107*(2), 192–205. https://doi.org/10.1016/j.obhdp.2008.02.009

30. Miller, V. D., Johnson, J. R., Hart, Z., & Peterson, D. L. (1999). A test of antecedents and outcomes of employee role negotiation ability. *Journal of Applied Communication Research, 27,* 24–48. https://doi.org/10.1080/00909889909365522

31. Asmub, B. (2008). Performance appraisal interviews: Performance organization in assessment sequences. *Journal of Business Communication, 45*(4), 408–429. https://doi.org/10.1177/0021943608319382

32. Seiter, C. (2014, December 9). The art and science of giving and receiving criticism at work: Understanding the psychology of criticism can help you give better feedback and better deal with negative reviews. *Fast Company.* https://web.archive.org/web/20150214124156/https://www.fastcompany.com/3039412/the-art-science-to-giving-and-receiving-criticism-at-work

33. Lindsey, N. (2012, November 7). Taking constructive criticism like a champ. *Forbes.* https://web.archive.org/web/20160413171001/http://www.forbes.com/sites/dailymuse/2012/11/07/taking-constructive-criticism-like-a-champ/#1bb0390a5145

34. Gibb, J. (1961). Defensive communication. *Journal of Communication, 11,* 141–148.

35. Sias, P. M. (2009). *Organizing relationships: Traditional and emerging perspectives on workplace relationships.* Sage.

36. Grenny, J. (2005). Talking Hi-Tech at Work. *T+D, 59*(11), 14.

37. Sims, C. (2015, August 1). Teaching millennials the Ps and Q of professional emailing. *Communication Currents.* https://web.archive.org/web/20200302192037/https://www.natcom.org/communication-currents/teaching-millennials-ps-and-q-professional-emailing

TEAM COMMUNICATION AND CONDUCTING MEETINGS

5

LEARNING OUTCOMES

After reading this chapter you will be able to:

1. Define small group communication

2. Know the advantages and disadvantages of working in a group

3. Describe the life cycle of teams

4. Identify how individual roles function within groups

5. Conduct and participate in a successful business meeting

6. Understand how small groups use ICT tools

© Rawpixel.com/Shutterstock.com

SELECT KEY TERMS

Small group
Groupthink
Forming
Primary tension
Storming
Secondary tension
Norming
Explicit norms
Implied norms
Conformity

Group roles
Task roles
Group building and maintenance roles
Individual roles
Performing
Adjourning
Meeting
Scheduled gathering
Structured discussion
Designated chairperson

INTRODUCTION

Lydia Jackson works for the University of San Angelo in the admissions office and has been charged with leading a group to create a new marketing campaign designed to increase enrollment by 10% over the next 5 years. While she has worked with groups in her department for years, this particular group is an ad hoc committee formed with many different people throughout the university. The committee is charged with creating a comprehensive plan including advertising material, programs, and events for increasing new student enrollment. As Lydia sits down to plan this process she considers the composition of the group. She'll need representatives from student affairs, student retention and advising, and many other areas of the university. How should she plan to convene this diverse group that will remain intact for the better part of a year? What types of activities should she plan for the first meeting? With tight schedules and large workloads, what is the best way to facilitate these meetings?

The material in this chapter will assist Lydia as she begins this process. Specifically, it will describe the advantages and disadvantages of group work, the steps of group formation, how to deal with conflict between the group members tied to their diverse perspectives, and specific steps for planning and facilitating meetings. As you read, formulate a plan for how she can successfully chair the committee.

Working in groups is not simple; it is in fact overwhelmingly complicated. The communication conundrums that groups face are many and varied. And the fact that not everyone within the group may have the same expectations of what should occur when the group gets together only adds to the confusion.

Making matters more complicated is the fact that the person we expect to be the leader, often the boss who likely called the meeting, is no more apt to be an expert communicator than you are. Most managers are people who have worked hard to achieve technical expertise in their given field and been rewarded with a promotion. They are often thrown into a new world of bringing people together, of moderating, of delivering good and bad news; in other words, they are now expected to be experts in communication, and it is a world that they are likely unprepared for.

And so the appropriate first step to understanding group work in a professional setting is to rid ourselves of the notion that this process is simple. Get rid of the idea that meetings

THE LEADER OF THE GROUP IS NO MORE APT TO BE AN EXPERT COMMUNICATOR THAN YOU ARE.

are always efficient. Lose the belief that there will always be an agenda, and that the agenda will be followed. Not everyone is going to participate equally, and some people's contributions will not necessarily be valuable or even on topic. Because here is the truth: Meetings that have clearly written agendas that are followed point by point, and allow everyone the opportunity to offer an insightful comment and provide group votes are not only fictional but also may not be the best way to efficiently accomplish group goals.

The value of working within a group does not lie in the ability to quickly rubber-stamp an agenda, nor does the value lie in coming up with only one solution. Group work, when operating at its best, can be messy, it can be long, and it can be tedious. But it can also produce new information, improve performance, bring people together, improve cultural understanding, and aid everyone involved in learning.

DEFINING AND UNDERSTANDING SMALL GROUPS

We often find ourselves communicating in groups. Although we do communicate intrapersonally (communicating with yourself) or in dyads (communicating in pairs), people are by nature social creatures. We are raised often in a family, our first group, and then continue to join other groups as our lives progress. From a business communication perspective, a **small group** is a *collection of people* working together, *interacting* with the *interdependent* purpose of accomplishing some common goal. The following sections define each of these terms and describe best practices for group formation.

Small group
> A collection of people, working together, interacting with the interdependent purpose of accomplishing some common goal.

COLLECTION OF PEOPLE

Small groups require, at a minimum, three people. When working in dyads, the communication process is very different. While interacting with only one other person, the communication process, although not easy, is greatly simplified. Breaks in the conversation naturally occur. Turn-taking only makes sense. But a third person will alter the dynamic greatly as roles are suddenly redefined.

The more people who are in the group, the more the dynamics change. Three is the minimum number, and although there is no hard-and-fast rule for a maximum number of

A THIRD PERSON CHANGES THE COMMUNICATION PROCESS DRAMATICALLY.

© Vasin Lee/Shutterstock.com

people in a small group, there seems to be a consensus that five to seven people make the ideal small-group size. The odd number is preferable, so that, like the Supreme Court, ties can be avoided if a vote is required. If the number of members is smaller than five, the group may not have the diversity needed to produce new and different ideas, perhaps even leading to **groupthink**. If the group is larger than seven, then there are some new dangers to face: (a) Members may feel that their role is reduced to the point that their presence is useless. They may become disenfranchised with the group, and if this happens, their presence may serve as a distraction rather than a contributing force. (b) The group may splinter—not just into two different factions but several. Multiple competing factions within the same group will only make it harder for the group to operate efficiently and effectively.

Clearly there are small groups out there of more than five to seven people such as PTA groups or even unions. But five to seven people are typically enough to offer diversity while still encouraging all involved to participate fully. Of course, group composition depends on the complexity and type of project or problem addressed. Regardless of size, maximizing quality interaction between group members is critical for success.

Groupthink
A major hindrance to group success when group members, for whatever reason, decide not to participate fully, or along with a decision, allowing only one voice to be heard during meetings.

INTERACTION

As discussed in Chapter 4, creating an open and supportive communication climate is essential to high functioning group interaction. Whether the group is meeting in person, via phone, email, or teleconferencing, the way group members communicate with one another, verbally and nonverbally, will define the relationships within the group. In this way group interaction is purposeful, goal-oriented, and relational. Traditionally group roles have been defined in large part by their face-to-face interaction. Through this interaction, roles will be defined and behaviors will be accepted or rejected. The close contact also allows for nonverbal signals to be more easily interpreted. However, as technology improves, the interaction between members will become more delicate. If not meeting face-to-face, the challenge in interpreting silence and tone becomes even more important. If communicating via email or text message, as is becoming more and more common, you will need to be aware that you often forfeit any intricacy in the language. As Mehrabian pointed out in *Silent Messages*,[1] anywhere from 65 to 93% of all communication is done through nonverbals. If you were joking in a very sarcastic manner during a meeting that the latest idea that your colleague suggested was a really "great idea," you might all have a good laugh. However, if this same message were typed and sent to a group via email, that "great idea," which is really a very poor one, might be seen to be gathering support. These contextual elements have a critical impact on group interaction, so the development of appropriate and effective messages that are appropriate for face-to-face and computer-mediated channels are critical to group success.

INTERDEPENDENCE

It is a cliché to say that a team is only as strong as its weakest link, but that does not make it any less true. Members of good teams and strong groups rely on each other, knowing that if one person is to fail, it is likely that the entire group will fail as well. To use a sports metaphor, if the offensive line fails to block for the quarterback, it does not matter how talented the quarterback is, for he will soon be crushed by an onslaught of defenders. To use an academic metaphor, if a group of five students decides to get together to plan a study session before a final and divides a 10-chapter textbook into five sections so that each

© Monkey Business Images/Shutterstock.com

member will have two chapters to read and report back on, only to have one member of the study group come to the meeting unprepared, the group will be unable to answer any of the questions concerning those two chapters. That means, at best, that the A the group could have gotten is now likely to be a B−. If two people do not pull their weight, the best that a group can expect to achieve on the final is a D−. Finally, in a business setting, if your small group has put together a presentation for potential investors and one of your members has failed to create the PowerPoint presentation as assigned, your small band of venture capitalists is not likely to get your funding, and the great idea that you had will go undeveloped.

The point of all of these examples is that all members of the group are interdependent. They rely on each other for success. Each member brings a specific skill set to the table that

© Life_ImageS/Shutterstock.com

serves as a working asset for success. Working in groups is an inevitable part of work life. This may not always be the popular sentiment, for many people feel that they work best alone. But this is unrealistic in any walk of life. One person cannot possibly play 11 positions on the football field or thoroughly read 10 textbook chapters in a night and hope to comprehend all of the information presented, or put together a comprehensive presentation for a group of investors as well as any group possibly could. Group work capitalizes on the diversity of skills and insights that are unattainable by working alone. That said, another important ingredient for group success is having a clear, common goal or mission.

COMMON GOAL

The previous examples also serve to illustrate another feature of group work. Each group has a common goal that they are trying to achieve. The football team is aiming to score a touchdown and win the game. The study group wants to pass the final; not just pass but excel. The entrepreneurs need to secure investors to begin working in earnest on their dream. Every group that you are in will have a common goal.

It is appropriate to note at this point that each of these groups is working toward achieving this common goal. There are lots of collections of people who just get together with no greater purpose than being together. These people may be your friends or your family, which in a different textbook may constitute a group. However, within a business context, the group should be working toward achieving a specific goal.

Now depending on the type of group, you may or may not have the freedom to choose your own goals. As students you will often be assigned to work in groups with little to no say about the actual activity. However, other times you will participate in a small group and have much control over the aims of the group. For example, if you decide to form a committee to fundraise for any number of activities, you are in charge of your own destiny.

Whether your group's goal was assigned or of your own choosing, the goal is perhaps the critical feature of group work. For without a goal, your group will languish in futility. Having a clear goal that is understood by all members will be crucial to group success. A goal will serve to set measurable bars of success and motivate members to attain that success. If the goal is not understood by all, then it will be even easier for the group to lose focus and get off task.

ADVANTAGES AND DISADVANTAGES OF GROUP WORK

Working in teams or groups can be a double-edged sword. Many of you, no doubt, shudder at the thought of working in teams. These fears do not automatically leave once you have left school. The same fears exist in business settings. You may be worried that members of your team will not fulfill their responsibilities, leaving the lion's share of a project for you. You may worry that your contribution will go unnoticed, lost in a sea of other paperwork. You may worry that your voice will be drowned out by overeager yet underqualified cohorts. However, when a group works together efficiently and effectively, the advantages will greatly outweigh any potential setbacks that you and your team may encounter.

ADVANTAGES OF GROUP WORK

Group Production There is a reason why so many people work in groups. And the reason is simple. As a group, we can accomplish far more than any one individual can. Tedious work (data entry, etc.) can be handled by a group minimizing the amount, time, and effort that any one person has to put in. Groups trying to do creative work (problem-solving, etc.) are better off than any individual, for they have each other to bounce ideas off of and people to double-, triple-, and quadruple-check their work. Think of any television show that is airing today, even reality television shows. All of them have a team of creative writers so that no one person will have the entire burden of creating a new show by themselves every week.

WHY IS IT ADVANTAGEOUS TO DO CREATIVE WORK WITHIN A GROUP?

© SeventyFour/Shutterstock.com

Even though groups can have high levels of productivity, not all tasks are best handled by a group. After all, a smart and capable person who is qualified may not need others to perform a simple task. Other people might actually be a hindrance if the job is to write a memo or answer a relatively simple question. If one person already knows the answer, calling together a committee to attempt to answer that same question would only serve as a waste of resources. However, more often than not, groups will have an advantage over the individual.

Team and Individual Satisfaction Working in groups has many benefits associated with it, and not all of them have to do with productivity. Group work is just as often a chance to do some social networking. The group structure provides an opportunity for members to meet not only at school or in the office, but also outside these formal environments. The more opportunity the group has to become friendly with one another and the more chances they have to chat and communicate with one another, the more likely they are to profess themselves satisfied with the group. The more satisfied with the group, the more satisfied members will be with their overall work experience.

Decision-Making and Commitment A small group is ideally constructed for decision-making. This may seem counterintuitive, as one person can easily make a decision, and adding more people to that mix will inevitably complicate the process. However, complication in this instance may turn out to be a good thing. Decision-making needs to be a collaborative process. When several people examine the situation, they may spot wrinkles that the original "decider" did not. However, if the group, after serious consideration of the problem, can come up with no better solution, you now have something more than you would have had originally. If only the "decider" reaches one conclusion, other group members may feel resentment at not being included in the decision-making process. When all members are allowed to participate and reach a joint decision, they are far more likely to be committed to the decision being made and more willing to support the decision if it later comes under fire.

Ownership The concept of ownership is intertwined with individual satisfaction and commitment. Ownership is the idea that people will have some control over their product. This is easily seen in an artist's work—a person who is allowed to create or express whatever he or she chooses. The business world conversely can be a place where little freedom is offered. It would not be unusual for an employee to be given an assignment in which they have little choice in how or why they are doing what they are doing. However, small groups can be a place where this sort of control is given to employees. When the group members are allowed to make their own decisions and exercise some control over what they are doing, they will feel a greater commitment to the product. That greater commitment can lead to a greater sense of satisfaction within the workplace.

Success Success breeds success. If group members think of themselves as successful, as having achieved some intermediate or long-term goals that they have set for themselves, they will become more satisfied and cohesive than they previously were. Even members who have actually had little to do with the success the group has achieved will still feel that same sense of satisfaction. Think of the backup center on last year's championship football team. This is a person who never saw the field and yet still ends up with the championship ring and a head covered with Gatorade and champagne. That person is now glowing in the warmth of victory and will have a renewed commitment to coming back the following year. Furthermore, others will wish to join the group because of the success, and those who are in the group will become more committed. In simplest terms, the more success the group has, the more committed to success the group will become.

© fizkes/Shutterstock.com

HOW DO OTHER MEMBERS FEEL IF A LONE "DECIDER" DETERMINES THE OUTCOME?

DISADVANTAGES OF GROUP WORK

The Ringlemann Effect Although productivity is greater for a group than for an individual, studies indicate that the productivity level for each individual group member will be lessened by the mere fact that they are working in groups. This is known as the *Ringlemann effect* or as social loafing. Group members, knowing that they have others to rely on to pick up the slack, might be less motivated.[2]

Ringlemann noticed this phenomenon and decided to test it using experimental methods. He had subjects pull a rope individually to see how hard they pulled. He then teamed up one subject with another and then another and so on. He found that when a person is working alone, they obviously pulled the rope using 100% of their maximum force. If a second person is added, each person pulled with an average of 93% of their maximum force. Add a third person to the group, and the effort drops to an average of 85% of their maximum force. If you add as many as eight people, each person exerted on average 49% of their maximum effort. Furthermore, the eight people demonstrated no more productivity than seven people. These results have been attributed to difficulties in both coordination between members and motivation among individuals.

Despite the drop in individual member productivity, the team is still more productive than the individual. Even if members are not giving their best efforts, more people working together are able to achieve more. The key to overcoming the Ringlemann effect is to be constantly vigilant. Be on guard. All members will need constant encouragement from all other members. This does not have to be destructive, harassing, never-ceasing criticism. If the group is going to run efficiently, respectful reminders, deadlines, and constructive feedback will need to be put in place.

Time Another challenge to group work is the issue of time. If you are still in school and are assigned group work, finding the time to get together outside class may be next to impossible, given the amount of outside responsibilities that many students are now shouldering. If you are working in a professional environment and are given the time to conduct meetings, that is still no guarantee that your time will be well spent. A survey done by Microsoft found that employees spend on average 5.6 hours per week, or 14% of the workweek, in meetings.[3] Of the employees surveyed, 71% said their time spent in those meetings was wasted. Furthermore, 39% of people said that meetings were a "productivity pitfall."

Getting together as a group is going to take time, and you are not always going to walk away feeling that something major has been accomplished. But this is one of the stereotypes that you are going to need to get away from if your group work is going to be successful. Time is what you need to invest for greater results in the long run. However, do not expect every meeting to be dynamic and fruitful.

Disharmony If you are asking seven people to sit in a room and come up with solutions to complex problems that not everyone agrees on, you are going to have to expect some feathers to get ruffled. The group, which hopefully is invested in the product that they are creating, will disagree about the best way to get things done. What's more, you are going to want employees who will stand up and say what they believe is right. The key to overcoming this disharmony is to realize that just because someone does disagree with you is no reason to lose your temper and begin berating your colleagues. You will need to strive to be respectful of your group members and the different perspectives that they bring to the table. Argue points on their merit; argue tenaciously, but do not lessen yourself and your group by resorting to profanity or even worse. The ability to manage conflict and provide constructive feedback is critical for group functioning.

Groupthink Groupthink is even worse than disharmony. Groups excel because so many different perspectives come together searching for a solution to a problem. But when group members give up their unique perspective to be only one voice, it can be very problematic. This process is known as groupthink, and it can happen for a number of reasons: (a) Group members may be very intimidated by an overwhelming personality within the group. If one group member, particularly a member in a leadership role, has strong feelings regarding a particular subject, then other members may not feel comfortable standing up to the leader. However, if the group is only there to rubber-stamp the opinions of one person, the group has already lost its function. Each person must be willing to speak their mind if the group is going to operate as effectively as possible. (b) Conversely, members may feel that they have little to contribute, that they do not offer any new solutions or perspectives, and so they best serve the group by supporting the more experienced and seasoned opinions. If this happens, then no alternate perspective can or will be offered, and the group is likely to continue to make the same decisions ending with similar results. (c) It is possible, especially considering the Ringlemann effect that members may not want to give their all to a particular project. They may view the group meeting as a chance to slack off while others do the hard work. If this is the case, then low-performing members may happily support the first solution offered.

Although presenting a unanimous front can be a powerful statement to the organization, you should be aware that if only one solution/opinion is being discussed in the group, your group is failing in its job of coming up with the best possible option/solution. How would you know if the solution decided on by the group is the best solution for this particular problem if no other solutions were discussed? It is difficult to altogether avoid the problem of groupthink, but in an effort to do so, your group may want to implement several of the following suggestions: (a) Create and follow an organized procedure that encourages all members to freely and easily participate in the decision-making process. (b) Before any

MANY PEOPLE FEEL MUCH OF THE TIME THEY SPEND IN MEETINGS IS WASTED.

© Andrey_Popov/Shutterstock.com

decision is made, discuss the potential negative consequences of that decision. Do not just think short-term but examine the long-term effects of your decision. (c) Make sure that all members who have doubts about the proposed solution have ample opportunity to express these doubts. (d) All members should be able to justify the rational reasons for taking a particular position. (e) Ask questions. Do not be afraid to delve into the reasons that people have taken a certain stance. Without questions, there will likely be no understanding of the problem or the solution.

MYTHS SURROUNDING THE SMALL GROUP

To further aid you as you begin to participate within small groups, it's important to dispel several myths that people bring with them to the process. If you do away with some of these false premises, then you will likely be better off.

Myth 1: There Is Always One Right Answer See if you can solve this old riddle. "A man and his son are going out for a drive when all of a sudden another car runs a light and crashes into the man and his son. An ambulance arrives shortly, and the man and son are rushed to the hospital. The father is bruised and worried sick because his son has been knocked unconscious. When the pair reaches the hospital, the boy is wheeled into surgery. The surgeon looks down at the boy and says, "I can't operate on this boy. He's my son.'" How is this possible? Usually the riddle is told to test for deeply entrenched preconceived notions about gender roles, for the answer usually is the surgeon is the boy's mother. But why would it not be acceptable for the answer to be the surgeon is gay and the boy is his adopted son? Or perhaps the boy is his stepson, his new wife's child from a previous marriage. The latter two answers are every bit as correct as the first, and yet most people will assume that there is just one correct answer. The truth is there is not just one answer to every question. In fact, sometimes there are several options. And the more solutions your group can come up with, the more options you will have for solving problems.

Myth 2: The Solution You Reach Must Be "The Best Solution" People often agonize over group decisions. The more people who are in the group, the more likely that the solution will have been tested and retested, poked and prodded until you as a group feel that the solution you have reached is the best solution out there. However, just because you put a great deal of effort into finding your solution does not mean that it is the best solution. If the group becomes convinced that it cannot be wrong and refuses to listen to any more suggestions, then they will have fallen into another trap. Better to think that your solution is best now but be open to more possibilities. Once you become so committed to your answer that you cannot even entertain other options you have seriously erred.

Myth 3: You Must Find "The Ultimate Solution" Somewhere between the second and fourth grades, you were asked to master your multiplication tables. When the teacher asked you what seven times eight was, the whole class could respond in unison, "56." And there was a right answer and a wrong answer. Later, when you got to college, your professors likely asked you to engage in critical thinking exercises—seeing if you could determine long-term consequences to your actions. Although there may not have been a perfectly clear answer at first, given time, you would reasonably determine what the correct path should be. But you will reach a point in your professional career when your group is going to be asked to solve a problem that perhaps has no good answer. The group is going to feel pressure to come up with a solution and not just a solution but the absolute right answer. If this is the case, you are in an impossible situation because not every problem has an ultimate solution. Many times, there is no easy fix, and problems can become overwhelming. Your group may not have been given the appropriate resources (money or technology) or have enough time to really get to the depth of any problem. And yet you will still feel compelled to give an answer because that is what you were asked to do. But you need to realize that not every problem has an answer or an answer that you are capable of reaching within the parameters given. If you are forming a neighborhood watch program to combat a rise in local crime, you may have several solutions: faster police response times, neighborhood alerts, and so on. But these ideas are not new, and crime still may continue to rise. The easy solution does not exist. Your group, despite its best efforts, may simply have encountered a problem to which there is no solution.

TEAM BUILDING

Listed among the positive aspects of working in small groups is the sense of commitment and personal satisfaction that comes when the group is working effectively and efficiently. In an effort to further encourage those same behaviors, it is essential to establish some guidelines for team building. The first necessity in team building is to establish the purpose of the group. What are your team's goals? Why are you getting together to work? Depending on the nature of your problem, this will in many ways help to shape what kind of team you will be building. Is the goal to create policy? Is the goal to improve performance in one particular department? Is your goal project specific? The answer to any one of these questions will help determine which sort of team you are building.

TYPES OF TEAMS

One-Time Teams The one-time team is a unique communication experience. Without the benefit of long-term planning, the group is forced to rely on an existing power structure that may not be to everyone's liking. The group should know going into this process that not everyone will get equal time in this meeting. This is not an opportunity to get together and discuss long-term plans. This group is called together to discuss a specific issue—an issue that can likely be handled in a relatively short time. Given the time constraints, team members must be willing to do away with a certain amount of ceremony and speak their minds quickly.

For a one-time team, all members must be willing to reach a conclusion at the end of the meeting. The point is to reach a conclusion, so all members of the team need to be well aware of the issues being discussed before they get to the meeting. They should all be invested in the outcome of the meeting but willing to compromise to reach a satisfactory conclusion.

Ad Hoc Committees Ad hoc committees have a few things in common with the one-time team; both are coming together for the first time with no previous history, and both are there to focus on one core problem. However, unlike one-time teams, ad hoc committees have the potential benefit of long-term planning. These meetings will progress in a much calmer, slower way than one-time teams. All members will informally be tested by other members to help determine leadership, social norms, and points of procedure for future meetings.

© Photographee.eu/Shutterstock.com

The unique aspect of the ad hoc committee is the focus on one core problem. The problem may be so large that it takes months or even years of meetings, but once the problem is solved, or the situation is improved, the group will disband. Take, for example, the Ad Hoc Committee on an International Convention against the Reproductive Cloning of Human Beings. The General Assembly of the United Nations called together this ad hoc committee "for the purpose of considering the elaboration of an international convention against the reproductive cloning of human beings."[4] The committee formed in 2002, and it took 3 years of meetings and consulting before they were able to attach three Annexes to Resolution 59/280 in 2005. The resolution passed overwhelmingly and the United Nations officially discouraged its members from conducting research or funding or encouraging experimentation resulting in human cloning. Once the resolution was passed, the group disbanded.

Negotiating Groups Situations arise in many walks of life that require people to take contrary sides on any number of issues. To better confront these daunting situations, small groups are often formed. These groups may be a small contingent of a larger group; take for example the Teamsters Union or the United Auto Workers Union. When there is cause for negotiation, the small group responsible for the negotiation meets, even though they speak for the larger group as a whole.

Negotiating groups do not just meet in massive labor disputes. They take place often in smaller everyday situations. An everyday event that often requires a negotiating group is the purchase of a new car. This is a situation in which customers find themselves faced with potentially spending thousands of dollars unnecessarily, for few people really have any idea about the value of a car, especially first-time buyers. Customers are confronted with an array of experiences strategically designed to get them excited about a potential new vehicle, all in an effort to produce the maximum amount of profit for the dealership and commission for the salesperson. After you smell the new car, go for a ride, and dream a little about what this car can mean to you, you will be confronted by a group of people. There will be the original salesperson, the salesperson's team leader, and a finance expert, as well as an insurance salesperson. The sales negotiating team is practiced and ready to deal.

Meanwhile, a savvy customer will perhaps feign indifference to a car they may actually be excited about, refuse to hand over the keys to their trade-in, and scoff at the first, second, or even third offer the dealer presents all in an effort to get themselves a better price. And faced with a seasoned team of salespeople, it is wise to at least consult with others who have been through the experience of buying a new car before. Bring in experts whom you trust, people to keep you sane during what could be a long negotiation.

Bear in mind that within a negotiation session it might appear likely that all sides are working amicably together. When studying communication, you should be aware that these negotiating sessions are fraught with misinformation and misleading nonverbal communication by both sides. Your team or group needs to be on the lookout for this and needs to remember that the goal is to get yourself or your team the best deal available.

Creative Teams One of the benefits of teamwork is the creative output that is often produced. "Brainstorming" sessions are a fundamental aspect of the creative process and is a term that was coined in 1953 by Alex Osborn, a partner in an advertising firm.[5] The goal of these brainstorming sessions was to produce as many ideas as possible. Members were encouraged not only to shout out any idea but also to add on suggestions to other group members' ideas. No idea was too radical or too impractical. No one in the group was allowed to be critical of others' ideas. The time for that would come later. The goal was to produce as much information as possible.

While in a professional setting, you will find yourself in a situation where you may have a need for any one of the previously mentioned groups. And although this list of group types is not exhaustive, it should give a good overview of some of the specific challenges and problems that groups are expected to overcome. Once the group has its goal, its purpose, the group may begin to come together and go through its own life cycle.

© bluedog studio/Shutterstock.com

HOW IS BRAINSTORMING FUNDAMENTAL IN THE CREATIVE PROCESS?

PHASES OF SMALL-GROUP COMMUNICATION

Although several theories exist describing the development stages of group work, this text will primarily focus on Bruce Tuckman's "Stages of Small Group Development Revisited," which is generally well accepted and easily demonstrated.[6] According to Tuckman, a group's life cycle will go through five distinct stages: forming, storming, norming, performing, and adjourning. These five stages are called a life cycle because they take the group from its infancy through its death and explain what behaviors are expected at each stage in its life. The life cycle metaphor is also apt because a group's measure of success is likely dependent on the group being able to grow into adulthood. If the group fails to reach adulthood and is stuck in its adolescent years, it is likely that the group will never achieve its primary purpose.

Forming The initial stage of group development, **forming**, is marked by members cautiously feeling their way into a new and potentially frightening situation. It is akin to a person sticking their toe into the water—testing the temperature before they dive into the pool. Members will have to balance individual and group goals as they meet new members. All members are likely to avoid conflict within this stage, for they do not wish to seem combative. Ernest Bormann describes primary tensions that may exist during the forming stage.[7] The **primary tensions** (which are perfectly normal) are feelings of unease as a group begins. People will "not know what to say or how to begin. The first meeting is tense and cold and must be warmed up. When groups experience primary tension, the people speak very softly; they sigh, and they are very polite" (p. 133). Although group members may appear disinterested in the early process, this is in all likelihood a facade. Group work marks a real opportunity for most people to prove their abilities and be recognized by both their peers and superiors. But until the primary tension is broken, the group will be unable to progress. The group will need to laugh and will need to socialize. So time spent at the beginning of the initial meeting goofing around, laughing, or participating in icebreaker activities is not time wasted but time spent building toward something better. When they are done warming up, or participating in icebreaker activities, the group should have oriented itself, have begun to think about a common goal, and be ready to get to work.

Storming Work will actually begin during the secondary stage of **storming**; it is then that the group will experience some discomfort because members will be asserting their personalities and trying to push their own agendas. When this happens, conflict is likely, and members' feelings might get hurt. Group members' roles will also be determined during this stage, and any push for a group goal is likely to also be a push for individual status within the group. Some groups will be eager to skip over this stage for fear of conflict; however, this would be a mistake. To avoid a passionate discussion for fear of conflict is to defeat the purpose of the group and to give into what Bormann calls **secondary tensions**. Secondary tensions are strains that the group experiences when members struggle in finding their role within the group, disagree about ideas, and have personality conflicts.[7] "Secondary tensions are louder than primary ones. People speak rapidly, they interrupt one another and are impatient to get to the floor and have their say; they may get up and pace the room or pound the table" (p. 135). These tensions need to be addressed and hopefully released or else the group will flounder, never progressing past the storming stage.

But conflict is important in creating an environment in which members feel comfortable expressing their opinions. This may seem counterintuitive in suggesting that conflict leads to an open environment where conversation is encouraged, but as Wheelan[8] and Wheelan

Forming
The initial stage of group development, marked by apprehension by its members and an overall tension throughout the group. The group must break this tension before it can proceed.

Primary tension
Ernest Bormann's term for the feelings of unease that group members feel when they initially meet. Members are unsure of social interaction rules and so are not sure how to act when first encountering a new group.

Storming
The second stage of group development. It is marked by actual work beginning, members trying to assert themselves, feelings perhaps getting hurt by other members pushing specific agendas.

Secondary tension
Ernest Bormann's term for the struggle that group members go through while trying to find their identity within the group. As opposed to primary tensions, secondary tensions are likely to be more aggressive in nature and lead toward open hostility.

TIME SPENT LAUGHING AND
JOKING IS TIME SPENT TOWARD
BUILDING A BETTER TEAM.

and Danganan[9] explain, if a group is able to get past the conflict, they will realize that each member is more committed to the group and that just because there is a disagreement, it does not mean the group will break apart. This will create a more secure feeling, and people will know that they can honestly offer their opinion in this environment.

To overcome these tensions, members must be able to fall back on the habits and relationships created during the forming phase of group development. Laughter is a good way to break tension, and social roles enacted during the norming stage may help break the tension simply by commenting on them. If humor does not work, the group will be forced to confront the problem head-on. This may mean a rational discussion during the meeting or a private discussion between the conflicting group members after the meeting.

Norming "Norms are the group's rules."[10] It is during the **norming** stage that the group begins to feel comfortable working together. They have established through their interaction a set of rules that will determine how they should behave during any given situation. The group will have learned how to deal with conflict and so should feel more comfortable expressing individual opinions. The group will have learned how to reach decisions, and so voting rituals will likely have been set. If the group chooses another method of decision-making besides a voting majority, then etiquette will have been created to allow differing opinions to be heard, and all sides to be granted the opportunity to present their point of view.

Norms will govern all behavior, not just decision-making processes. That is why it is important to establish the difference between **explicit norms** and **implied norms**. Explicit norms are rules that have been clearly stated and/or written and are agreed on by all involved parties. These may be rules handed down by an authority figure such as your teacher saying that you are not allowed to use your cell phone during class. Or they may be rules that the group has agreed to such as the procedure for reviewing the minutes of a previous meeting. Implied norms are rules that have not been discussed or written out but are still agreed on by the group through nonverbal interaction. As these rules are unwritten and unspoken, new members are going to break them unknowingly. When this happens, conflict will arise, and the new member will be confused as to what the problem is. For example, if you find a person sitting in your seat during class, you might stare and wonder how that person could be so insensitive. Or if a student breaks the implied dress code

Norming
The third stage of group development. It is marked by the group coming together and beginning to be productive. Rules for behavior will be firmly established during this point.

Explicit norms
Rules that have been clearly stated or written, and all members are expected to know them.

Implied norms
Rules that have not been written or clearly stated, and all members are expected to know them.

by wearing a tuxedo or formal cocktail dress to class, you could reasonably ask what the student had planned. This uncertainty can lead to stress, anger, or even conflict.

Once the norms have been established, the group can begin to work in harmony. However, a heavy premium is going to be placed on conformity to the norms. **Conformity** is choosing to adhere to the already socially accepted behavior or majority behavior. In our society, conformity is expected. If you choose not to conform to the social norms, you risk being alienated by your peers. An acceptable level of nonconformity is healthy for the group.

According to Dentler and Erikson[11] and Pavitt and Curtis,[12] deviant behavior by some members serves as a release for tension, a reminder of what acceptable behavior is, a basis for comparison that conforming members can be rewarded for, and last that the deviant member gives the conformists a problem to solve (p. 177).

Also, although it would be easy to assume that the group would want all members to conform to its ideals, it is in fact advantageous to have some members who are nonconformists. If all members of the group have gelled and are in constant agreement, the group will have succumbed to groupthink and will no longer be able to function effectively. Bear in mind that constant nonconformity will serve to disrupt the group, but occasional nonconformity is what every group needs. If the group is going to continue to be efficient, certain norms will need to be questioned from time to time. For example, if there is a standing weekly meeting scheduled with your group, but there has been no progress made from one week to the next, then there is no reason to have the meeting. At least one nonconformist in the group needs to have the courage to say that this is an issue.

Conformity
Adherence to the socially accepted behavior rules or the majority behavior rules.

AN ACCEPTABLE LEVEL OF NONCONFORMITY IS HEALTHY FOR THE GROUP.

© Rawpixel.com/Shutterstock.com

Group roles
Certain behavior is expected from all group members. Once a behavior is expected from an individual member, that member has officially been assigned the role.

Task roles
A specific category of group roles that focuses on the goal completion.

Discussion of conformists and nonconformists transitions very naturally into a discussion of **group roles** in general. At this point in the group development life cycle, social roles will have been set, and members will begin to expect certain behaviors of each other. Like an actor cast in a supporting role, no one expects that person to show up one day and play the lead.

In 1948, Kenneth D. Beene and Paul Sheats compiled a list of 25 roles that members are likely to take on when interacting in a group situation.[13] The roles have been broken down into three different categories: **Task roles**, which are roles that are focused on goal completion; **group building and maintenance roles**, which focus on interpersonal relationships and group harmony; and **individual roles**, which focus on personal agenda to the possible detriment of the group. Table 5-1 provides a list of all 25 roles and a sample message that would come from each.

Bear in mind that members are usually not relegated to only one role. A person who is an encourager can also be a gatekeeper or an information seeker. A harmonizer who often uses comedy may also be a follower when it comes to decision-making. Each of these parts has the potential to play an important role in group development, whether that role is a task role, a group building role, or an individual role. However, this list is far from exhaustive. Over the years as business has changed, so have the roles people play in small-group communication. McCann and Margerison,[14] in studying high-performance groups, observed that members are often assigned roles or assume roles because they are already proficient in a certain area. For example, "organizers," people who are naturally good at making plans, will work to make sure people stay on top of their deadlines. "Advisors," people good at researching, will compile information for the group and be able to disseminate that information to help direct future plans. Once roles and norms have been established, then the group may proceed to the next stage.

TABLE 5–1: GROUP ROLES

Role/Definition	Sample Message
1. Task Roles	
Initiator–Contributor	Constantly pushing new ideas, always looking for a new direction for the group. *"Let's examine the effects of President Trump's immigration policies for law enforcement."*
Information Seeker	This person is a researcher, constantly searching for new information and better information for the group. *"Has anyone found evidence that supports our premise that is not from Wikipedia?"*
Opinion Seeker	Always seeking the opinion of other group members and checking for potential disagreements among members and looking to address them as soon as possible. *"What do you think about the direction we are going?"*
Information Giver	Perhaps not a researcher but able to synthesize information and distribute it to the group. *"Sacramento State University has increased its tuition 60% in the last 3 years."*
Elaborator	Expands on and clarifies the ideas of other members. *"I want to make sure the rest of the group understands exactly what you are getting at."*
Coordinator	Connects the hypothetical to the real world. Tries to make the problem something tangible. *"You cannot compare public transportation in New York and Los Angeles because the cities, although both big, are different in so many ways."*

TABLE 5–1: GROUP ROLES

Role/Definition	Sample Message
Orienter	This person's role is to keep the group on task. *"That was very funny, but we should really be focusing on the task at hand."*
Evaluator–Critic	Attacks the argument that the group is presenting. This is not done in a negative way but with the intent of pointing out flaws in the plan so that it may be adjusted. *"The governor may want to legalize marijuana, but he does not have the support of key members of the legislature."*
Energizer	Needs to keep the group moving and will exert extra effort when the group is beginning to drag. *"I will be happy to do this research but who is going to work on the presentation?"*
Procedural Technician	This person will act as a type of coordinator between the group members, making sure that meetings are scheduled when people can attend, that the location is adequately stocked, and so forth. *"The meeting is going to be held at Karen's house next Thursday. Who can bring some snacks?"*
Recorder	People may also think of this as the secretary. The recorder will take the minutes and/or detailed notes. *"It was agreed at last week's meeting that all parties would have their assignments ready tonight."*
2. Group Building and Maintenance Roles	
Encourager	Constantly building up the self-esteem of other members—the cheerleader of the group in some ways. *"Way to go, Clara. That was a great idea."*
Harmonizer	Peacekeeper. Will work with other members to help settle differences, often using humor. *"Why don't you tell us how you really feel?"* (sarcastic remark following an argument)
Compromiser	Is looking for everyone to be happy and will try to modify ideas/plans to please all. *"I know that you might be too busy to finish your assignment so how about we all divide up your section?"*
Gatekeeper and Expediter	Ensures that everyone in the group has an equal chance to participate in the conversation. *"We have not heard from John in awhile."*
Group Observer	Provides a running commentary about the group's actions. *"We are really making progress here."*
Follower	A person who goes with the flow. Will not volunteer a new opinion. *"That sounds great—what you guys are talking about."*

TABLE 5–1: GROUP ROLES

Role/Definition	Sample Message
3. Individual Roles	
Aggressor	Unlike the evaluator–critic, this person attacks ideas with the intention of aggrandizing themselves, not with the interest of the group in mind. *"I think this plan is a bad one. Why aren't we doing this the way I suggested?"*
Blocker	Tries to veto any idea that comes forward without offering any alternative. *"I don't like any of these ideas."*
Recognition Seeker	Tries to enhance individual status, not by working, but by citing past accomplishments. *"The last three group projects I led all got A's."*
Self-Confessor	Makes him- or herself the center of attention by constantly talking about him- or herself while not necessarily talking about work. *"The other night, I was out way too late. Do you know what I mean? I am always out too late."*
Playboy	Incapable of being serious. Is constantly making jokes and distracting others. *"Why don't we knock off early? We can pick this up tomorrow."*
Dominator	Monopolizes the conversation with attempts to prove his/her own brilliance. Characterized with long speeches and excessive opinion giving. *"It is my opinion that we should . . ."*
Help Seeker	Expresses insecurity often. Turns that into a cry for help. *"I am really not very good at this . . . Would you help me make this presentation?"*
Special-Interest Pleader	Has a private agenda that he/she puts above the group's interest. Will continue to push special agenda to the detriment of the team. *"Why don't we re-explore my earlier ideas? I really think that is the way to go."*

Performing When a group has reached the **performing** stage, they have firmly set their goals, found out what accepted behaviors are, and know what their roles should be. The group is focused and firing on all cylinders. This stage is defined by its productivity. But because of the high level of productivity, it is also at this point that those roles and norms may need to be violated. With so much focus on the final goal and such a push to reach that goal in a hurry, new problems may arise. When last-minute details pop up, a member who is primarily a harmonizer may need to quickly change gears and become a coordinator or an information giver. The key to success here is to be flexible. Do not be locked into playing one role. Efficient groups are able to adjust on the fly, and this becomes critical during this phase.

Performing
The fourth stage of group development. It is marked by extreme productivity and the slight breakdown of group roles.

This phase is also marked by high enthusiasm with group members and high loyalty to the group. As discussed earlier, success breeds success. As the group becomes more productive, the members will feel more excited about how much they have achieved and will be eager to achieve more. And because of that success, they will want to be more loyal to the group. The performing stage is very exciting because, if for no other reason, the goal is nearly at hand.

Adjourning Once the goal has been accomplished, the group may begin to disband, or **adjourn**. When people leave an effective team, they will simultaneously feel both a sense of pride at having accomplished something meaningful and a sense of loss at having to walk away from newfound friends and colleagues. Keeping up personal relationships is difficult when people meet regularly, but that challenge is compounded when members no longer see each other on a regular basis. This last stage is truly why the metaphor of the life cycle of the group works because when a group metaphorically "dies," naturally there will be a sense of loss. When the group breaks up, people will miss each other.

Adjourning
The final stage of group development. It is marked by a sense of pride at having accomplished the group's goal and a sense of loss at the disbandment of the group.

IN THE PERFORMING STATE, THE GROUP MAXIMIZES ITS PRODUCTIVITY.

©fizkes/Shutterstock.com

TABLE 5–2: STAGES OF GROUP DEVELOPMENT

Stage	Definition
1. Forming	Initial stage of group/team development. Marked by members feeling their way into a new and potentially frightening situation. Members balance individual and group goals as they meet new members. All members likely to avoid conflict to seem non-combative.
2. Storming	Secondary stage of group/team development. Members assert their personalities and try to push their own agendas. Conflict is likely and members' feelings might get hurt. Group members' roles will be established at this point.
3. Norming	Group begins to feel comfortable at this point. Have established a set of rules (norms) to determine how they should behave in a given situation. Group will have learned to deal with conflict and can express individual opinions. Voting rituals will be set.

TABLE 5-2: STAGES OF GROUP DEVELOPMENT

Stage	Definition
4. Performing	Group has firmly set their goals, found out what accepted behaviors are, and what their roles should be. Group is focused and firing on all cylinders. This stage is defined by its productivity. At this stage, roles and norms may need to be violated. The key to success is to be flexible. Efficient groups are able to adjust on the fly.
5. Adjourning	The final stage of group development. It is marked by a sense of pride at having accomplished the group's goal and a sense of loss at the disbandment of the group.

RUNNING AND PARTICIPATING IN A SUCCESSFUL MEETING

On an average workday, 11 million meetings occur. And many employees wish that they had that time back. That said, a primary tool that small groups use to conduct their work is the business meeting. Sadly, meetings that have so much potential to be productive and successful are so often dismal failures. Employees dread a daily drain on their productivity, and they view meetings as one of the primary drains.

Meetings fail for a number of reasons:

- The meeting was unnecessary in the first place.
- There was no purpose to the meeting.
- There was no time to prepare for the meeting.
- People who needed to attend the meeting were absent.
- Ineffective leadership.

This list is far from exhaustive, but these are all problems that are easily remedied and, if solved, can lead to greater job satisfaction, better economic decisions, and less wasted resources. The first step in having a successful meeting is to define what a meeting is because a meeting is more than people sitting in a room together. A **meeting**, as defined by Engelberg and Wynn,[15] is "a scheduled gathering of group members for a structured discussion guided by a designated chairperson" (p. 327). Keep in mind the critical elements of this definition: (a) **scheduled gathering**, (b) **structured discussion**, and (c) **designated chairperson**. All three of these elements are important and call for further elaboration. Obviously, the meeting needs to be scheduled because an unscheduled meeting is not a meeting at all, but rather a collection of random people sitting in a room together. The second element of the definition is slightly more complicated. The term *structure* implies different things to different people. Structure may mean highly rigid and controlled to some people but that is not the intent in this definition. Although some meetings may take on a highly structured discussion in which each person is allowed 1 minute to offer their opinion on a particular subject, other meetings may have a minimally structured discussion—one

Meeting
A scheduled gathering of group members for a structured discussion guided by a designated chairperson.

Scheduled gathering
A purposefully held meeting that was prearranged.

Structured discussion
Unlike idle chatter, structured discussion is a guided conversation with a specific purpose.

Designated chairperson
The person who is there to make sure the group stays on task and that the group keeps going in an agreed-on direction.

where a general idea is kicked around for an hour or two. Brainstorming sessions, although they do have some particular rules, would have to be considered minimally structured. But there is still a structure to guide the discussion. Without this structure, there will be no basis for discussion on any particular topic. Finally, the idea of a designated chairperson needs explanation. The chairperson may not be the group "leader" but may act more as a moderator does during a presidential debate. The person is there to make sure the group stays on task and that the group keeps going in an agreed-on direction. This person may be elected or appointed, but it is necessary that someone is there to guide the discussion. Now that a definition for a meeting has been established, all incidental gatherings may be eliminated from the discussion, and the focus can be turned to eliminating the aforementioned problems from meetings.

WHAT ARE THE THREE ELEMENTS OF A MEETING?

© Rawpixel.com/Shutterstock.com

STEPS FOR PLANNING SUCCESSFUL MEETINGS

The first step in having a successful meeting is planning. And the first question that you need to ask yourself as you plan a meeting is this: "Do we even need to meet in the first place?" If the answer to that question is no, then stop creating the agenda. The meeting is not necessary. But if the answer is yes, then you have another question to ask yourself: "Do we need to meet face-to-face?" This question may appear simple, but it has great financial ramifications. Suppose a face-to-face meeting is necessary and that the meeting will last approximately 3 hours. If 10 people will attend the meeting, all of whom make $10 per hour (an amazingly low figure, even in today's economic climate), the meeting has already cost you or your employer $300, not including the time it took to gather information and put the presentation together. And nothing is guaranteed to be accomplished at the end of the 3 hours. So, think carefully about whether you need to meet face-to-face. If you need to make a major decision and gather information, or provide training, or need immediate feedback, then call the meeting. Otherwise postpone or cancel altogether. Other means are available to you to gather simple answers or to pass on a new social norm.

If you still decide that a meeting is necessary, then it is incumbent on the person who has called the meeting to do some serious planning. Not only will planning need to take place, but also more critical questions will need to be asked. For example, what is the purpose of the meeting? If the purpose is distribution of information, you may not need to have a meeting. If the information can be emailed to colleagues and you will be available and are willing to answer any queries via email, then do not hold the meeting. However, if the purpose of the meeting is to create a new product line or ad campaign, then the face-to-face meeting will need to be called. Determining the purpose of the meeting will go a long way in helping the moderator of the meeting keep the group on task and focused. If the goal of the meeting is unclear, then the moderator is likely to be confused as well.

If you know the purpose of the meeting, then you will find yourself asking another important question. Who should attend this meeting? Are specific people already familiar with the product line that you are trying to launch? Do company accountants need to be present to discuss financial limits of the ad campaign? If certain people need to be at your meeting and they find themselves unable to attend, you need to postpone the meeting. There is no point in calling a meeting if the key players cannot be in attendance. It would be akin to a graduate student calling a thesis defense meeting when his or her thesis committee could not attend. Time is always going to be one of the difficult aspects of teamwork, but it is one that needs to be dealt with realistically.

Now let's suppose that the necessary players can meet tomorrow morning or 3 weeks from now. Given the choice between meeting sooner rather than later, people may often feel overeager and decide to meet the next day. This can be a crucial mistake that leads to an ineffective meeting. All sides need a chance to prepare for the meeting. To call a last-minute meeting is not only unfair to the people attending the meeting but it is also unfair to you, the person calling the meeting. As has been previously pointed out, many people will spend their days counting the minutes in a meeting rather than actively participating. Give yourself the greatest chance for success, and that means taking the appropriate amount of time to prepare and distribute a well-thought-out agenda.

Meeting agendas are an extremely important tool for running meetings. If you don't have an agenda, don't expect people to attend or be happy about attending your meeting. Agendas serve to provide a structure for the meeting itself and often highlight announcements, old business, new business, and specific decisions that need to be made. These documents provide attendees with information about what they need to be prepared for and should include any attachments or supplementary material needed. There is a lot to know about preparing a strong agenda. First, carefully consider what must be accomplished in the meeting and do not overschedule. Consider placing time limits on how long each item should take and if something needs more time, make an adjustment and then shift other items to the next meeting. No one likes to be held too long in a meeting as it is a serious drain on productivity. Second, seek input on the agenda from those attending the meeting and get feedback on which topics to include. Third, assign different agenda items to those responsible so that you can maximize participation and hear from key contributors. Finally, send the agenda and supporting material out in advance providing enough time for each attendee to read the material. Members need to know why they are there and how to prepare. If they feel they are there just to sit back and be spectators, then they "should stay at their desks and do their work."[16] Keep in mind that a well-developed agenda can go a long way toward a smooth functioning meeting, even for people who may not be the strongest facilitators. Tables 5-3 and 5-4 provide sample structures for creating an agenda. Many organizations may have a standard protocol for agendas, but if not, feel free to develop a structure that meets your meeting objectives and maximizes participation.

RESEARCH NOTE

MEETINGS AND TECHNOLOGY: THE IMPORTANCE OF TELEPRESENCE

In the workplace, individuals have a variety of technologies readily available for communication or meetings. These technologies range from the most commonplace and affordable, such as telephones and email, to newer technologies, such as virtual conferencing and even robotics. Portable digital phones are now capable of video conferencing in addition to sending and receiving text messages, shared applications, and standard voice communication. A number of emerging media are designed to provide individuals with a more immersive communication or conferencing experience, characterized broadly as *telepresence*. Traditional media such as the telephone, radio, and others offer a degree of presence as well. Specifically telepresence occurs through the use of technology and creates within the user a psychological state where the actual media used becomes transparent in the interaction.[a] These definitions suggest at least two aspects of telepresence that are important for this section. First, telepresence is an experience that occurs when the conveyance of information in an environment is perceived to be non-mediated. This is felt as a sort of being a part of the environment that is presented through some technology. Second, telepresence is thought of as a psychological state (one that is experienced) which exists along a continuum—meaning that one can experience more or less presence.[b] Stated differently people can be more or less aware that their communication is mediated; therefore, an immersive environment is created not only from the technology used but also through the psychological state of the individual.

You might wonder why it is important to reduce the appearance of mediation. As noted by Matthew Lombard, telepresence in business offers the advantages of saving the time and emotional labor involved with traveling for a business meeting in addition to the costs associated with business travel. Telepresence has implications for several other aspects of business communication such as persuasion, social learning, task enjoyment, and attention. One of the most common effects of telepresence is enjoyment; however, there is little research on the relationship between telepresence and enjoyment because we tend to take this effect for granted.[c] Intuitively, if we enjoy the mediated experience more as if it were real, that should also create other positive outcomes for the organization and employees. Additionally, involvement is also associated with telepresence, which also has obvious benefits for the workplace.

The most common business application involving telepresence is its use for meetings. Cisco, for example, markets a line of products under the description of telepresence solutions.[d] They promote high-definition video and enhanced audio, in addition to sharing multimedia applications. Cisco offers options from dedicated telepresence rooms to mobile device solutions all with the goal of creating a more immersive environment to enhance outcomes of meetings and collaborations. However, the company does compete with similar technologies which are not being marketed as telepresence, but offer many of the same features. Issues of cost, mobile technologies, and advantages in the cloud are allowing more companies the ability to have the look and feel of being in the same place as other meeting attendees along with all the benefits.[e] Although most individuals using such technologies to create immersive environments may not use the term telepresence, the idea of using technologies to reduce the appearance of mediation is attractive to a variety of organizations.

Another promising use for telepresence involves training and is an area of considerable research. If a person can complete a training seminar without having to fly to a central location and has similar outcomes as a face-to-face training session, there are cost and time savings for the organization. Studies have shown that telepresence is beneficial to learning and teaching to an extent that it is being used in medicine as well as business.

Telepresence robots are also being used in business. Companies such as Suitable Technologies are marketing these devices with the goal of making meetings and telecommuting more immersive. The ability to move around a physical business environment and facilitate scheduled or impromptu meetings are advantages that telepresence robots have compared to immersive videoconferencing technologies. Such telepresence devices give more autonomy to the user and reduce the restrictions of being confined to one room. It is uncertain how commonplace telepresence robots will be. Currently they have a novel use while offering many, if not more, of the benefits of traditional telepresence systems.

Technologies in the workplace will continue to evolve, not only to transmit messages, but also to provide a sense of "being there" or "being there with others." As they do, the possibility for higher levels of satisfaction in mediated workplace communication will become more focused in addition to the cost and access of such technologies becoming more attainable.

[a] Bracken, C. C., Pettey, G., Guha, T., & Rubenking, B. (2008, May). Sounding out presence: The impact of screen size, pace and sound. Paper at the annual conference of the International Communication Association, Montreal, Canada.

[b] Westerman, D., Spence, P. R., & Lachlan, K. A. (2009). Telepresence and the exemplification effects of disaster news. *Communication Studies, 60*(5), 542–557. doi:10.1080/10510970903260376

[c] Bracken, C. C., & Skalski, P. D. (2009). *Immersed in media: Telepresence in everyday life*. Routledge.

[d] Savitz, E. (2012). 5 Reasons Cisco And Polycom Are In Trouble In Telepresence. https://web.archive.org/web/20120508162254/http://www.forbes.com/sites/ciocentral/2012/05/03/5-reasons-cisco-and-polycom-are-in-trouble-in-telepresence/

[e] Lombard, M. (2010). The promise and peril of telepresence. In Bracken C., & Skalski, P. (Eds). *Immersed in media: Telepresence in everyday life*. Routledge.

TABLE 5-3: SAMPLE AGENDA I

Pandexter Nail Company
Executive Board Meeting Agenda
Wednesday, June 25, 2020
8:00 a.m. Board Room

I. Approval of Minutes
II. Old Business
    A. Conflict of interest forms
    B. Travel request forms
    C. Dress code revisions
III. New Business
    A. New product line—time line for installation
    B. Sales team initiative—where are we now?
    C. International conference—reservations needed ASAP
IV. CEO's Report
    A. Budget
    B. Marketing campaign
    C. Future goals
V. Adjournment

TABLE 5-4: SAMPLE AGENDA II

Speech Communication Department
Faculty Meeting Agenda
Wednesday, April 16, 2020
3:00 p.m. Center Hall 100

I. Approval of Minutes
II. New Business
    A. Committee reports
    B. Faculty senate
    C. Curriculum
    D. Calendar committee
III. Director's Report
    A. End of the year party
    B. Global studies—study abroad proposals due by May 1
    C. Budget—expect a 4.2% cut for 2020
    D. New grant proposals due now
    E. Office updates take place next week
IV. Administrative Reports
    A. Coordinator, Undergraduate Studies
    B. Director, Speech Communication Center
    C. Advisors

CHAIRING A MEETING

If you have clarified the purpose of the meeting and created an agenda, determined where and when it should be held and who should be attending, and received confirmation that those group members will be there, then you, acting as chairperson, have accomplished a great deal. But there is still a major obstacle to overcome, that is the actual running of the meeting. As the acting chairperson, you will have several responsibilities to deal with: You will need to open and close the meeting, you will need to deal with difficulties within the discussion, you will need to be conscious of meeting logistics, and ideally you will follow the agenda while still being flexible and smart enough to allow discussion to flow off the charted agenda if it is still productive. These separate duties all need to be elaborated on.

The logistics of running a meeting are daunting. Even a task as simple as getting started on time can be challenging. If several of your group members tend to be tardy, you may need to provide the group members with a recommended arrival time and a hard meeting time. This will simultaneously send the message that there is an exact time when this meeting will occur, but also provide some time to get the social networking aspects of the group work out of the way. Members who wish to chat may show up early to do so, but once the meeting begins, it is all business.

When opening the meeting, the chairperson needs to be considerate of time constraints and quickly get to the point. Thank the group members for coming and being on time, introduce the purpose for the day's meeting, and appoint a minute taker/recorder. Table 5-5 provides an example of meeting minutes that could be followed. Different organizations have different structures for meeting minutes that vary in the level of detail, so if you are taking minutes, follow standard form. The key decisions made and action items are the most important notes to be recorded and all minutes should be circulated and checked for accuracy at the next scheduled meeting. Once a recorder is established, the chairperson will then either hand over the reins to the first presenter or, if there is no presenter, throw out the first discussion question—something that will get group members involved. Please be aware that some members may not be eager to volunteer. If that is the case, the chairperson may have to delicately pass the question to an individual instead of asking for volunteers. This may save time compared to waiting for the next person to jump up and answer. Closing the meeting is just as important. You will be able to sense when the group is getting fidgety, losing their patience and productivity. As the chairperson, you should briefly review the information covered during the meeting; discuss whether any assignments, duties, or responsibilities were assigned during the meeting; and if another meeting is necessary, ask the members while you have them all in the same room when the next time is that they are all available. Once that information is attained, thank everyone for their contributions and adjourn.

One of the major responsibilities of running a meeting is to make sure that you stay on the agenda. To use our earlier financial example, if a meeting starts 15 minutes late because some members are tardy and runs 45 minutes long because people tended to wander off point, that is another $100 just in salary costs. You as chairperson need to balance the cost of these delays against the information that is being produced. If group members are creating new ideas in a new direction, but you find that you are slightly off the agenda, then ask yourself what the relative worth is of the ideas being produced. Perhaps a group member is telling a humorous story that has nothing to do with the agenda items but is serving to unite the group and bring them closer together. What is the value of that bond? As chairperson you will have to answer those types of questions in real time as they occur. Be aware that this situation may happen; do not be afraid to interrupt and say "We need to get back on track," but do not do so just for the sake of finishing the meeting right on time. If

TABLE 5–5: SAMPLE MEETING MINUTES

Speech Communication Department
Faculty Meeting Minutes
March 4, 2020

The Speech Communication Department met on Wednesday, March 4, 2020, in Center Hall 100.

Call to Order: Dr. Mitch Blake called the meeting to order at 3:00 p.m.

Faculty/Staff Present: Suzanne Brown, William Thomas, Mathew Davis, Andrea Lee, Mitch Blake, Britanny Connor, Danielle Streeter, Brian Richards, Eric Murphy, Todd Thompson, Barbara Turner, Cindy Russell, Teresa Joan, and Glenn Putnam.

I. Approval of Minutes

Dr. Barbara Turner motioned to approve the minutes from the January 22nd faculty meeting and Dr. Cindy Russell seconded the motion.

II. New Business

A. Committee Reports

1. Faculty Senate (Teresa Joan)
   a. New student center approved
   b. Budget cuts—4.5% approved by chancellor
   c. School of the Arts has been approved
   d. Faculty Assembly is discussing post tenure review process

2. Assessment (Cindy Russell)
   a. Assessment survey has been implemented and data will be collected next month. Watch for emails.

3. PRSSA (Cindy Russell)
   a. Group has two field trips to NYC planned. There will be workshops and networking opportunities. Panel discussions regarding job interviewing available as well as a networking lunch.

III. Director's Report

A. Budget

1. $100K in lapse salary (adjuncts, overloads, DE summer classes, etc.)
2. $124K Operating Budget (faculty travel, office supplies, maintenance agreements, postage, student employees, part-time employees)
3. Possibilities
   a. Eliminate DE classes
   b. Raise undergraduate admission standards
   c. Eliminate master's program

B. Canceled classes and make-up days

1. April 29 make-up day for January 30
2. April 30 make-up day for January 29
3. Email sent from Chancellor regarding these make-up days.

C. Global Studies

1. Study abroad—proposals due by May 1
2. Be thinking ahead to summer 2021. If interested, please let Director know

IV. Administrative reports

A. Assistant Director: Summer I and II schedules are done. These will be printed out and placed in your mailbox next week. Please read and sign to show your approval.

B. Summer GA assignments are still being done.

Meeting adjourned at 4:55 p.m.

© Monkey Business Images/Shutterstock.com

THE MEETING CHAIRPERSON
SHOULD OPEN THE DISCUSSION
AND QUICKLY GET TO THE POINT.

facilitating the meeting becomes too difficult, you might consider appointing someone to be a process observer. This person can keep a check on the time, ask the group to refocus, point out if others have not been able to participate, or make the group adhere to its standard rules or principles for meetings. Having this role separate from leading the group through an agenda can be very helpful as it also reduces power imbalances. The role of process observer can be rotated and truly ensures that everyone is aware of good meeting practices with regard to participation.

Perhaps the most difficult task that the chairperson takes on is trying to deal with difficult group members. You will certainly need to wear the gatekeeper hat while acting as chairperson. Certain group members will not want to participate, and you will need to try to prod answers out of them. Other members may wish to dominate the floor, thinking of you as competition rather than a helpful moderator. A smart moderator may assign the dominant member another job that will not allow that person the time to participate, such as the role of recorder. Side conversations that arise during the meeting may prove especially distracting. People who are content to text during the meeting rather than participate will also be an issue. As an effective moderator, you may attempt to address these problems before they occur; however, a warning may not be enough. If that is the case, the whole group may have to use nonverbals to get the deviant members to comply. A silent room that has all eyes glaring at one person who is playing solitaire on their phone may be enough to shame that group member into putting away their phone.

EFFECTIVE PARTICIPATION IN A MEETING

Even if you are not the designated chairperson of the meeting, being an effective participant in any meeting is a skill that you should want to hone. First, remember to be on time. Consider the effort and planning that went into getting the meeting itself into becoming a reality. Second, be in the right frame of mind when attending the meeting. Make sure to review the materials including the agenda and other preparation materials prior to the meeting date and time. Your time in the meeting will be much more productive if you can utilize that time to the best of your ability, and that comes with being prepared. Third, clarify the outcomes of the meeting. Asking the chairperson in advance if you can assist them and then during the meeting remaining focused on the goals will allow the meeting to both remain productive and allow you to get more out of the meeting at the same time. Fourth, be attentive to group roles and goals. As mentioned earlier in this chapter, individuals will take on task, group building, and individual roles. In your participation, focus on your task and group building roles. This will allow the meeting to be productive and your role within it to be productive. Finally, ensure that you contribute in a positive and meaningful manner. Meetings are about work and you should be prepared to carry your weight.

Meetings that are ineffective are nothing but a drain on company resources, both in time and money. But effective meetings will produce a greater quantity of work as well as a higher quality. Although this chapter offers several hints on how to run and participate in a successful meeting, you must also remember the information presented at the beginning of the chapter. Group work is difficult; it is messy and a potential waste of resources. Not every member will give their all because they are working in a group. But efficient and effective groups will lead to greater productivity, which will lead to greater success, which will lead to greater employee loyalty, which will end with greater employee satisfaction. In addition to being skilled meeting facilitators and participants today's employees must also master ICT (Information Communication Technology) as it is critical to small group functioning. The following section reviews common tools available and provides tips for communicating competently with these evolving channels.

ICT AND SMALL GROUPS

Group and teamwork is aided by different forms of information communication technology termed *collaborative technologies*. These technologies can include instant messaging, forums and social media features, online meeting space, video conferencing, information repositories, and much more. Organizations are investing in these systems especially as employees become more geographically dispersed across continents and time zones. Additionally, with such a high number of employees telecommuting, collaborative systems are key to group productivity and success. While email will continue to be a popular form of communication, these collaborative technologies offer much more in terms of telepresence, immediacy, information sharing, and productivity. Programs such as Slack, Lync, SharePoint, Jive, Asana, Jabber, and Workplace by Facebook offer employees new and innovative ways to work remotely with both cloud applications and organizations' custom on-site applications. These tools allow teams to communicate frequently, crowdsource for solving problems, manage projects, and share files. A recent *Forbes* magazine article also highlighted the boom of virtual and augmented reality applications for business.[17] These technologies are not just for gaming purposes. For example, some applications allow you to change your background when livestreaming for meetings which means you can show content to other members. You can also expect to see more Smart Virtual Personal Assistants (SVPAs . . . think Siri or Alexa) that can create task lists, take notes in meetings, schedule meetings, and send reminders. They can also scan email for important information and create and distribute meeting agendas. While there are still some challenges and expense to using collaborative technologies, organizations claim high levels of productivity, reduced decision-making time, and better solutions to problems.[18] Additionally, these tools may make work life balance more attainable for employees as work processes are more efficient and the need and expense for travel is reduced. That said, while these tools have the ability to streamline project work, organizational leaders need to stay attentive to issues with technology implementation and communication overload.[19] While many employees are moving away from email and toward collaborative technologies, communication overload is still a problem. Specifically, since most people are most comfortable with email, they continue to use it even when it is not the most efficient form of communication for completing tasks. Managers should encourage their employees to use the tools but should also make sure employees are not overloaded with them. One way of avoiding the use of too many separate collaboration software programs is to look for products that integrate multiple features such as file sharing, teleconferencing, and project management tools.

According to Harvard Business Review, there are several tips worth considering when adopting and utilizing new collaborative technologies[20]:

- **Commit to using standardized tools** or company supported tools since adding too many different applications can become burdensome. Have teams stick to using the same technology to do their work.
- **Consider the best tool for the message**. If something does not require a quick answer, then avoid choosing instant messaging that might pull someone off task (Use both synchronous and asynchronous forms of communication).
- **Get together face-to-face whenever you can**. Consider quarterly or bi-annual meetings for more complicated tasks such as goal-setting. This allows the group time to conduct important work, but also time to connect socially.
- **Ask that all team members use the video feature** of team meetings instead of some just calling into the meeting. This makes interaction consistent and allows for screensharing.
- **Develop communication protocols** for how the team will function. These protocols might include which technology to use and how, but could also mean developing rules for how teams interact and engage such as not being on your phone during meetings, requiring everyone to participate, circulating agendas ahead of time, starting and stopping meetings on time, agreeing on a common language (especially important for international teams), and so forth.
- **Build collaboration routines** such as weekly meetings or progress updates that occur on the same days and times but that also rotate to accommodate employees in different time zones. Also, leaders should integrate one-on-meetings instead of relying solely on team meetings to allow for feedback, connection, and goal setting.
- **Find ways to foster connection** between team members such as beginning meetings with updates from each member, celebrating successes, or integrating team-building activities.

Finally, just as we discussed the importance of email netiquette and fostering strong workplace relationships in Chapter 4, it is equally important to consider competent communication using collaborative technologies, particularly videoconferencing. While some tips probably go without saying such as avoiding being late, working to make eye contact with meeting goers, avoiding eating during meetings, and working to include all members, there are other tips you might not have considered. An article in *The Wall Street Journal* highlighted the following rules of etiquette for videoconferencing[21]: (1) avoid typing, using your phone, or working on other things during a videoconference as it is a distraction to other attendees and it becomes obvious when you are not paying full attention; (2) make eye contact with the camera when talking directly to meeting participants, otherwise, try to stay focused on the screen so as not to miss important information; (3) avoid interruptions by placing a sign on your door or cubicle letting others know you are in a meeting, or if working from home, keep pets and family members away; (4) keep your microphone muted to keep out background noise; (5) avoid technical difficulties by arriving to the meeting ahead of schedule and knowing how to end the call when finished; and, (6) be aware of what others can see in your background which also includes appropriate attire and professional or neutral background (wearing pj's or teleconferencing from your bed is a bit much).

CONCLUSION

As mentioned at the beginning of the chapter, Lydia Jackson has a big job ahead of her as she convenes an ad hoc committee at her university to develop a new admissions campaign. Based on the information in this chapter, Lydia can expect the group to progress through the stages of team formation including forming, storming, norming, performing, and adjourning. Because she's at the beginning of the process, she should plan activities that will allow the group members to get to know one another and also allow the group to determine its own goals and objectives. During these processes, Lydia will not be surprised by the roles and conflict that emerge. However, she now understands that conflict can be a constructive form of dialogue and a way for new ideas to come to the forefront and avoid groupthink. Even more importantly, Lydia recognizes the important role she will play in planning for their meetings. Specifically, she will prepare agendas and material in advance and provide committee members with adequate time to prepare for meetings, and she will only call face-to-face meetings when appropriate. She has also decided to appoint a process observer, a person who will make sure that the meeting is staying on track with the agenda and within the set time limits. Finally, she understands that the group needs to come together on a social as well as a task basis, so she will work to incorporate some unstructured activities in the meetings that will help bring people together, while tapping into their creative potential.

Group work and meetings can be extremely productive, but before you convene a group or call a meeting, be sure that this is the appropriate step to take. Meetings and group work are seen as a drain because they are often used in an ineffective manner. Meetings and group work are opportunities for members to contribute to the overall success of the company in a real way. These events are opportunities to form lasting social relationships with coworkers leading to greater job satisfaction. Despite all of these benefits from group work and meetings, people still see the majority of this time as a waste. And so before the meeting is called, before the group is convened, think. Ask yourself: Is the meeting really necessary? What is the purpose of the group? If you know the purpose of the group, and the meeting is necessary, you are well on your way to creating a positive work environment in which your team will thrive.

Notes

1. Mehrabian, A. (1981). *Silent messages: Implicit communication of emotion and attitudes* (2nd ed.). Wadsworth.

2. Ingham, A. G., Levinger, G., Graves, J., & Peckham, V. (1974). The Ringlemann effect: Studies of group size and group performance. *Journal of Experimental Social Psychology, 10,* 371–384. https://doi.org/10.1016/0022-1031(74)90033-X

3. Microsoft Press Release. (2005). *Survey finds workers average only three productive days per week*. Author.

4. United Nations General Assembly, Ad Hoc Committee on an International Convention against Reproductive Cloning of Human Beings. (2005). *United Nations declaration on human cloning*. Office of Legal Affairs United Nations. https://web.archive.org/web/20060217202035/http://www.un.org/law/cloning/index.html and https://doi.org/10.1515/9783110182521.379

5. Osborn, A. F. (1953). *Applied imagination: Principles and procedures of creative problem-solving*. Scribner's.

6. Tuckman, B. W., & Jensen, M. A. C. (1977). Stages of small group development revisited. *Group and Organizational Studies, 2,* 419–427. https://doi.org/10.1177/105960117700200404

7. Bormann, E. G., & Bormann, N. C. (1996). *Effective small group communication* (6th ed.). Gordon Press.

8. Wheelan, S. A. (1994). *Group processes: A developmental perspective*. Allyn & Bacon.

9. Wheelan, S. A., & Danganan, N. B. (2003). The relationship between the internal dynamics of student affairs leadership teams and campus leaders' perceptions of the effectiveness of student affairs divisions. *NASPA Journal, 40,* 93–112. https://doi.org/10.2202/1949-6605.1258

10. Engleberg, I. N., & Wynn, D. R. (2007). *Working in groups*. Houghton Mifflin.

11. Dentler, R. A., & Erikson, K. T. (1959). The functions of deviance in groups. *Social Problems, 7,* 98–107. https://doi.org/10.2307/799160

12. Pavitt, C., & Curtis, E. (1990). *Small group discussion: A theoretical approach*. Gorsuch Scarisbrick, Publishers.

13. Beene, K. D., & Sheats, P. (1948). Functional roles of group members. *Journal of Social Issues, 4,* 41–49. https://doi.org/10.1111/j.1540-4560.1948.tb01783.x

14. Marerison, C. J., & McCann, D. (1989). How to improve team management. *Leadership & Organization Development Journal, 10*(5), 2–42. https://doi.org/10.1108/EUM0000000001142

15. Engleberg, I. N., & Wynn, D. R. (2007). *Working in groups*. Houghton Mifflin.

16. Henkel, S. L. (2007). *Successful meetings: How to plan, prepare and execute top-notch business meetings*. Atlantic Publishing Group.

17. Newman, D. (2018, May 17). 3 technology trends driving adoption of collaboration tools. *Forbes*. https://web.archive.org/web/20180517214322/https://www.forbes.com/sites/danielnewman/2018/05/17/3-technology-trends-driving-adoption-of-collaboration-tools/

18. Goodwin, B. (2014, March 3). No more email? Why companies are turning to collaboration technology. *Computer Weekly*. https://web.archive.org/web/20150424224341/https://www.computerweekly.com/feature/No-more-email-Why-companies-are-turning-to-collaboration-technology?vgnextfmt=print

19. Greene, J. (2017, March 13). Beware collaboration-tool overload; Employees are struggling to cope with an abundance of tools, prompting providers to try to simplify things for them. *Wall Street Journal* (Online).

20. Watkins, M. D. (2013, June 27). Making virtual teams work: Ten basic principles. *Harvard Business Review*. https://web.archive.org/web/20160309131818/https://hbr.org/2013/06/making-virtual-teams-work-ten/

21. French, S. (2016, March 14). Ten rules of etiquette for videoconferencing; Don't let the small screen fool you there are right ways and wrong ways to behave. *Wall Street Journal*.

SECTION II

BUSINESS COMMUNICATION TECHNOLOGY

CHAPTER 6: Communication Technologies

CHAPTER 7: Social Media

COMMUNICATION TECHNOLOGIES

LEARNING OUTCOMES

After reading this chapter, you should be able to:

1. Describe the importance of the terms *what*, *how*, and *when* as they apply to communication technologies.

2. Discuss the impact of the Internet on communication in the business place.

3. Discuss the impact of wireless communication technologies on the way people communicate in the business place.

4. Describe how to choose and effectively use communication technologies.

5. Describe several communication technology-related job, career, safety, and health concerns.

6. Describe assistive technologies that enable disabled individuals to communicate more easily and effectively in the business place.

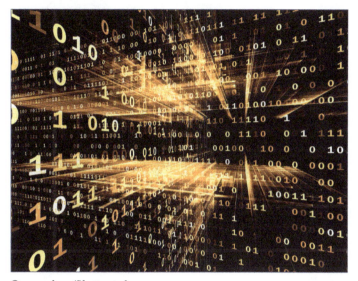

© agsandrew/Shutterstock.com

SELECT KEY TERMS

INTRODUCTION

You are strongly encouraged to know what communication technology exists and is forthcoming, how to use communication technologies effectively and efficiently, and when to use them. Each of these forms of knowledge will be critical to your success in the professional business world. The Internet, WiFi, and a host of wireless communication technologies have vastly changed the way much of the communication occurs in the business place. Be careful, however, not to get so comfortable with communicating electronically that you overlook the importance of face-to-face communication in a variety of domestic and international settings. Furthermore, don't feel the need to be connected to the technology all the time for work. It is healthy both physically and mentally to enjoy some downtime, which many would call vacations and weekends.

The intent of this chapter is to provide you with an overview of business communication technologies. This goal is realized through discussions regarding the following topics: keeping up with technological developments, significant communication technology developments of the past, the Internet and World Wide Web, communicating via wireless technologies, using communication technologies effectively, and some cautious communication technology predictions.

This chapter is not the only place we discuss business communication technologies in the book. Technologies related to specific communication topics are discussed in appropriate locations elsewhere in the book. For example, technologies that support teams' efforts, business meetings, business presentations, and other topics are discussed in the related chapters.

© everything possible/Shutterstock.com

KEEPING UP: WHAT, HOW, AND WHEN

It has been said there are only two certainties in life—death and taxes. While most would agree that death and taxes are inevitable, they are not the only certainties. Change is also an unavoidable certainty, as history reminds us. This is especially true of change in communication technologies. While recent changes in communication technologies do not constitute the first of their kind, the magnitude of recent changes, coupled with the rapid pace at which they are being introduced, poses a sizable challenge to organizations and employees. Furthermore, many of these technologies are changing the ways we communicate in the business place.

No matter the type or size of organization you work for, you need to keep up with communication technologies. Keeping up can be summed up in three words—*what, how,* and *when.*

WHAT

The term *what,* as used here, implies you should stay abreast of both current and projected communication technologies. You should consider reading specialized magazines, such as *Smartphone & Pocket PC, Smart Computing, PCWorld, or Pen Computing,* which covers mobile computing communication. These magazines and others like them focus exclusively on technological developments, issues, and trends. Another specialized technology magazine to consider is *PC Magazine,* a digital publication that can be accessed at www. pcmag.com. In addition, consider browsing periodicals such as *Fortune, BusinessWeek, and the Wall Street Journal* to locate articles about communication technology developments and trends. You can also visit money.cnn.com/technology/ to read about communication technology developments. Finally, you could take a communication technology workshop or class or attend a major electronics show such as the annual International Consumer Electronics Show.

HOW

Here the term *how* implies you should learn *how* to use both current and projected communication technologies. Your best bet is to either take a workshop or class or sit down with a friend or colleague who is willing to teach you. On the other hand, you might be the type of person who likes to teach yourself. This approach is a practical option for many.

WHEN

Here the term *when* pertains to two things. First, the term implies you will learn whichever specific communication technology is most appropriate for each communication situation you face. This information is presented later in the section titled "Choosing the Appropriate Communication Medium," where insights into how to make "when" choices are shared. An example would be making the decision to send an e-mail about a short, routine matter instead of conducting a videoconference. Second, the term *when* speaks to knowing when it is unwise to use electronic communication devices because doing so is considered unacceptable behavior as described in Figure 6-1.

FIGURE 6-1: AVOID USING COMMUNICATION TECHNOLOGIES WHEN ...

Can you identify specific settings in schools and businesses where it is not in a student's or employee's best interest to be texting or browsing the Internet? No matter your response, it is in your best interest to know. Otherwise, you run the risk of compromising your learning potential and grades, ability to persuade faculty to write recommendation letters, employment stability, and ability to achieve desired career goals! Each of these represents a big price to pay for careless use of communication technologies.

Most college and university instructors discourage students from using electronic communication devices during class unless they are being used for specific, class-related purposes. For example, an instructor may want you to access information using your tablet or laptop, use your smartphone as a substitute device for a clicker, or work on a collaborative document from a wiki site during class. However, few instructors appreciate it when students use electronic devices for other purposes during class when they should, instead, be listening and joining in class discussions.

Even in organizations where there is a proliferation of communication technologies, there are settings in which using electronic devices such as smartphones, tablets, laptops, etc. is discouraged. For example, most managers justifiably do not want employees using such devices during presentations, meetings, and training sessions. One reason is the potential of distracting speakers, meeting chairpersons, trainers, and others seated nearby. Another reason involves missed opportunities and associated costs. Yet another reason has to do with lost knowledge. For example, when employees text or catch up on their e-mail during presentations, business meetings, or training sessions, they are not acquiring the information and ideas speakers, fellow meeting participants, and trainers are sharing. Finally, managers, presenters, etc. do not appreciate the rudeness and unprofessional nature of such actions. Inappropriate use of electronic communication devices can tarnish an employee's image in the eyes of his or her superiors and even tarnish his or her employer's image.

Make sure you know when and where at school and in the workplace it is appropriate to use electronic communication devices, and avoid using them in those settings where they should not be used. Unfortunately, many of today's communication technologies, such as smartphones and texting, are addictive for some. For example, seasoned employment recruiters routinely mention job candidates who answer their smartphones during job interviews. Wise job candidates control the desire to answer their phone when it rings during a job interview by leaving the phone in their car or at home.

Keeping up with current and projected communication technologies is important to businesspeople and organizations. In today's business environment neither individuals nor organizations can compete adequately if they do not keep up. This is not a new challenge for businesspeople or organizations. For example, around the time PCs were first developed in the late 1970s there were businesspeople who did not keep up with the new technology. Shortly thereafter some of these employees were replaced with others who were keeping up. Essentially it is no different today. Businesspeople who desire to remain marketable and useful need to keep up with current and projected communication technologies, and businesses that desire to be successful and grow need to do the same.

Just as ancient Rome's highways were important communication lines many centuries ago, the Internet and the associated communication technologies are important in today's organizations. It is essential to stay current with Internet-based communication technologies so one does not end up (as some would say) "as road kill on today's information superhighway."

Keeping up with communication technology developments is one of the major challenges you will face during your professional business career. Adopting an approach for "keeping up" that is rooted in the words *what, how,* and *when* will help you manage this challenge.

SUMMARY: SECTION 1— KEEPING UP: WHAT, HOW, AND WHEN

- Your willingness and ability to keep up with current and projected communication technology developments are critical to your career and to your organization's success.
- The term *what* implies you will stay abreast of both current and projected communication technologies.
- The term *how* implies you will learn how to use communication technologies effectively.
- The term *when* implies you will learn which specific communication technologies will be most appropriate for each communication situation you face.

SIGNIFICANT COMMUNICATION TECHNOLOGY DEVELOPMENTS OF THE PAST

Since so many of the communication technology developments of the past affect the ways people communicate in today's business place, it is useful to reflect on some advances that made a major impact. A brief historical look will leave you with a better appreciation for current communication technologies and a broader base from which to speculate on future developments.

Looking into the past reminds us that (1) communication technology development is not unique to our time, (2) many communication technologies currently in use are simply improved versions of past developments, and (3) people have a long history of searching for ways to improve on existing communication technologies and develop new communication technologies. Figure 6-2 provides a brief look at the major technological developments that have had profound effects on how we communicate today.

FIGURE 6-2: COMMUNICATION TECHNOLOGIES THAT LAID THE FOUNDATION

- **Printing Press.** Gutenberg's invention of moveable type in the 15th century made it possible to reproduce books, written documents, pictures, and images more quickly and accurately, thus leading the way to the mass distribution of information.

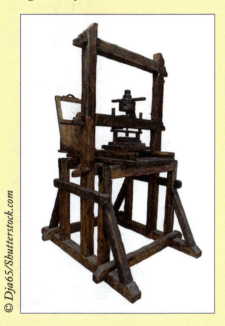

- **Telegraph.** Prior to the invention of the telegraph in 1837, messages were transmitted in a variety of ways, including smoke, drum signals, and carrier pigeons. The first successful telegraph machine was patented by Samuel Morse in 1837 and became functional in 1844.

- **Fax Machine.** The first commercial fax (facsimile) machine became available in 1865. However, fax machines did not achieve widespread use in most U.S. businesses until the 1980s when faster, less-expensive machines were introduced.

FIGURE 6-2: COMMUNICATION TECHNOLOGIES THAT LAID THE FOUNDATION

- **Telephone.** Alexander Graham Bell thought of the idea in 1874 and developed a working telephone in 1876. The first commercial line was installed in the United States in 1877 and 140 years later the telephone is the second most widely used communication medium in U.S. businesses.

© Chuck Rausin/Shutterstock.com

- **Typewriter.** The first successful typewriters were marketed in 1874. Electric typewriters were introduced in the 1920s, although they were not in widespread use until the 1940s. Electronic typewriters, with limited memory capacity and a few word processing features, appeared in 1971. Typewriters were the pre-PC workhorses.

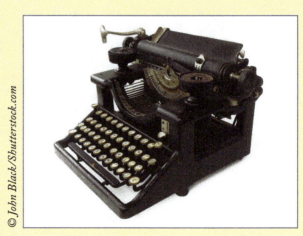

© John Black/Shutterstock.com

FIGURE 6-2: COMMUNICATION TECHNOLOGIES THAT LAID THE FOUNDATION

- **Personal Computer.** PCs hit the market in the early 1980s and are still our computing workhorses. Before then, there were basically two types of computers in use in businesses—mainframes and minicomputers. Both of these were very expensive and, in the case of the mainframes, they were very large.

© Oleksandr Lysenko/Shutterstock.com

- **Internet.** In 1969, the first two remote computers were connected to create the nascent ARPAnet—the first computer network. This project was funded by the U.S. Defense Advanced Research Projects Agency (DARPA).[1] By the early 1970s, the main Internet-based business application was e-mail. Other early applications included posting and searching for information and file transfers. As time passed, companies developed LANs (local area networks) that gave employees access to e-mail, databases, and the Internet and to WANs (wide area networks) that allowed them to access company data and applications from remote locations.

© Sergey Nivens/Shutterstock.com

Over the years, other technological developments have also impacted the way people communicate in the business place. Some of these technologies have since been retired to museums, storage closets, and landfills. However, others continue to play prominent roles in today's organizations. Can you identify which of the following technologies are still viable in today's business place: dictaphones, mimeograph machines, photocopiers, calculators, word processors, cell phones, voicemail, videoconferencing, scanners, personal digital assistants (PDAs), spreadsheets, desktop publishing?

SUMMARY: SECTION 2— SIGNIFICANT COMMUNICATION TECHNOLOGY DEVELOPMENTS

- While some of the significant communication technology developments are no longer commonplace, most still exist in various forms.
- Learning about past developments reminds us that humans have a long history of searching for new and improved communication tools and will continue to do so.
- The communication technology developments briefly mentioned in this section include moveable type, telegraph, telephone, fax machine, typewriter, personal computer (PC), and the Internet.

THE INTERNET AND WORLD WIDE WEB

Internet
A self-regulated network connecting millions of computer networks around the globe.

World Wide Web
(the Web) A collection of standards and protocols linking massive amounts of information on the Internet, thus enabling user access.

The **Internet** is a self-regulated network connecting millions of computer networks around the globe.[2] The Internet easily comprises the largest computer network in existence. Some people refer to the Internet as the Net, while others refer to it loosely as the **World Wide Web** or the Web. However, the Internet and the Web are not the same thing. The World Wide Web is a subset of the Internet. It is a collection of standards and protocols (rules) that link massive amounts of information located on the Internet across millions of discrete locations. The Internet was first introduced in 1969 and the World Wide Web in 1990.

© nasirkhan/Shutterstock.com

Information on the Web is available in a number of forms. Each web page can be a combination of text, pictures, illustrations, charts, graphs, and audio and video clips. It is common for web pages to contain **hyperlinks** (*links*), which are links to other web pages. Users simply click on the link and a *browser* retrieves the intended page.[3]

THE INTERNET'S IMPACT

The Internet has had profound effects on organizations as well as on governments and individuals. It is conceivable that the magnitude of the impact the Internet will ultimately have on U.S. organizations and society for that matter will exceed the combined impact the telegraph, railroad system, and Industrial Revolution had on the United States during the 19th century.

The Internet owes much of the credit for its rapid growth in popularity to a number of supporting developments in recent years ranging from affordable communication technology and WiFi to mobile devices such as smartphones and tablets. Of course, the early boost came from the introduction of the PC (personal computer) and the ensuing PC revolution which resulted in PCs being placed in great numbers in organizations, schools, libraries, and homes. Improvements to communication satellites and growth in their numbers supported Internet use, as did increased quality and use of fiber optic cables. Important support for Internet growth also came from the ability to digitize information of all forms ranging from text and photos to audio and video clips.

Finally, here is one more impact of the Internet worth noting. It sure has saved a lot of trees. In 2015 it was estimated that it would take 136 billion pieces of paper to print the content of the Internet. This would involve killing eight million trees and, if placed in a single stack, the paper print-out would stand 8,300 miles high.[4]

THE INTERNET AND ORGANIZATIONS

Most organizations use the Internet and a variety of other communication networks in an integrated manner to accomplish their objectives. Organizations have an interest in providing integrated networks that "enhance the ability of their employees to find, create, manage, and distribute information."[5] An organization, for instance, may access one or more intranets and extranets in addition to the Internet.

An **intranet** is a companywide computer network that facilitates internal communication, providing an efficient means of information distribution, collaboration, and access to databases. For example, intranets may contain information ranging from policy manuals and meeting minutes to job and project instructions. Intranets provide privacy and confidentiality through the use of *firewalls* that block outside Internet users from accessing internal information.[6] Intranets are popular in organizations for a number of reasons, including their speed and internal control over their structure and contents.

An **extranet** is a network that links the intranets of business partners via the Internet in such a way that the result is a private network.[7] For example, extranets provide electronic communication links among companies and select customers, suppliers, distributors, investors, and other strategic partners. They also provide efficient access to a number of professional associations. Just as intranets facilitate internal communication, extranets facilitate communication among a host of external business partners. In addition, extranets provide efficient, rapid access to vast amounts of external information in highly secured networks.

WAYS THE INTERNET ENHANCES COMMUNICATION

Several of the major ways businesses use the Internet that enhance communication are presented in Figure 6-3. While reading through the list, keep in mind that many of the uses are supported by intranets, extranets, and the Web as well.

FIGURE 6-3: COMMON WAYS BUSINESSES USE THE INTERNET TO ENHANCE COMMUNICATION

- Sending and receiving e-mail messages
- Sharing and retrieving information
- Conducting research
- Accessing databases
- Accessing computer programs
- Developing and transmitting newsletters, brochures, and other documents
- Social networking
- Building strong public relations
- Providing customer service
- Developing and transmitting policy and procedure manuals
- Designing, developing, and maintaining web pages
- Facilitating online discussion groups
- Supporting Internet telephones
- Enabling collaborative computing that lets people share information (e.g., through e-mail systems, collaborative software systems, videoconferencing, electronic white boards, electronic meeting systems, and computer-aided decision-making systems) without the traditional time and space constraints[8]
- Accessing specialized legal information and government regulations
- Providing online bulletin boards
- Providing and accessing distance learning training
- Buying, selling, trading, and tracking investments
- Posting job openings
- Maintaining résumé databases
- Recruiting employees
- Supporting a number of e-commerce functions such as e-marketing
- Access/use apps

Three of the uses mentioned in Figure 6-3 warrant a closer look, due to the impact that they are having: e-mail, research, and e-commerce.

E-mail E-mail refers to electronically-generated messages and documents that are sent over the Internet, intranets, and extranets. E-mail is currently the most widely used communication medium in U.S. businesses.[9] Organizations use e-mail in a variety of ways. Some of the more common uses include coordinating work, sending attachments, keeping others informed, following up on earlier communication, sending the same message to many people simultaneously, and e-marketing.[10]

Organizations around the globe enjoy several benefits from e-mail. Included among these are:

- E-mail reduces the costs associated with distributing information to large numbers of employees or other stakeholders as well as the costs associated with paper preparation, duplication, and distribution.
- E-mail is a tool that supports and increases teamwork and collaboration because people can communicate easily and efficiently with others.
- E-mail, in conjunction with the Web, enhances research efforts.
- E-mail supports the mobility and flexibility benefits associated with mobile communication technologies such as laptops, cell phones, smartphones, and tablets.[11]

However, e-mail does pose some problems and challenges. Two of these that warrant mentioning are interpersonal disconnection and information overload.[12]

Interpersonal disconnection refers to a problem directly related to the use of e-mail in organizations. As employees send e-mails with greater frequency, they will likely engage in fewer face-to-face encounters, videoconferences, and phone conversations. The lack of nonverbal cues such as facial expressions and varying tones of voice has resulted in some employees feeling less connected to their fellow workers and organizations.[13] Employees may also feel less connected to clients and other stakeholders. Instant messaging, texting, blogging, and tweeting have all added to these problems. Furthermore, the overall quality of communication is compromised.

To encourage face-to-face communication, some companies now set aside a few "e-mail-free days" each month. Social interaction in the workplace is important to most people and, as can be expected, requires at least a minimal level of face-to-face and oral communication. To do otherwise potentially threatens employees' commitment and productivity levels as well as their overall job satisfaction. While there is no doubt that e-mail is a very popular and valuable business communication tool, we need to be careful not to use it to the extent that it creates interpersonal disconnection.

Information overload refers to situations in which businesspeople routinely receive more e-mail messages (or other communications) than they can effectively read, respond to, and act on. This situation is further exacerbated when employees go on vacation. For example, it is not uncommon for some employees to return from a vacation only to find hundreds of new e-mail messages waiting for them to process. To avoid such situations, some employees do not use all their allotted vacation time to relax. Some sort through and respond to incoming e-mail. Try not to take your e-mail on vacation with you. We all need downtime away from both the workplace and work tasks to rest, relax, and recharge our batteries. To do otherwise invites problems ranging from stress-related health problems to decreased productivity and burnout.

In response to the problem of information overload, a variety of techniques are recommended to manage the problem. Several of these techniques are shared in Chapter 8 in the section entitled *Managing High-Volume E-mail*.

Conducting Research If done correctly, conducting research on the Internet is cost efficient and time efficient. These efficiencies are especially evident when you contrast conducting research with today's electronic tools to a time not long ago when wading through hardcopy books, directories, journals, and magazines or squinting your eyes in an attempt to gather information from microfilm and microfiche were the norm.

Some of the same concerns researchers had in the past still exist in the Internet era, however. For example, researchers still need to question the validity of the information

interpersonal disconnection A potential problem directly related to the popularity of e-mail whereby users engage in fewer face-to-face and telephone conversations.

information overload A situation in which people routinely receive more information and messages than they can effectively read, respond to, and act on.

they acquire. Businesspeople and students, alike, face this challenge and are cautioned not to automatically assume that since information is posted on the Internet, it is credible. Your two best lines of defense for assuring the information you gather is valid are (1) gathering it from reliable Internet sources and (2) validating information you gather from the Internet through additional sources you know to be reliable, whether located on the Internet or elsewhere. For example, information posted on *Fortune* magazine's and the *Wall Street Journal's* websites can typically be relied on as being valid, whereas information posted on the websites of tabloids located near grocery store checkout stands may not be as reliable.

Be careful not to plagiarize. **Plagiarism** is the passing off as one's own the writings and ideas of others. Some of the common reasons some writers plagiarize are listed below:

- Some writers do not realize they are doing so.
- Some writers procrastinate during writing projects to the point of leaving themselves too little time to handle citations properly.
- Some writers think that if they located the information on the Internet, it is free and clear for the taking.
- Some writers are too lazy or careless to cite where needed.
- Some writers are simply unscrupulous.[14]

Be careful! Be especially careful not to plagiarize information found on the Internet. While it may be tempting to do so, especially when you are in a hurry, downloading information verbatim from online sources directly into your documents without citing these sources is plagiarism. Geraldine E. Hynes reminds us in her book *Surfing for Success in Business Communication* that writers should cite their sources when they (1) quote word-for-word, (2) closely paraphrase, or (3) repeat a series of phrases from documents posted on the Internet.[15]

E-commerce   E-commerce (electronic commerce) refers to buying and selling products, services, and information over the Internet.[16] For example, many consumers log onto Amazon.com to buy books, music, and other items. When they do so, they are shopping in an e-commerce environment.

© Neirfy/Shutterstock.com

Another term that broadens the meaning of e-commerce is e-business. **E-business,** while addressing buying and selling activities, also implies servicing customers, collaborating with business partners, and conducting electronic transactions within an organization. The common thread that runs through all three of these functions is communication—electronic communication via the Internet.

plagiarism
The passing off as one's own the writings and ideas of others.

e-commerce
(electronic commerce) The transactions involved in buying and selling products, services, and information over the Internet.

e-business
A broader term for e-commerce that implies servicing customers, collaborating with business partners, and conducting electronic transactions within an organization as well as addressing buying and selling transactions.

While businesses developed around an e-commerce/e-business structure come and go like other forms of business, the concept holds great potential. Much of e-commerce success rests on the strength, diversity, and growth of the Internet. This is not to suggest that any time soon people will no longer shop in retail outlets and malls as they do today. Most people still like some face-to-face interaction with others, and many find the traditional approach to shopping to be a social outlet. Whatever the reasons, don't look for dot-com businesses to put retail outlets and malls out of business any time soon. E-commerce is growing in popularity. Every year greater numbers of people let their fingers do the shopping via the Internet.

Just how much impact this "e-structure" will have on businesses and customers is yet to be fully seen. Many believe it will have profound effects. Some even suggest e-commerce may result in a new industrial order. This point was made several years ago by former Vice President Al Gore when he said,

> *We are on the verge of a revolution that is just as profound as the change in the economy that came with the Industrial Revolution. Soon electronic networks will allow people to transcend the barriers of time and distance and take advantage of global markets and business opportunities not even imaginable today, opening up a new world of economic possibility and progress.*[17]

In many respects, Mr. Gore's predictions regarding the Internet were very accurate.

Current e-business growth is being fueled by a number of forces, including strong global competition, low-cost labor in many countries, the changing nature of the workforce, innovations and new technologies, and rapid decline in technology costs.[18] Benefits also stimulate growth. Some of the more noticeable benefits of e-commerce include the ability to expand into new markets, including global markets; reduced overhead; improved customer service; and reduced paper and transportation costs.[19] In summary, e-commerce is a new way to do business.

BARRIERS TO THE INTERNET

Despite the many applications and benefits the Internet offers, there are some barriers. Three in particular include restricted information flow, achieving sufficient broadband, and personal use by employees.

Restricted Information Flow This refers to governments that block access to many Internet sites and services within their borders. In his Cyberspace Independence Declaration, John Perry Barlow declared, "We are creating a world that all may enter without privilege or prejudice accorded by race, economic power, military force or station of birth."[19] However, Barlow's prediction still hasn't been fully realized. Some governments have learned how to regulate what information can be accessed by their businesspeople and citizens.[20] After all, the Internet is not owned and controlled by any one nation, organization, group, or individual. Each nation is left to determine how unfettered the information flow will be within its borders.

Achieving Sufficient Broadband *Broadband* refers to fast connections on the Internet. In the same vein, *bandwidth* refers to how fast Internet content can be delivered. Simply stated, there are still several areas in the world that do not have broadband access due to a combination of pricing, economic, and technical problems. On a positive note, the number of such areas is decreasing.

Non-work Use by Employees The Internet provides a nearly limitless source of websites, activities, information, chat capabilities, and social networking sites. Unfortunately, this wealth of activities, information, and distractions has contributed to major ethics and productivity problems in the U.S. workplace. The problem has to do with employees using the Internet for non-work purposes while at work. The problem has become prevalent enough that dismissing employees for inappropriate use of the Internet in the workplace is not unusual.

Just how common is this problem? Russ Warner, CEO of ContentWatch, reports that 64 percent of U.S. employees browse non-work related websites such as Facebook, Linke-dIn, Google+, and Pinterest every day at work.[21] Among workers who browse non-work websites, those ages 18–35 do so most frequently with 73 percent reporting such activity. Respondents across all age ranges gave the following reasons for doing so: they don't feel challenged enough in their job, they work too many hours, the company doesn't give suffi-cient incentive to work harder, they're unsatisfied with their career, and they're just bored.[22] Shopping, conducting job searches, making travel arrangements, visiting social networking sites, downloading music, and viewing porn are among the more common reasons for visit-ing the Internet for non-work purposes, each of which can easily land an employee in the unemployment line!

While most employees keep personal Internet use to a minimum at work, others appear to be less committed to their workplace obligations. As can be expected, employees who use the Internet for non-work purposes contribute to lost productivity, which ultimately harms everyone in the company.[23]

Many businesses have responded to this problem by developing policies on inappro-priate use of the Internet at work. Such policies typically pertain to misuse of company- and employee-owned electronic communication devices. Employees who own laptops, netbooks, tablets, and smartphones are expected to forgo using them for personal reasons while at work.

Other measures employers take to reduce the problem include blocking certain websites on employees' office computers, electronically monitoring employee use of the Internet, limiting employee access solely to an Intranet, and blocking employee access to the Internet entirely. Clear policies and measures reduce the instances of Internet misuse in the work-place. Clearly, such activity is greatly reduced when employees simply embrace their ethical responsibilities and work-related obligations to their employers.

SUMMARY: SECTION 3— THE INTERNET AND WORLD WIDE WEB

- The Internet is a self-regulated network connecting millions of computers worldwide.
- The Internet is popular throughout the world and has profoundly affected orga-nizations, governments, and individuals.
- Intranets, extranets, and websites were developed using Internet technology.
- Businesses use the Internet in many ways to enhance communication efforts. Among them are sending and receiving e-mail, facilitating online discussion groups, providing distance learning, recruiting employees, and supporting e-commerce functions.
- Major barriers to full and equal access to the Internet include inadequate access in poor and rural areas of the United States, restricted information flow in many countries, limited broadband support, and misuse of the Internet by employees.

COMMUNICATING USING WIRELESS TECHNOLOGIES

© Tyler Olson/Shutterstock.com

It was not that long ago that most electronic communication tools depended on wires, cables, and modems to facilitate communication and information exchange. That was the age of the wired office. Given the right network configurations and electronic communication devices, combined with cloud computing, many of today's communication technologies function untethered. Businesspeople now conduct a large portion of their communication using wireless communication devices linked to personal area networks (PANs), local area networks (LANs), and wide area networks (WANs), and there are no indications that this trend will go away any time soon. It is much more likely that we will populate the world with billions more wireless electronic communication devices in the years to come.

Advances in communication technologies and network development, along with availability of WiFi and affordable technologies, enable businesspeople to perform many of their job responsibilities while moving from office to office, while traveling, and from their homes. From these varied sites, wireless technologies make it possible for them to send and receive text messages and e-mails; access social media sites; participate in conference calls and videoconferences; collaborate on group projects using group support systems (e.g., SharePoint, Google Docs, wikis, SkyDrive); share data files; and browse the Internet.

WIRELESS COMMUNICATION DEVICES

The most common devices with wireless communication capabilities that support uses such as those mentioned above include conventional and data-enabled cell phones, smartphones, laptops, netbooks, and tablets. Most of these devices have been standard business tools for a number of years, while others are relatively new entries. For example, **smartphones**, which merge cell phone and personal digital assistant (PDA) technologies, such as early models of the *BlackBerry*, are used extensively in today's businesses. Another example of a relatively new entrant is the **tablet**. These practical, affordable communication devices are another popular wireless communication tool in today's office. And just as the merging of cell phone and PDA technologies gave us smartphones, tablet and smartphone technologies have begun to merge, resulting in devices such as Samsung's Galaxy Note, which is a hybrid of a smartphone and tablet. Basically, this device has smartphone features and users can also write on the screen using a stylus. The current list of wireless communication devices has grown tremendously in a short time and will keep growing as people further embrace wireless, mobile technologies in the workplace and in their personal lives.

Five wireless communication devices that are making a noticeable impact on mobile communication: netbooks, tablets, cell phones, smartphones, and **Internet phones.**

Netbooks Netbook computers have been on the fringe of general laptop options, but now a new generation of netbooks is gaining market share. Netbooks are considerably smaller than normal laptops, with screen sizes that range from 5–13 inches and weigh as little as 2–3 pounds. **Netbooks** are highly portable devices whose main functions are to access e-mail, browse the Web, and use Web-based applications. Netbooks were originally

smartphones
Mobile phones offering advanced capabilities.

tablet
Relatively small touch pad computers with capabilities ranging from Internet access to standard PC functions.

Internet phones
Devices delivering voice communications over IP networks such as the Internet.

netbook
Small laptop whose main functions are to access e-mail, browse the Web, and use web-based applications.

marketed as companion devices for laptop users who kept their data on the Web and mostly ran Web applications rather than software saved onto the computer itself. Now netbooks compete with laptops. Netbook popularity is driven partly by its low cost. An average netbook costs about $300. Thanks to technological advances, the lines between netbooks and laptops are becoming blurred. With increased processing power and additional features, some industry watchers suggest that netbooks are becoming little more than cheaper, smaller laptops.[24]

Tablets Tablets are also referred to as Tablet PCs, Webpads, and Touch Pads. There are a variety of tablets on the market, and the number keeps growing as more models are in various stages of development. Tablets are small touch pads with capabilities ranging from Internet access to standard PC functions. Users typically perform functions with their fingers or a stylus. They can also use a screen-based keyboard or attach a separate keyboard and mouse. Some tablets even respond to voice commands. Like several models of smartphones, tablets have a built-in camera and video recorder. Some models have a voice-activation feature. Most tablets have a 9-inch screen, are about 10x7½x½ inches in size, and weigh about one pound. Most of their surface is screen. Smaller tablets are also available. For example, Apple's Mini-iPad and Google's Android Tablet both have 7-inch screens. In contrast, Fuhu's nabi Big Tab HD 24 is the largest tablet with a 23.6 inch screen and weighs in at 10.5 pounds. It is designed predominately for children and families. Given that Apple received complaints about its first iPad weighing too much (roughly 1.5 pounds), the nabi Big Tab HD 24 is not necessarily intended to be a mobile tool—although the early portable PCs (luggables) that made their way onto the market in the early 1980s weighed closer to 40 pounds and businesspeople were happy to have them. Just imagine how much people would complain today about 40-pound portable communication devices!

Given tablets' low cost and wide range of features, some industry watchers suggest that tablets will eventually be the mobile electronic communication device of choice, eroding netbook and laptop sales. In 2015 tablets started outselling PCs, due in large part to their relatively-low cost, capabilities, features, and versatility.

Mobile Phones Long gone are the days when our ability to place and receive phone calls was limited to land line phones, pay phones, and costly long-distance charges. Today, mobile phones are very popular around the globe in and outside of the workplace. One might say that mobile phones are ubiquitous. For example, most Americans do not leave home without their mobile phones. And, if they do forget and leave their homes or offices without them, they're covered. While out and about, they buy a disposal mobile phone with airtime for a few dollars. However, disposable phones typically lack most of the features of conventional mobile phones.

Mobile phones are most frequently referred to as cell phones and smart-phones, although many tablets also have phone capabilities. Tablets with phone capabilities include LG G Pad, Sony Xperia Z2, Samsung Galaxy Tab S, Apple iPad Air 2, Amazon Fire HDX 8.9, and Nvidia Shield Tablet.[25] Cell phones might simply be thought of as mobile phones with basic calling capabilities, whereas smartphones are cell phones with a host of features and capabilities that continue to increase with what seems to be the never-ending development of apps. Approximately 30 percent of Americans currently own one or more cell phones and approximately 66 percent own one or more smartphones. Cell phones and smartphones are popular communication devices due in great part to their mobility, small size, low cost, and ease of use.

Most smartphones have at least the basic functionality of PCs, making it possible for users to check and send text and e-mail messages, participate in IM exchanges, access social media, access company files, receive Internet faxes, and browse the Internet while engaged in a phone conversation. Smartphones also have scheduling and lists and notes features as well as GPS capability. Furthermore, smartphone digital and video cameras support Instagram, Pinterest, and YouTube needs. Last, but not least, Smartphones support a number of videoconferencing-related technologies including Video Chat, Snapchat, Skype, and FaceTime.

Mobile apps have vastly expanded mobile phone capabilities in recent years. At the current pace apps are developed, it is nearly impossible to keep up, although businesspeople are encouraged to do so with those that are applicable to business. Keeping up, in this regard, is most challenging given the rate new business apps are introduced. While there is not enough room in this book to address all of the current business apps, there is room to share what are considered to be several of the most useful business apps. These are presented in Figure 6-4. Possibly you are already familiar with most of them. If not, this is as good a time as any to get started.

FIGURE 6-4: USEFUL BUSINESS APPS FOR YOUR SMARTPHONE

Communication Apps
- **MobileDay** - conference caXll dialer app
- **GoToMeeting** - virtual meetings app

Enterprise Productivity/Internal Collaboration Apps
- **Slack** - team communication app
- **Jira** - issue and software tracking app
- **Asana** - e-mail-less project management app
- **Trello** - organizing app

Social Media Apps
- **Snapseed** - photo editing app for brands that are regular posters to social media sites
- **Wordswag** - Instagram word art and type over images app

Personal Productivity Apps
- **Concur** - expense reporting app
- **Expensify** - expense reports app
- **Evernote** - note-taking/collaboration app
- **TheFreeDictionary** – extensive dictionary app

Contact Management/Business Social Networks Apps
- **LinkedIn** - professional networking app

Mobile Payments/Wallet Apps
- **Apple Pay** - payment service app
- **PayPal** - payment service app

Mapping/GPS Apps
- **Google Maps** - map app

Travel Apps
- **Uber** - automobile transportation app
- **Car2Go** - car rental app
- **Localeur** - virtual tour guide app

News/Entertainment Apps
- **HBO Go** - entertainment app that is a good one for frequent business travelers
- **Chromecast** - entertainment app that is good for business travelers

Source: Aaron Strout, "Top 20 Most Useful Mobile Business Apps For 2015," April 30, 2015, http://marketingland.com/top-20-most-useful-mobile-business-apps-for-2015-126124.

Smartphones are typically larger than cell phones and come in a variety of sizes and shapes. Many models use touch-sensitive screens, while some even have slide-out keyboards. With the emergence of the iPhone, third-party development of applications, known as apps, have proliferated. Apps can be anything from games to driving directions to music lists. New apps are developed daily that help drive smartphone sales and, in turn, reduce the number of electronic devices people carry with them. GPS systems, digital cameras, video cameras, music players, voice recorders, PDAs, and electronic book readers are all examples of devices that have steadily been replaced by smartphones that have these features.

FIGURE 6-5: MOBILE PHONE CHALLENGES

- Concerned that others may hack your phone conversations while you are walking around your office, riding on the commuter train, or having coffee at a café?
- Knowing when and where it is appropriate to place and receive phone calls. Everywhere is not the answer. As a general rule, it is rude to place and respond to phone calls during face-to-face conversations, business meetings, presentations, business dinners, training sessions, and job interviews whether you are the recruiter or the job applicant.
- Being a courteous caller. Phone calls should be placed and received in a relatively quiet place where you are not disturbing others whether they are in the workplace cubicle next to yours, on the elevator, or next to you on a commuter train.
- Being aware of your surroundings while crossing streets. Unfortunately, some are so distracted by their mobile phone conversations, as well as texting, that they unknowingly step out in front of vehicles or fall through uncovered manholes. Death often results in these situations.
- Avoiding the urge to participate in phone conversations (and texting) while driving. Doing so is considered to be the equivalent of driving drunk and has resulted in numerous injuries and fatalities over the years. Possibly one day such driving safety concerns will be eliminated by smart cars that will essentially drive themselves. Imagine being able to put your car on auto pilot, pick up your smartphone, and talk or text without safety concerns.[26] For mobile phone safety tips, visit http://www.cellphonesafety.org/safer/tips.htm.
- Achieving seamless telephony for global travelers. This matter pertains to world phones.

World phones are cell phones with global roaming capabilities. The ideal world phone would enable a businessperson to place and receive wireless mobile phone calls to and from any location around the globe. Currently, world phone reception is available in some but not all global locations. However, the need to provide seamless telephony for global travelers exists, and progress continues in that direction.[27]

Internet Phones Internet phones are made possible, in part, due to Voice over Internet Protocol (VoIP), which refers to the delivery of voice communications over IP networks such as the Internet. These are also sometimes referred to as voice over broadband or Internet telephones. They are programs that allow people to talk to each other over the Internet. They are not really wireless communication devices like cell phones and smartphones;

world phones
Cell phones with global roaming capabilities.

© ra2studio/Shutterstock.com

however, they do enable communication over the Internet through wireless communication devices. The appeal of Internet telephones is the reduction or elimination of long-distance costs associated with conventional phone calls.

Without going into detail, the ability to communicate via Internet phones presumes that users have the appropriate software and hardware. These add-ons range from sound cards, speakers, and microphones to the software. The Internet phone is fairly new. It was introduced in 1995 by VocalTec. Despite some bugs in the technology, Internet phone use is growing, and market analysts predict that it has a bright future.[28]

Are you addicted to your mobile phone? If you find the term "addicted" to be a bit strong, how about replacing it with the term "deepening dependence" instead. The term addicted has such negative connotations for some. As discussed here, these two terms have similar meanings: the extremely anxious feelings many people suggest they would have if their mobile phone wasn't available or they couldn't use it with a relatively high degree of frequency. Recent Gallup polls concluded that almost half of American smartphone users "can't imagine" life without their device.[29]

FIGURE 6-6: IN THE EVENT OF A FIRE

In the event of a fire in your home, what would you save first? In a recent smartphone relationship survey, 53 percent of the respondents said that in the event of a fire, they would save their smartphones first. Really! This speaks to some level of addiction? Each of us just might want to pose this question to our loved ones, roommates, etc., just to see where we rank on the "save list" should a fire break out.

Source: Jae Yang & Veronica Bravo, "Rescuing smartphone," Motorola Smartphone Relationship Survey, USA Today, August 21, 2015, p. B1.

SMARTPHONE ADDICTION
Lorem ipsum dolor sit

© Zygotehaasnobrain/Shutterstock.com

In addition, a study spanning Africa, China, and the United States that focused on the reasons behind digital distractions confirmed that addiction is one of the main reasons people text and the like in inappropriate settings.[30] If you are uncertain as to whether you are addicted to your mobile phone, so to speak, the following questions will likely help you arrive at an answer.

- Have you ever returned home to get your mobile phone after discovering you left home without it?
- Do you get noticeably stressed if your mobile phone battery is low? (When asked in a survey, 92 percent of Americans said they do.)
- Would you feel noticeably stressed if you did not have access to your mobile phone for several hours? Several days? (When asked in a survey, most Americans said they do. However, the length of time varies as could be expected.)

- What is the approximate number of times you check your mobile phone daily for phone and text messages? This is based on a 16-hour day. (Based on survey results, the typical American checks his or her mobile phone 103 times daily for phone and text messages which averages out to checking for them every seven minutes.)
- Are you using your mobile phone wisely (e.g., avoiding using it in inappropriate settings such as college classes, corporate training sessions, business meetings, etc.)?
- Are you using your mobile phone safely (e.g., avoiding using it while driving, crossing streets, etc.).

Your responses to the above questions should give you some sense of where you stand on the mobile phone addiction question. Hopefully you determined that you are not addicted. If you determined that you are, however, help is on the way. Figure 6-7 contains suggestions on how to beat the addiction or at least minimize it.

FIGURE 6-7: BEATING SMARTPHONE ADDICTIONS

- First, recognize the problem. Studies have linked smartphone dependence to stress anxiety and poor cognitive performance.
- Set short-term goals. Don't try to go cold-turkey for an extended period of time. Instead, wean yourself starting with a half-hour between stealing peeks. Then progressively increase the length of time between peeks.
- Spread the word. Tell your contacts what you are attempting to do. This will likely influence the frequency with which they contact you and expectations regarding how quickly and how often you will respond.
- Shut it down before bed. Reading on a bright screen in a dark room will not only delay sleep but can also cause less deep sleep and make you less alert the next day. In addition, reading on bright screens in dark places frequently has also been linked to detached retinas![31]

Smartwatches Smartwatches are a relatively new addition to the wearable communication technologies market, a market that has existed for several years. In fact, wearable computing and wearable technologies conferences are routinely held around the world and have been for a number of years. Some examples include WT (wearable technologies) Conferences, GizWorld Conferences, International Symposium on Wearable Computers (ISWC) conferences, and IDTechEx Wearable Conferences.

Smartwatches offer many of the same features as smartphones, but the availability of these varies among models. As can be expected, more expensive smartwatches often offer more features.

Businesspeople use smartwatches for a number of purposes ranging from checking e-mail and alerts to accessing business files. The hands-free nature of smartwatches is a very practical benefit.

On the downside, there are a number of drawbacks to smartwatches. For example, they are relatively expensive in contrast to netbooks, tablets, and smartphones. However, prices will eventually come down. In addition, early smartwatches were larger than most people preferred. This concern should diminish as smaller, voice-activated smartwatches hit the marketplace. Then too, there is the obvious concern about battery life. Screen size is another obvious drawback. For example, just how realistic is it to expect that most people will be able

Wearable Technology Conference
http://wearablestech-con.com/

© wavebreakmedia/Shutterstock.com

to or even want to read e-mail messages and business documents on small 1.5- to 1.6-inch screens. There is another potential drawback that some might actually consider to be a benefit of smartwatches and that is the ability to easily check alerts and e-mails during meetings and training sessions. Most managers no more appreciate employees doing such things on smartwatches than on smartphones, tablets, and laptops during meetings and training sessions. Lastly, there are the potential drawbacks of never being disconnected that wearable technologies such as smartwatches pose. This point is made in the article "Never Offline."

© monicaodo/Shutterstock.com

Given the above-mentioned drawbacks, will smartwatches become widely used in the business world? Probably not if the drawbacks are not addressed. However, if manufacturers do address these concerns, ranging from cost and size to battery life, smartwatches just might become a popular mainstay.

© mindscanner/Shutterstock.com

THE IMPACT OF WIRELESS COMMUNICATION TECHNOLOGIES

Today's vast array of relatively low-cost, wireless communication technologies, combined with WiFi, has had a monumental impact on how communication occurs in the business place. Three ways organizations are impacted are presented below.

Working Away from the Office Possibly the most noticeable impact is the relatively new-found freedom businesspeople have experienced as a result of being freed from conventional, wired offices. For example, they no longer need to be tethered to stay in touch. Wireless communication devices have already and will continue to have a profound impact on how, where, when, and how frequently businesspeople communicate no matter the physical distance between business partners.

Wireless communication technologies are also playing a prominent role in transforming an ever-growing number of traditional U.S. office workers into telecommuters. **Telecommuters** refers to employees who perform some portion of their work away from the office while linked to it electronically. Before the advent of wireless communication technologies, telecommuters typically worked from their homes (or other fixed locations) using computers, fax machines, and telephones linked to their office through wired modems. Today's telecommuters who perform all or a significant portion of work from their homes are likely to use a combination of wired and wireless communication devices.

Telecommuting is increasingly popular with workers, businesses, and governments. The proliferation of communication technologies; potential cost savings related to buying, building, leasing, and maintaining office buildings; overcrowded streets and highways; deteriorating air quality; rising fuel and energy costs; and fear of terrorist attacks have together fueled telecommuting growth and popularity in the United States.[32] While employers see cost savings and potential benefits to the environment, most workers relish the idea of working in more relaxed and safer settings. Those who telecommute from their homes typically enjoy forgoing the expenses, hassles, and needed time associated with commuting and not needing to purchase as many expensive business clothes. Many also like the schedule flexibility typical of many telecommuting positions.

A set work schedule and a professional mindset are key to successful telecommuting for most people, whether the work is partially or fully performed from one's home. Without these, productivity typically suffers noticeably.

Even though today's communication technologies support telecommuting for many, it is not the right work structure for all employees. Those who do not adapt well to telecommuting are typically less productive and often eventually leave the company voluntarily due to dissatisfaction with their work environment. While businesses can relatively easily and inexpensively convert traditional workers into work-at-home telecommuters to "e-mobilize" their workforce, telecommuting will not bring out the best in all business employees. For example, some employees cannot be productive and meet deadlines without a structured schedule that involves traveling to and from an office during traditionally designated hours. Still others have difficulty separating work responsibilities from home and social distractions. In addition, it is common for some telecommuters to feel isolated because of the loss of daily contact with others, which leads to job burnout for some. For additional information on the challenges of working from home, visit http://www.glassdoor.com/blog/5-telecommuting/ and http://www.mnn.com/money/green-workplace/blogs/5-telecommuting-challenges-and-how-i-solved-them.

For obvious reasons, employers and employees need to be realistic about the extent to which telecommuter work is embraced. Survey instruments investigating the downsides and the benefits of telecommuting can be administered and followed up with interviews to determine an employee's suitability for telecommuter positions.

Once the decision is made to shift certain employees to telecommuter status, it is wise to closely monitor their productivity and job satisfaction for a while to determine if the change in job structure is working out as planned.

Just as telecommuting is not the right work structure for some employees, it does not support all job tasks. For example, work activities such as important meetings and presentations do not fit into the telecommuting work structure.

Telecommuter
An employee who performs some portion of his or her work away from the office while linked to the office electronically.

17 Tools For Remote Workers, Kevan Lee
http://www.fastcompany.com/3038333/17-tools-for-remote-workers

Moving Around the Office Untethered Just as wireless communication technology has made it possible for businesspeople to move around freely away from the office, it has opened the doors to mobile communication within the office. In wireless offices, workers are no longer tethered to desktop PCs, telephones, and defined office spaces such as cubicles. However, even in wireless offices, some closed-off spaces remain for status, quiet-time purposes, private meetings, conference calls, and videoconferences.

In wireless business environments, the trend is moving in the direction of working in common, open spaces rather than in isolated cubicles and offices. These large open spaces frequently look more like casual living rooms than traditional offices filled with desks and filing cabinets. Instead, these open spaces may be filled with comfortable furniture and flat-panel screens hanging from the walls.[33] This all sounds wonderful, but be careful not to settle into an exceptionally comfortable chair after a big lunch. You know what that will do to your productivity while you are napping!

Savings Associated with Wireless Offices The reduction or elimination of costs associated with setting up and maintaining wired offices is another way wireless communication technologies impact organizations. In the traditional wired office, much cost and effort went into running wires and cables to individual offices and cubicles to hook into an array of wired communication devices. Additional costs were incurred when employees were occasionally relocated within their buildings, requiring some rewiring. Wired offices also have the cost associated with hiring technical support personnel to maintain the systems.[34]

As popular and pervasive as wireless communication technologies are in the business place, it is wise to stay current. An excellent way to stay current is to routinely read magazines dedicated to wireless and mobile communication topics. Such magazines include *Wireless Business & Technology*, *Smartphone & Pocket PC*, and *Mobile Computing*. In addition, magazines and newspapers such as *Fortune*, *PC Magazine*, *BusinessWeek*, and the *Wall Street Journal* routinely include articles, editorials, and even extensive sections devoted to wireless communication technologies and processes. There are also a number of websites that contain information about wireless communication and wireless communication devices.

SUMMARY: SECTION 4— GOING MOBILE: WIRELESS COMMUNICATION TECHNOLOGY

- The combination of smaller computer chips and a number of communication networks, such as PANs, LANs, and WANs, have led the way for a host of wireless electronic communication devices.
- Wireless electronic communication devices currently in use include cell phones, smartphones, world phones, Internet phones, laptops, notebooks, netbooks, and tablets.
- While cell phones and smartphones are ubiquitous, be mindful of their many courtesy and safety issues.
- Wireless communication devices play a prominent role in transforming an ever-growing number of U.S. office workers into telecommuters, as well as providing them with mobility within offices.

USING COMMUNICATION TECHNOLOGIES EFFECTIVELY

The sophistication and potential of the Internet combined with today's electronic communication technologies cannot be ignored. Their effects on the business place and elsewhere are numerous and are continuously changing how we work, play, relax, and interact with others. However, if we want to fully realize the potential benefits, we need to use these technologies effectively. Suggestions pertaining to how to use electronic communication technologies effectively are presented below.

CHOOSING THE APPROPRIATE COMMUNICATION MEDIUM

The importance of selecting the appropriate medium for each communication situation or setting was discussed at length. With all this talk about the Internet and electronic communication technologies further discussion of this topic is needed.

While electronic communication devices are the right media choice for some situations, they are not best for all situations. We need to be careful not to become so enamored with electronic communication technologies that we automatically choose them at the expense of effective communication.

The concept of information richness or media richness helps us make more effective communication media choices. **Information richness** refers to how robust a communication medium is. Some communication media are rich, some are lean, and the rest fall in between. The richest form of communication is face-to-face communication. It is considered the richest because most people find it to be the most natural way to communicate, and it contains the full range of nonverbal cues in addition to the spoken word. Immediate feedback is another benefit of face-to-face communication. Less robust media (e.g., text messages, e-mails, tweets) are lean and should be limited to messages regarding routine matters.

Given the rationale presented above, holoconferencing is the second richest communication medium followed, in descending order, by videoconferencing, Skype and video chat exchanges, phone conversations, conference calls, instant messaging, e-mailing, texting, tweeting, and blogging. **Holoconferences** are telepresence-based videoconferences in which screen images are replaced with 3-dimensional images of participants who are not physically present.

Be careful not to become so enamored with the convenience and cost- and time-saving benefits of electronic communications technologies that you skimp on face-to-face communication. Remind yourself that when a situation is important, complex, or controversial, there is no electronic substitute for face-to-face communication. Even videoconferencing falls short to face-to-face communication in terms of participant comfort level and relationship-building potential.

CONTROL COMMUNICATION TECHNOLOGY, RATHER THAN ALLOWING IT TO CONTROL YOU

As wonderful as the Internet and electronic communication devices are, they have their shortcomings and challenges. Recall the challenges pertaining to mobile phones and telecommuting that were discussed previously. Additional challenges are presented below.

information richness
Refers to how robust a communication medium is.

holoconferences
Telepresence-based videoconferences in which screen images are replaced with 3-dimensional images of participants who are not physically present.

Information Overload Challenges Information overload results when individuals receive too many electronic messages to realistically process. This situation often results in the receiver becoming overwhelmed by the volume of information. Businesspeople must be sensitive to how many messages can be processed realistically given their daily demands on their time. Several techniques for managing e-mail volume are discussed in Chapter 8 (Writing Electronically). In addition, we each need to search for and access information wisely in databases and on the Internet. The better we understand our purpose for gathering the information, the less likely we are to gather unneeded, excess information. In addition, the better we know how to navigate databases and the Internet, the less overwhelmed we are likely to become when conducting research.

Polyphasic Activity Challenges **Polyphasic activity** refers to doing more than one thing at a time (e.g., multitasking). This is typical of humans. For example, carrying on conversations while walking or driving is polyphasic activity. Multitasking is a way of life in the workplace and for many people in their personal lives. What does this have to do with communication technologies? Today's communication technologies often make polyphasic activity a reality—a detrimental reality. For example, it is possible to participate in a conference call, check and respond to e-mail, and browse the Internet simultaneously. However, performing so many different activities simultaneously typically compromises the effectiveness of how each is handled. The point is that even though much of today's communication technology supports extensive polyphasic activity, we must be careful not to compromise the effectiveness of our efforts by overextending ourselves.

Balancing Work and Personal Life Challenges Joan Greenbaum, author of *Windows for the Workplace: Computers, Jobs, and the Organization of Office Work in the Late 20th Century*, identified a growing technology-related problem. She suggested that because today's technology has empowered businesspeople to work anywhere at any time, many are working everywhere and all the time.[35] Some even feel guilty when they are not working most of the time. This is especially true of telecommuters who work extensively from their homes. The result is they are not getting away from their work, so they are not building in enough downtime to fulfill their personal needs and re-energize. Maintaining such a continuous work schedule for any serious length of time can easily result in negative outcomes ranging from increased feelings of stress and depression to medical problems such as ulcers and high blood pressure as well as job and career burnout. It is neither healthy nor logical for employees to be constantly connected to the workplace no matter whether employers require their employees to do so or employees voluntarily choose to do so. By 2015 the potential negative effects of such workplace actions led the German government to pass a law that restricts businesses from e-mailing employees after 6 p.m. on week nights and on weekends as a means of reducing worker stress.

So, what can you do to maintain your sanity and health as well as function effectively in work environments in which you are likely to overextend yourself? Consider scheduling set work times, and then do your best to stick to them. In turn, set aside time for personal matters, friends, and family and do as little work as possible during those times. In addition, do not allow yourself to be on call constantly. Furthermore, give yourself permission to disconnect from your electronic communication devices when you are not working. For example, do not get into the habit of checking your text messages, e-mails, voicemail, and various social media sites every waking hour of every day and night. Lastly, do not feel compelled to carry your laptop, tablet, smartphone, and/or smartwatch with you everywhere you go. It is healthy to disconnect periodically as described in Michael Harris's book *The End of Absence*.

The End of Absence
http://www.endofabsence.com/

Brevity, Tone, and Carelessness Challenges It is generally understood that we are expected to keep electronic messages and posts brief. Thus, we are encouraged to write relatively short e-mail messages, text messages, and social media posts as well as leave brief voicemails. The potential problem with this sweeping expectation is providing too little information to communicate our messages and posts adequately. To minimize this potential problem, have others read your messages and posts carefully to determine if clarity exists.

Improper tone is also a potential problem when developing electronic messages and posts. The tone-related problems include using a tone that is too informal or is less than tactful. For most of us, our early experiences with e-mail involved sending informal messages to family and friends. Furthermore, this informal tone was likely reinforced when we wrote text messages, tweets, and posts. The end result was very likely an informal writing style that worked well with your family and friends, but is too informal for most business e-mail messages. For some reason, many people do not state things as tactfully in electronic messages as they should. This is especially characteristic of e-mail, in which electronic alter egos have been known to take control in counterproductive ways.[36] Good advice when developing electronic messages that just might help you avoid tone issues is to assess your tone carefully before sending or posting.

Lastly, a careless writing style is typically looked upon unfavorably in the business world. However, when developing electronic messages for family and friends, many of us developed a careless writing style, a style that is frowned upon in the professional workplace. This means we should adhere to basic writing mechanics rules (e.g., grammar, punctuation, spelling) when developing electronic messages in business settings. To minimize this potential problem, before sending or posting, edit electronic messages and posts carefully with special focus on writing mechanics and accuracy.

Telephone Challenges There is probably no finer example of the potentially impersonal nature of electronic communication devices than what we are currently witnessing with the telephone. What started out in 1876 as such a simple, effective communication device has evolved into a device containing a host of features that present their own set of problems. Several of the more commonly mentioned telephone irritants are presented in Figure 6-8.

FIGURE 6-8: TELEPHONE IRRITANTS

- Not controlling background noise when using speaker phones.
- Automatically responding to call waiting calls when conversing with others.
- Not giving others your full attention during conference calls.
- Not giving a caller the choice to be placed on hold, and placing callers on hold for extended times (longer than one minute).
- Placing computer-generated calls and advertisements to people's offices, mobile phones, and homes.
- Subjecting callers to long, involved phone menus.
- Not providing callers with a telephone menu option to speak with a person.
- Placing telemarketing calls at dinnertime, during evenings, and on weekends and holidays.
- Placing and answering calls in inappropriate settings ranging from college classes and corporate training sessions to business meetings and job interviews.

Without exception, each of the telephone irritants mentioned in Figure 6-8 can be eliminated. The lesson in all this is that phone usage decisions should result in people treating others respectfully.

FIGURE 6-9: UNETHICAL USE OF THE TELEPHONE

Most people do not appreciate receiving unsolicited calls from telemarketers, fundraisers, and politicians during dinnertime, evenings, weekends, and holidays. In addition, most people do not appreciate receiving computer-generated calls making requests, advertising products and services, or endorsing politicians. Just because today's technology makes it possible for us to place unwanted calls so easily and inexpensively does not mean we should do it.

Technology Uses Challenges The issue here has to do with employees' perceptions about and proficiency with electronic communication technologies. Do you believe all business employees are comfortable and proficient with a wide range of electronic communication technologies? While most business employees adapt well to electronic communication technologies, some don't. In fact, some prefer a technology-free existence. Figure 6-10 reinforces these points through a list of 10 common "techno-types" that were identified by Dr. Francine Toder, emeritus faculty of California State University Sacramento. If you have not already thought about it, take this opportunity to identify which techno-type or combination thereof best describes you. Then, reflect on how your attitude toward technology will affect your career.

FIGURE 6-10: TECHNO-TYPES

- **The Imposter.** Imposters play around on computers, hoping that their lack of knowledge goes undetected.
- **The Challenger.** Challengers are angered by technology and afraid that it may be used against them.
- **The Resister.** Resisters prefer the simplicity of a tech-free existence. (Resisters are the most common techno-type!)
- **The Technophobe.** Technophobes are paranoid about technology.
- **The Procrastinator.** Procrastinators use technology for the easiest tasks and never go for the max.
- **The Addict.** Addicts eat, sleep, and drink technology.
- **The Driver.** Drivers use tech skills to outpace everyone.
- **The Player.** Players are grown-up gamers who live to play.
- **The Dreamer.** Dreamers harbor unrealistic expectations for technology.
- **The Hermit.** Hermits prefer electronic communication in lieu of face-to-face contact.

Source: From Tech Types *by Paula Felps. © 2000 by Paula Felps. Reprinted by permission.*

Are all business employees receptive to telecommuting and productive when placed in a telecommuting work environment that has them working out of a spare bedroom or converted garage in their home? Some structured, self-disciplined employees are satisfied, productive employees in telecommuting environments. In contrast, others do not adapt well to such environments.

It is important that managers keep employees' communication differences, preferences, strengths, and weaknesses in mind when making decisions regarding integrating electronic communication devices into the workplace and making telecommuting assignments. Bringing employees in on the decision-making process as it relates to technology choices and telecommuting shows them how they will potentially benefit personally from the proposed changes. Suffice it to say, e-mobilizing a company's workforce requires more thought and effort than simply distributing smartphones, laptops, netbooks, and tablets en masse.

Technology Over-Reliance Challenge Millennials (those born between 1982 and 2004) are now the largest segment of the American workforce, and it has been suggested that one of the biggest issues they are having in the workplace is over-reliance on electronic communication. When surveyed, 91% of millennials reported that they aspire to be leaders, and over half (58%) of those respondents indicated that they think the most important leadership skill is communication. Furthermore, 51% indicated that communication is one of their strongest skills. Given their reliance on electronic communication, are these millennials' overall communication skills as strong as they believe them to be? Or, is it possible that some of them, while having strong electronic communication skills, are lacking in other areas such as face-to-face communication, listening, and presentation skills, to name a few? All communication conducted in the business place cannot and should not done electronically. Thus, there is still a strong need for all business personnel of all ages to have strong communication skills whether they are communicating electronically or otherwise.[37]

Technology-Related Job Security and Career Concerns While most of today's communication technologies hold great potential for increased productivity, when misused they can lead to job loss and even threaten careers. Figure 6-11 contains a number of communication technology job security and career threats you are encouraged to keep in mind as you move through your working years.

FIGURE 6-11: TECHNOLOGY-RELATED JOB SECURITY AND CAREER THREATS

- Reduced productivity resulting from being connected too frequently (e.g., 24/7 connectivity).
- Job/career burnout from being connected too frequently (e.g., 24/7 connectivity).
- Job/career fallout from using communication technologies during business meetings, presentations, and training sessions (e.g., texting, tweeting, answering phone calls, browsing the Internet). The vast majority of U.S. managers discourage employees from doing so.
- Job/career fallout from using communication technologies for personal (non-work) reasons in the workplace (e.g., e-mailing friends, downloading music, browsing porn sites, e-shopping, and sexting which is on the rise among 20–26 year-olds in the United States).

Technology-Related Health and Safety Threats As mentioned previously, today's communication technologies hold great potential for increased productivity. However, today's communication technologies also pose health and safety threats when misused. Figure 6-12 contains several communication technology health and safety threats you are encouraged to keep in mind as you move through life. Each of us is vulnerable to these technology-related health and safety threats.

FIGURE 6-12: TECHNOLOGY-RELATED HEALTH AND SAFETY THREATS

- Vision impairment associated with viewing small screens with a fairly high degree of frequency. Hopefully you will be able to do most of your reading from good-sized monitors and even then increase the type size to ease eye strain. In addition, you are encouraged to take more frequent breaks than you would normally take to rest your eyes. Finally, consider purchasing a pair of glasses designed for small screens including e-books.
- Hearing loss associated with frequent use of mobile phone earpieces and ear buds.
- Carpal tunnel syndrome damage (repetitive motion nerve damage) associated with too much keyboarding—especially on small netbook keyboards and small mobile phone keypads. One relatively new entry to the list of carpal tunnel syndrome afflictions that you definitely do not want is "cellphone elbow." This can occur if you talk on a mobile phone for a long time while holding your neck crooked and your elbow bent.[38] Maybe it is time to buy a headset!
- Detached retinas resulting from using electronic communication devices such as mobile phones and tablets with a relatively high degree of frequency in dark settings. Turn on some lights!
- Stress-related health problems (e.g., high blood pressure) resulting from being on call 24/7, whether required to do so by your employer or exercising self-imposed behavior.
- Safety concerns associated with placing smartphone and cell phone calls, participating in phone conversations, texting, blogging, or tweeting while walking, jogging, running, and driving. You can Google the related injuries and fatalities statistics if you wish. The numbers are high and depressing as can be expected. Despite the related safety claims, voice-activated technology features in cars do not insure complete safety even after drivers end their calls. There is typically a transitional period (liminal space) of approximately 20-30 seconds following such calls during which drivers are still distracted before they once again focus their attention on driving.

Communication technologies are yours to use safely and effectively or to misuse at potentially high professional and personal costs. Here's hoping you use current and future communication technologies in ways that promote your career aspirations and your health and safety as well as that of others.

ASSISTIVE TECHNOLOGIES

assistive technologies Electronic devices enabling people with physical disabilities to communicate more easily and effectively.

Great strides have been made in the development of **assistive technologies** that enable people with a variety of disabilities to communicate more easily and effectively. Figure 6-13 contains some examples, but this is by no means an all-inclusive list of assistive technologies.

FIGURE 6-13: ASSISTIVE TECHNOLOGIES

- **Hearing.** For people who are either deaf or hearing challenged, TTY (text telephone) technology is helpful. Incoming calls are converted to text. Captioning capabilities on videos and similar technologies are also practical.

© alphaspirit/Shutterstock.com

- **Speaking.** For people who are either deaf or speaking challenged, TTY (text telephone) technology is also helpful. For outgoing calls, they can keyboard their message, and their phone partner receives a computer-generated voice message.
- **Seeing.** For people who are blind or visually challenged, *JAWS* screen reading software converts text to voice. Apple's *VoiceOver* works in a similar way. There are also printers that print text in Braille.

Figure 6-13 provided you with a quick glimpse at assistive technologies. A more inclusive list of assistive technologies follows.

Alternative input devices allow individuals to control their computers through means other than a standard keyboard or pointing device. Examples include:

- **Alternative keyboards.** Featuring larger- or smaller-than-standard keys or keyboards, alternative key configurations, and keyboards for use with one hand.
- **Electronic pointing devices.** Used to control the cursor on the screen without the use of hands. Devices used include ultrasound, infrared beams, eye movements, nerve signals, or brain waves.
- **Sip-and-puff systems.** Activated by inhaling or exhaling.
- **Wands and sticks.** Worn on the head, held in the mouth, or strapped to the chin and used to press keys on the keyboard.
- **Joysticks.** Manipulated by hand, feet, chin, etc. and used to control the cursor on screen.
- **Trackballs.** Movable balls on top of a base that can be used to move the cursor on screen.
- **Touch screens.** Allow direct selection or activation of the computer by touching the screen, making it easier to select an option directly rather than through a mouse movement or keyboard. Touch screens are either built into the computer monitor or can be added onto a computer monitor.
- **Braille embossers.** Transfer computer generated text into embossed Braille output. Braille translation programs convert text scanned-in or generated via standard word processing programs into Braille, which can be printed on the embosser.

- **Keyboard filters.** Are typing aids such as word prediction utilities and add-on spelling checkers that reduce the required number of keystrokes. Keyboard filters enable users to quickly access the letters they need and to avoid inadvertently selecting keys they don't want.
- **Light signaler alerts.** Monitor computer sounds and alert the computer user with light signals. This is useful when a computer user cannot hear computer sounds or is not directly in front of the computer screen. As an example, a light can flash alerting the user when a new e-mail message has arrived or a computer command has completed.
- **On-screen keyboards.** Provide an image of a standard or modified keyboard on the computer screen that allows the user to select keys with a mouse, touch screen, trackball, joystick, switch, or electronic pointing device. On-screen keyboards often have a scanning option that highlights individual keys that can be selected by the user. On-screen keyboards are helpful for individuals who are not able to use a standard keyboard due to dexterity or mobility difficulties.
- **Reading tools and learning disabilities programs.** Include software and hardware designed to make text-based materials more accessible for people who have difficulty with reading. Options can include scanning, reformatting, navigating, or speaking text out loud. These programs are helpful for those who have difficulty seeing or manipulating conventional print materials; people who are developing new literacy skills or who are learning English as a foreign language; and people who comprehend better when they hear and see text highlighted simultaneously.
- **Refreshable Braille displays.** Provide tactile output of information represented on the computer screen. A Braille "cell" is composed of a series of dots. The pattern of the dots and various combinations of the cells are used in place of letters. Refreshable Braille displays mechanically lift small rounded plastic or metal pins as needed to form Braille characters. The user reads the Braille letters with his or her fingers, and then, after a line is read, can refresh the display to read the next line.
- **Screen enlargers, or screen magnifiers**. Work like a magnifying glass for the computer by enlarging a portion of the screen which can increase legibility and make it easier to see items on the computer. Some screen enlargers allow a person to zoom in and out on a particular area of the screen.
- **Screen readers.** Are used to verbalize, or "speak," everything on the screen including text, graphics, control buttons, and menus into a computerized voice that is spoken aloud. In essence, a screen reader transforms a graphic user interface (GUI) into an audio interface. Screen readers are essential for computer users who are blind.
- **Speech recognition or voice recognition programs.** Allow people to give commands and enter data using their voices rather than a mouse or keyboard. Voice recognition systems use a microphone attached to the computer, which can be used to create text documents such as letters or e-mail messages, browse the Internet, and navigate among applications and menus by voice.
- **Text-to-Speech (TTS) or speech synthesizers.** Receive information going to the screen in the form of letters, numbers, and punctuation marks, and then "speak" it out loud in a computerized voice. Using speech synthesizers allows computer users who are blind or who have learning difficulties to hear what they are typing and also provide a spoken voice for individuals who cannot communicate orally, but can communicate their thoughts through typing.

- **Talking and large-print word processors.** Are software programs that use speech synthesizers to provide auditory feedback of what is typed. Large-print word processors allow the user to view everything in large text without added screen enlargement.
- **TTY/TDD conversion modems.** Are connected between computers and telephones to allow an individual to type a message on a computer and send it to a TTY/TDD telephone or other Baudot equipped device.[39]

If you do not have a disability that impedes your ability to communicate easily and effectively with others, you have likely given little thought to assistive technologies like those mentioned in Figure 6-13. That is understandable. However, awareness of and familiarization with such technologies better positions you to help others by informing them of applicable technologies. For those with disabilities, such technologies have a profound and positive impact on their ability to communicate on the job as well as in their personal lives. Those who develop such technologies should be applauded!

SUMMARY: SECTION 5— USING COMMUNICATION TECHNOLOGY EFFECTIVELY

- Choose the best communication medium for the situation, which does not always mean an electronic communication device.
- Be sensitive to the negative effects of uncontrolled information overload and polyphasic activity.
- Strike a balance between work and personal life by scheduling non-work times and being willing to disconnect from your e-mail and cell phone for a time.
- Just because some electronic communication devices support brief messages, do not assume brevity is synonymous with clarity. Do not get careless with your tone and grammar when using electronic devices.
- When used improperly, telephone technology chases away customers and business partners.
- When possible, assign electronic communication devices to individuals best suited to use them effectively and productively.
- Use as needed and/or inform others of assistive technologies that enable people with a variety of disabilities to communicate more easily and effectively.

SOME CAUTIOUS COMMUNICATION TECHNOLOGY PREDICTIONS

Given the rapid rate at which communication technology developments occur, making predictions about what's to come is downright dicey business. As we all know, all predictions do not come to fruition. However, there are strong signs and trends supporting the communication technology predictions listed in this section.

You may laugh at the following prediction that was made several years ago because, in contrast to today's technology offerings, it sounds a bit silly. In a 1949 issue of *Popular Mechanics* magazine they predicted that "Computers of the future may weigh no more than 1.5 tons."[40] The sizes and weights of today's laptops, netbooks, and tablets certainly validated the 1949 prediction. In 1949 computers were mainframe computers that weighed thousands of pounds—often filling entire rooms. You can now see why people in 1949 longed for smaller, lighter computers.

It is important that people continue to make predictions and strive to turn them into reality. It is through this creative process and willingness to explore the unknown that improvements to existing technologies and development of new technologies occur. Imagine for a moment how different things would be in the workplace, our homes, and elsewhere if Alexander Graham Bell had not pursued the development of the telephone or Thomas Edison and others the development of the light bulb. The effect on organizations and elsewhere would be profound to say the least. So, the next time you read about or hear someone talk about research in the area of futuristic developments such as transporter systems and time travel, do not be too quick to think they are delusional and dismiss the possibilities. Instead, imagine the impact that such developments will have in the workplace and elsewhere. In other words, dare to dream!

Listed here are several communication technology predictions. Time alone will obviously tell for certain if they transpire. As an aside, no attempt was made to list these predictions in any perceived order of importance.

- The popularity of e-mail, texting, instant messaging, and numerous social media applications in the workplace, as well as in our personal lives, will continue.
- Social networking sites ranging from Facebook, LinkedIn, Instagram, Pinterest, and YouTube will increase in popularity and applications in and outside of the business world.
- Cloud computing will continue to grow at a fast pace. For example, between 2015 and 2018 International Data Corporation (IDC) projects that public cloud services revenue will double to $127 billion.[41]
- E-commerce sales will continue to grow in the United States and globally. While current U.S. e-commerce sales figures exceed $300 billion, they are projected to reach approximately $500 billion by 2019. Global e-commerce sales figures are approximately $2 trillion currently and are expected to reach approximately $2.5 trillion by 2019.
- The combined effects of the Internet and electronic communication developments will further global business interaction, much like e-mail, mobile phones, and social media have done thus far.
- Traditional single-function cell phones will continue to be replaced by smartphones and along with the smartphones will come more features and access to an even-larger number of apps.
- As smartphones and related service plans grow in popularity, more people will trade in, so to speak, their cell phones for smartphones. As mentioned earlier, cell phones can be thought of as essentially being mobile phones with basic calling capabilities, whereas smartphones also have extensive features.
- The number of landline phones will decrease as mobile phones meet the need.
- Despite the popularity of small-screened smartphones and tablets, large screen PC monitors have not gone away and appear to be gaining some traction. For example, Samsung offers a 29-inch ultra-wide curved screen LED monitor. While small screens are practical when on the go, large-screen monitors offer in-office users a more eye-friendly experience.
- With the steady demise of landlines and increased mobility within the business community, greater numbers of people will rely on external batteries to charge their

mobile phones and other electronic communication devices as needed. The *Power Castle 12000*, *Power Castle 13000*, and *Power Castle 14000* external batteries are well received and each weighs less than one pound.

- A greater number of multipurpose devices such as smartphones and tablets will be introduced.
- A greater number of established technologies will merge, giving way to new electronic communication devices, much as the combining of cell phone and PDA technologies led to the advent of smartphones.
- Tablets will continue to erode PC sales. Tablet sales surpassed PC sales in 2015. However, the PC is still considered to be workhorse in the office much like the typewriter was before PCs were invented.
- Handheld electronic devices that offer both smartphone and tablet features and capabilities may one day replace smartphones and tablets as we currently know them. Samsung's *Galaxy Note* is an example of one such device. The screen is larger than the typical smartphone, but smaller than a standard tablet screen.
- The number of apps for smartphones, tablets, and smartwatches will grow.
- The number of e-books will increase along with the number of e-book readers such as *Kindle Paperwhite*, *Kindle Fire HD*, *Kindle Touch*, *Kindle Fire Touch*, and *Nook Simple Touch*. **E-books** are books transmitted digitally and read on computers and e-readers. **E-readers** are electronic tablets designed for reading digitally transmitted e-books.

e-books
Books transmitted digitally and read on computers and e-readers.

e-readers
Electronic tablets designed for reading digitally transmitted e-books.

©Sergy Nivens/Shutterstock.com

- The number of college textbooks are available as e-books (including this textbook) will continue to grow.
- The number of public and private school systems that equip their students with e-book readers and e-books, in place of hardcopy textbooks, will continue to grow.
- Speech-recognition developments will lead to an even greater number of electronic communication devices that can be accessed orally, like most tablet users are currently able to do. *Dragon Dictate for Mac* and *Google Dragon* are examples of speech recognition software used with PCs, and *Bing Voice Search*, *Dragon Search*, and *Shoutout* are examples of speech recognition software used on mobile devices such as smartphones. Of course, these are just a few!
- Tablets and notebooks will eventually be activated by gestures.
- Interactive digital whiteboards called smartboards (e.g., Hitachi's StarBoard) will continue to grow in popularity in businesses and schools. **Smartboards** are large,

smartboards
Large, interactive, electronic screens containing practical applications for business meetings and presentations.

interactive, electronic screens containing practical applications for project teams, business meetings, presentations, and training sessions. They first became available in 1997.

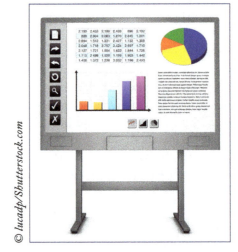

© lucadp/Shutterstock.com

- Self-erasing paper may become more commonplace. This is paper on which you write, but in a few hours it is invisible, which is practical for privacy and security reasons.
- A greater number of electronic meeting technologies will offer alternatives for conducting business meetings. While conference call and videoconference technologies have made great inroads in the business world and are widely used, other technologies such as telepresence systems will grow in popularity. These systems actually place holograms (3-dimensional images) of your distant meeting partners in front of you in your geographic location.
- The continuous size reduction of transistors and computer chips will lead to smaller, yet more powerful electronic devices.
- More traditional tower-based desktop PCs in businesses will continue to be replaced with virtual desktops. Virtual desktops consist of a monitor, keyboard, and small connector box tied to a server.
- The number and quality of assistive devices (technologies) that help people with disabilities communicate more easily and effectively will continue to grow.
- Wireless communication devices will continue to e-mobilize growing numbers of office workers around the globe. In response, the number of traveling and home-based telecommuters will grow significantly.
- Greater numbers of business offices will adopt more open-environment working settings with fewer cubicles and traditional walled-in work spaces. Examples of technologies that should be prevalent in such settings include: smart glass that morphs into media screens, 3-D printers that produce small prototypes, subtitled conference calls, hologram tables, conference call suites with computer programs that translate languages instantaneously, and programs that will enable office workers to navigate computer screens with the flick of the wrist.[42]
- The number of people who are injured or killed by drivers of cars, buses, trains, planes, helicopters, boats, and other motorized vehicles while using mobile phones (e.g., smartphones) while driving will rise.[43]

- The number of cities, states, and countries in which citizens voluntarily reduce their use of mobile phones to place calls and text while driving will increase. You may believe this is wishful thinking; however, strong signs of this are appearing in Great Britain and Los Angeles, for example. In such places, participating in phone conversations and texting while driving are increasingly considered to be socially unacceptable behaviors.
- The number of countries, states, and municipalities outlawing drivers from placing cell phone calls, participating in cell phone conversations, and text messaging while driving will continue to rise.[44] Such bans first went into effect in the late 1990s.
- Digital pens will grow in popularity as their price drops. These pens record what you write and store it digitally. You can then download what you wrote. Most digital pens will also record your graphics and drawings. Some pens also have video and audio recording capabilities.
- Electronic pencils like the Apple Pencil that works in tandem with Apple's iPad Pro will likely grow in popularity. The Apple Pencil works like a regular pencil and supports the creation of art, animations, blueprints, and more.
- Virtual reality systems applications will increasingly fill entertainment voids as well as provide business applications ranging from making it possible for consumers to virtually test products before purchasing them to virtual mirrors in which consumers can see themselves in different clothing options without having to try them on.
- The number of wearable communication technologies will increase and be smaller (e.g., smartwatches, ear buds, headsets). Another example is Google's Glass which are glasses containing a computer. Through voice and touch the wearer can access the Web, place and receive calls, send and receive text messages, take photos, and access a host of other computer-based applications. Google is currently working on developing contact lenses with similar capabilities. Apple is working on developing wearable computers.[45]
- Telepathy—brain-to-brain communication—just might become a reality. According to Jerry Adler, researchers are breaching the boundaries of the mind, moving information in and out across space and time. Sounds like something out of a *Star Trek* movie, not a potential reality. Personally, I don't think others really want to know my every thought![46]
- Growing numbers of humanoid robots with modifiable personalities will be active members of our workforce that we will communicate with routinely.
- The number of jobs requiring creativity and complex human exchanges will increase as computers acquire some of the most advanced cognitive and physical human skills (e.g., humanoid robot plumbers, surgeons, robo-bosses, etc.). Many humans' ability to work may come down to what they can do better than computers.[47]
- The exponential growth in computing power will result in humans having the capability to create superhuman intelligence by 2045 which will result in the end of the human era shortly thereafter. Sounds like something out of a *Terminator* movie. You have heard of artificial intelligence, right? Experts in the field are currently warning us about the dangers of it and are making similar *Terminator* references about the real possibility of systems like Cyberdyne. Now how's that for an upbeat prediction to end on?![48]

Whether you personally find the above predictions to be far-fetched and unlikely to happen does not change the fact that, in our constantly changing, global marketplace, businesspeople and businesses need to stay abreast of electronic communication technologies if they want to remain competitive and viable. As mentioned at that beginning of this chapter, you need to know what communication technology is currently available, how to use it, and when to use it to keep up. Even that is not enough, however! You should be aware of projected technological developments—developments that will profoundly affect your career and the organizations you either work for or own and operate.

Keeping up with communication technology predictions is not all that easy unless you have a crystal ball. And, since most of us do not have a crystal ball to gaze into, you should consider, among other sources, reading about predictions and technology research and developments in *Technology Review* articles. *Technology Review* bills itself as "the authority on the future of technology." MIT has been publishing this magazine since 1899. (From 1899 until 1998 it was *The Technology Review*.) Other good sources for technology predictions and technology research and development updates are *Popular Mechanics* and *Popular Science*, magazines with long histories of making technology predictions.

SUMMARY: SECTION 6— WHAT'S NEXT? SOME CAUTIOUS PREDICTIONS

- The only thing certain about a prediction is that it will or will not produce the intended outcome.
- The popularity of the Internet and e-commerce will continue to grow, leading the way to further globalization.
- Social media will continue to fill several business needs.
- Combination devices and electronic tablets of all sorts will replace conventional PCs.
- Speech-recognition developments will change the way we interact with electronic communication devices and the Internet.
- Telepathy is close to a reality.
- Wireless communication devices, including wearable technology, will continue to e-mobilize office workers.
- Growth in computing power and the advent of humanoid robots could easily threaten job opportunities and even human identity as we know it.

Notes

1. Michael J. Miller, "Living History," *PC Magazine* 21, no. 5 (March 12, 2002): 153.

2. Efraim Turban, Jae Lee, David King, and H. Michael Chung, *Electronic Commerce: A Managerial Perspective* (Upper Saddle River, NJ: Prentice-Hall, 2000), 507.

3. John R. Levine, Carol Baroudi, and Margaret Levine Young, *The Internet for Dummies*, 4th ed. (Foster City, CA: IDG Books, 1997), 63.

4. "Work Number," *Southwest The Magazine* (June 2015): 45.

5. Internet World Stats: Usage and Population Statistics, Top 20 Internet Countries By Users, http://www.internetworldstats.com/top20.htm, 2012. Robert Kreitner and Angelo Kinicki, *Organizational Behavior*, 5th ed. (Boston: Irwin McGraw-Hill, 2000), 503.

6. Ibid.

7. Turban et al., *Electronic Commerce*, 507.

8. Kreitner and Kinicki, *Organizational Behavior*, 504.

9. Ibid., 483.

10. Doug Bedell, "From QWERTYUIOP, An E-mail Revolution," *The Dallas Morning News*, February 19, 2002.

11. Kreitner and Kinicki, *Organizational Behavior*, 504.

12. Paula Felps, "Hearing-Impaired Embrace Instant Messaging," *The Dallas Morning News*, February 20, 2001.

13. Ibid.

14. Kreitner and Kinicki, 505.

15. DeTienne, *Guide to Electronic Communication*, 14–19.

16. Turban et al., *Electronic Commerce*, 506.

17. Ibid., xxvii.

18. Robert Insley, "Managing Plagiarism: A Preventative Approach," *Business Communication Quarterly*, 74, no. 2, (June 2011): 184–85.

19. Ibid.

20. Jeremy A. Kaplan, Bruce Brown, and Marge Brown, "Pocket to Palm," *PC Magazine 20*, no. 1 (December 11, 2001), 143.

21. Cheryl Conner, "Employees Really Do Waste Time at Work," July 17, 2012, http://www.forbes.com/sites/cherylsnappconner/2012/07/17/ employees-really-do-waste-time-at-work/.

22. Ibid.

23. Conrad H. Blickenstorfer, "Webpads," *Pen Computing 28*, no. 1 (Winter/Spring 2002): 72.

24. David Shier, "Siemens SIMpad SL4," *PocketPC 5*, no. 2 (May 2002): 17.

25. Xiomara Blanco, "Best tablets with cell service," March 14, 2012, Updated May 20, 2015, http://www.cnet.com/news/best-tablets-with-cell-service/.

26. Timothy Captain, "Wireless Messaging Services," *Laptop* 45, no. 3 (March 2002): 71.

27. Ibid.

28. Erica Ogg, "Time to Drop the Netbook Label," *CNN Technology* (August 20, 2009), http://w.cnn.com/2009/TECH/ptech/08/20/cnet.drop.netbook.label/index.html.

29. Katy Steinmetz, "Beat Your Smartphone Addiction," *Time*, July 27, 2015, 25.

30. Leida Chen, Ravi Nath, & Robert Insley, "Determinants of Digital Distraction. A Cross-Cultural Investigation of Students in Africa, China, and the U.S.," 23, Issue 3-4, (March 2014): 145.

31. Steinmetz, 25.

32. Ibid.

33. Jennifer M. George and Gareth R. Jones, *Understanding and Managing Organizational Behavior*, 3rd ed. (Upper Saddle River, NJ: Prentice-Hall, 2002), 289.

34. Tynan, "Technology in America—Office," 107.

35. Brickenstorfer, "Webpads," 72.

36. Ibid.

37. Rex Huppke, "Millennials want to lead; they just need a hand," *The Dallas Morning News*, July 26, 2015, 2D.

38. Nancy Churnin, "Call for Relief from Your Cell," *The Dallas Morning News*, September 29, 2009.

39. Microsoft Accessibility, "Types of Assistive Technology Products," https://www.microsoft.com/enable/at/types.aspx.

40. Andrew Hamilton, "Brains that Click," *Popular Mechanics* 91, no. 3 (1949).

41. "The Cloud Corp.," www.fortune.com/adsections , pp. S1, S3, & S6.

42. "Brave New Work: The Office of Tomorrow," *Fortune* 64, no. 1 (January 16, 2012): 49–54.

43. Ibid.

44. Nick Bilton, "Wearable Computers Are the Next Big Devices, Report Says," *The New York Times*, April 17, 2012.

45. Ibid.

46. Jerry Adler, "Mind Meld," *Smithsonian*, May 2015, 45–51.

47. Geoff Colvin, "In the Future Will There Be Any Work Left for People to Do?," *Fortune*, June 16, 2014, 193-202.

48. Lev Grossman, "sin.gu.lar.i.ty n: The moment when technological change becomes so rapid and profound, it represents a rupture in the fabric of human history," *Time*, February 21, 2011, 42-49.

7

SOCIAL MEDIA

LEARNING OUTCOMES

After reading this chapter, you should be able to:

1. Describe the most popular social media sites.

2. Describe how the nine most popular social media sites are used in organizations.

3. Describe various ways several popular types of social media are used in businesses.

4. Write effective social media content.

5. Discuss barriers to effective social media posts

6. Write effective social media policies.

7. Follow the rules of social media netiquette.

© Manczurov/Shutterstock.com

SELECT KEY TERMS

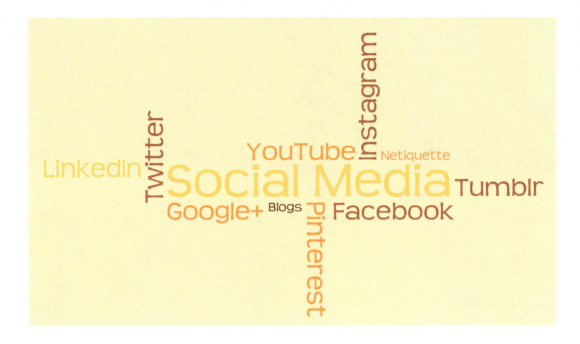

INTRODUCTION

Social networking is growing in popularity around the globe. According to global computer and telecommuting research company The Radicati Group, the number of social networking accounts is projected to grow to 5.2 billion by 2018.[1] Within organizations, social media platforms such as **Facebook, Twitter, LinkedIn,** and **Google+** are having profound effects on how needs are met and communication occurs. Social media is used in organizations for a host of purposes ranging from customer service, public relations, and marketing to acquiring customer feedback, increasing brand awareness, and locating job candidates. Effective writing is key to social media posts and while some writing suggestions pertain to all social media platforms, others are unique to specific platforms. Adhering to social media **netiquette** rules is also important when communicating with others via social media.

The intent of this chapter is to provide you with information regarding social media. This goal will be realized through discussions regarding the following topics: social media overview, the role of social media in organizations, social media writing suggestions, and social media netiquette.

SOCIAL MEDIA OVERVIEW

What is **social media**? Hahn Nguyen did a nice job of capturing the essence of *social media* when she described it as the collective of online communications channels dedicated to community-based input, interaction, content sharing, and collaboration.[2]

© nasirkhan/Shutterstock.com

In short, social media makes it possible for individuals and organizations to form communities, communicate with each other, and produce and share content online. In addition, social media helps people increase their personal and professional networks and connect with others who share their interests. Furthermore, social media helps individuals and organizations stay in touch with friends and stakeholders with whom they may otherwise have difficulties doing so. Communicating with others via social media is often referred to as *social networking*.

social networking
The process of communicating with others via social media.

Facebook The most popular online social networking service and website.

Twitter An online social networking and microblogging service.

LinkedIn
An online business-oriented social networking service.

Google+
An online social networking and identity service.

netiquette
Rules about the proper and polite way to communicate with other people when using the Internet.

social media
Collective of online communication channels dedicated to community-based input, interaction, content sharing, and collaboration.

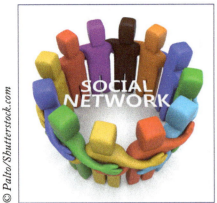

Social networking in organizations is often hosted on a number of popular social media platforms including *Facebook, Twitter, LinkedIn,* and *Google+.* Such sites typically require individuals and organizations to create a profile that typically includes demographic information, interests, preferences, pictures, and updates about current events or happenings. Most social media sites provide tools for users to create and facilitate content, upload pictures and videos, create blogs, review media, and share opinions and comments. Users can also group themselves depending on geographic location, interests, heritage, topics of interest, or professional and social associations. In turn, these groups facilitate communication and management of subgroups within larger social networks.

In organizations around the globe, social media is having profound effects on how needs are met and communication occurs. In addition, most organizations are actively searching for additional social media uses and opportunities.

Small businesses owners and operators, in growing numbers, are also discovering how social media sites can promote their businesses. While some small business owners write, blog, and post their own *Twitter* and *Facebook* entries, others simply do not have the time for it. This situation has fueled a number of support businesses that specialize in providing advertising and public relations services through social network sites including *3 Green Angels, Everywhere LLC, Red Square Agency Inc.,* and *ThinkInk LLC.*

As a means of maximizing social media's potential benefits, many organizations have developed social media strategies, policies, and codes of ethics. There is a difference between a policy and a code of ethics. For example, a blogging policy covers what a person can and cannot say for legal or company reasons; whereas a blogging code of ethics gives instructions on how to act in the **blogosphere**. The code of ethics works in tandem with blogging etiquette.[3]

blogosphere
The universe of blogs.

Speed, convenience, low cost, and the ability to reach large numbers of people simultaneously are among the major reasons why social media has become an increasingly popular tool in organizations. Furthermore, affordable and easily accessible communication technologies such as smartphones, smartwatches, laptops, and electronic tablets, combined with widespread availability of WiFi and the Internet, have contributed to the growing popularity of social media in organizations. Thus, it should come as no surprise that the vast majority (90%) of businesses are using at least one type of social media.[4]

FIGURE 7-1: BENEFITS OF BUSINESS SOCIAL NETWORKING

1. **Return on Investment.** Private social media networks provide organizations with a return on investment for all their people. Such networks can reveal hidden gems; people who lack the nerve to talk aloud but have ideas and expertise to share. Social media networks can encourage and reward online contributions so that the hidden gems can reveal themselves through their contributions.
2. **Unlocked Information Silos.** Many large organizations develop **information silos**, which are departments that are self-contained. As a result, extensive connections across the organization do not happen. With private social media networks organizations can break down silos. They can let interaction, knowledge sharing, and collective problem solving become the normal communication pattern throughout the organization.

186 Chapter 7: Social Media

FIGURE 7-1: BENEFITS OF BUSINESS SOCIAL NETWORKING

3. **Improved Teamwork.** Sales is such a competitive occupation. Traditionally, compensation plans reward individual sales achievement. Cross-fertilization of successful strategies through the deployment of customer relations management (CRM) tools runs counter to this "all-for-one" sales mentality. A private social media network that encourages mentorship and rewards cooperative behavior can create winning sales teams that share strategies and compensate top salespeople for helping the "newbies." This represents a significant cultural shift for the normal sales organization. It means new compensation plans that acknowledge and reward both individual sales achievements and collective knowledge sharing contributions.

4. **Increased Customer Engagement.** The new business model is "customer web-centered." It has always been true that it is easier to sell to an existing customer than it is to recruit a new one. Hence the relationship with existing customers is something that private social networking addresses. Through a private social media network, customers can be invited into online communities. These communities may include other customers with similar challenges. Communities can become great listening posts for organizations to learn about common customer problems. They are also great places to do collective sales pitches.

5. **Better Employee Morale.** Private social media networks begin with individuals creating profiles, and these profiles can reveal great ways to discover hidden talents. We tend to pigeonhole people by job title but most of us are much more than our jobs. For example, I write music and do orchestration when I am not working with clients. People in the accounting department or in shipping may also enjoy music or play instruments. This type of discovery can pay huge dividends in improving morale within an organization. It can even impact the bottom line when you find out that someone is experimenting with open source software application development at home and has come up with a new widget or gadget that can be shared with others in the organization with similar interests, leading to who knows what.

Source: Rosen, Len. "Business Social Networking: Public and Private – There is a Place for Both," CMS Wire Aug 19. 2009. Sept 5, 2009. <http://www.cmswire.com/cms/enterprise-20/business-social-networking-public-and-private-there-is-a-place-for-both-005304.php>.

Despite the popularity of social media, businesspeople still need to determine which communication medium is most appropriate for each situation. Sometimes social media is the right choice, whereas other times it may be another communication medium such as face-to-face communication, e-mail, texting, a phone call, or a videoconference. Jim Blasingame, one of the world's foremost experts on small business and entrepreneurship, offers some practical advice to help you make good media choices. He encourages businesspeople to use the following two approaches when making communication media choices: (1) ask yourself which communication medium best suits the circumstance and (2) ask your customers and clients which communication medium they prefer.[5]

SOCIAL MEDIA CATEGORIES

The most common use of social media in businesses is to facilitate internal communication, followed by communication with customers, and then communication with external partners.[6] To facilitate internal communication, some organizations develop private social media networks to meet their needs. Some organizations hire others to develop their internal social media networks, while others use programs such as *Wall.fm* and *Ning* to do so. *Wall.fm* is an online service for building and hosting social media networks, and *Ning* is an online platform that can be used to create custom social media networks. In contrast, social media interaction with customers and other external partners typically occurs through public social media networks such as *Facebook*, *LinkedIn*, *Google+*, and others.

FIGURE 7-2: NETWORKING VIA SOCIAL MEDIA

Facebook, Twitter, and LinkedIn are great social media platforms for networking. According to Ashley Jones, owner of Skylight Creative Group, if interaction with these platforms is done correctly, organizations can gain lots of attention, fans, followers, and clients. Such is the case with social media. Here are several tips Ashley Jones offers for networking via social media.

- **Don't post something just to post it.** Make sure your content is relevant and/or interesting.
- **If you're using social media to network, stay professional.** Don't get too casual or personal.
- **Use the tools to their full potential.** Don't expect people to come to you if you are not engaging.
- **Don't spam.** This is self-explanatory.
- **Don't post too frequently.** Most people are already bombarded with updates, messages, etc.
- **Don't just post the same thing across different social media platforms.** If you are posting the same thing on several social media platforms, nobody will follow you on all of them.
- **Keep your content fresh.** Update at least once a week.
- **Follow up with connections.** Respond to posts, comments, and messages.

Networking should be a mutually beneficial experience, so if someone helps you, return the favor.

Source: Ricker, Susan. "How to network via social media." CareerBuilder. October 23, 2012.

MAJOR CHALLENGES SOCIAL MEDIA POSE

Despite the positive inroads social media has made into organizations, as can be expected, it also poses several challenges. Three of these challenges worth noting are described below.

1. **Honing traditional writing skills and acquiring new skills.** People read differently online than they do offline. Thus, adapting online copy to meet readers' needs is one of the challenges of writing for social media. Within this chapter, you will find specific writing suggestions that are applicable to all social media platforms as well as other writing suggestions that are applicable to specific social media platforms.

2. **Merging the basic writing process steps with the speed, convenience, and writing protocols associated with social media in ways that result in effective posts.** Much like e-mail and texting, social media encourages the development of short posts. As a result, some related problems are not uncommon. For example, in their quest to develop short posts, some writers ignore basic rules of grammar and punctuation and even get careless with spelling. In addition, some writers fall into the habit of not editing and revising their posts. Such carelessness can easily result in poorly written, confusing posts that contain too little detail to achieve clarity and/or leave readers with poor perceptions of their communication partners' writing abilities and professionalism. In turn, carelessly written posts can easily reflect poorly on the organization being represented. And if all that isn't enough to cause problems, such carelessly written posts can also damage writers' job stability and job growth potential.

3. **Being realistic about the importance of building relationships.** Strong relationships with stakeholders (e.g., colleagues, clients, suppliers) are crucial to long-term business success. Job stability and career growth are also influenced by relationships formed in the workplace. With this in mind, it is a good idea to remind ourselves that the most effective way to build strong relationships in the professional workplace is through face-to-face interaction. Herein lies the challenge! Be careful not to communicate so much on social media and other electronic media that you fail to build strong relationships with stakeholders due to insufficient face-to-face interaction. Otherwise, you might be eroding professional relationships and your chances of achieving the level of career growth you desire. As it pertains to building professional relationships, are there viable alternatives to face-to-face communication? While it is not a perfect substitute for face-to-face interaction, videoconferencing (e.g., *Skype*) is an alternative.

I trust you agree that the challenges described above are significant and should be taken seriously. Your task now is to benefit from your new-found awareness of them by keeping them in mind.

SUMMARY: SECTION 1—
SOCIAL MEDIA OVERVIEW

- Social media makes it possible for individuals and organizations to form communities, communicate with each other, and produce and share content online.
- Social media is having profound effects on how needs are met and communication occurs in organizations around the globe.
- Speed, convenience, low cost, and the ability to reach large numbers of people simultaneously are among the major reasons why social media has become an increasingly popular tool in organizations.
- The most common use of social media in businesses is to facilitate internal communication, followed by communication with customers, and then communication with external partners.
- Benefits of business social media networks include return on investment, unlocked information silos, improved teamwork, increased customer engagement, and better employee morale.

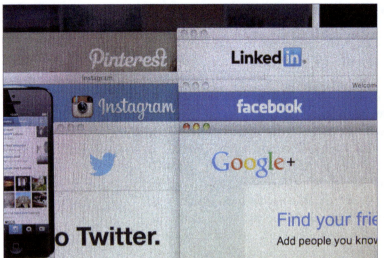

THE ROLE OF SOCIAL MEDIA IN ORGANIZATIONS

The vast majority of businesses worldwide use one or more types of social media. As mentioned previously, the most common use is to facilitate internal communication, followed by communication with customers and external partners in that order. Typical internal uses of social media include increasing knowledge sharing, building employee morale, improving collaboration and productivity within work groups, enhancing employee engagement, building communities (e.g., employees with common interests), and facilitating organizational culture changes.[7]

Common external uses, also mentioned earlier, range from customer service, public relations, and marketing to acquiring customer feedback, increasing brand awareness, and locating job candidates. Marketing, in particular, is a very popular use of social media. Such marketing falls under the umbrella of *digital marketing* which includes marketing via social media, display ads, online searches, and e-mail. According to Forrester Research, it is projected that spending on digital marketing will reach $103 billion in 2019, which is nearly double the 2014 figure, and will soon surpass spending on television advertising.[8]

Pinterest An online social curation and social networking service.

Tumblr An online microblogging platform and social networking website.

Instagram An online mobile social networking service that supports photo- and video-sharing.

FIGURE 7–3: THE 15 MOST POPULAR SOCIAL MEDIA SITES

1. Facebook
2. Twitter
3. LinkedIn
4. **Pinterest**
5. Google+
6. **Tumblr**
7. **Instagram**
8. VK
9. Flickr
10. Vine
11. Meetup
12. Tagged
13. Ask.fm
14. MeetMe
15. ClassMates

Source: "Top 15 Most Popular Social Networking Sites," www.ebizmba.com/articles/social-networking-websites, *March, 2015*

MOST WIDELY-USED SOCIAL MEDIA SITES IN ORGANIZATIONS

Facebook, Twitter, LinkedIn, Pinterest, Google+, Tumblr, Instagram, YouTube, and *blogs* are currently among the most widely used social media sites for businesses. Brief descriptions of each, along with how they are used in businesses, follow.

© www.BillionPhotos.com/Shutterstock.com

- Facebook
  Facebook is an online social networking service that was founded in 2004 and is currently the most popular social media site with well over one billion active users worldwide. In addition to posting text-based messages, Facebook users can also post photos and videos. Facebook is used externally in businesses predominately as a customer service tool, a public relations tool, to identify target markets, to promote company websites, to screen job candidates, and to identify viable potential job candidates.

© Annette Shaff/Shutterstock.com

- Twitter

  Twitter is an online social networking and microblogging service that was founded in 2006. Twitter has over 300 hundred million active users worldwide and currently supports a large number of languages. Twitter enables users to send and read short, text-based messages (tweets). Twitter users can also post photos and videos. Twitter is used externally in businesses predominately as a customer service tool and a public relations tool. Twitter is also used to seek information from large numbers of people (*crowdsourcing*) and obtaining feedback. It is also used to increase brand awareness and monitor brand reputation. Twitter also offers businesses a powerful products and services feedback tool.

© tanuha2001/Shutterstock.com

- LinkedIn

  LinkedIn is an online business-oriented social networking service that was founded in 2002 and has several hundred million active users worldwide. LinkedIn is considered to be the world's largest professional network catering predominately to business professionals. LinkedIn is used externally in businesses predominately to identify business job candidates, for professional networking purposes, to feature business events (e.g., professional conferences), to increase branding/marketing presence in the marketplace, to build new relationships with potential customers, to increase company exposure, to promote their businesses, and to acquire customer feedback and insights.

How to Use LinkedIn for Business video https://www.youtube.com/watch?v= yM5K0ytrDDA

© Evan Lorne/Shutterstock.com

- Pinterest

  Pinterest is a social networking service that was founded in 2010 and has several million active users worldwide. Pinterest provides a service whereby users can discover, collect, share, and store visual images. Pinterest is used in businesses predominately for advertising and conducting market research. Currently, approximately one-third of online adults use Pinterest, which reminds businesses of the growing popularity of photos and visual images.

© tanuha2001/Shutterstock.com

- Google+

  Google+ is a social networking and identity service that was founded in 2011 and has over a half billion active users worldwide. Google+ users can also post photos in addition to text-based messages. In many ways, Google+ is similar to Facebook. Google+ is used externally in businesses predominately as a customer service tool, for direct contact with customers, to identify target markets, and for internal and external communication.

© tanuha2001/Shutterstock.com

- Tumblr

  Tumblr is a microblogging platform and social networking website that was founded in 2007 and hosts several hundred million blogs worldwide. With Tumblr, users can post multimedia (e.g., videos, photos, music), links, and other content to a short-form blog. Tumblr is used in businesses predominately for implementing marketing campaigns, highlighting products and services, promoting brands, customer service, and creating blogs.

© 360b/Shutterstock.com

- Instagram

  Instagram is an online mobile social networking service that supports photo- and video-sharing. Users can also include comments and share feedback. Instagram was founded in 2010 and has several hundred million active users worldwide. Instagram is used in businesses predominately for marketing, advertising, conducting marketing research, and for internal purposes such as morale building. Currently, approximately one-third of online adults use Instagram which reminds businesses of the growing popularity of photos and video.

© tanuha2001/Shutterstock.com

- YouTube

  YouTube is a free online mobile social networking service that supports video-sharing. YouTube was founded in 2005. The popularity of YouTube videos is typically measured by the number of times each video is viewed as well as subscriber status. YouTube is used in businesses in a number of ways both externally and internally. YouTube is currently used in businesses predominately for product and services advertising, retail promotion, direct sales, product support, recruiting, posting bulletins, internal training, and employee communications. [9]

© Your Design/Shutterstock.com

- Blogs

  Blog is short for "web log," a type of user-generated website that acts as a communication and networking medium for the masses. It is a type of self-publishing via the Internet done through easy-to-use Internet applications and websites. Blogs are built for flexibility and designed to be short and frequently updated, unlike long essays or prose. Although blogs have been championed by social networks for personal use, they have made a significant impact on the business world, the journalism world, and in academia where they are being used in the classroom. All these blogs that the public has access to reside in the *blogosphere*, which is the universe of blogs. The blog was independently invented in 1997. Blogs are used in businesses predominately for marketing, tracking customer/client satisfaction, brand building, and as a customer service and public relations tool.

© nasirkhan/Shutterstock.com

The main type of business blog is the *corporate blog*, which is often used as an e-newsletter, viral marketing campaign, and open channel between businesses and consumers. The most popular types of blogs are *external blogs* and *internal blogs*. External blogs can be seen by anyone with an Internet connection, whereas internal blogs can be seen only by organizational employees and designated stakeholders.

EXTERNAL BLOGS

One of the biggest distinctions in external corporate blogs is who writes them. According to Chris Anderson, author of *The Longest Tail: Why the Future is Selling Less of More*, the best business blogs are not written by top managers or marketers, but by mid-level employees.[10] They are often more entertaining, more honest, and are less likely to repeat everything in the latest ad campaign or mission statement. They can also be more informative about the inner workings of the company. Consulting company Accenture directs new recruits to its Careers page, which displays blogs written by employees in various departments so that recruits can get a taste of the day-to-day activities of a new management consultant. Or, they can read the rants of a recruiter so they know what not to do.

One big draw of external blogs for companies is the feedback they receive from consumers. Because bloggers comment on blog posts and the relative anonymity of the Internet, consumers are less reluctant to tell companies exactly what they think. This can be invaluable information that was formerly only available through expensive polls and surveys. It is also instant or sometimes pre-emptive. Bloggers can tell a company what they think of a product before it hits store shelves, for example. That is the real key to successful blogs; a conversational style that solicits and receives feedback.

INTERNAL BLOGS

Internal blogs are used by companies so that only employees or a select group of people can see a particular blog. These are usually password protected, and sometimes are on a local intranet. Internal blogs are a good starting place for companies that are testing the waters of blogging. They can be used as testing grounds for speed, content, frequency, and authorship before a company enters the blogosphere. Although they can be a warm up for external blogs, internal blogs also have a place internally once a company is comfortable with the medium. Sample ways internal blogs are used in organizations are presented in Figure 7-4 below.

Internal blogs are great for acting as time-ordered business records that have many uses. They are also great for project members or leaders who can track projects and ideas without adding an extra archiving step. New project members can easily get an overview of the project and how it is developing. Possibly the most valuable use is for legal discrepancies. If a decision or action was subject to questions, the business would have clear and thorough documentation.

There is even a term that captures the essence of blogging effectiveness. The term is **hedonometer**. It refers to a computerized sensor that surveys the Web to measure the collective happiness of millions of bloggers.

hedonometer
A computerized sensor that surveys the Web to measure the collective happiness of millions of bloggers.

FIGURE 7-4: WHAT TO DO WITH YOUR INTERNAL BLOG

Communications and technology expert Shel Holtz provides us with the following list of ways you can use an internal blog:

- **Alerts.** Don't you hate getting those e-mails that let you know when the server's going to be down? People who need to know can subscribe to [the] list server status Weblog. Instead of having to send out those e-mails, IT can simply request that employees subscribe to their blog.
- **Projects.** Companies have terrible institutional memories when it comes to projects. Anybody who needs to delve into a project's records to find out how a decision was reached a year ago is probably out of luck. Project teams can set up a group blog to maintain an ongoing record of decisions and actions. Project leaders can also maintain a blog to announce to the rest of the company the current status of the project.
- **Departmental.** Departments can maintain blogs to let the rest of the company know of current offerings or achievements. Imagine the marketing department being able to submit a simple post to its own blog announcing the availability of new marketing brochures or other collateral material.
- **News.** Employees can contribute industry or company news to a group blog or cover news they have learned in their own personal blogs.
- **Brainstorming.** Employees in a department or on a team can brainstorm about strategy, process, and other topics over blogs.
- **Customers.** Employees can share the substance of customer visits or phone calls. When sharing such information with fellow employees, remain professional; even when the customer was difficult.
- **Personal Blogs.** Even though it sounds like a timewaster, a personal blog can prove valuable in the organization. Consider an engineer who reads a lot and attends meetings of his professional association. He updates his blog with summaries of the articles he's read in journals (with links to the journal's website) and notes he took at the meeting. Employees who find value in this information will read the blog; those who don't care—anybody who isn't an engineer, perhaps—aren't missing anything if they don't. And if he posts a few articles that have nothing to do with work, well who said work can never be fun?
- **CEO Blogs.** What a great way for the CEO to get closer to employees. Imagine a new CEO hosting a blog called "My First Hundred Days" in which she writes about her experiences daily and lets employees comment in order to help her get acclimated.

Source: Weil, Debbie. The Corporate Blogging Book: Absolutely Everything You Need To Know About Blogging to Get It Right. *New York, NY: Penguin Group, 2006.*

SOCIAL MEDIA DRAWBACKS

While the social media platforms described previously provide businesses with numerous benefits, there are potential drawbacks to specific social media platforms that should be kept in mind. For example, with *Facebook* negative comments about products and services are potentially viewed by large numbers of current and potential customers and clients which can, in turn, can have negative effects on sales and public relations. Similar observations can be made about *Google+*, *Tumblr*, and *Instagram*. "Manning the phones" so to speak with *Twitter* is potentially very costly when one considers the time needed to support all those back-and-forth tweets. Then, there are those *LinkedIn* users who compromise the networking potential *LinkedIn* offers when they do not join groups and associations and actively participate in discussions taking place within them. There are even potential drawbacks with *Pinterest*. For example, since the vast majority of *Pinterest* users are female, this can create a drawback for businesses that are not targeting female audiences exclusively. *Pinterest* is aware of this and is taking measures to increase the number of male users. Thus far they are making good headway in reaching this goal.

Here, we are reminded that there is a place for common sense measures when our goal is to eliminate, or at least minimize, social media hacking.

FIGURE 7–5: SOCIAL MEDIA COMMON SENSE SECURITY REMINDERS

We all know that one of the potential perils of posting information on the Internet is cyber theft. In short, some individuals or organizations will attempt to access information that you did not intend for them to access. Furthermore, some individuals and organizations have become very skilled at hacking into such information. With all this in mind, here are four common sense security reminders that just might reduce or eliminate the damage hackers can cause.

- Be aware that your information can be hacked. Don't be naive or unaware. By being aware, you will be much more likely to take measures to minimize the potential occurrence and/or damage.
- Reset passwords often using those that cannot easily identified. Then, keep them private!
- Keep antivirus software updated.
- Don't post/transmit information you don't want the wrong people and organizations to acquire (e.g., sensitive legal documents).

© Ivan Lukyanchuk/Shutterstock.com

There are also some potential drawbacks that span all social media platforms to varying degrees. For example, social media users are generally encouraged to develop and post brief messages/content. *Twitter* with its 140-character message limit is a good example. In the quest for brevity, which is so pronounced with social media, clarity can be easily compromised when too little is said to communicate clearly. Then too, there are potential health concerns associated with social media use. For example, excessive use of the technologies used to communicate on social media can result in health issues ranging from repetitive motion nerve damage (*carpal tunnel syndrome*) and vision deterioration to detached retinas and chronic shoulder and lower neck pain. If nothing else, common sense should remind us that spending significant amounts of time looking at small screens and composing on small keypads will eventually lead to health issues that could have been avoided. Furthermore, there are potential safety issues associated with social media use. For example, excessive use of the technologies used to communicate on social media can result in safety issues ranging from driving-related accidents (e.g., *tweeting while driving*) to pedestrian-related accidents (e.g., *unknowingly stepping out in front of oncoming traffic while tweeting*).

The good news is that most of the above-mentioned drawbacks can be eliminated or at least controlled. Awareness of their existence and potential damaging effects is a good starting point for all of us. For me, the most important among them are the potential health and safety issues.

FIGURE 7-6: ONLINE INCIVILITY: SOCIAL MEDIA'S DARK SIDE

Unfortunately some customers and clients use social media platforms to express disrespectful, rude, and/or malicious thoughts about organizations, products, services, and/or personnel. While organizations need to be open to feedback and can benefit greatly from feedback they receive via social media, less-than-civil feedback can be annoying, frustrating, and challenging to deal with. Organizations are challenged to identify which of these posts they should respond to and how they should respond. For example, in his book *BIFF: Quick Responses to High Conflict People*, Bill Eddy recommends responses that are *brief, informative, friendly*, and *firm*. It is imperative that organizations address these issues in their social media policies and codes of ethics.[11]

There have also been instances of employees who post inappropriate material on social media platforms. What should employees avoid posting? According to the National Labor Relations Board, they should not put up posts that damage a company, disparage its products or services, reveal trade secrets, or reveal financial information. Furthermore, they should not post information about clients or customers. In addition, employees should not put up posts that are racist, homophobic, sexist, or discriminate against a religion. As a means of reducing such instances, companies are encouraged to develop written social media policies that spell out what employees can and cannot post along with specific examples.

In regard to the issue of online incivility, Andrea Weckerle's book *Civility in the Digital Age: How Companies and People Can Triumph Over Haters, Trolls, Bullies, and Other Jerks* is a timely source you should consider reading before going to work in the professional workplace. This book focuses exclusively on disrespectful, rude, and/or malicious posts directed at organizations and how they should be handled.

Source: "What workers can, can't say on social media," The Associated Press – The Dallas Morning News, 4/5/15, 4D.

SUMMARY: SECTION 2— THE ROLE OF SOCIAL MEDIA IN ORGANIZATIONS

- The vast majority of organizations worldwide use one or more types of social media.
- Typical internal uses of social media include increasing knowledge sharing, building employee morale, improving collaboration and productivity within work groups, enhancing employee engagement, building communities (e.g., employees with common interests), and facilitating organizational culture changes.
- Common external uses of the social media platforms include uses ranging from customer service, public relations, and marketing to acquiring customer feedback, increasing brand awareness, and locating job candidates.
- *Facebook, Twitter, LinkedIn, Pinterest, Google+, Tumblr, Instagram, YouTube,* and *blogs* are currently among the most widely-used social media sites in organizations.
- The main type of business blog is the corporate blog.
- The most popular business blogs are external and internal blogs.
- To limit potential damage from hackers, take common sense security measures.
- Social media policies can help companies and their employees deal with disrespectful, rude, and/or malicious posts directed at their organizations.

SOCIAL MEDIA WRITING SUGGESTIONS

The majority of this section is devoted to specific social media writing suggestions. Some of these suggestions are applicable to all social media, while others are specific to each of the nine social media platforms highlighted in this chapter (*Facebook, Twitter, LinkedIn, Pinterest, Google+, Tumblr, Instagram, YouTube,* and *blogs*). In addition, some coverage is also devoted to the following writing suggestions: writing professional bios for social media sites, writing social media policy, writing basics, and barriers to effective writing for social media sites.

Before presenting specific writing suggestions, however, it's a good idea to remind ourselves of the basic challenge business writers face whether they are writing for social media or other media. They are challenged to write effective messages and posts that their readers will interpret as they wanted them to be interpreted and, in turn, they will act upon their messages and posts as desired. By writing clear, professional-quality social media posts, business writers reduce the risk of confusing and frustrating their readers as well as negatively influencing their readers' perceptions of their businesses. Thus, when writing for social media, business writers need to devote sufficient time to developing their posts so the result is clear, professional-quality communication.

Figure 7-7 contains writing suggestions pertaining to all social media platforms. Following Figure 7-7, you will find writing suggestions that pertain specifically to each of the major social media sites highlighted in this chapter. These include *Facebook, Twitter, LinkedIn, Pinterest, Google+, Tumblr, Instagram, YouTube,* and *blogs.*

FIGURE 7-7: WRITING SUGGESTIONS PERTAINING TO ALL SOCIAL MEDIA PLATFORMS

- Craft posts that others will find valuable enough to share with friends and colleagues.
- Craft posts that center on your audiences' questions and concerns.
- Write strong, clear headlines.
- Write longer posts—at least long enough to achieve clarity.
- Write longer posts that include long-tail keywords to increase search queries.
- Consider writing longer posts as a means of increasing backlinks.
- Build in time between draft writing and editing blog posts to improve the quality of the posts.
- Include images (e.g., photos, graphics) in longer posts to keep readers' attention.
- Avoid repetition, unless you are using the technique for emphasis purposes.
- Put share buttons at the bottom of every post and page to make it easy for readers to share.

Source: Bennette, Cari. "10 Writing Tips for Great Social Media Posts," Socialmouths, 10/14/14, http://socialmouths.com/blog/2014/10/14/10-writing-tips-great-social-media-posts/

How to Write Social Media Content http://www.wikihow. com/Write-Social- Media-Content

WRITING SUGGESTIONS SPECIFIC TO FACEBOOK, TWITTER, LINKEDIN, PINTEREST, GOOGLE+, TUMBLR, INSTAGRAM, YOUTUBE, AND BLOGS

You are encouraged to keep the following writing suggestions in mind when communicating via each of the social media platforms listed below.

Facebook Writing Suggestions

- Be natural and avoid boring posts.
- Be topical, timely, and relevant.
- Write posts that appeal to your target audience (e.g., talk about topics they are interested in).
- Be visual by including photos, videos, links, etc.
- Keep posts relatively short—80 characters or fewer is encouraged.
- Bring emotions into Facebook posts.
- Ask questions to engage readers.
- Post inspirational quotes. They are popular attention getters.
- Post full links (URLs) when posting to an external website.
- Be yourself so readers feel like you are talking to them directly.
- Include a call for action to encourage readers to become invested in you, your brand, or your event.[12 & 13]

Twitter Writing Suggestions

- Start with a headline that is clear, catchy, and relevant.
- Be personable and conversational.
- Tweet links containing timely, relevant information.

- Use acronyms cautiously. Don't assume everyone understands what they mean just because you do. When in doubt, spell them out.
- Use abbreviations cautiously. Don't assume everyone understands what they mean just because you do. When in doubt, spell them out.
- Don't abuse basic writing rules (e.g., grammar, using all lowercase letters, etc.). Doing otherwise looks unprofessional.
- Spell words properly. Misspelled words reflect poorly on you and the organization you represent.
- Don't use **emoticons** and **emojis** because they look unprofessional. Emoticons are representations of facial expressions (e.g., smiley faces), whereas emojis are like emoticons in that they include facial expressions but also include common objects (e.g., cars), animals, places, etc.
- Don't be too quick to post a tweet. Write it and then let it sit for a while. Come back to it and do some editing. Then post it.
- Use hashtags that are related to your event or industry. Don't compromise your credibility by using hashtags that aren't related to your message.[14, 15, 16, & 17]

emoticons
representations of facial expressions (e.g., smiley faces).

emojis like emoticons in that they include facial expressions but also include common objects (e.g., cars).

FIGURE 7–8: SIX SECRETS TO ONLINE SUCCESS WITH TWITTER

1. **Immediacy.** Real-time flow of comments and adaptability to mobile handsets makes tweeting more immediate than blogging.
2. **Brevity.** Limiting messages to 140 characters makes them easier to produce and easier to digest.
3. **Pull and Push.** The ability of users to choose whose tweets they follow makes it less random than e-mail.
4. **Searchability.** Messages can be searched, making the content more accessible than the comments on a social network.
5. **Mixing the Public and the Personal.** A user's personal contacts are on equal footing with public figures' contacts.
6. **Retweeting.** By copying and retransmitting messages, users can turn the network into a giant echo chamber.

Source: Waters, Richard. "Sweet to Tweet." Financial Times. February 27, 2009.

LinkedIn Writing Suggestions

- Write for your target audience—the *LinkedIn* demographic.
- Don't post too frequently. Schaffer recommends doing so on a weekly basis.
- Include visuals when and where appropriate.
- Include short, clear, professional headlines.
- Keep your posts in the 30-to-1000 word range.
- Tell a story. Don't just list facts and figures.
- Don't just cut and paste your résumé and cover letter.
- Don't exaggerate or knowingly make false statements about your work experiences, skills, and accomplishments.
- Optimize your LinkedIn profile.
- Include a company page.[18, 19, & 20]

LinkedIn Invitation Writing Suggestions

- Tell the person you want to connect with how you know or know of him or her.
- Personalize your invitation to connect in some way.
- Find something in common with your potential connection.
- Be enthusiastic.
- Be honest.
- Read your potential connection's profile and then reference something in it.[21]

LinkedIn Profile Writing Suggestions

- Include a professionally taken headshot (photograph) so you are portrayed in the best light.
- Develop a strong headline that will get you noticed.
- Include experiences that contain keywords that others are using to find someone like you.
- Customize your URL so you are able to add it to your e-mail signature, résumé, cover letter, letterhead, business cards, and marketing literature.
- Write an engaging, interesting, impressive summary.
- Customize the design of your profile's background.[22 & 23]

LinkedIn Summary Writing Suggestions

- Do not leave your summary section blank!
- Before writing, know what you want your summary to communicate.
- Before writing, know what you want your readers to do.
- Before writing, identify needed content and then gather it together. This would include lists of your most important accomplishments, values and passions, workplace strengths, qualities and skills that differentiate you from others, and honors and awards.
- Break up your summary with graphics, headers, etc.
- Use all 2000 characters you have available to you.
- Include your contact information![24, 25, & 26]

Pinterest Writing Suggestions

- Write longer descriptions that are at least 300 characters long.
- Include a link that further describes a product or service.
- Include the product or service price.
- Include hashtags and keywords that will increase your exposure.
- Include a short call to action.
- Mention those Pinterest users whose work you shared.
- Include appropriate, tasteful humor when the opportunity arises.
- Write clear, persuasive comments.
- Include your business information.
- Complete your profile.
- Keep your business-related boards separate from your personal-interest boards.
- Pin images that are applicable.
- Use various types of content throughout your boards.
- Spread your content out over several boards so followers can more quickly pinpoint content that interests them.[27, 28, & 29]

<u>Google+ Writing Suggestions</u>

- *Google+* posts are mini-blogs so don't make them too short. Kennedy recommends they be one-to-three paragraphs long.
- Use boldface and italicizing features to help your readers move around in and through your posts more easily.
- Include keywords and hashtags so you can be more easily found.
- Include visually appealing images to keep readers' interest and support your goals.
- Start with a headline that is clear, catchy, and relevant.
- Use acronyms cautiously. Don't assume everyone understands what they mean just because you do. When in doubt, spell them out.
- Use abbreviations cautiously. Don't assume everyone understands what they mean just because you do. When in doubt, spell them out.
- Don't abuse basic writing rules (e.g., grammar, using all lowercase letters). Doing otherwise looks unprofessional.
- Spell words properly. Misspelled words reflect poorly on you and the organization you represent.
- Don't use emoticons (e.g., smiley faces). They look unprofessional.
- Don't be too quick to post. Write a post and then let it sit for a while. Come back to it and do some editing. Then post it.
- Create a *Google+* page where you can provide information about your business and services. Link this page to your company website.[30 & 31]

<u>Tumblr Writing Suggestions</u>

- Choose a blog name that describes the theme of your blog.
- Choose or develop a theme that enhances and supports your purpose.
- Write blogs that target specific niches.
- Write blogs that serve a specific purpose.
- Know your target audience.
- Use a conversational tone.
- Link keywords in your blog to related pages on your company website.
- Pace yourself realistically by determining how much you will post and how often so you can settle into a regular, practical rhythm that you can maintain for the long-term.
- Craft your posts carefully so they are professional and engaging.
- Include images to assist in grabbing and keeping your readers' interest.
- Include keywords and hashtags so you can be more easily found.
- Start with a headline that is clear, catchy, and relevant.
- Use acronyms cautiously. Don't assume everyone understands what they mean just because you do. When in doubt, spell them out.
- Use abbreviations cautiously. Don't assume everyone understands what they mean just because you do. When in doubt, spell them out.
- Don't abuse basic writing rules (e.g., grammar, using all lowercase letters). Doing otherwise looks unprofessional.
- Spell words properly. Misspelled words reflect poorly on you and the organization you represent.
- Don't use emoticons (e.g., smiley faces). They look unprofessional.

- Don't be too quick to post. Write a post and then let it sit for a while. Come back to it and do some editing. Then post it.
- Provide contact information for your company.[32 & 33]

Instagram Writing Suggestions

- Edit your captions before posting.
- Edit your comments before posting.
- Include hashtags and keywords that will increase your exposure.
- Include a short call to action.
- Write clear, persuasive posts.
- Include your business information.
- Keep your posts about your brand.
- Run giveaways and promotions.
- Respond to other users' comments.[34, 35, & 36]

YouTube Writing Suggestions

Here are some suggestions pertaining to writing YouTube descriptions.

- Write short (concise) descriptions. YouTube has a 5000 character limit on descriptions, but do your best to write no more than two short paragraphs.
- Write compelling descriptions. Otherwise, people may look no further.
- YouTube descriptions should be searchable. Keywords are critical to this! Consider using Google's *AdWords* keywords tool if you need help with finding the right keywords.
- Use links extensively. They provide ways to promote your other videos as well as drive traffic to your other social media sites.
- Use timestamps. These work well with longer step-by-step videos and when you have a special announcement at a certain part of the video.
- Give credit where credit is due. If it is not already in your video, in your description you should mention individuals you collaborated with or who otherwise helped you with your video (e.g., director, cinematographer, make-up, etc.).[37]

Blog Writing Suggestions

- Know what you want to write about.
- Be narrow in focus.
- Be broad and complex enough that you do not run out of things to say.
- Keep content fresh.
- Keep writing style entertaining and conversational.
- Take risks on controversial topics if you want to increase the number of links to your post.
- Establish the appropriate tone. If it is too dry, they won't read it. If it is too informal, it might affect your organization's professional image.
- Update posts frequently. Updating corporate blogs once a week is recommended.

Blog Writing Suggestions: Don'ts

- Do not defame or discuss your colleagues and their behavior.
- Do not write anything defamatory.

- Do not write personal blogs on company time.
- Identify your blog as a personal blog and state that the views are your own.
- Do not reveal confidential information.
- Do not reveal trade secrets.[38]

WRITING PROFESSIONAL BIOS FOR SOCIAL MEDIA SITES

When writing bios for social media sites, keep them relatively short—essentially a few sentences. Here are some suggested ways to write a professional bio.

- Show, don't tell: "What have I done" > "Who I am". Essentially, don't just tell the reader you possess some desired quality such as leadership. Instead, give a good example of when you demonstrated that quality—a situation in which you were a good leader.
- Tailor your keywords to the specific audience you are targeting.
- Keep your language current. Avoid using overused words and phrases such as clichés.
- Answer one question for the reader: "What's in it for me?"
- Focus on the knowledge, skills, and experiences you bring as a means of gaining and keeping readers' attention.
- Update your bio frequently; preferably every quarter or so.[39]

WRITING SOCIAL MEDIA POLICY

© phoenixman/Shutterstock.com

Familiarity with social media policies increases the odds that employees will use social media effectively. Furthermore, well-written social media policies serve as models for the clear writing that employers expect from their employees. Nancy Flynn, author of *The Social Media Handbook*, offers a number of practical tips for writing effective social media policies. These are presented below.

- **Use Clear and Specific Language.** Avoid using language that is open to interpretation by employees.

- **Include Content Rules.** Here are some examples:

  - No illegal content.
  - No harassment or discrimination based on race, religion, age, etc.
  - No disclosure of confidential company, executive, or employee data.
  - No exposure of customers' personal financial data to outside parties.
  - No whining or complaining about the company, customers, or business.

- **Define Key Concepts and Terms.** Don't assume everyone understands the related terms and concepts. Just imagine the problems that could result from misunderstanding terms such as *confidential data* and *trade secret*, to name a few!
- **Use Plain English.** Here are some examples of how to do so. Avoid confusion, frustration, and misunderstandings by using short words in place of long words when you have the option to do so. Avoid including legal jargon and go easy on the use of technical terms. You can't always avoid using technical terms, but if you are not certain that others are familiar with them give a brief definition following the term. Then, there is the matter of abbreviations and acronyms. A good general rule regarding using abbreviations is don't. As for acronyms, spell them out the first time you use them in a social media policy followed by the acronym in parentheses. After that, just use the acronym.
- **Write With Accuracy.** Present accurate, reliable information.
- **Write Concisely.** Write social media policies that are short, simple, and straight to the point, all the while understanding that enough information must be included to achieve clarity.
- **Write Social Media Policies in Which Clarity is Evident.** Clarity, along with accuracy, are key components of well-written social media policies.
- **Adhere to Standard Writing Protocols.** Stick to standard writing protocols such as basic rules of grammar, punctuation, and spelling. It is difficult to embrace policies that are carelessly written!
- **Enhance Policy Readability by Using Effective Design Techniques.** Here are some examples:

  - Boldface headlines and subheads to emphasize important points.
  - Use bulleted or numbered lists.
  - Include a table of contents with lengthy policy documents.
  - Include a glossary containing social media, technology, and regulatory terms.[40]

Andrea Weckerle, author of *Civility in the Digital Age*, offers several additional tips for drafting robust and legal social media policies. She suggests that the following be incorporated into social media policies.

- An explanation for why a policy is created in the first place.
- An explanation for portions of a policy that may be controversial.
- What platforms the policy covers (e.g., company's social media channel, company's website).
- Which employees the policy covers (e.g., full-time, part-time).
- The importance for employees to avoid conflicts of interest and the appearance of conflict of interest.

- The importance of employees adhering to existing laws and to consider bringing legal questions or concerns to their supervisor and/or company's attorney.
- The importance for employees not to misuse their professional position for personal gain.
- Which employee actions will be frowned upon (e.g., intentionally defamatory statements, expressing threatening behavior, stating intentional lies that can harm the company).
- What the consequences of an employee's violation of the organization's social media policy may be.
- What the consequences of a user's or visitor's violation of the organization's social media policy may be.
- A requirement that employees should make it apparent that the views expressed on their personal social media sites are their own and not those of their employer, unless clearly stated otherwise.
- Any special expectations or requirements that the company or organization may have based on its respective industry.[41]

FIGURE 7–9: BEST TIMES TO POST ON SOCIAL MEDIA SITES

Analytics app SumAll researched the best time to post to the nine social media platforms listed below. Here are the findings.

- Facebook   1–4 p.m.
- Twitter   1–3 p.m.
- LinkedIn   5–6 p.m.
- Pinterest   8–11 p.m.
- Google+   9–11 a.m.
- Tumblr   7–10 p.m.
- Instagram   5–6 p.m.
- Blogs   10:30–11:30 a.m.
- YouTube   Submit video at 1 p.m. as it will often take up to one hour to upload and process the video. This way your video will be available during peak time which is 2 p.m.

Sources: Lee, Kevan. "Instagram for Business: 12 Answers to the Biggest Questions About Timing, Hashtags, and More," posted online, http://blog.bufferapp.com/instagram-for-business, June 11, 2014. Bonini, John. "What's The Best Time to Publish a Blog Post," posted online, http://www.impactbnd.com/blog/whens-the-best-time-to-publish-a-blog-post, January 6, 2014. Robertson, Mark R. "YouTube Traffic Patterns and Uploading Recommendations," http://www.reelseo.com/youtube-traffic-analysis-seo/November 12, 2007.

WRITING BASICS

There are also a number of writing basics that can improve the quality of your social media posts, bios, profiles, and policies. These writing basics categories include:

- Following the Three-Step Writing Process
- Analyzing the Audience
- Choosing the Right Communication Medium
- Overcoming Writer's Block
- Developing Goodwill
- Choosing the Right Words

- Using a Variety of Sentence Types
- Including Images, Photos, Graphics, and Videos
- Editing
- Proofreading
- Writing Collaboratively

The above topics, with the exception of the last one, are discussed in detail in Chapters 9 and 10.

FIGURE 7-10: SOCIAL MEDIA JOBS

With the advent and popularity of social media, new jobs evolved. Eight examples are presented below.

- **Advertising, Promotions, and Marketing Manager.** Employees in these positions plan programs to generate interest in a product or service and work with art directors, sales agents, and financial staff members. They also direct and coordinate advertising and promotion campaigns, as well as introduce new products to the marketplace. In addition, they also manage digital media campaigns which often target customers through the use of social media, websites, and live chats.
- **Blogger.** Employees in this position are responsible for opinionated, stylish writing and frequently posting new content to the Internet. Their duties may also include developing and/or revising text for other venues, including online communities, press releases, Web articles, and video blogs.
- **Community Manager.** Employees in this position create and execute social media strategies to accomplish real business objectives for brands.
- **Content-Marketing Manager.** Employees in this position write and promote business blogs, e-books, and white papers. This includes watching conversations on Twitter to figure out which topics are driving conversations.
- **Meeting, Convention, and Event Planner.** Employees in these positions coordinate all aspects of professional meetings and events which includes being familiar with social media.
- **Public-Relations Manager and Specialist.** Employees in these positions create and maintain a favorable public image for their employer or client. They write material for media releases, plan and direct public relations programs, and raise money for their organizations which includes being familiar with social media.
- **Social-Networking Analyst.** Employees in this position engage with customers and acquire new followers and fans. They also scour the Web finding content that is most relevant to their follower base that will help them get a good conversation started.
- **Social Media Manager.** Employees in this position are responsible for deciding what content to feature on social media channels. Daily tasks include posting, responding to community discussions, and combating spam.

Source: Ricker, Susan. "8 jobs in social media." CareerBuilder. October 23, 2012.

BARRIERS TO EFFECTIVE WRITING FOR SOCIAL MEDIA SITES

Familiarization with the typical barriers will help you write more effective social media posts, bios, profiles, and policies. Here are some of the common writing barriers that can have negative effects on social media posts and content.

- Not having a realistic attitude regarding the importance of writing effectively.
- Not analyzing one's audience sufficiently before crafting social media posts.
- Not choosing the best social media platform(s) for the purpose.
- Not being familiar with and/or willing to apply basic writing fundamentals (e.g., including sufficient details to achieve clarity, writing concisely, using a reader-centered tone).
- Not being familiar with and/or willing to apply writing mechanics (e.g., rules of grammar, capitalization).
- Not concerning oneself with proper spelling.
- Not applying appropriate writing strategies (e.g., persuasive strategy).
- Not posting during the most effective time range.
- Not requesting feedback and/or contact.
- Not being completely honest as described below.

Making false statements and/or exaggerations in social media posts, bios, and profiles is strongly discouraged. Not only is doing so unethical, it can have damaging effects on organizations and even result in expensive legal judgments. Most of us realize that making false statements and exaggerations on social media is unacceptable and unprofessional. If we are not cautious, however, we may knowingly or inadvertently stretch the truth when developing social media content to make our organizations, products, services, and even ourselves sound better than they/we are. For example, some job hunters make false statements and exaggerations on their *LinkedIn* sites and résumés in an attempt to persuade potential employers to grant them job interviews. This is not to suggest that most job candidates do so! However, to suggest that no job hunters do so would be naïve. For example, in a 2015 *Jobvite* survey 20 percent of adults with post-graduate education, 18 percent of adults with a college degree, and 9 percent of adults with a high school education or less admitted to inflating their job skills on social media when searching for jobs.[42] Whether one is searching for a job on social media or developing his or her résumé, the "lies, exaggerations, and land mines analogy" serves as a good reminder to stick with the truth. The analogy suggests that while lies and exaggerations on social media sites and résumés, much like buried land mines, may go unnoticed at first, they can detonate at any moment proving fatal to job searches, job stability, careers, and long-term credibility.[43]

SOCIAL MEDIA NETIQUETTE

With the advent of the Internet and social media, several new words were added to our collective vocabularies. *Netiquette* is one such word. **Netiquette** refers to "rules about the proper and polite way to communicate with other people when using the Internet."[44] The list of netiquette rules is lengthy and not limited to just those that pertain to social media. Here, however, our interest is focused on those that pertain specifically to social media etiquette; especially those that are writing-related. Here are several such social media netiquette rules.

- Fill out your online profiles completely with information about you and your business.
- Use a different profile or account for your personal connections.
- Create a section on your main profile detailing who you are seeking to befriend and ask visitors to abide by that information.
- Offer information of value. Don't just talk about yourself and your company.
- Pick a screen name that represents you and your company well.
- Don't put anything on the Internet that you don't want your future boss, current clients, or potential clients to read.
- Never write or post social media content when you are overly tired, jet lagged, intoxicated, angry, or upset.
- Compose your posts, updates, and tweets in a word processing document so you can check grammar and spelling before you send them.[45]

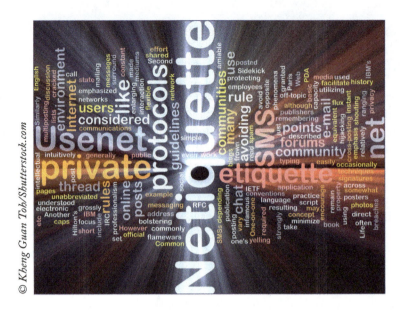

© Kheng Guan Toh/Shutterstock.com

Figure 7-11 contains additional social media etiquette suggestions that are specific to blogs, but most of which are also applicable to other social media platforms.

Nancy Flynn, author of *The Social Media Handbook*, sums up social media etiquette as follows. Adhere to the rules of social media etiquette. Be polite, polished, and professional. Write, post, and publish content that is 100 percent appropriate, civil, and compliant.[46]

SUMMARY: SECTION 4—
SOCIAL MEDIA NETIQUETTE

- *Netiquette* refers to rules about the proper and polite way to communicate with other people when using the Internet.
- *Social media netiquette* refers to rules about the proper and polite way to communicate with other people over social media.
- Examples of social media netiquette rules include offering information of value and never posting social media content when you are overly tired, jet lagged, intoxicated, angry, or upset.
- Examples of blogging etiquette include: do not use your blog to let off steam, do not blog anonymously, do not comment unless you have something legitimate to add to the conversation, and be gracious to readers and commenters.
- Generally speaking, be polite, polished, and professional.

Notes

1. Sara Radicati, Editor, "Email Statistics Report," The Radicati Group, Inc., http://www.radicati.com/wp/wp-content/uploads/2014/01/Email-Statistics-Report-2014-2018-Executive-Summary, April 2014.

2. Hanh Nguyen, "What Is the Definition of Social Media?", http://mysocialmediareview.blogspot.com/2014/08/what-is-definition-of-social-media.html, August 15, 2014.

3. Author unknown, "Social Networking Sites Account for More than 20 Percent of All U.S. Online Display Ad Impressions," September 1, 2009, http://www.reuters.com.

4. Amy M. Young and Mary D. Hinesly, "Social Media Use to Enhance Internal Communication: Course Design for Business Students," *Business and Professional Communication Quarterly*, 24 No. 4, (2014): 426–439.

5. Jim Blasingame, "High Tech or High Touch: It's Really Not Complicated," *The Wall Street Journal*, October 6, 2009.

6. Young and Hinesly, *Business and Professional Communication Quarterly*, 426.

7. Young and Hinsley, *Business and Professional Communication Quarterly*.

8. Mitchell Schnurman, "Schnurman: The great digital hope for ad agencies," *Dallas Morning News*, pp. 1D & 6D, July 21, 2015.

9. M. Miller, *YouTube for Business: Online Video Marketing for Any Business* (Indianapolis, IN: Que Publishing, 2011), 18–25.

10. Chris Anderson, *The Long Tail: Why the Future of Business Is Selling Less of More* (New York: Hyperion, 2006).

11. Bill Eddy, *BIFF: Quick Responses to High Conflict People* (HCI Press, 2012, Kindle edition).

12. Geoff Desreumaux, "10 Tips to Write Engaging Facebook Posts," http://wersm.com/10-tips-to-write-engaging-facebook-posts/, January 13, 2014.

13. Jazeel Ferry, "Tips for Writing Tweets and Facebook Posts Before Your Event or Conference," http://blog.eventifier.com/tips-for-writing-tweets-and-facebook-posts-before-your-event-or-conference/), August 6, 2014.

14. C.G. Lynch, "Twitter Tips: How to Write Better Tweets," http://www.computerworld.com/article/2524316/networking/twitter-tips--how-to-write-better-tweets/, April 30, 2009.

15. Seth Lieberman, "Twitter writing: Five Tips to Win in 140 Characters," http://adage.com/article/btob/twitter-writing-tips-140-characters/287329/), December 19, 2012.

16. Ferry, "Tips for Writing Tweets and Facebook Posts Before Your Event or Conference."

17. Paul Edwards and Sarah Edwards, "Social Media Marketing," *Quick Study*, BarCharts, Inc., 2011.

18. Neal Schaffer, "9 Tips to Writing Posts That Get Read on the LinkedIn Publishing Platform," https://www.linkedin.com/pulse/20140313210407-235001-9-tips-to-writing-posts-that-get-read-on-the-linkedin-publishing-platform/, March 13, 2014.

19. Edwards and Edwards, "Social Media Marketing."

20. Jada A. Graves, "16 Things You're Doing All Wrong on LinkedIn," *U.S. News & World Report*, (June 23, 2014): 1-18.

21. Ariella Coombs, "7 Tips for Writing A Great LinkedIn Invitation," http://www.careerealism.com/linkedin-invitation-tips/, October 25, 2014.

22. Donna Serdula, "What Makes a LinkedIn Profile POWERFUL?", http://www.linkedin-makeover.com/linkedin-profile-samples/).

23. Edwards and Edwards, "Social Media Marketing."

24. William Aruda, "Three Steps To Writing The Perfect LinkedIn Summary," http://www.forbes.com/sites/williamarruda/2014/09/07/three-steps-to-writing-the-perfect-linkedin-summary/, September 17, 2014.

25. Brenda Bernstein, "5 Essential Tips for a KILLER LinkedIn Summary," http://www.careercast.com/career-news/5-essential-tips-killer-linkedin-summary.

26. Graves, *U.S. News & World Report*.

27. Mitt Ray, "6 Tips for Writing Effective Pin Descriptions on Pinterest," http://socialmarketingwriting.com/6-tips-for-writing-effective-pin-descriptions-on-pinterest/, January 6, 2014.

28. Lisa Pluth, "5 Ways Pinterest Success Comes From Great Writing," http://socialfresh.com/writing-on-pinerest/, April 19, 2012.

29. Danielle Cormier, "25 Things That Make You Look Dumb on Pinterest," http://blogs.constantcontact.com/pinterest-for-business/, August 15, 2013.

30. Reba Kennedy, "Google Plus: Tips for Writing Google+ Posts and Why You Should Care About Google+," http://rebakennedy.blogspot.com/2013/09/google-plus-tips-for-writing-google.html, September 11, 2013.

31. Edwards and Edwards, "Social Media Marketing."

32. Jamie Clark, "11 killer tips for a successful Tumblr blog," http://www.creativebloq.com/tumblr/secrets-successful-tumblr-blog-3132101, March 8, 2013.

33. Edwards and Edwards, "Social Media Marketing."

34. "Instagram Tips: Comments," http://blog.instagram.com/post/13978983262/comments.

35. Kevan Lee, "Instagram for Business: 12 Answers to the Biggest Questions About Timing, Hashtags, and More," https://blog.bufferapp.com/instagram-for-business, June 11, 2014.

36. Brittney Helmrich, "Instagram for Business: Everything You Need to Know," http://www.businessnewsdaily.com/7662-instagram-business-guide.html, January 21, 2015.

37. Ed Carrasco, "5 Tips For Effective YouTube Video Descriptions," http:///newmediarockstars.com/2013/06/5-tips-for-effective-youtube-video-descriptions/, June 13, 2013.

38. Nancy Flynn, *Blog Rules: A Business Guide to Managing Policy, Public Relations, & Legal Issues* (New York: American Management Association, 2006).

39. Courtney Seiter, "How to Write a Professional Bio For Twitter, LinkedIn, Facebook, & Google+," https://blog.bufferapp.com/how-to-write-a-professional-bio-for-twitter-linkedin-facebook-google+/, February 5, 2014.

40. Nancy Flynn, *The Social Media Handbook* (San Francisco: Pfeiffer, A Wiley Imprint, 2012), 175–177.

41. Andrea Weckerle, *Civility in the Digital Age: How Companies and People Can Triumph Over Haters, Trolls, Bullies, and Other Jerks* (Indianapolis, Indiana: Que Publishing, 2013), 254–256.

42. Jae Yang and Karl Gelles. "Inflating Job Skills on Social Media," *USA Today*, February 20, 2015.

43. Mark Wrolstad. "Lying on Resumes: Why Some Can't Resist," *The Dallas Morning News*, December 22, 2001.

44. Merriam-Webster Dictionary (online).

45. Lydia Ramsey, "Top 12 Rules of Social Media," http://www.businessknowhow.com/internet/socialmediaetiquette.htm)

46. Sarah E. Needleman, "Firms Get a Hand With Twitter, Facebook," *The Wall Street Journal*, October 1, 2009.

SECTION III

BUSINESS WRITING

WRITING ELECTRONICALLY

8

LEARNING OUTCOMES

After reading this chapter, you should be able to:

1. Discuss how to write effective business e-mail messages.

2. Manage an overloaded e-mail inbox.

3. Describe how to write effective business instant messages.

4. Describe how to write effective business text messages.

5. Describe ways to write effective company websites.

6. Discuss netiquette rules that pertain to writing electronically.

© GaudiLab/Shutterstock.com

SELECT KEY TERMS

INTRODUCTION

Writing electronically in the business place has its challenges. First is honing traditional writing skills and acquiring new writing skills as needed. Second is merging the writing process with the speed, convenience, and protocols of electronic communication to achieve effective documents. Third is being realistic about the importance of building relationships. It is important that you are familiar with your employer's e-policies that pertain to electronic communication. In addition, keep in mind that e-mail and texting are considered to be informal communication mediums that are best used for routine matters. Furthermore, do your best to write high-quality material for company websites for obvious clarity and corporate image reasons. Finally, be very familiar with netiquette rules and suggestions that pertain to writing electronically.

The intent of this chapter is to provide you with information on writing electronically. This goal is realized through discussions of the following topics: electronic writing in organizations, writing effective e-mail messages, instant messages, text messages, websites, and choosing the right medium.

ELECTRONIC WRITING IN ORGANIZATIONS

Electronic writing refers to developing and transmitting messages and documents via electronic communication technologies such as e-mail, instant messaging, text messaging, and websites as well as social media sites which are addressed in Chapter 7. Speed, convenience, and cost efficiencies are among the main reasons electronic communication has become so popular in U.S. organizations and elsewhere.

electronic writing Developing and transmitting messages and documents via electronic technologies such as e-mail, instant messaging, text messaging, and websites.

© schiva/Shutterstock.com

Despite the speed, convenience, and cost efficiencies, electronic writing also has some challenges. Three of these challenges are described below.

1. **Honing Traditional Writing Skills and Acquiring New Skills.** Readers read differently online than offline; thus, you must adapt your online copy to meet readers' needs. Specific writing suggestions are covered in this chapter for *e-mail*, *instant messages*, *text messages*, and *websites*.

2. **Merging the Writing Process with the Speed, Convenience, and Protocols of Electronic Communication to Achieve Effective Documents.** Electronic communication media such as e-mail, instant messaging, and websites encourage the development of short messages and inadvertently invite some to ignore rules of grammar, punctuation, and spelling rules while doing so. In addition, many writers do not edit and revise their electronic messages before sending them. Too often the result is poorly written messages that contain too little detail to achieve clarity, leaving readers with a poor perception of their communication partner's writing abilities. Be careful. Poorly written communications can be career killers.

3. **Being Realistic about the Importance of Building Relationships.** Before expanding on this challenge, please understand that in the U.S. business place strong relationships with stakeholders (e.g., colleagues, clients, suppliers, investors) are crucial to job stability and career growth. Building business relationships is best accomplished through face-to-face interaction. Herein lies the challenge. Avoid doing so much of

© ARENA Creative/Shutterstock.com

your communicating (written or otherwise) electronically that you fail to build strong relationships with your stakeholders. Most would agree that communicating electronically is appealing and efficient on several levels. However, communicating too frequently via e-mail, instant messages, text messages, websites, and social media can easily compromise your ability to achieve your career goals. Despite our good intentions, however, we cannot always meet with others face-to-face. When you cannot, but should, at least place a phone call or hold a videoconference instead of e-mailing or texting. Phone calls and videoconferences are more personal and support relationship building better than e-mail and text messages do.

Formality plays an important role in selecting the best medium for each writing situation. Written documents and messages are frequently viewed as being *formal*, *informal*, or *semiformal*. For example, letters are considered formal documents. Documents and messages developed and transmitted electronically (e.g., e-mails, e-memos, instant messages, and text messages) are generally considered to be informal. Awareness of such differences in perception is important because readers' formality expectations vary and must be taken into consideration. For example, for an important message to an external client, you would be expected to send a formal document, in this case, a hardcopy letter. In contrast, if you need to send a brief message with routine, straightforward information to a subordinate within the company, an informal written medium such as e-mail is a good choice. Or, if you and a fellow worker, who are both on the same job level, need to discuss some points pertaining to a routine, noncontroversial matter, IM would be the informal medium of choice. Before moving on, let's look at one more example that lands you midstream on the formality spectrum. If you need to send a message to subordinates about changes to internal procedures, a semiformal document is necessary. In this case, it would be a memo.

For now, e-mail is the most widely used communication medium in U.S. organizations, which is exactly why it receives the most coverage in this chapter. E-mail will one day be knocked out of the top spot. Humans have a long history of inventing new technologies that, in turn, replace previously popular technologies. PCs replacing typewriters is a good example of this phenomenon. This is not to suggest, however, that e-mail will be replaced in the top spot anytime soon. However, at the rate new electronic communication technologies are being introduced it is always a possibility. As to when this will occur is anyone's guess. In the meantime, if you are preparing for a business career or are already working in the business world, knowing how to use e-mail effectively is very important.

In this chapter you will learn how to write effective, reader-friendly e-mail messages, instant messages, text messages, and website content. Competency in these areas will enable you to capitalize on the potential of each of these electronic communication tools, while avoiding the inherent pitfalls. Since electronic communication will certainly comprise a large percentage of your business communications in the professional workplace, mastering the basics now will give you a competitive edge.

SUMMARY: SECTION 1— WRITING ELECTRONICALLY IN ORGANIZATIONS

- Electronic writing (e.g., e-mail messages, instant messages, text messages, website content) is growing in the business world.
- Electronic writing challenges include honing traditional writing skills and acquiring new skills; merging the writing process with the speed, convenience, and protocols of electronic communication to achieve effective documents; and being realistic about the importance of building relationships.
- Formality plays an important role in selecting the best medium for each writing situation.
- E-mail is the most widely used communication medium in U.S. organizations.

E-MAIL

E-mail is a method of exchanging digital messages from one author to one or more recipients.[1] E-mail is the predominant communication medium in U.S. organizations and elsewhere for that matter, and no wonder why. It is a fast, convenient, and inexpensive way to reach one or multiple recipients with a few clicks of the mouse. Owing to its popularity, e-mail has replaced messages that were once transmitted exclusively through hardcopy letters and memos. E-mail has also replaced the need to send faxes as often. Some even send sensitive correspondence via e-mail, although you must be careful to remember that e-mail is not a private medium.

© amasterphotographer/Shutterstock.com

e-mail
A method of exchanging digital messages from one author to one or more recipients.

The prevalence of e-mail means that more workers than ever are writing. Even entry-level employees who used to be exempt from most writing activities now write e-mails to accomplish a host of activities from explaining procedures to coworkers to apologizing to a customer for a billing error.[2]

Where once we picked up the phone to communicate business and personal information, today we routinely send e-mail messages instead. By replacing phone calls with e-mails, however, a process has been created by which informal conversations are recorded and formal business decisions are documented electronically.[3] The result is an unprecedented amount of documented business communication that can be used against an employer or employee should a workplace lawsuit be filed.

The convenience of e-mail comes at a price for employers in the form of increased liability concerns. In response, many companies have reduced their exposure to legal "e-disasters" by establishing and enforcing policies that govern employees' electronic writing. These policies are discussed next.[4] On the employee side, the convenience of e-mail means that much of your relationship with coworkers, customers, and supervisors may rest on your e-mail exchanges.[5] In this writing-centered environment, e-mail is no longer the equivalent of a casual lunch conversation, and your ability to quickly organize and clearly express ideas in e-mail becomes important to your overall success in any organization. In today's electronic workplace, written communication makes a competitive difference.[6]

© mkang/Shutterstock.com

To write effective e-mail messages, you *must* think before you send. Therefore, the standard rules that apply to all business writing (e.g., appropriate tone, logical organization, grammatical correctness) are important to follow when you write e-mails. When written with consideration for your audience, e-mail is a productive communication tool that allows you to make a direct, positive, and polite connection with your reader. This, in turn, will win you the attention and goodwill of coworkers, customers, and other stakeholders.[7] The trick is to develop an effective e-mail style that supports effective business communication.

SELECTING THE RIGHT MEDIUM: TO E-MAIL OR NOT TO E-MAIL

Not all messages should be sent by e-mail. While corporate e-mail cultures differ, some rules on whether to e-mail the message apply across the board.

Consider the formality or informality of the message context. For instance, when introducing yourself or your product to an organization, the proper route to take is still a formal letter, report, or proposal. In addition, even though e-mailing a thank-you note following a job interview is usually acceptable, sending a promptly mailed, handwritten thank-you note would definitely garner more attention and would be more appropriate.[8]

E-mailing a thank you for a job well done is always appreciated, but a face-to-face thank you is better. Likewise, important job requests, such as requests for a raise or promotion or a resignation announcement, should be done face-to-face.[9] An e-mail that requests a raise would most likely be considered spineless or not be taken seriously. A request for a sick day should be made over the phone in most offices.[10]

On the other hand, e-mail is widely used to communicate routine, daily business messages since it is cost efficient and fast. Direct requests or informative messages to coworkers; companywide announcements, like the time and place of the holiday party or the next staff meeting; or a change in an organization's travel policy can all be sent safely by e-mail as long as everyone in the office has access to it.[11] Equally safe to send by e-mail are major personal announcements, like the happy news of a new mom or dad or the sad news of a death in a coworker's family. Other announcements, like graduations or birthdays, probably do not warrant a companywide e-mail.[12]

Do not use e-mail, however, if your message meets one of the criteria listed below. Instead, make a phone call or immediately hold a meeting. Place a phone call or schedule a meeting if:

- Your message requires an immediate response. You cannot assume that your recipient will answer his or her e-mail right away. It is inappropriate to send a follow-up message demanding to know why a recipient has not responded to your message.[13]
- You want to hear the tone of your communication partner's voice so you can read between the lines.
- Your message has many discussion points and needs an extended response or extended negotiations to resolve.
- You want your comments to be private. No message that is private, confidential, or sensitive should be sent by e-mail.[14] We all know that others can hack e-mail if they really want to. So if we don't want it out there, we shouldn't send it off into cyberspace.
- You are concerned about **phishing**, which is the act of sending an e-mail to a user falsely claiming to be an established legitimate enterprise in an attempt to scam the user into surrendering private information that will be used for identity theft.[15] This is simple. If you question the authenticity of an e-mail that made its way into your inbox, don't respond to it. However, it is best not to open it at all!

phishing
The act of sending an e-mail to a user falsely claiming to be an established legitimate enterprise in an attempt to scam the user into surrendering private information that will be used for identity theft.

When deciding whether to send an e-mail message, ask yourself if your need is for speed, cost efficiency, and/or mass distribution. Speed, cost efficiency, and mass distribution are e-mail's strengths. If you need your reader to receive your communication in a few seconds rather than a few days—especially if you have a tight deadline and want to work up to the last minute—e-mail is the way to go. Remember, though, that a quick message does not necessarily mean a quick reply. The recipient is under no obligation to answer your message quickly even though good e-mail etiquette recommends responding to e-mail promptly.

If you have multiple recipients for that 20-page report, consider e-mailing it as an attachment rather than making 50 copies for distribution. It is a good idea to determine first if your attachment will arrive in its entirety. If not, you might consider sending portions of it as separate attachments.

E-mail is also a good tool for communicating across time zones and continents. Rather than calling your business contact in Germany in the evening, e-mail lets you and your international recipient conduct business during your respective normal business hours.[16]

MANAGING HIGH-VOLUME E-MAIL

Given its many benefits, the following question may sound extremely odd. In regard to e-mail, have we humans created a monster? Well, not in the sense of a Frankenstein monster, but possibly in terms of the number that are sent and received in the business world daily and how much time it has consumed in the daily lives of business employees in the workplace. For example, the number of e-mails sent and received daily in the business world in 2015 was approximately 109 billion—a number which is predicted to increase to approximately 140 billion by 2018.[17] As for the e-mail impact on an individual level, a McKinsey Global Institute poll found that the typical office worker spends an average of 2.5 hours of his or her workday writing, reading, and sorting out e-mail messages.[18] And, e-mail traffic is projected to grow. According to the global computer and telecommuting research company, The Radicati Group, between 2014 and 2018 the number of e-mail messages business employees will send and receive each work day will grow from 121 to 140 which averages out to sending 5 and receiving approximately12 during each working hour.[19] You know the amount of e-mail traffic is high when some employees justify reading and sending work-related e-mails during non-work hours such as evenings and weekends while others hesitate to take all of their allotted vacation time because they dread the thought of facing down overloaded e-mail inboxes when they return to the office.

Help is on the way! Some of the e-mail workload is currently being replaced by text messages, instant messages, and social media. In addition, you might be encouraged by companies such as Yammer, Chatter, Convo, and HipChat that are, according to Leena Rao, "openly waging war on email" by providing and promoting alternative communication approaches for e-mail.[20]

Given the high volume of incoming e-mail activity, you are among the lucky few if you have an assistant who sorts through your incoming e-mail, deletes unnecessary messages, and forwards summaries of the important messages to you. If not, you alone must decide how to deal with all those e-mails that arrive in your inbox daily. Good luck with that! However, help has arrived. The following tips can help you manage that overloaded inbox.

- Follow the Last In, First Out rule. Read the last e-mail in a series of e-mails in case the issues from the previous e-mails have been resolved. If you need to reply to the series, read them all first before you reply.[21]
- If you are away from the office for a few days and return to an overflowing inbox, respond to the last day's e-mail first; these responses will not be late. As for the other e-mails, since you are already late in replying, adopt a last in/first out order after you prioritize by sender or subject.
- On first reading, do something with your e-mail even if it is only to group "Read Later" e-mails into a separate folder rather than leaving them to clutter your inbox.
- Deal with all non-urgent messages at one time rather than taking time out to deal with each message as it comes up during the day.[22]
- Use the archive function to inspect e-mails not previously saved and either delete or archive them. Set up the function to delete nonessential e-mails that are older than a specific number of days.
- Delete chain letters and spam. Unsubscribe to mailing lists that you rarely read.
- Set up other e-mail accounts, outside of your office e-mail, for ordering online and for personal correspondence.
- Use filters to prioritize your mail into separate folders. Some suggestions for ways to organize your mail include:
  - Separate internal office mail from outside mail that does not include your company's domain name.
  - Separate mass mailings from those addressed directly to you. Route messages in which you were cc'd or bcc'd to a mass-mailing folder.

- Create a separate folder for family e-mail after you are sure your company's electronic policy allows you to receive personal e-mail at work.

• If you are going to be away from the office and your e-mail account for an extended period, activate an automatic "Out-of-the-Office" reply. That way, anyone who needs your answer right away will know not to expect it. This feature will help you keep messages from building up in your inbox while you are away.[23]

E-POLICIES AND POTENTIAL E-MAIL LIABILITY ISSUES

To reduce potential liability associated with e-messages, organizations develop **e-policies** that address matters ranging from corporate-level wheeling and dealing to employee jokes. E-mail with its shoot-from-the-hip qualities of speed and mass distribution exponentially increases this potential for liability. International Data Corp. estimates that millions of U.S. workers send billions of e-mail messages daily.[24] Not all these messages are related to work. According to an Elron Software survey, many employees with Internet access report receiving inappropriate e-mails at work, including e-mails with racist, sexist, pornographic, or inflammatory content. Whether solicited or not, these types of messages in employees' electronic mailboxes can spell e-disaster for the company and the sender.[25]

Evidence of executives and companies stung by their own e-mails abound. One such example is a Chevron Corp. case in which sexist e-mails, like "25 Reasons Beer Is Better Than Women," circulated by male employees cost Chevron $2.2 million to settle a sexual harassment lawsuit brought by female employees.[26]

In another case involving *The New York Times'* shared services center in Virginia, nearly two dozen employees were fired and 20 more were reprimanded for violating the company's e-mail policy. They had sent and received e-mails with sexual images and offensive jokes.[27] In this case, one of the fired offenders had just received a promotion while another had just been named "Employee of the Quarter." These kinds of incidents cost any company negative publicity, embarrassment, loss of credibility, and, inevitably, loss of business.[28]

Another example was a lawsuit against American Home Products Corp. over a rare but often fatal lung condition some consumers developed after taking the company's diet pills. Insensitive employee e-mails contributed to the company's decision to settle the case for more than $3.75 billion dollars, one of the largest settlements ever for a drug company.[29] One e-mail printed in the *Wall Street Journal* expressed an employee's concern over spending her career paying off "fat people who are a little afraid of some silly lung problem."[30] This example shows how important it is to review and revise your e-mails for potentially inflammatory content before sending.

Still another example involves unauthorized use of a company's computer system for a mass e-mailing. At Lockheed Martin, an employee sent 60,000 coworkers an e-mail about a national day of prayer and requested an electronic receipt from all 60,000. The resulting overload crashed Martin's system for six hours while a Microsoft rescue squad was flown in to repair the damage and to build in protection.[31] The company lost hundreds of thousands of dollars, all resulting from one employee's actions. The employee was fired for sabotage. And, the list of corporate e-mail disasters goes on.

Most companies do recognize that careless e-mails can cost them dearly. If one poorly worded, thoughtless e-mail gets in the hands of defense attorneys in a lawsuit, the company may have to pay up to the tune of a six-to-ten-figure settlement. With these kinds of productivity, profit, and public relations disasters resulting from e-mail

e-policies
Guidelines for using electronic communication.

and Internet use, it is not surprising that employers are implementing e-policies. Whether a company consists of two part-time employees or 2,000, the best protection against lawsuits resulting from employees' access to e-mail, IM, and the Internet is a comprehensive, written e-policy, one that clearly defines what is and is not acceptable use of the organization's computers.[32] According to Nancy Flynn, Internet guru and policy consultant, the best policies are straightforward, simple, and accessible.[33] These e-policies inform employees of their electronic rights and responsibilities as well as tell them what they can expect in terms of monitoring. While employees believe they have a right to privacy where their e-mail is concerned, the federal Electronic Communications Privacy Act (ECPA) states that an employer-provided computer system is the property of the employer, and the employer has the right to monitor all e-mail traffic and Internet activity on the system. Currently, over half of U.S. businesses monitor employee e-mail and Internet activity. Monitoring programs can determine if e-mail is being used solely for business purposes.

Some companies monitor every keystroke made on every keyboard by every employee. Electronic monitors screen for words that alert managers to inappropriate content and some monitors can be configured to spot "trigger" words that indicate everything from profanity and sexually explicit or racially offensive language to the exchange of sensitive information, such as trade secrets and proprietary information.[34]

Although sanctioned by the ECPA, monitoring has its downsides. For example, employees may resent being unable to send an occasional personal e-mail to check on their kids or to make dinner reservations online without violating company policies. The feeling of being watched can hurt morale and eventually may cause good workers to quit, which means lost money for the company.[35] Some employees are striking back at e-policies, claiming protection under state statutes that include a right to privacy.

Finally, even monitoring programs cannot ferret out the hostile tone or the badly worded document open to misinterpretation, especially when being dissected by opposing lawyers. The haste and recklessness with which we tend to write e-mail, along with its high volume, exacerbate an old problem: mediocre writing skills. Only careful attention to employees' writing habits can halt the production of bad e-mail documents.[36]

Policies that govern e-mail use often incorporate electronic writing policies, electronic etiquette (netiquette) guidelines, company-use-only guidelines, and retention policies that outline how long e-mails are saved before they are automatically deleted from mail queues and mail host backups.[37] Some companies purge all e-mail messages older than 30 days and do not keep backup tapes of e-mail. Some experts advise companies to retain no e-mail since a lawsuit could require a review of all backed-up e-mail.[38] However, some industries such as financial firms are governed by federal securities laws that require them to retain e-mails relating to the firm's overall business for three years.[39]

What is clear is that more organizations and employers are implementing e-policies. Therefore, as an employee, you need to familiarize yourself with your employer's e-policies and follow them closely. Since every document you write, including e-mail and IMs, is not only a reflection of your professionalism but also a reflection of your organization's credibility, you need to reflect corporate goals by writing clear, clean e-mails that observe company policy. In addition, before firing off that first e-mail at your job, take time to learn your organization's e-mail culture.

GETTING FAMILIAR WITH THE E-MAIL CULTURE OF YOUR ORGANIZATION

Corporate e-mail culture varies greatly.[40] Some companies use e-mail as their main form of communication; others use it only occasionally. Some companies do not mind if you send personal messages via e-mail; in others, it is a dismissible offense. Some top executives welcome e-mails from staff; others follow a strict hierarchy of who can message whom. Therefore, when you move to a new job, take time to observe the e-mail culture for answers to the following questions so you avoid e-mail mistakes or, worse yet, the e-mail career killer (ECK). A good example of an ECK is sending your new boss a jokey "let's get acquainted" e-mail, only to discover his or her dislike for using e-mail except for formal communications.

- Notice the tone of the e-mails among coworkers. Is it formal or informal? Do they use e-mail for socializing, joking, and gossiping, or is it reserved for formal, job-related messages?
- What is the e-mail chain of command? Can staff skip over their supervisors and e-mail suggestions or questions to upper management?
- How are urgent or sensitive messages usually communicated?
- Do all employees have access to e-mail? Do they check it regularly?
- How are staff-wide announcements made, via e-mail? bulletin board? memo? intranet?
- Are personal announcements, such as "My house is on the market" or "I just found the cutest puppy; any takers?" acceptable over companywide e-mail?
- What are the company's written policies on e-mail, IM, and Internet use? Is any noncompany-related browsing allowed? To what extent are e-mail, IM, and Internet use monitored?[41]

Become familiar with your employer's e-culture as soon as possible. If you are uncertain about where the organization stands on such matters, do not guess. Ask your immediate supervisor or an HR representative.

WRITING EFFECTIVE E-MAIL MESSAGES

The fiction that quick, poorly-written business messages are acceptable is fostered, in part, by the medium itself. Unlike writing memos and letters where we tend to be more guarded and take time to write thoughtfully, e-mail often brings out the worst of our bad writing habits. As Gregory Maciag, president and CEO of ACORD, the nonprofit industry standards association, points out, the medium can hamper communication: "In place of thoughtful content, we send and receive short bursts of often grammatically and emotionally challenged communiqués that we sometimes regret."[42] Additionally, writing consultant Dianna Booher laments: "They log on; they draft; they send."[43] To avoid creating confusion, misunderstandings, and hurt feelings with your e-mails and to ensure that you get the busy reader's attention, think and plan before you draft an e-mail message, then revise it before you hit Send.

DRAFTING E-MAIL MESSAGES

Competition for the electronic readers' attention grows daily with tens of millions of e-mail users online. The challenge for those who send e-mails is to get their targeted readers' attention. To help you get your reader's attention, follow the guidelines discussed here, beginning with the all-important subject line.

Subject Line Some busy executives get hundreds of incoming e-mails a day. To get through them quickly, they look at the subject line. If that grabs their attention, they scan the first screen. Messages that do not get the reader's attention at the subject line run the risk of never being read or of being deleted. To avoid "e-mail triage":[44]

- Always include a clear, informative subject line. It should communicate the topic of the message, and, like the subject line of a memo, it should be specific and brief. A subject line such as "Staff meeting changed to 3 p.m." provides the necessary information. A subject line such as "Meeting," "Information," "Guidelines," or "Hey" convey nothing. If you use "URGENT" or "!" too often, you reduce the urgency of the message in the reader's mind, and he or she eventually ignores it.[45]
- Be brief. Write the important points of your topic in the first half of your subject line. In an inbox, only the first 25–35 characters of the subject line usually appear. In a string (thread) of exchanged e-mails, change the subject line if the subject changes. That way, if you have to refer to an old e-mail, you won't have to reread every message with the same "Re."[46]

Body The first thing to appear in the body of your e-mail may be your **e-mailhead** (e-mail letterhead; see Figure 8-1 for an example). E-mailheads appear routinely when e-mail is used to transmit formal contracts, proposals, offers, and other business transactions. Companies that provide eletterheads, like Dynamic E-mail Stationery from StationeryCentral.com, offer graphically enriched e-mail that reflects your corporate identity.[47]

When you use an e-mailhead, be sure you have a clear purpose for including it, such as making it clear that the message is from your company. Otherwise, the reader may object to the wasted lines.

Always include a salutation. Including a greeting at the start of your message personalizes it, plus it establishes your role in the message's history.[48] If you normally address a person by his or her title or if you do not know the person well, include his or her title when addressing them: "Ms. Jones," "Dr. Smith," "Prof. James," etc.

FIGURE 8–1: E-MAILHEAD

To: recipient@byco.com
From: Mia Deal (mdeal@herco.com)
Date: 201____
Subject: Offer to Purchase Smartboards
       Her Company Inc.
       3024 Main Street
       Chicago, IL 54890
Dear Mr. Brown:
text
text
Sincerely,
Mia Deal
Marketing Manager
(mdeal@herco.com)

If you are unsure how to address a person, err on the side of formality (this cannot be stressed enough). Being too formal will not offend even the most informal of people and will satisfy the most traditional formalists. However, if you are too informal at the outset, you run the risk of ruining your credibility with that person or organization. You can always change the salutation in subsequent messages if the recipient indicates that informality is fine.

Although business correspondence greetings like "Dear Sirs" are outdated forms in the United States, greetings are more formal in other countries, such as Japan and Germany.

Keep the body of your message short, no more than 25 lines (approximately 250 words) or one screen's worth of words.[49] A sharp contrast to this is the approximately 1,100 word e-mail message an executive vice president at Microsoft sent announcing the layoff of 12,500 employees.

For longer documents, send an attachment. However, some companies do not accept attachments for fear of viruses, so check with your recipient first. If you must attach a document to an e-mail, use clear headings in that document to break up the text and allow for skimming.

Remember there is a live person on the other end of your communication, so get right to the point in the first or second sentence and support your main idea with details in the next paragraph. Begin your e-mail with your main idea or request. Most important, keep the body of the message brief and to the point. Focus on developing one topic only, and make responding easy. For example, phrase a message so that your reader can respond with a quick "yes" or "no."[50]

In summary, make your message reader-oriented to help your recipient grasp your message quickly:

- Begin with your bottom-line, main idea, or a precise overview of the situation. If you want the reader to take action, begin by making your request. Include the requested action in the subject line for emphasis. If the message is for the reader's information only and needs no follow-up, put "FYI" in the subject line.
- Keep messages under 25 lines long, and use short sentences.
- Use white space before and after your main idea to highlight it.
- Use short sentences and short paragraphs that cover one idea. Separate short paragraphs with white space.
- Use bulleted or numbered lists to help readers quickly differentiate multiple points or directions.[51]

Signature Block Always close with something, even if it is only your name. Simple closings, though, like "Regards" or "Best wishes," add a touch of warmth to this otherwise cold medium. Add credibility to your message by adding a signature block after your name. For consistency, create a signature file (.sig) containing, at a minimum, your name, title, and address. You could also include phone and fax numbers; your web address or website; an advertising message, slogan, or quote; your business philosophy; or ASCII art created from text and symbols. However, many organizations have eliminated these slogans and quotes from employees' signature files in an effort to steer clear of potential litigation. The best advice is to know and follow your organization's policy. Avoid duplicating material in the signature that is already in your e-mailhead, if you use one.[52]

EDITING AND REVISING E-MAIL MESSAGES

It is in the editing phase that writers have the opportunity to convert an average-to-poor e-mail message into an effective e-mail message. It is not a step to be rushed. Here are some editing tips that should help you produce effective e-mail messages.

- Build some time in between the drafting and editing phases.
- Edit when you are rested.
- Edit when you are not rushed.
- Don't edit when you are upset or noticeably distracted.
- Do several separate editing passes. With each pass, focus on just one or two potential areas of improvement (e.g., *message organization, writing mechanics, spelling*). Identifying 100 percent of the message's weaknesses simultaneously in a single editing pass is difficult to accomplish. By making separate focused editing passes, you are far more likely to identify what should be revised.
- With each editing pass, read the e-mail message word-for-word. Don't just skim over the message.
- If the e-mail message is important, have others edit it also.

While editing, make sure your tone is appropriate to your audience. E-mail is an impersonal medium that is fertile ground for misunderstandings and hurt feelings. Temper your messages with politeness and objectivity. Strive for a professional, yet conversational tone. Use personal pronouns ("I," "you," "me") to humanize the connection. To humanize your e-mail, avoid the "**e-tone.**" Nancy Friedman, a consultant and trainer, invented the term "e-tone" to refer to the miscommunication that occurs when you have one tone of voice in mind as you write e-mail, but your recipient reads it with a totally different tone. Friedman urges e-mail writers to use words that express feelings—"please," "thank you," "I'm happy to report," or "sorry to say"—to tell them how you feel.[53] Friedman contends that even sensitive topics, such as apologies, can be addressed in e-mail if done properly.

Also check to make sure you have not overused punctuation marks that can cause misunderstandings. For example, a subject line in an e-mail to a professor that says "Grades???????" might sound as if you are unhappy with your grade, when your intent was to merely find out what your grade is. Similarly, overuse of the exclamation point can offend people because it can make you sound pushy or overexcited!!!!!!!!

Finally, be sure the e-mail you are about to send does not contain a reckless or emotional outburst. For example, do not send an e-mail in which you stridently complain about your boss to a coworker because the offensive e-mail could get forwarded, accidentally or on purpose, to your maligned boss.

PROOFREADING E-MAIL MESSAGES

Proofread your e-mail carefully. Do not let poor spelling and typos detract from the credibility of your message. Use the grammar and spell checker, but then reread the message yourself before you hit Send. You cannot depend on a grammar or spell checker to catch every error. Some basic proofreading tips that will help you identify those oversights include:

- Proofread when you are not rushed.
- Proofread when you are rested.
- Do separate, focused proofreading passes (e.g., *once for misspelled words, once for spacing problems*, etc.)

e-tone
> Refers to the miscommunication that occurs when the writer has one tone of voice when writing the e-mail, but the recipient reads it in a totally different tone.

- With each proofreading pass, read the e-mail message as opposed to merely skimming.
- If the e-mail message is important, have others proofread it also.

Contrary to popular belief, businesspeople do pay attention to typos, no matter what the medium. Typos and grammatical errors undermine your credibility and the credibility of your e-mail message, and they subject the message to misinterpretation. Sloppy writing shows a lack of respect for your reader. Remember that some decision makers go out of their way to catch spelling or grammatical errors in business documents. Catching careless coworkers' errors in office e-mail is a common pastime in many organizations.[54] To avoid being the joke of the day, proofread. Take the following example:

"If emale is writon with speeling mestakes and gramitckal errors, you mite git the meening, however, the messige is not as affective, or smoothly redable."

After proofreading, always ask yourself, Would I want to see this message in a *New York Times* cover story or taped to the office refrigerator? If not, do not send it.

Now let's look at a poorly written, persuasive e-mail message (Figure 8-2). The message situation is based on a request to an individual to be the keynote speaker at the annual conference of the Association for Business Communication. This should be a relatively easy message to write. However, the poorly written sample below reminds us that, when we are careless, we can easily weaken our chances of meeting our objective!

FIGURE 8–2: PERSUASIVE E-MAIL MESSAGE (POORLY-WRITTEN VERSION)

Subject: Keynote Speaker Request

What a beautiful day! Spring is oficially here, and we can finally put away our winter clothes. And, since you are likely in a good frame of mind, it is a good time to ask a favor of you.

The 85th Annual International Conference of the Association for Business Communication will be held in Providence, Rhode Island this coming October 2-5. The theme of the conference focuses on communicating on social media for business purposes. Your name was mentioned as a potential KEYNOTE SPEAKER! We assumed you would like the added publicity. So, how about it? Will you speak at the conference on October 2? We will pick up your travel expenses and put you up in a decent hotel relatively-near the conference site!

Contact us. Have a nice day!

Before reading further, take a few minutes to identify the weaknesses in the poorly written e-mail message above.
Now, let's look at some of some of letter's weaknesses.

- Spelling error: should be "officially" not "oficially" in line one of the message.
- Subject line error: while clear, it signals the request too early
- Strategy error: did not stay on topic in opening paragraph.

- Strategy error: request was strongly hinted at in the first paragraph (". . . ask a favor of you").
- Strategy error: desire was not built adequately before stating request.
- Strategy error: little was done in the way of integrating appeals to build reader desire.
- Netiquette error: the words "keynote speaker" should not be in all caps.
- Netiquette error: overuse of the exclamation point weakens its emphasis.
- Clarity problem: basic details were missing (e.g., location, time of day or evening, length of talk, honorarium, flight details, ground transportation details, meal arrangements, hotel location, etc.).
- The writer's name was not included.

Now, let's look at an improved version of the same e-mail message (Figure 8-3).

FIGURE 8-3: PERSUASIVE E-MAIL MESSAGE (IMPROVED VERSION)

Subject: Your Social Media Expertise Has Come To Our Attention

Your book, *The Social Media Revolution*, is drawing many favorable comments from business managers. Thank you for making such a fine contribution and, in turn, helping so many in the business place keep up to date with social media.

The Association for Business Communication will hold its annual international conference in Providence, Rhode Island on October 2–5. Several of the 600 members currently enrolled for the convention have expressed an interest in meeting you and hearing your thoughts on how to communicate effectively on social media. Those of us on the association's board concur with our members. With this in mind, we are extending to you an invitation to give the keynote speech at the Thursday evening gala dinner from 7–7:30 p.m. on October 2. There, we would like you to share your thoughts regarding how to communicate effectively in businesses on social media. We are prepared to offer you $5,000 honorarium as well as cover your travel, food, and lodging expenses.

We sincerely hope you will accept our invitation. Please contact me with your decision by April 20 at (240) 420-7575 or at rgreer005@gmail.com. We look forward to having you join us in Rhode Island this fall; a time when the weather is pleasant and nature provides added beauty as the leaves change colors.

Ronald Greer, President
Association for Business Communication

Now, take a few minutes to identify the strengths in this improved version of the e-mail message.

- Subject line: on topic and grabs reader's attention without hinting at the request.
- Strategy compliance: the opening paragraph gains attention via complimentary, reader-centered comments.
- Strategy compliance: the opening paragraph is on topic.

- Strategy compliance: the opening paragraph has a friendly tone.
- Strategy compliance: clear, strong desire was built prior to making the request (e.g., *favorable comments, fine contribution, members interested in meeting you*).
- Strategy compliance: request was clearly stated.
- Strategy compliance: made it easy for the reader to respond by giving contact information in the closing paragraph.
- Strategy compliance: the closing paragraph contained forward-looking talk.
- Strategy compliance: the closing paragraph had a positive tone.
- Strategy compliance: building desire continued through the closing paragraph (e.g., *honorarium, Rhode Island is beautiful in early October*).
- Netiquette compliance: no shouting (words in all caps).
- Netiquette compliance: free of abbreviations and emoticons.
- Spelling compliance: no misspelled words.
- Grammar compliance: free of mechanical errors.
- Clarity compliance: message is clear.

OBSERVING E-MAIL NETIQUETTE

We are all encouraged to follow the rules of netiquette (electronic etiquette) when developing and sending e-mail messages. **Netiquette** refers to etiquette rules governing electronic content and use. Netiquette rules apply to all electronic communications—blogs, social media, e-mail, text messages, etc.—business or personal.[55] These rules of polite behavior have sprung up alongside the etiquette that governs our off-line behavior and have quickly become a universally understood behavioral standard that transcends cultures, businesses, and geographical boundaries.[56]

Avoid Flaming Avoid publicly criticizing people in e-mail or discussion groups using inappropriate language. An e-mail **flame** is a hostile, blunt, rude, insensitive, or obscene e-mail. Flames are immediate, heated reactions and have no place in a business environment. If you are upset or angry, cool down and rewrite your hastily written, angry message before it damages you and your organization.[57] Remember that any e-mail you send—whether strictly business, gossip, complaints, or personal issues—could wind up in your boss's inbox.

netiquette
Guidelines for acceptable behavior when using electronic communication via e-mail, instant messaging, text messaging, chat rooms, and discussion forums.

flame
A hostile, blunt, rude, insensitive, or obscene e-mail.

© Kheng Guan Toh/Shutterstock.com

Avoid Shouting Shouting is using all CAPS in your message. An e-mail with the line THE MEETING WILL BEGIN AT 3PM will be interpreted as demanding and obnoxious. Conversely, do not write in all lowercase letters. Stick to standard capitalization in e-mail.

Avoid Spamming Spamming refers to posting junk or unsolicited e-mail posts to a large number of e-mail addresses.

Avoid Acronyms and Abbreviations in E-mail Do not use acronyms and abbreviations unless you are e-mailing good friends. If you do use them, always explain what they mean. It seems that with increasing volumes of e-mail coming across computer screens daily, the substance of each communication drops, so that the average e-mail message now looks something like this: "OMG did u c K's latest x LOL!!!!!!!!!!" or "I'm on my way. I'll be there soon," has now degenerated to "im on my way!!!!!!!! Ill be thr son!!!!!"[58] Remember that e-mail not only reflects your level of professionalism, but also lives on in backups that could come back to haunt you.

Watch What You Forward Forward is perhaps the most dangerous command on your e-mail program, second only to Reply All. While forwarding is a time-saving way to share information, used without thinking, it can turn into an ECK. Think twice before forwarding e-mail. Although forwarding is sometimes necessary for business reasons, most people do it more often than they need to.[59] For example, refrain from passing on chain letters, jokes, rumors, and wacky stories unless you know your recipient shares your love of this Internet flotsam and jetsam.[60] Many e-mail users resent having jokes and stories fill their inboxes. Respect your reader's time and ask before you forward.

Do not forward all or parts of messages without the consent of the sender as well as the intended recipient. Remember that anything a person writes is copyrighted the minute the author writes it, whether it is an article from the *Wall Street Journal* or the musings of your best friend and coworker.[61] Would you send a photocopy of a handwritten letter to someone else? Phillip Zimmermann, creator of Pretty Good Privacy encryption, says the same thought and respect should go into forwarding e-mails.[62]

Ask Before You Send an Attachment Some organizations prohibit e-mail attachments due to hidden viruses. Before you send an attachment, ask if the reader would prefer receiving the material as an attachment or in the text of the message.[63] In addition, do not simply send an attachment without explaining what it is in the body of the e-mail. "See attached" or a blank e-mail with an attachment raises suspicions that it might be a virus. In such a situation, the recipient will most likely delete the message without opening the attachment.

If You Need an Immediate Response or Action to Your E-mail, Use the "Receipt Notification" Option *Receipt notification* lets you know when the reader opens the message. However, some readers resent the use of receipts, saying that receipts imply a lack of trust on the sender's part. Your better option might be to phone the recipient, letting them know that a pressing e-mail is on its way and that you would appreciate a quick response.[64]

FIGURE 8-4: INTERNATIONAL E-MAIL NETIQUETTE

- Before you begin writing, determine your reader's needs. You may have to translate your message into your reader's language.
- Be careful with dates and times. Most Europeans would interpret 3/5/17 as May 3, 2017 (with the month appearing in the middle), rather than March 5, 2017. The Japanese, in contrast, sometimes use a year/month/day format. To avoid misunderstanding, write out the name of the month as in March 5, 2017 or 5 March 2017.
- Most countries use a 24-hour system, so be sure to use that time format when setting up videoconferences, conference calls, and IM meetings: "The conference call will begin at 13:00 on 3 March 2017."
- Since most countries use more formal written communications than the United States does, be formal when you e-mail internationally. Address people by their surnames and titles, and use a formal tone throughout your message. To help you sort out titles used in different countries, like *"Monsieur"* or *"Madame"* or *"Herr,"* check a reference work, like Peter Post and Peggy Post's *The Etiquette Advantage in Business*.[70]
- Use specific language and avoid acronyms, abbreviations, business or technical jargon, and humor. They do not translate well.
- Before using monetary denominations, state the currency (e.g., US$10,000).
- Give country codes for phone numbers. The U.S. country code is "1 (e.g., 001-608-123-4567)."
- Use generic names rather than brand names (e.g., photocopy rather than Xerox).
- Be specific when you mention geographical locations: Use New York rather than East Coast.
- When indicating time, be sure to indicate which time zone you mean. For example, "I'll call you at 6 p.m." could mean your time or theirs.

Source: Adapted from Samantha Miller, E-mail Etiquette *(New York: Warner Books, 2001) and Nancy Flynn,* The ePolicy Handbook *(New York: American Management Association, 2001).*

If You Want Your Reply to Go Only to the Sender, Hit "Reply," Not "Reply All." If you hit *"Reply All,"* your message will go to all the recipients on the list. Getting messages not meant for them irritates many listserv members. They might send you a flame for this netiquette breach e-mail. If you want your reply to go only to the sender, type in that person's address. Be considerate of people's privacy.

Only CC People Who Need to Read the E-mail Many managers and executives complain about being copied on messages they do not have to read. Unless your boss has requested it or it is standard practice for your workgroup, keep message CC's to a minimum.

Beware of the blind copy (BCC). BCCing means you can sneak a copy of a message to someone without the main recipient knowing, since the BCC'ed person does not appear in the main recipient's header. You have no assurance that the person BCC'ed will keep the message "secret."[65]

Before E-mailing Over Your Boss's Head to Upper Management, Know What Is Customary in Your Office   In most cases, your boss wants to be kept in the loop when you are e-mailing up the chain of command, so let him or her know about ideas, requests, or questions that you plan to send to upper management. Tell your boss before you e-mail up the command chain, rather than by CCing him or her.[66]

Do Not Use Company E-mail to Circulate Personal Requests   Instead, use bulletin boards or a Web message board to post personal requests.[67]

International E-mails Pose Language, Culture, Time Challenges   Before writing and sending an e-mail message internationally, think about your reader's communication needs.

SUMMARY: SECTION 2— E-MAIL

- The popularity of e-mail in the business community is extensive and growing worldwide.
- When deciding whether to send an e-mail, consider how formal or informal the situation is and your need for speed, mass distribution, and privacy.
- Know the tips on how to manage high volumes of e-mail to avoid getting overwhelmed.
- Employers are developing e-policies to protect themselves from lawsuits. Know your company's e-policies and why they were designed.
- Become familiar with your organization's e-mail culture before you send e-mails.
- Know how to write effective e-mails to communicate your thoughts clearly and to avoid misunderstandings. Rather than drafting and immediately sending a message, take time to plan, draft, and revise before you send it via e-mail.
- Abide by the rules of e-mail netiquette to avoid offending recipients and to support message clarity.
- Before you send messages to international business partners, familiarize yourself with the rules of international e-mail netiquette.

INSTANT MESSAGING

instant messaging (IM)
Exchanging text messages in real time between two or more people logged into a particular instant messaging service.

Instant messaging (IM) involves exchanging text messages in real time between two or more people who are logged into a particular instant messaging service.[68] The two defining characteristics of IM, presence awareness and near real-time operation, make it a compelling alternative to phone calls and e-mail. It has been reported that 60 percent of business phone calls never reach their intended recipients.[71] This obvious deficiency in phone calls helps to explain the growth of instant messaging in businesses.

MAJOR BENEFITS OF IMS IN BUSINESS

Combining the real-time benefits of using the phone with the convenience of e-mail, IM offers a variety of advantages to the corporate communicator.[69] IM's popularity as a business communication tool can be explained by its quickness, flexibility, and versatility.

IM Is Quick A sender can detect whether a user is online, send an IM, and institute a back-and-forth conversation, virtually, in real time.[70] Unlike e-mail that can remain unanswered in someone's overloaded inbox for days, IM can detect someone's presence online, which is good for an for immediate response. IM also eliminates long e-mail threads.[71]

IM Is Flexible Many people can be in on the same conversation. In that way, work groups can use it to get tasks done quickly.

Along with making team communication easier, IM allows users to have more than one message thread going at a time. IMs are so easy to handle that you can be on the phone and still respond to them. In terms of security, with commercial-grade IM software, users have the option of archiving IMs for legal or management reasons or purging them to avoid being susceptible to court-ordered discovery processes.[72]

© Kheng Guan Toh/Shutterstock.com

IM Is Versatile IM facilitates communication among geographically distributed workgroups; it improves communication with business partners and suppliers; it quickens response time between customer service and support departments and customers; and it facilitates cross–business unit communication.[73] Users can even send files via most IM applications when a report, contract, or invoice needs to be quickly reviewed or approved.[74] As a collaborative tool, IM easily enables team members to meet in a dynamic space, share files, set up whiteboards, and discuss changes. The space disappears when users are finished. Collaboration is much easier than in the pre-IM days.[75]

The buddy list, an IM staple first developed by AOL, has become "*presence management*" in business contexts, where detecting who is online to answer a question or to buy a product in real time means increased productivity and profits.[76] **Presence management** refers to being able to determine if others are online and available. Companies like AT&T, IBM, Boeing, the U.S. Army and Navy, the National Cancer Institute, and a host of other high-tech, financial, and retail companies use IM to assemble virtual teams from locations around the world. IMs allow employees to communicate with coworkers, clients, customers, and other business contacts from their virtual offices.[77] Retailers like Landsend.com and 1-800-flowers.com use IM to answer customer questions when they arise. It is faster than e-mail and cheaper because customer reps can reply more quickly.[78] HP, Gateway, and Mail Boxes Etc. also use chat in their sales and service.

A good example of a business that thrives virtually by using IM is the CPA firm of Carolyn Sechler. She heads a 14-member virtual office workforce that serves 300 clients, primarily nonprofit organizations and technology entrepreneurs, in several states and countries.[79] From her home office, Sechler works with CPAs from Alabama to British Columbia. She meets with her core team of four every two weeks using her IM service, ICQ. She believes in making people feel comfortable: "At 9 a.m. we all tune in—and we can archive the chats. What's the point of making people go anywhere when they can be comfortable?"

IM is the tool that makes her virtual business possible, a business that has grown 10–15 percent every year. Sechler says that she has used ICQ since its inception. She keeps a "buddy list" of team members up and running on her computer so that they can communicate throughout the day. She can exchange quick messages or files with any of them by IM—a faster service than e-mail—and they can have "impromptu conversations" that bring together four, five, or six members into one chat area. According to Sechler, being accessible

presence management Being able to determine if others are online and available.

online strengthens ties with clients, circumvents crises, and lets the firm find out early about new consulting opportunities.[80]

Despite IM's benefits in the business place, some companies do not allow employees to install IM services because they believe non-work IMs will distract employees from their work. Non-work IM interruptions can be avoided by using the privacy functions on your IM service or by having two IM services—one for work and the other for family and friends.

HOW TO USE IM

Instant messaging works this way: A small piece of client software is loaded onto a PC, smartphone, or other device and maintains a constant connection to a central hosting service. Anyone who is logged onto the service is flagged as online. The software includes a "buddy list" that enables the user to store the nicknames (everyone has a nickname on IM) of clients, coworkers, and other business contacts. When a buddy is online, the name or icon lights up. The user clicks on the icon to send the buddy an IM or a file attachment.[81] After that, messages fly back and forth, all in the same window that scrolls up as the conversation continues. Unlike e-mail, which can take time to reach its destination, IMs reach their destination instantly even if the person is continents away.

You can also control when others can send you a message. Privacy options include saying that you are away at lunch and that you don't want to be bothered. You can even block the fact that you are online.

IM is great for those messages that are too brief to pick up the phone or too urgent to try to play phone tag. In many cases, IM has replaced phone use for short transactions.[82] Since it does not require your full attention, you can even talk on the phone while messaging other people.

Another useful feature allows you to invite several people into the same session. Unless you need the archiving function to save the message, these messages usually disappear when you log off.

© Iculig/Shutterstock.com

FIGURE 8–5: INSTANT MESSAGING BENEFITS THE HEARING IMPAIRED

Instant messaging as well as e-mail, texting, and social media have greatly benefited people with hearing impairments within and outside of the workplace. According to Grant W. Laird Jr., founder, owner, and CEO of the Dallas-based Deaf Network, "Instant messaging has become one of the primary means of communication among members of the deaf community as well as between the deaf and hearing population."[17] Instant messaging is viewed by many in the deaf community as having opened up the lines of communication and leveled the playing field.[18] For additional information, visit these deaf resource websites: www.deafnetwork.com and http://deafcelebration.org/.

WRITING EFFECTIVE INSTANT MESSAGES

Businesspeople typically expect that instant messages be relatively short. With this in mind, be careful not to cause confusion and frustration by taking shortcuts that are ill advised. For example, abbreviations, whether standard or created on the fly, should not be included in business instant messages. Furthermore, a careless writing style (e.g., poor grammar, misspelled words) can leave message recipients questioning your level of professionalism and your credibility. With business instant messages, a careless writing style can easily result in message recipients judging writers' level of professionalism and credibility. In addition, company image is also threatened by poorly written text messages for similar reasons. Here's a list of suggestions to keep in mind when writing business instant messages.

- Write short instant messages. This is what IM recipients expect.
- Start your message with a greeting (e.g., Hello, Hi) and mention your recipient's name.
- Do not include confidential information that you don't want hacked.
- Write clear messages, which means, in part, including enough detail to get the job done.
- Use a polite, friendly tone.
- Adhere to grammar rules.
- Adhere to punctuation rules.
- Adhere to number usage rules.
- Do not type in all caps whether it is a single word or an entire sentence. Doing so looks unprofessional.
- Avoid shorthand measures (e.g., LOL, GR8) because they are typically perceived as being unprofessional and can easily contribute to misunderstandings.
- Avoid acronyms unless you know your reader is familiar with those you use.
- Avoid using technical jargon unless you know your reader is familiar with it.
- Avoid using slang which can easily lead to misunderstandings.
- Don't use abbreviations because they often cause confusion and misunderstandings.
- Don't use emoticons because they are considered to be unprofessional in business writing.

- Avoid misspellings because they speak to a careless, unprofessional writing style.
- Use humor cautiously. If you expect it can be misinterpreted, don't include it.
- Indicate that you are signing off (e.g., Signing off now.).
- Include your name at the end of instant messages.
- Edit, revise, and proofread your instant messages before sending them.

INSTANT MESSAGING NETIQUETTE

You are encouraged to adhere to the following netiquette rules when developing and transmitting business instant messages.

- If someone is marked as unavailable or if you have received an away message from that person, refrain from messaging until they return. Although you may be in a chatty mood, a coworker or family member may be busy and unable to respond promptly. If the recipient uses the same IM service for work and personal messages, the person cannot shut it down since it is a work tool, like the phone. If they are at work and available, be courteous and ask them if they have time to chat, "Got a minute?" If they do not, do not be offended. Ask them to message you when they are free. If you are on the receiving end, don't be afraid to let people know you are busy. Learn to say "no" or ask them to message back later.[83]
- When responding to someone's message, it is a good idea to type your answer, send it, and then wait for the recipient's reply before sending another message. That way, things will not get confusing because you each respond to one idea at a time.
- Know when to stop. Do not let a thread go on and on. A simple "got to go" or "bye" should be sufficient to end the conversation.
- Do not use IMs for long messages. Betsy Waldinger, vice president at Chicago-based OptionsXpress Inc., spends a lot of her day working on an online customer service chat system. She recommends either sending short messages or breaking up long ones over many screens. Typing long messages keeps the person at the other end waiting while you type. IM should not replace e-mail. Use IM for quick-hit messages that require fast responses. Use e-mail for longer discussions.[84]
- If you work in an office where IM is part of the culture, send a message before you drop in on someone. This gives the other person a chance to say whether the visit would be convenient.
- Don't share bad news in an IM.
- Be courteous.
- Log off IM when you are not using it. Otherwise, you may come back to find messages waiting and senders wondering why you are ignoring them.
- Do not hide online. Some managers use the ability to be invisible online as a way to watch employees. This is a quick way to discourage workers from using IM. Being on or off IM is not a good way to determine whether your remote employees are working. Be courteous, and if you are on, be visible. Use the service busy icons, like "Do Not Disturb" or "Busy" to indicate your availability.[85]
- Use two carriage returns to indicate that you are done and the other person may start typing.[86]
- Remember that chat is an interruption to the other person. Use it only when appropriate.

- Be careful if you have more than one chat session going at once. This can be dangerous unless you are paying attention.
- Like e-mail, set up different accounts for family and friends and for work-related IMs.

Instant messaging is a popular communication tool as was previously mentioned. To fully realize its benefits and our purposes for instant messaging, however, you are encouraged to practice the above-mentioned instant message writing suggestions and adhere to the above-mentioned instant message netiquette rules.

SUMMARY: SECTION 3— INSTANT MESSAGING

- Major benefits of instant messaging include its quickness, flexibility, and versatility.
- IM is a viable alternative to phone calls. It cuts costs and keeps people in touch no matter where they are. IM is great for those messages that are too brief to pick up the phone or too urgent to try to play phone tag.
- When deciding whether to IM, consider how formal or informal the situation is and your need for speed, convenience, and privacy.
- Know how to write effective IM messages so as to communicate your thoughts clearly and to avoid misunderstandings.
- Abide by the rules of instant messaging netiquette to avoid offending recipients and to support message clarity.

TEXTING

A **text message** is a short message that is sent electronically to a cell phone or other device.[87] Text messaging has gained wide popularity in the United States and elsewhere since its inception. The first text message (Merry Christmas) was sent on December 3, 1992. Although usually sent from one mobile phone to another, text messaging is often integrated into IM software so that messages can be sent via an IM, but received on a mobile phone. Text messages are no longer limited to text. Video clips and pictures, which are often captured with a mobile phone, are easily integrated into these messages.

text message
A short message that is sent electronically to a cell phone or other device.

© Fine Art/Shutterstock.com

BUSINESS USES OF TEXTING

Text messaging is popular in the U.S. business community for many reasons. First of all, text messages are relatively inexpensive compared to phone messages. While lengthy and more-involved messages do not lend themselves to text messaging, texting is a practical option for shorter and less-involved messages. Another advantage of texting is its ability to communicate in real time. When sending e-mail messages and instant messages, if the recipient is away from his or her computer or his cell phone lacks Internet capability, they cannot be reached. Generally speaking, text messaging offers mobility as well as e-mail functions such as texting several people simultaneously. Text messaging is used extensively in industries, such as real estate, construction, and transportation. Each of these industries has people working in the field who are not connected to a computer all the time. They are able to receive alerts, updates, and quick messages throughout the day without having to rack up phone bills.

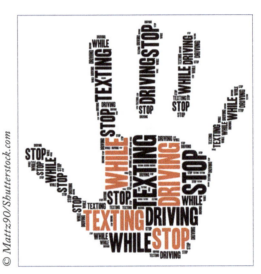

© Mattz90/Shutterstock.com

FIGURE 8-6: TEXTING WHILE DRIVING, WALKING, AND JOGGING

As you know, today's mobile communication technologies and WiFi availability make it possible for drivers to send and receive text messages, as well as participate in phone conversations while operating vehicles ranging from cars, motorcycles, and buses to trains, planes, and helicopters. Unfortunately, there are numerous documented cases of accidents resulting in injuries and fatalities tied directly to such ill-advised use of mobile communication technologies. While some of these drivers lived to tell their side of the story in court, others were not so lucky. Texting and placing phone calls while driving defies both logic and responsible citizenship. It is basically selfish, narcissistic behavior. However, this has not stopped some drivers from taking chances with their fate as well as the fate of others! In response, some countries, as well as several U.S. municipalities and states, are considering or have passed laws making it illegal for drivers to text and/or participate in phone conversations while driving. The U.S. government considers such measures periodically, but has yet to pass such laws.

Drivers in some countries have made great headway on this issue aside from related laws. For example, in the United Kingdom texting while driving is socially unacceptable behavior. In essence, UK citizens are policing themselves on this matter. There appears to be a similar trend in Los Angeles. These are positive signs.

Hopefully you are not risking your safety and the safety of others by practicing such dangerous behaviors. And hopefully the defensive driver in you is constantly on the lookout for other drivers who are not as considerate.

© karen roach/Shutterstock.com

While driving recently, I observed an additional texting-related distraction. It was a humorous, yet serious bumper sticker. It read, "Honk If You Love Jesus. Text While Driving If You Want To Meet Him!" No matter how tasteless you might find this bumper sticker, it is one more reminder to those who read it to be responsible, careful drivers.

Then, there are the potential dangers associated with texting while walking and jogging. The most serious of these is inadvertently stepping out or jogging out onto a street or road into the path of oncoming traffic, stepping through an uncovered manhole, or walking into a light post, tree, or other immobile object. Do you text while walking? If so, you are a *text walker* which is the term used for people who text while walking.

© mimagephotography/Shutterstock.com

Furthermore, the term *text walking* has entered our vocabularies. It refers to the act of texting while walking which apparently is commonplace enough in Belgium that they are adding text walking lanes to their sidewalks. There is also a term that describes specific walking differences between text walkers and other walkers. The term is *text walking gate*, and it reminds us that text walkers typically walk 25 percent more slowly than other walkers, take smaller steps, and raise their feet higher at curbs. The prevailing belief is that text walkers subconsciously take these measures to form a safety bubble around them which frankly won't help a bit if they don't look up before crossing streets and roads!

In the United States the most common business use of text messaging is to communicate with consumers through retail or reality TV shows. Text message marketing has a foreseeable future, whether it be for advertisements or product notifications. Once purchases are made, buyers can then be easily notified of order confirmations, shipping, back orders, etc., through text messages.

WRITING EFFECTIVE TEXT MESSAGES

In their haste to send short text messages, some writers develop unclear messages that reflect poor writing habits. While using a careless writing style when texting family and friends is typically acceptable, using such a writing style in business text messages is strongly discouraged. With business text messages, a careless writing style can easily result in message recipients judging writers' level of professionalism and credibility. Furthermore, company image is also threatened by poorly written text messages for similar reasons. Here's a list of suggestions to keep in mind when writing business text messages.

- Ask if it is a good time for you and your recipient to have a text chat.
- Write short text messages. This is the standard expectation.
- Do not include confidential information that you don't want hacked.
- Start your message with a greeting (e.g., Good morning) and mention your recipient's name.
- Write clear messages, which means, in part, including enough detail to get the job done.
- Use a polite, friendly tone.
- Adhere to grammar rules.
- Adhere to punctuation rules.
- Adhere to number usage rules.
- Do not type in all caps whether it is a single word or an entire sentence. Doing so looks unprofessional.
- Avoid textese (e.g, LOL, BRB, OMW, W8, CID, GR8) because it is considered unprofessional and can easily contribute to misunderstandings. Recently I noticed a drink coaster in a local restaurant. It had a reminder printed on it that applies to using textese in text messages. It read, "2 much txting mks u 1 bad splr." What an insightful message!
- Avoid acronyms unless you know that your reader is familiar with those you use.
- Avoid using technical jargon unless you know your reader is familiar with it.
- Avoid using slang which can easily lead to misunderstandings.
- Don't use abbreviations because they often cause confusion and misunderstandings.
- Don't use emoticons because they are considered to be unprofessional in business writing.

- Avoid misspellings because they speak to a careless, unprofessional writing style.
- Use humor cautiously. If you expect it can be misinterpreted, don't include it.
- Include your name at the end of text messages.
- Edit, revise, and proofread your text messages before sending them.

TEXTING NETIQUETTE

You are encouraged to adhere to the following netiquette rules when developing and transmitting business text messages.

- Make sure your communication partner is receptive to texting. While millennials are very receptive to texting, that doesn't mean everyone else is. Some people prefer e-mail, others prefer phone conversations. You get the point!
- Don't send text messages regarding important, complex, and controversial business situations and matters. These should be dealt with using more robust, formal communication forms such as face-to-face conversations and videoconferences.
- Text at a time that is reasonable. For example, don't send early-morning (e.g., 6 a.m.) text messages to individuals who are not morning people. And, be sensitive to time differences when texting international business contacts.
- Do not discuss legal matters via text messages.
- Be courteous.
- If you desire an immediate response, consider placing a phone call or sending an instant message rather than texting. While most people respond to text messages, they don't always do so immediately.
- Don't be too quick to get upset with an individual who doesn't respond to your text message. They may have simply overlooked your text message in the midst of juggling all of their responsibilities.
- Don't be a texting nag by resending a text message when you don't feel a person has responded as quickly as you wanted them to respond. Call them instead.
- Do not send bad news via text messages. Sharing bad news warrants a less-casual communication medium such as a face-to-face conversation.
- Don't text in inappropriate settings such as during training sessions, meetings, and presentations. Doing so shows a high degree of disrespect for trainers, fellow meeting participants, and speakers.
- Excessive texting while out to lunch with fellow employees is discouraged.
- Don't text while driving. Doing so is extremely dangerous and inconsiderate of others' safety.
- Before you send a text message, make sure your autocorrect feature has not distorted your message. [88 & 89]

Text messaging certainly has its benefits as mentioned previously and offers businesses a viable communication tool. To fully realize its benefits and our purposes for texting, you are encouraged to practice the above-mentioned text message writing suggestions and adhere to the above-mentioned text message netiquette rules.

SUMMARY: SECTION 4— TEXTING

- Texting is a viable alternative to sending e-mail and placing phone calls. Text messaging can cut costs and keep people in touch no matter where they are.
- When deciding whether to send a text message, consider how formal or informal the situation is and your need for speed, convenience, and privacy.
- Don't text while driving. It is not worth the risk to you and others!
- Know how to write effective text messages so as to communicate your thoughts clearly and to avoid misunderstandings.
- Abide by the rules of text messaging netiquette to avoid offending recipients and to support message clarity.

WEBSITES

website
A set of interconnected Web pages starting with a homepage.

A **website** is a set of interconnected Web pages that build from a homepage. Websites are commonplace in today's businesses and are used predominately for sharing information, advertising products and services, online retailing, and tracking visitor demographics. *Amazon* and *L.L. Bean* are good examples of online retailing businesses. Whether it is *Amazon*, *L.L. Bean*, or other company websites, visual features such as photos and videos are powerful tools for attracting customers much like high-quality, color photos are in hardcopy catalogues. Furthermore, many websites also offer audio features which certainly provide additional marketing tools.

© marekuliasz/Shutterstock.com

WEBSITE WRITING SUGGESTIONS

What follows are some suggestions to keep in mind when developing written materials for business websites.

- **Reduce the Clutter.** Simple, easy-to-navigate websites are typically appreciated, whereas cluttered, hard-to-navigate websites can quickly frustrate potential customers and, in turn, chase them and their consumer dollars to competitors' websites, products, and services.

- **Most People Who Browse the Internet Skim.** This means they do not read content in its entirety. Nor are they big on scrolling. What does this mean to those who write Web content? Write concise, skimmable text. Grab your readers' attention quickly. Make your main points on the first screen. If you don't, your reader will likely be off to one of the millions of other sites, just clicks away.
- **Write Concisely.** Web readers do not want to wade through excess verbiage, so write concisely. However, do not do so at the expense of clarity. Include the level of detail needed to achieve this goal also.
- **Write with Design in Mind.** Include keywords, subheads, bulleted lists, and short paragraphs. Use clear, informational headlines. Then provide objective, supporting details. Experts say that your Web page is too text heavy if you can place your open palm over a block of text on your website without touching a graphic image.
- **Write Comprehensively.** While it seems like a contradiction, Web writing also demands comprehensiveness. Web browsers will stay around if they like what they see.
- **Use Links to Interior Pages Where You Can Tell the Rest of Your Story.** Use links to keep them hooked. However, keep links to a minimum and always provide a link back to your home page.
- **Avoid Puffed, Exaggerated "Marketese" and Stuffy, Bureaucratic Prose.** Write in a conversational voice, do not talk down to Web readers, and do not exaggerate your product or service.
- **Use the Web's Interactivity.** Build your website so your readers can react to your site through e-mail feedback or discussion boards, and use drawings, graphics, animation, audio, or video where they enhance your words.

Your website must serve the business community's needs. Knowing how to write effective website content will serve you well in this environment.

SUMMARY: SECTION 5— WEBSITES

- Websites are commonplace in today's businesses.
- Company websites are used predominately for sharing information, advertising products and services, and online retailing.
- The quality and ease of use of company websites contributes greatly to their effectiveness.
- Know how to develop effective websites and write effective website content.

CHOOSING THE RIGHT COMMUNICATION MEDIUM WHEN SO MANY ELECTRONIC WRITING CHOICES ARE AVAILABLE

Imagine you are a businessperson who wants to communicate with existing and/or potential customers or clients. Given the many electronic and non-electronic options available to you, how do you select the right medium? Do you choose e-mail, IM, text messaging, or a website? Or, do you post your message on a social media site such as LinkedIn or Facebook? Do you place a phone call instead or have a face-to-face meeting? Or, do you saturate the market, so to speak, by transmitting your message over digital media, in the hopes that

FIGURE 8-7: POTENTIAL E-WRITING HEALTH THREATS

Excessive electronic writing can potentially cause physical damage. This is not to say that electronic writing technologies are bad or that they should not be used. However, we are reminded that misuse of them can be most serious. Here are three examples of potential health threats for your consideration.

- **Carpal tunnel syndrome.** This is repetitive motion nerve damage that often occurs in individuals' thumbs and wrists as a result of too-frequent keyboarding (e.g., texting) on small smartphone, tablet, and notebook keypads.
- **Chronic Neck and Shoulder Pain.** A form of this has been found to result from excessive keyboarding on electronic tablets during which time our fingers and wrists are hovering above the keypad. It appears that our inability to rest our wrists while keyboarding is the culprit.
- **Vision Problems.** Viewing small screens (e.g., smartphones, tablets, netbooks, etc.) too frequently invite vision problems. Common sense reminds us that straining our eyes frequently while viewing small screens will ultimately take its toll. In addition, there has been an increase in the number of people experiencing detached retinas due to viewing small screens frequently in ill-lighted settings. There is an irony in the detached retinas/digital small screens threat in that the retina acts like an electronic image sensor in a digital camera, converting optical images into electrical signals.

Hopefully you are not going for the potential physical threats trifecta described above. Nerve damage, chronic neck and shoulder pain, and vision problems are not easily and inexpensively repaired. It's worth thinking about!

current and potential customers and clients will spot you? With so many choices, making the right media choice can certainly be overwhelming!

Jim Blasingame, one of the world's foremost experts on small business and entrepreneurship, offers some practical advice to help you make good media choices. He encourages businesspeople to use the following two approaches when making communication media choices: (1) ask yourself which communication medium best suits the circumstance and (2) ask your customers and clients which communication medium they prefer.[90] Regarding Blasingame's second approach, remind yourself that not all of your clients or customers will share your interest in and your ability to use each electronic communication tool you are comfortable using. Nor do they all have access to the technology you prefer to use. For example, many people around the globe lack access to the Internet by circumstance or choice, including some in the United States.

Notes

1. Wikipedia.
2. Nancy Flynn, *The ePolicy Handbook* (New York: American Management Association, 2001), 1.
3. Flynn, 49.
4. Ibid, 50.
5. Dianna Booher, *E-Writing: 21st Century Tools for Effective Communication* (New York: Pocket Books, 2001), 1.
6. Ibid., 2.
7. Ibid, 12.
8. Samantha Miller, *E-Mail Etiquette* (New York: Warner Books, 2001), 103.
9. Ibid., 105.
10. Ibid., 103.
11. Ibid., 102.
12. Ibid.
13. Flynn, 101.
14. Booher, 13.
15. Webopedia, http://www.webopedia.com/TERM/P/phishing.html
16. Flynn, 89.
17. Leena Rao, "Email: Unloved. Unbreakable," *Fortune*, 5.1.15 (May 1, 2015): 55-56.
18. Daniel Bates, "You've got (more) mail: The average office worker now spends over a quarter of their day dealing with email," July 20, 2012, http://www.dailymail.co.uk/sciencetech/article-2181680/Youve-got-mail-The-average-office-worker-spends-over-a-quarter-of-their-day-dealing-with-email.

19. Author unknown, "Emails expected to rise to 140 a day in 2018," May 4, 2014, http://www.news.com.au/finance/work/emails-expected-to-rise-to-140-a-day-in-2018/story-e6frfm9r122.

20. Rao, 55.

21. Miller, 22; Booher, 33.

22. Miller, 31; Booher, 36.

23. Booher, 41.

24. Flynn, 3.

25. Ibid., 4.

26. Ibid., 7.

27. Ibid.

28. Ibid.

29. Ibid., 50.

30. Ibid.

31. Ibid., 9.

32. Ibid., 81.

33. Ibid., 34.

34. Michael R. Overly, *E-policy: How to Develop Computer, E-policy, and Internet Guidelines to Protect Your Company and its Assets* (New York: American Management Association, 1999), 27.

35. Alan Cohen, "Worker Watchers Want to Know What Your Employees Are Doing Online," *Fortune* (June 1, 2001): 70–81, http://infoweb7.newsbank.com.

36. Valli Baldassano, "Bad Documents Can Kill You," *Across the Board* 38 (September/October 2001): 46–51.

37. Flynn, 54.

38. Ibid., 52.

39. "Some Wall Street Firms Did Not Retain Required E-mails–NYT," (May 7, 2002), http://www.reuters.com.

40. Miller, 94–95.

41. Ibid., 95.

42. Gregory A. Maciag, "E-mail Might Be the Killer Application, but Poorly Managed, It Could Bury You," *National Underwriter* 106 (March 18, 2002): 33–35.

43. Booher, 9.

44. David Angell and Brent Heslop, *The Elements of E-mail Style* (New York: Addison-Wesley, 2000), 18–19.

45. Ibid., 19–20.

46. Ibid., 19.

47. "Promote Corporate Identity Through E-mail," *Business Forms, Labels & Systems 40* (March 20, 2002): 18.

48. Angell and Heslop, 21–22.

49. Ibid., 20.

50. Ibid., 24.

51. Ibid., 15–32.

52. Ibid., 117.

53. Dawn Rosenberg McKay, "E-mail Etiquette," *Online Netiquette Uncensored: Courtesy #3*, http://www.onlinenetiquette.com.

54. Flynn, 146.

55. Nancy Flynn, *The Social Media Handbook: Policies and Best Practices to Effectively Manage Your Organization's Social Media Presence, Posts, and Potential Risks* (San Francisco: Pfeiffer, 2012), 327.

56. Flynn, 97.

57. Ibid.

58. David Spohn, "E-mail Rules of Engagement" (May 18, 2002), http://webworst.about.com.

59. Miller, 43.

60. Ibid.

61. Ibid., 51.

62. Brian Sullivan, "Netiquette," *Computerworld* 36 (March 4, 2002): 48.

63. Flynn, 99.

64. Ibid., 100.

65. Ibid., 99.

66. Ibid.

67. Ibid., 107.

68. PC Magazine Encyclopedia (online).

69. Mandy Andress, "Instant Messaging," *InfoWorld* 24 (January 7, 2002): 36.

70. Suzanne Gaspar, "RUOK w IM?" *Network World* 19 (February 25, 2002): 40.

71. Matt Cain, "META Report: The Future of Instant Messaging," *Instant Messaging Planet* (April 29, 2002).

72. Ibid.

73. Andress, 36.

74. Brad Grimes, "Peer-to-Peer Gets Down to Business," *PC World* 19 (May 2001): 150–154.

75. David LaGesse, "Instant Message Phenom Is, Like, Way Beyond E-mail," *U.S. News & World Report* 130 (March 5, 2001): 54–56.

76. Laura Schneider, "Is There Room in Your Cubicle for Instant Messaging?" *What You Need to Know About*, http://chatting.about.com.

77. Jim Sterne, "People Who Need People," *Inc.* 22 (2000): 131–132.

78. Michael Hayes, "What We Sell Is Between Our Ears," *Journal of Accountancy* 191 (June 2001): 57–63.

79. Ibid.

80. Bradbury, 41.

81. Lagesse, 56.

82. Laura Schneider, "Instant Messaging: Annoyance or Necessity?" *What You Need to Know About*, http://netconf…about.com.

83. Brian Sullivan, "Netiquette," *Computerworld* 36 (March 4, 2002): 48.

84. Jeff Zbar, "The Basics of Instant Messaging Etiquette," *Net.Worker News* at www.nwfusion. com accessed on May 13, 2002.

85. Ibid.

86. "Netiquette Guidelines," http://www.dtcc.edu.

87. Mirriam-Webster Dictionary (online).

88. Jacquelyn Smith & Vivian Giang, "7 Rules Of Texting Etiquette Every Professional Needs To Know," September 18, 2014, http://www.businessinsider.com/texting-etiquette-rules-every-professional-needs-to-know-2013-9.

89. Dana Manciagli, "Texting etiquette: 6 rules to follow while texting at work," January 23, 2015, http://www.9news.com/story/money/business/2015/01/24/texting-etiquette-6-rules-to-follow-when-texting-at-work/22276643/.

90. Jim Blasingame, "High Tech or High Touch: It's Really Not Complicated," *The Wall Street Journal*, October 6, 2009.

PLANNING AND DRAFTING BUSINESS DOCUMENTS

9

LEARNING OUTCOMES

After reading this chapter, you should be able to:

1. Explain how academic writing differs from business writing.

2. Discuss the purposes of various types of written media.

3. Describe the three-stage writing process.

4. Discuss techniques that will help you break through writer's block.

5. Discuss ways to achieve good message organization.

6. Specify drafting techniques that will help you adapt your message to your audience.

© assistant/Shutterstock.com

SELECT KEY TERMS

INTRODUCTION

Business writing stresses audience awareness, political sensitivity, speed, and fluency. Furthermore, the two usual purposes of business writing are to inform and to persuade.

Good business writers typically follow the three-stage writing process—planning, drafting, and revising. Good planning involves audience analysis, determining the appropriate writing medium, and identifying organizational devices. Drafting involves writing the "rough draft" of the message or document.

The intent of this chapter is to provide you with information on how to effectively plan and draft business documents, including how to move past writer's block and how to manage the drafting process in organizations. These goals will be realized through discussions regarding the following topics: how academic writing differs from business writing, stage one of the writing process (planning, defining your purpose, analyzing your audience, organizing your ideas, and choosing the best medium), and stage two of the writing process (drafting, getting started, moving past writer's block, drafting to support your purpose, types of supporting detail, drafting with your audience in mind, creating goodwill, drafting with organization in mind, building paragraphs, and managing the drafting process in organizations).

HOW ACADEMIC WRITING DIFFERS FROM BUSINESS WRITING

Although both business writing and academic writing depend on complex thinking and writing strategies, business writing differs in many respects from academic writing. While academic writing encourages you to express yourself, business writing stresses purposefulness, audience awareness, speed, concision, and fluency.

Just as the culture of the writing classroom influences the writing produced in that class, the organization's culture influences how you write each document—its appearance, content, purpose, and tone. A company's internal and external e-mail messages, social media posts, text messages, memos, letters, reports, and proposals not only support the organization's business but also communicate the company's philosophy and public image. For these reasons, good business writing demands that its practitioners develop a social awareness of their organizational environment.

Business Writing
http://writing2.
richmond.edu/writing/
wweb/business/started.
html

THE THREE-STAGE WRITING PROCESS

Another difference between academic and business writing pertains to the writing process. The writing process comprises three stages—*planning, drafting*, and *revising*. In the academic classroom, the writing process is just as important, if not more so, than the final document. In the business world, however, the final product is what matters. The process itself is secondary; but is still important in that it drives the final product.

In business settings "writing" often means only the actual phrasing of ideas into words. In many organizations, prewriting or planning activities, such as creating an outline or gathering information, are not considered part of the writing. This narrow view of writing can cause scheduling problems because, as you know, the actual writing time on a particular document involves more than writing; it also involves planning and revision activities before the document is complete. Therefore, writers in organizations need to define their purpose and audience and organize their ideas quickly in order to move onto the **drafting** process.[1]

As a business writer, you must adapt your writing to the demands of your organizational community, developing several composing styles to fit each writing situation. Your ability to produce well-written documents in an organizational setting will depend to a great extent on how effectively you understand and manage the writing process.

STAGE 1 OF THE WRITING PROCESS: PLANNING

Planning involves defining your purpose, analyzing your audience, organizing your ideas, gathering information, outlining, and choosing the best medium. Document clarity and effectiveness depend, in large part, on the thought and effort put forth in this stage.

Prewriting decisions about purpose, audience, and organization vary from being a matter of a few minutes of reflection before writing a routine letter to performing extensive audience analysis, researching, communal brainstorming, note taking, reviewing previously completed documents, and creating extensive outlines before writing a complex proposal. It is important to generate ideas before you start writing. There are several ways to do this, including freewriting, listing, and clustering.[2]

drafting
The first pass at writing a document.

planning
The prewriting activity; typically includes defining your purpose, analyzing your audience, organizing your ideas, and choosing the right medium.

© Gunnar Pippel/Shutterstock.com

Freewriting occurs when the writer notes all the message ideas that flow through his or her mind without lifting the pen from the paper or pausing at the computer. *Listing* is just that—listing! Simply take a few minutes to list everything you want to include. **Clustering** involves more focus and attention than freewriting and listing. When you generate ideas through clustering, you establish the relationships among the parts of your message.

DEFINING YOUR PURPOSE

Business writing is done for a purpose. Starting to write without knowing your purpose is like starting on a trip without knowing your destination. Writing without a clear purpose is frustrating for you, but it is even more frustrating for your readers who become impatient and less receptive as they try to figure out what you wrote and what you want. Thus, identifying your purpose is the first step in the *planning stage*.

The cornerstone of good organization is a clearly stated purpose, which is your reason for writing. To determine your purpose, ask yourself, What do I want my audience to do or to learn after reading this message? Put yourself in your reader's place. What would you as a reader ask on receiving this document? Do I read it, route it, or skip it? What's in this for me?[3] To help you determine your purpose, fill in a worksheet like the one presented in Figure 9-1.

FIGURE 9-1: COMMUNICATION PURPOSE WORKSHEET

The purpose of this (document type) _____

Is to (writer's purpose) _____[4]

So that (reader's purpose) _____

If the document has been requested, a short reminder can lead into your purpose: "Here is the opinion you requested on the recent changes in job descriptions." In contrast, unsolicited writing requires more explanation: "I am writing because I am concerned about the report ..." or "I am concerned about the recent report ..."

As you identify your purpose, ask yourself, So what? and Who cares? This helps you ensure that what you say has significance for you and for your readers.

The two general purposes of business writing are (1) to inform and (2) to persuade. For example, most memos inform readers, whereas proposals persuade readers. These purposes often exist in a single document. While the central purpose of business proposals is to persuade readers, informing them is a secondary purpose in most. When writing an informational letter to his clients, an insurance agent's central purpose may be to inform them of the products and services his organization offers. However, his secondary purpose is likely to persuade them to take advantage of these products and services.

For experienced business writers, arriving at the document's purpose is a routine part of the writing process because business writing is almost always done in response to a specific request or situation. And certain kinds of documents are written again and again, so your purpose for writing becomes almost second nature.

FIGURE 9-2: PLAN THEN WRITE

In his book, *Write Up the Corporate Ladder*, Kevin Ryan introduces the Plan Then Write method as a process that professional writers use to "achieve the highest standard of excellent business writing." Here are the steps.

Step 1. Plan.

- Choose a format.
- Define your subject by making a bulleted list of your main point and supporting points.
- Determine your audience (Who are your readers? What do they know and not know about your subject?).
- State your purpose (What is your reason for writing?) and state your call to action (What do you want your audience to do?).

Step 2. Write (and keep writing and rewriting until you have a final draft).

Keep these guidelines in mind:

- Start with the easy parts.
- Focus on "thinking clearly on paper," not writing rules. Writing is the act of problem solving using your writer's intuition as a guide.
- Change your plan as you discover new ideas.
- Make liberal use of bulleted lists and subheads.

Step 3. Edit 1. Revise and proofread your final draft.

Step 4. Edit 2. Give your final draft to an experienced or professional proofreader. (If you are unable to give your final draft to an experienced or professional proofreader, a second pass at revising and proofreading it will typically net improvements.)

Source: Kevin Ryan, Write Up the Corporate Ladder: Successful Writers Reveal the Technique That Helps You Write with Ease and Get Ahead. (New York: American Management Association, 2003) 15–16

SUMMARY: SECTION 1— PLANNING YOUR PURPOSE

- Business writing differs from academic writing in that business writing stresses audience awareness, political sensitivity, speed, and fluency as being very important.
- Good writers follow the three-stage writing process: planning, drafting, and revising.
- In the planning stage of writing, you first define your purpose—why you are writing.
- The two usual purposes for business writing are to inform and to persuade.

ANALYZING YOUR AUDIENCE

Your audience is closely tied to your purpose, and analyzing it is the second step in the planning stage. Good business writers write documents from their readers' points of view, asking *who* will read this document and *how* will they use it? Your answers to these questions will help you structure the document so your readers can quickly process the information.

Audience analysis in organizations is more important today than ever before. The lightning speed of the Internet and other communication advances makes information instantaneous and overwhelming. This means business readers must juggle the demands of more information in less time. For business writers this trade-off presents special challenges that did not exist before. Writers must compete for their readers' attention by creating documents that grab their attention and keep it. Every element, from the interest and clarity of the text to the document design, becomes important in the competitive business environment of the 21st century.

Business writers are encouraged to imagine their intended audiences. For example, in the preface to the SEC's *A Plain English Handbook*, Warren Buffet suggests, "Write with a specific person in mind." According to Buffet, when he sits down to write an annual report, he imagines talking to his sisters who "though highly intelligent … are not experts in accounting or finance. They will understand plain English, but jargon may puzzle them."[5] In imagining this kind of "every woman" audience, Buffet succeeds in writing reports that are jargon free and that address what the readers want to know.

CLASSIFYING YOUR AUDIENCE

The first step in audience analysis is to classify your audience in terms of what they will do with your message. Note who will read, route, or make decisions based on your message. These audiences may not be of equal importance, but a successful business message should try to accommodate the needs of all of its readers. The four basic audience classifications are *primary, secondary, gatekeeper,* and *watchdog.*

Primary Audience Your **primary audience** has the power to make decisions necessary for you to accomplish your purpose and to ensure the appropriate actions are taken. A primary audience may be a single person or many persons and may be from any level in the organization (your peers, your superiors, or your subordinates) or an external reader (a client). The primary audience is the decision maker who acts or does not act on your conclusion and recommendation. The primary audience has the authority to do what you want done.[6]

Secondary Audience Who else will see your document? Because departments in an organization are interrelated, you involve a number of persons when you send a report to a primary audience. The **secondary audience** is made up of those individuals who will be affected by your message or who will implement your decision or will implement the directive of the primary audience. The secondary audience may have commented on your message in its various drafts and may have to act on the basis of your message even though they were not included in the approval process.[7]

Gatekeeper Audience The **gatekeeper's** function is to route your message. This person has the power to stop your message before it goes out. Sometimes the gatekeeper is someone higher up in the organization. In some instances, gatekeepers may be first- or

primary audience
The readers for whom you develop your document.

secondary audience
The readers who will be affected by your message or who will implement your decision or the decision of the primary audience.

gatekeeper
People who route and re-route your documents.

second-level managers who must review the document and sign off on it before it is distributed. Often gatekeepers do not read the report; however, they do file it away for future reference.[8]

Watchdog Audience This group is an external audience that is not directly affected by the message, but has substantial political, social, or economic power over the primary audience that will ultimately approve your message. An example of a **watchdog audience** would be industry reviewers whose positive reviews are important to you and to your organization's credibility.[9]

While it is important to classify your readers according to the roles they play in the development of your document, you should also be able to adapt quickly to an audience that you may not immediately recognize as important. For example, the Pacific Gas and Electric's watchdog audience, discussed in Figure 9-3, was ultimately its most important audience.

watchdog audience
External critics not directly affected by a message (e.g., an advertisement), but who have substantial political, social, or economic power over an industry.

FIGURE 9-3: THE WATCHDOG AUDIENCE CAN BITE

If your watchdog audience includes Erin Brockovich, watch out. As a clerk for the law firm of Masry and Vititoe, Brockovich was puzzled over why medical records would be included in a real estate file. This led her to the residents of the town of Hinckley, California. The story of her investigation and legal triumph was dramatized in the Oscar-winning movie *Erin Brockovich*.

Brockovich was able to track down internal memos and other documents that connected the corporate offices of Pacific Gas and Electric (PG&E) with PG&E's Hinckley Compressor Station. The Hinckley Station had been contaminating the groundwater with the toxic chemical Chromium 6 for more than 30 years before Brockovich got involved in putting the missing pieces of the case together.

Many of Hinckley's residents and domestic animals that drank the polluted water and breathed the contaminated air were getting or had gotten sick and some had even died by the time Brockovich first visited the town to investigate. In the end, PG&E compensated the named plaintiffs $333 million in damages—the largest legal settlement in U.S. history to that time—in addition to agreeing to clean up the environment and to stop using chromium.

Erin Brockovich is an American legal clerk and environmental activist. She is currently working as a consultant to law firms in the United States and Australia. To learn more about Brockovich, visit her website at www.brockovich.com.

IDENTIFYING THE NEEDS OF YOUR AUDIENCE

The second step in audience analysis is to identify your reader's needs. Analyze your audience to determine what, if anything, in their background or experience might prevent your message from getting through. To do so, determine their background knowledge, experience, and training; what information they need to know; what your audience's attitude is toward you and your message; how interested they are in your message; and which demographic and psychographic characteristics are relevant. After you complete the profile, use the results to adjust your message to meet the specific needs and expectations of your audience.

First, what are their background knowledge, their experience, and their training? Recent studies have shown that background knowledge is the key to reader understanding. If you are writing to an audience of your peers, you will probably spend little or no time filling in background information. On the other hand, if your audience has high background needs, you may have to define key terms, eliminate jargon, and use concrete examples that relate your points to things with which your audience is familiar.[10]

For example, if you are developing a new computer program and you are writing a progress report to your immediate supervisor who is familiar with the project, you probably do not need to spend time on background information or definitions. If, however, you are the same programmer faced with the task of writing documentation for a user manual for consumers, you need to use plenty of concrete examples containing little or no jargon to instruct them on how to use your program.

FIGURE 9-4: AUDIENCE ANALYSIS WEB STYLE

As a website visitor you are being watched. Online advertisers have a tool that makes Big Brother seem infantile. Through "cookies" technology, the data collectors—Engage, BroadVision, DoubleClick, and Net Perceptions—collect a mind-blowing amount of information about you, everything from names and addresses to where you are going, what you are doing when you get there, and what you are spending while you do it.

As a website owner and developer, this is great news—if you can afford it. You can make every audience feel like an audience of one as you personalize every customer's experience and serve them ads and special offers they are sure to love. "Hello there, H.T. Customer. Look what we've got for you today!" Try www.broadvision.com or www.doubleclickbygoogle.com or www.perception.net/ for more information on the marketing tools of the future. The U.S. Census Bureau Statistical Abstracts is a helpful source for audience analysis information. Visit www.census.gov/compendia/statab/.

Second, what information do they need to know? Many business writers make the mistake of telling everything they know about the subject rather than considering what their audience really needs or wants to know. Unfortunately, how much you know often has little connection with what your audience wants and needs to know. Some audiences need little supporting information; they want only the bottom line. Others have high information needs. For them provide enough evidence, statistics, and sources to make your message credible and convincing.[11]

For example, if your primary audience comprises busy executives, begin with your purpose, use short paragraphs with clear topic sentences for easy scanning, keep tabular data to a minimum and place it on the same page as the reference whenever possible, and put the detailed information in appendices at the end of the report. Conversely, if your primary audience is your immediate supervisor who must be convinced that your methodology, data quality, and conclusions are correct, provide those details in the body of the report.

Third, what is your audience's attitude toward you and your message? Their attitudes and emotions toward you and your message are important considerations. If they are positive or neutral toward you and your message, you can usually expect a positive reception. In this situation, use direct organization—begin with your main idea first—then reinforce their positive attitude by stating the benefits they will gain from the message.

On the other hand, if tempers have been flaring over recent changes within the organization or over a power struggle between departments, your audience may have a fearful, anxious, or hostile reaction to your message. In this case, use the indirect method to organize your message and begin with your evidence first. This helps your readers understand and accept the recommendations at the end of your message.[12]

For example, when presenting good news about an across-the-board salary increase, use the direct method since you can be fairly sure that your audience will react positively to the news. Conversely, audiences may have a hostile reaction to news about salary cuts unless you can convince them first that salary cuts are needed to prevent across-the-board layoffs.

Fourth, how interested are they in your message? If your audience is neutral or uninterested in what you have to say, you may gain their attention and build their interest by beginning with an attention-getter that emphasizes what's in it for them, build the reader benefits into the body of your message, and in the conclusion make it easy for them to act.[13]

Interest levels typically vary. For example, company managers from a different department may be interested in reading your report on a project they know little about. In contrast, members of your own department may be uninterested in the same report because they are already familiar with the project.

Fifth, which demographic and psychographic characteristics are relevant? Especially when you are directing your message to a large audience composed mainly of strangers, determine their **demographic** characteristics—gender, age, occupation, income—and **psychographic** characteristics—personality, attitudes, and lifestyle. Taking this kind of cultural information into account can help you organize and compose your message in a way that helps your readers accept what you have to say.[14]

Analyzing your audiences for their roles and background expectations helps ensure that the message you send is the one that they receive. If you are already familiar with your audience—your supervisor, your peers of several years—you probably do not need an extensive analysis. At other times, you may find that your audience is too large and diverse to meet each member's needs effectively. In that case, write for the needs of the decision makers and the opinion leaders in the audience.

SUMMARY: SECTION 2— ANALYZING YOUR AUDIENCE

- The first step in audience analysis is to classify your audience according to what they will do with your message. The four major audience classifications are: primary, secondary, gatekeeper, and watchdog.
- The second step in audience analysis is to identify the needs of your audience: (1) What is their background experience? (2) What information do they need to know? (3) What is their attitude toward the subject of your message? (4) How interested are they in your message? (5) What demographic and psychographic characteristics are relevant?

ORGANIZING YOUR IDEAS

The third step in the planning stage is organizing your ideas. After you have analyzed your audience, organize your information with their needs in mind. Find out how your audience will use your document, then organize your information logically from their point of view. If they will use the document for reference only, organize the information to make it easy for them to get in, get their answer, and get out.[15] If you are persuading your readers to take action, organize the information so they can see how taking action will benefit them. Your readers will not appreciate a ricochet approach to writing. They expect a smooth, logical flow of information.

© Nataliya Hoya/Shutterstock.com

ACHIEVING GOOD ORGANIZATION

Achieving good organization is a necessity for any business writer. It helps your audience understand and accept your message. Follow these two steps to organize your material with your audience in mind.

1. Limit your purpose.
2. Organize your ideas using the direct or indirect organization pattern.

Limit your purpose. Suppose your manager asks you, the company's head website developer, to prepare a report about your major competitor's website. You spend five days of grueling research and writing to come up with a 20-page report on every aspect of the site from the size of the graphics on the home page to a description of all 100 links. When you hand him the report, he asks, "What's all this? I only needed to know the size of the graphics on their home page." Save yourself a lot of time and trouble by clarifying the purpose of the document you were asked to produce before planning and drafting. To save yourself and your reader time and trouble, limit your purpose to one main idea that you develop with three or four major supporting points.

Choose the direct or indirect method to organize your ideas. Two ways to organize business documents involve using the direct (deductive) and the indirect (inductive) methods.

Direct Method of Organization When you use the **direct method** of organization, state the purpose of the message—your main idea—at the beginning. In the next paragraph, follow up with supporting details. The direct method is the most efficient way to convey your message to your reader.[16] The memo in Figure 9-5 is organized using the direct method and lets you know up front why you are reading it. The information in this memo is easy to grasp because it is presented in the way that most people comprehend information. Therefore, the direct method is easy to read.

FIGURE 9-5: MEMO ORGANIZED USING THE DIRECT METHOD

As of December 4, we will begin the transformation to a team-based structure. If you are interested in becoming a team leader, please see your department manager for an application. Submit your application to the HR department by December 8.

We will evaluate the applications according to each individual's qualifications. The qualifications we are looking for in a team leader are:

- A willingness to give each project 110%
- An ability to lead coworkers in meetings and projects without causing hostility
- A team spirit as shown in past team projects
- No evidence of hidden agendas on past team projects

Team leaders will have extra responsibilities for which they will receive an additional $2,000 per year. These responsibilities include the following:

- Support and lead a team of 5–7 coworkers
- Act as a liaison between team members and management
- Meet monthly with other team leaders and management to discuss ideas for making teams more productive

Everyone interested is encouraged to apply.

Indirect Method of Organization Using the **indirect method**, begin your message with your evidence or explanation before presenting your purpose or main idea. By working backward, you lead your reader to understand the reasons behind your purpose—the main idea—before you present them with the main idea. The memo in Figure 9-6 is organized using the indirect method. Compare Figures 9-5 and 9-6 and how they approach the same situation.

FIGURE 9-6: MEMO ORGANIZED USING THE INDIRECT METHOD

As you are aware, for the last several months, we have been looking into moving to a team-based structure in all departments. After several meetings, we have decided that teams, when used effectively, give management the opportunity to constructively respond to employees' ideas and concerns. We also learned that team leaders are essential in making this strategy work.

Team leaders need performance and leadership skills to effectively lead a team as large as seven coworkers. Team leaders will act as the liaison between team members and management, representing the concerns of their team members while enacting management policies.

We have decided that team leaders will receive an additional $2,000 per year to compensate them for their extra responsibilities. As of December 4, we will move to a team-based structure.

If you are interested in becoming a team leader, please see your department manager for an application. Applications are due to the HR department by December 8.

Use the direct method when you expect your audience will be receptive or neutral toward your ideas. Routine and good news, orders and acknowledgments, informational reports, and nonsensitive memos benefit from the direct method of organization. The direct method:

1. Saves the reader time. Messages that take too long to get to the point lose readers who cannot spend time trying to understand them.
2. Sets the details of the message in context. The reader is not left frustrated and wondering, What's the point?

E-mail messages typically follow the direct method. E-mail has become many people's default form of contact, and why not? It's fast, simple, cheap, and independent of time zones and geography.[17]

Use the indirect method when your audience will be unreceptive, displeased, or even hostile toward your message. Use the indirect method when (1) presenting bad news, (2) persuading an audience of strangers, (3) persuading an audience that will be unreceptive or even hostile toward your message, and (4) writing to a superior.[18] The indirect method:

1. Spares the reader's feelings. Since the main idea appears at the end, the reader is more prepared for it.
2. Encourages a full reading. Presenting evidence and explanations first preserves the reader's ego and lessens the negative reaction to the negative purpose, stated at the end of the message.
3. Avoids offending a reader in a superior position and allows the reader to slowly comprehend your sensitive or negative information.[19]
4. Builds suspense, but should be used only when you know your reader will stick with you to that last most important idea.

There are exceptions to choosing the method of organization. For example, if your situation logically calls for the indirect method, but you know your reader prefers reading the message "straight up," use the direct method.

FIGURE 9-7: CHOOSING A FORMAT

In Kevin Ryan's book, *Write Up the Corporate Ladder*, he suggests that the first step in the planning stage is to choose a document format. A *format*, he says, is the outline, layout, or presentation of a document or other publication; the way in which something is presented, organized, or arranged. A format, as described here, is often transformed into a *template* as a means of standardizing document formats. Here are sample subheads for a sample business letter template:

Date
Return Address
Salutation or greeting
Body of the letter
Close
Signature block

Ryan states that templates have many advantages, some of which are:

1. They prevent writer's block by allowing the writer to move around within the document and start writing where he or she has the most immediate information.
2. They speed up the writing process by establishing a logical flow of ideas and information. When you have filled in the subheads, Ryan says, you are done writing.
3. You know which types of information to gather and where to place them.
4. Since each section in the template acts as a prompt for the data you need, templates guarantee your documents will always be complete and that you will not omit important information.
5. Your readers know what to expect and where to quickly find information.
6. Templates help eliminate wordiness by providing structure and guidelines. Wordiness is often a result of not knowing when to stop writing and feeling as if your report or letter needs to be longer.

Ryan reminds us that documents that are produced regularly and contain the same basic information in each are excellent candidates for templates, while documents that include information that changes each time they are created are inappropriate for templates.

Source: Kevin Ryan, Write Up the Corporate Ladder: Successful Writers Reveal the Technique That Helps You Write with Ease and Get Ahead. (New York: American Management Association, 2003) 29–32.

WAYS TO ORGANIZE YOUR IDEAS

Because much business writing is solicited by others, you must read or listen to the request or solicitation carefully. Often the request itself implies a way to organize the document. For example, if your manager asks you to look into the advantages and disadvantages of purchasing a new office printer, your best bet would be to organize your response around the advantages and disadvantages of purchasing a new printer.

If an organization is not implied in the request, use lists, outlines, and planning guides to organize your ideas. For writing projects that require more planning than a routine reflection on the who, why, what, when, where, and how of the message, business writers must decide on the organization ahead of time, especially in light of the constant interruptions and disruptions of writing in the workplace.[20] Even the organization of routine messages can get lost when the writer, plan in head, gets interrupted midsentence and then returns, perhaps hours later, to an incomplete sentence and the original mental plan now gone. Stop-and-go writing, common in the workplace, is frustrating unless you jot down a plan, however rough, before you begin.[21]

If you cannot discern what organization will best serve the reader, then group and unify the document's ideas yourself. In such a situation, the following organizational devices can help you create an organizational plan and stick to it.

Lists   One way to organize a business document is a listing.[22] Many business writers claim to organize their ideas by listing them first. Listing is helpful if it actually arranges the material logically. However, most lists simply note information rather than arrange it. The examples below show the difference between a list and an arrangement. Arrangement here refers to the logical sequencing of items listed. The examples below represent the writer's attempt to organize his ideas regarding an inquiry into health insurance coverage.

List	Arrangement
1. all 50 employees dislike HMOs	1. what information is needed
2. a description of company operations	2. why you need it
3. current provider's limitations	3. when you need it

Comparing the two examples, we instinctively feel that the arrangement is more organized than the list because each item in the arrangement is united by a unifying principle—that of inquiry.

Outlines   In contrast to lists, formal outlines provide an organizational pattern and a visual and conceptual picture of your writing. A well-crafted outline helps you organize a complex document by providing a visual image of how your ideas logically flow. An outline cuts down on your writing time because it provides an ordered overview of your document.

The disadvantage of a formal outline is that it can be too constraining. Many writers complain that outlining takes too long and inhibits their ideas. For example, when writing a report, some writers do not know what they are going to say until they say it. Writers who obsess over creating the perfect outline may be avoiding writing the document itself.

An outline can be written using either topics or complete sentences. A **topic outline** uses words or phrases for all entries with no punctuation after entries. A **sentence outline**

topic outline
Uses words or phrases for all outline ideas with no punctuation after the ideas.

sentence outline
Uses complete sentences with correct punctuation to organize the outline.

uses complete sentences with correct punctuation for all entries. A topic outline is easy and fast to write. A sentence outline presents a more detailed overview—including topic sentences—of your work and makes drafting the actual paper faster and easier.

Planning Guides Another way to organize your ideas is to develop and use planning guides that fit your workplace writing situation. Fred Reynolds, writing consultant and professor at City College, CUNY, helped a writer develop the correspondence planning guide below. Since the writer's work focused mainly on correspondence, Reynolds helped him develop a planning guide that he could fill in prior to drafting. The writer could return to the guide for direction and refocusing when his drafting was interrupted, which it frequently was.

FIGURE 9-8: PLANNING GUIDE

Correspondence Planning Guide
File Reference:

_____

Purpose:

_____

Major Points I Want to Make:

_____

_____

Further Action Needed:

_____

_____

Source: J. F. Reynolds, "What Adult Work-World Writers Have Taught Me about Adult Work-World Writing, in Professional Writing in Context, e. J. F. Reynolds C. B. Matalene, J. N. Magnotto, D. C. Samson, Jr., and L. V. Sadler (Hillsdale, NJ: Lawrence Erlbaum, 1995), 1–31.

No matter what organizational method you use, once completed, it should enable you to move through the drafting stage of the writing process more quickly and efficiently.

SUMMARY: SECTION 3— ORGANIZING YOUR IDEAS

- Achieve good organization in the prewriting stage by limiting your purpose, and choosing the direct or indirect organizational pattern.
- Choose a method to organize your ideas: listing, outlining, or planning guides.

CHOOSING THE BEST WRITING MEDIUM FOR THE SITUATION

The fourth step in the *planning stage* is choosing the best medium. First, let's familiarize ourselves with the most common types of written media in organizations which are e-mail messages, letters, memos, reports, social media, text messages, and websites.

WRITING MEDIA OPTIONS

E-mail An e-mail message typically deals with routine matters that are not as important as business letters. E-mail is a popular communication medium in organizations for obvious reasons. For example, its speed and ability to reach a number of people at the same time are valued, along with the convenience and permanence of writing.

E-mail's strengths, however, reflect its pitfalls. People often use e-mail as they would a conversation; they react immediately, writing without thinking about organization, grammar, and the effect their words will have. Because it lacks the important nonverbal behaviors that make up face-to-face communication—vocal inflection, eye contact, and gestures—it can generate overreactions and misunderstandings.[23] E-mail is not a private medium so writers must be careful what they include in their messages. E-mail is discussed at length in Chapter 8.

Letters Business letters are sent most frequently to external communication partners, but some are also sent internally, most typically to superiors. Business letters speak to a variety of non-routine situations, in contrast to memos that typically address routine matters. In that sense, letters are a more formal medium than e-mails, text messages, tweets, and blogs. They are also more private. According to the late Malcolm Forbes, a good business letter can get you money, get you off the hook, or get you a job.[24] Since business letters frequently go to external audiences, they are important reflections of the company image. According to Emily Post, "[T]hey are the single most impressive written ambassador for your company."[25] Letters are discussed at length in Chapter 11.

Memos A memo (memorandum) is an informal written communication sent within an organization for quickly communicating news, policies and procedures, directions, information placed on record, and employment-related information. Memos are the backbone of an organization's daily communication. No matter whether they are hardcopy or e-memos, the fact remains that for brief, one-way communication, the memo remains an efficient form of communication at all levels.[26] Memos are not private. They stay around in filing cabinets and on computers for years. If your message is private, send a letter or communicate verbally. For busy office denizens, make your memos reader-friendly by making your subject line specific, discussing only one topic in each memo, and organizing information around clear topic sentences to allow for skimming. Keep the length to one page or less. Memos are discussed in Chapter 11.

Reports These are formal documents that convey information to help others make informed, sound decisions. Reports are typically either informational or analytical, which means some pass along information, while others offer readers conclusions and recommendations based on information gathered. Reports come in many formats and range from a few pages to over a hundred. Reports are discussed at length in Chapter 12.

Social Media Posts These are the predominate form of writing at social media sites. Facebook is a very popular social media platform used in businesses predominately for customer service, public relations, and marketing. LinkedIn is a specialty social media platform that caters to business job applicants and professionals. For example, users can upload résumés and present a professional online identity, whereas businesses can search for viable job candidates. LinkedIn is also a good site to bring together employees, clients, suppliers, and other stakeholders. Social media is discussed at length in Chapter 7.

Text Messages These are also known as short message service (SMS). Texting is popular in the U.S. business community for a variety of reasons. For example, text messages are relatively inexpensive and enable people to communicate in real time. In addition, employees are able to receive alerts, updates, and quick messages throughout the workday. Texting is discussed at length in Chapter 8.

Websites A website is a set of interconnected Web pages. Two common business purposes for websites are sharing information and selling goods and services. Here are some suggestions to keep in mind when writing for business websites: Write concisely, write with design in mind, and make use of the Web's interactivity. These and other suggestions are discussed at some length in Chapter 8.

MAKING THE WRITING MEDIUM CHOICE

Base your medium choice on your audience's expectations and necessity. Do not fall into the habit of simply using the communication medium with which you are most comfortable and skilled. In addition, do not assume that the most cost-effective medium will always get the job done for you and your organization. For example, if you had to communicate to a partner on a sensitive and important matter, you should meet with him or her face-to-face in lieu of communicating via e-mail—a medium devoid of nonverbal cues and privacy.

While electronic communication devices are the right media choice for some situations, they are not the right choice for all situations. We need to be careful not to become so enamored of electronic communication devices that we choose them without thinking, at the expense of effective communication . The concept of information richness (media richness) provides us with a useful way of making effective media choices. *Information richness* refers to how robust a communication medium is. Some communication media are considered to be rich, and some are thought to be lean, while others reside along that continuum. For example, face-to-face communication is the richest form of communication because most people find it to be the most natural way to communicate. In contrast, less-robust media (e.g., text messages, tweets, e-mail messages) are lean media. Such media should be used for routine matters. The trick is to not get too comfortable with any one medium to the point where you use it for most situations without a thought. Let your audience's/receiver's preferences and/or the situation guide you in such decisions.

Finally, there is the question of formality when choosing among the various writing media. Essentially it comes down to determining the level of formality the situation warrants. For example, if the situation you need to address in writing is non-routine and a level of formality is expected, you should turn to business letters and reports and go with a formal tone. On the other hand, if the situation you need to address in writing is routine and formality is not a high expectation, you should consider sending an e-mail message or post to a social media site and go with a less formal, conversational tone.

AUDIENCE EXPECTATIONS

Before sending your message, determine which way your audience would prefer to receive it, then send it that way. Meeting your audience's message expectations helps ensure they receive and read the message promptly. In situations where you are sending written communication to international business partners and are not sure about formality expectations write in a formal style and avoid the conversational tone.

Before sending a message or document, consider whether it is necessary. Most businesspeople are already inundated with too many messages and documents as it is, without having to wade through those that are unnecessary. Here are four tips for deciding when to send a message:

© Korn/Shutterstock.com

1. Avoid writing the message or document if you possibly can.
2. If you must send a message, for every minute you spend considering your message content, spend 10 minutes considering your audience. *How* you say something is *more important* than what you say.[27] Memos and e-mail, especially, are more likely to be perceived as negative and nasty than is verbal communication.[28]
3. Do not assume that written communication is confidential. Assume that your writing will be passed on.
4. Do not falsely equate writing with action. Writing about something is not the same as actually doing something.[29] Do not assume that you are off the hook just because you've written something.

SUMMARY: SECTION 4— CHOOSING THE BEST WRITING MEDIUM FOR THE SITUATION

- There are several media from which to choose when delivering written content. Choose the one that best suits your situation: memo, letter, report, e-mail, text message, blog, website, social networking site (e.g., LinkedIn, Facebook), and Twitter.
- When considering one medium over another, think about your audience's expectations and the necessity of sending the message.

STAGE 2 OF THE WRITING PROCESS: DRAFTING

You have now arrived at Stage 2 of the writing process—the *drafting stage*. You have completed the planning stage and are ready to write.

© vit-plus/Shutterstock.com

When writing the *rough draft*, resist that inner English teacher voice. If you analyze and nit-pick each sentence as you write, your writing will be a slow, tortuous process. Instead, focus on writing what you want and need to say; while not forgetting that during the revising stage you can improve how you say it. While drafting, do not stop to worry over the placement of a comma or creating the perfect phrase. Instead, do your best to keep moving forward, guided by the direction and purpose you have already determined in the planning stage. Matters such as comma placement and perfect phrases are best resolved in the revising stage. As draft copy writers we should take comfort in knowing that there is an arsenal of writing support software readily available to assist us during the revising stage.

Most experts agree that writing a rough draft should take less time than revising. Do not waste precious time during the drafting stage that could be better used during the revision stage—the stage that holds the potential of converting a poor-to-average document into a good-to-excellent one. During the *drafting stage*, just let the ideas flow onto your paper or screen as quickly as possible.

GETTING STARTED: MOVING PAST WRITER'S BLOCK

After defining your purpose, profiling your audience, and organizing your ideas, you are ready to draft your document. However, sometimes no matter how much planning you do, you will have trouble getting started. When this happens, you are experiencing **writer's block** which refers to times when writers have difficulty getting started writing.

writer's block
Describes the situation when a writer has difficulty getting started writing.

© Ollyy/Shutterstock.com

Why does writer's block occur? People experience writer's block for a number of logical and illogical reasons. Some examples are presented in Figure 9-9. Understanding why you experience writer's block will help you recognize the condition and select an approach to help you overcome it.

So, how do you overcome writer's block when it appears to have a stranglehold on you? A good idea is to try an approach that worked for you in the past or that has worked for others. Some examples are presented in Figure 9-10.

Writer's block is something all writers struggle with at times. The trick is to accept that it will happen occasionally, determine the cause, and then control it. In the process, cut yourself some slack. Do not beat up on yourself too much while struggling with writer's block. Instead, tackle the condition logically and move forward with the task at hand.

© Rido/Shutterstock.com

FIGURE 9-10: COMMON WAYS TO OVERCOME WRITER'S BLOCK

- If you do not like to write, give yourself a pep talk and just do it. Just because you do not like to write, does not mean you are a terrible writer.
- If you lack confidence in your writing skills, realize that once you get started and knock out the draft copy, helpful writing assistance software is available.
- If you are a perfectionist, that does not change the fact that you need to knock out a draft copy before working your perfectionistic magic in the revision stage. So, get your hands dirty by writing a typical, imperfect draft copy. In the process of doing so, *freewrite* without concern for spelling, grammar, and punctuation, all of which can be corrected later. Besides, nobody is typically looking at or judging your writing at the draft copy stage. Give your ego a much-needed rest and let the words flow.
- If you are procrastinator, be tough on yourself and do not buy into that cliché that goes, "You do your best writing at the last minute." This is the time for a reality check, which is telling you to get started.
- If you planned poorly and that appears to be at the root of your writer's block, go back and redo the planning stage the right way before attempting to move forward. Your renewed efforts should net you a clear purpose for your writing project, which is an arch enemy of writer's block. While planning, develop an outline. Having an outline in front of you is a good way to overcome writer's block.
- If the document is important and you know it must be well written, do not let fear freeze you. No matter what your hang-ups are, it is likely that you need to get on with it. Much like the procrastinator described above, get tough on yourself. A good starting point is to write the easiest part first, such as the report's cover page or your résumé's contact information section. Those no brainers are painless to write and get your mind and fingers moving.
- If the root of your writer's block is a distraction, either remove the distraction or move to a different location.
- Scheduling uninterrupted blocks of time is a good idea.
- If fatigue is the reason for your writer's block, which is certainly legitimate, set the project down and come back to it when you are rested

© ImageFlow/Shutterstock.com

DRAFTING TO SUPPORT YOUR PURPOSE: TYPES OF SUPPORTING DETAIL

You have come up with your purpose for writing—your main idea—and now you must support it with enough detail to explain your points and support your generalizations. You have to do all this without becoming tedious and losing your reader. Although your supporting details may come naturally to you in routine situations, you should be familiar with the types of support you can use to help your reader understand and accept your purpose. For that reason, make your evidence as specific as possible. Seven common types of supporting detail in business documents are (1) factual evidence, (2) examples, (3) expert opinion, (4) definition, (5) description, (6) analogy, and (7) narration.

Factual Evidence Factual evidence and statistics are the most convincing kinds of support in business documents. To be effective, factual support should clarify and support your purpose.

Examples Giving examples is probably the most common way to develop generalizations, abstract ideas, and unfamiliar concepts. Usually examples do not provide a complete catalog of instances, but give enough to suggest the truth of the idea. In general, the less familiar the concept, the more examples the reader needs to understand the concept.

Expert Opinion The opinion of a recognized authority can add compelling support to your purpose. Expert opinion can be based on primary research (research you have gathered yourself, or expert testimony) or on secondary sources (journals and magazines). Just be sure that the person or source on which you are relying is a recognized authority in your field.

Definition If your audience consists partly or entirely of non-specialists, define technical terms the first time you use them to demystify the reading experience. For example, in a marketing plan to be circulated to an external audience, you would define terms such as *Generation Y* (the 60 million people in the United States born between 1979 and 1994). You might also point out that this population segment is smaller than the 72 million baby boomers that make up their grandparents' generation, but triple the size of Generation X, people born in the United States between 1961 and 1982.

Description Description means using concrete, specific details that appeal to one or more of the five senses (sight, sound, smell, taste, and touch). In business writing, the goal of writing is to convey the information as objectively as possible so the reader and writer interpret the terms and concepts the same way.

Analogy Development of your details by analogy means to draw a comparison between items that appear to have little in common. Business writers use analogies to make the unfamiliar seem familiar, to provide a concrete understanding of an abstract topic, and to help the audience see the idea in a new light.

Narration Supporting with narration means using a story or part of a story to support your purpose. A story is usually arranged in chronological order, starting with what happened first, second, third, etc.

FIGURE 9–11: CAPITALIZING ON WHEN, WHERE, AND WHAT

Writing effectively with a high degree of consistency is challenging for most of us and is even more challenging for those who don't like to write and/or don't feel necessarily skilled at doing so. No matter your attitude about writing and perceived skill level, you can certainly benefit from writing during the time range you do your best writing, at the location where you do your best writing, and using the writing tool with which you do your best writing. That makes sense! Right? In the business place you won't always be able to be as selective, but with the mobility today's electronic communication technologies have provided some of your writing can be done away from the office and even during non-traditional work times.

DRAFTING WITH YOUR AUDIENCE IN MIND: CREATING GOODWILL

unbiased language
Words that do not reinforce a prejudice.

Adapting your message to the needs and wants of your audience contributes to goodwill. You can make your writing reader friendly by developing a tone of goodwill. You create a tone that expresses your goodwill toward your reader by (1) using the you-attitude, (2) emphasizing reader benefits, (3) being positive, (4) using **unbiased language**, and (5) being polite.

DEVELOPING A YOU-ATTITUDE

Developing a **you-attitude** means writing from your reader's point of view. Just as law-yers create empathy for their clients in the minds of the jurors, visualize what your read-ers want or need to know and then write your message in terms of them, substituting *you* for the *I* and *we* of the self-centered or company-oriented messages. Compare the following examples.

Company Oriented: Our company can offer you an environment that is always challeng-ing. We've got the best record in the business.

You Oriented: If you are a hard worker, you should do well here.

Company Oriented: Grassbusters is offering one month of free lawn services if you agree to sign up with our service for one year. Call us now to get your free inspection and quote. We are the best lawn service in town.

You Oriented: You can have your yard perfectly clipped and groomed for one month, absolutely free if you sign up with Grassbuster's top-of-the-line lawn service for one year. You deserve the pride and peace of mind that a perfectly groomed lawn brings. Call today for a quote.

I Oriented: I am sending information on peripheral options available for the computer I sold you.

You Oriented: In the next few days, you'll receive complete details on the capabilities and prices of the options available for your new computer.

When you concentrate on the reader, you are putting your empathy skills to work for you. No matter your field, you need to empathize with your audience. For example, accounting firm recruiters use client-responsiveness writing exercises as assessment tools in the hiring of new accountants.[30] Accounting firms believe students need to learn how to respond sensitively to client needs. Similar concerns surface in the insurance industry where writing letters that are legally proper yet still convey a sense of humanity and caring is a constant challenge.[31]

Whatever your goal, your readers will appreciate a warm and sincere tone.

> **you-attitude**
> Writing from your audience's point of view.

ABUSING THE YOU-ATTITUDE

Overuse of the you-attitude can make you sound pushy: Imagine a staccato voice barking out the following message. "Do you have a job? Do you have 99 dollars? Do you want a new car? Then this is your lucky day, baby!" Sound familiar? This is a good example of how over-using *you* can turn off your audience by making them feel manipulated.

In a more apt example, Brockman and Belanger showed that in letters asking recruiters to participate in a résumé research project, phrases designed to emphasize the reader, like "influential firm" rather than "firm" and "your valuable service" as opposed to simply "your advice," were viewed in many cases as "blatant attempts at flattery and manipulation." In Brockman and Belanger's study, the recruiters preferred the letter without these phrases.[32]

When giving criticism, using *you* can sound too blunt. Using *you* in an accusatory way could offend your reader.

Blunt: You can rest assured that with the old damage on your car, no dealer would ever think of offering you anything near book value.

Less Blunt: The old damage on your car will make it difficult to get full value for your car.

Blunt: You really made a mess of that presentation.

Less Blunt: Presentations can be tricky. Let's see what steps can be taken to improve your next one.

When criticizing another person's performance, it is best to leave out the "you." Concentrate on how your reader can improve, rather than pointing out his or her mistakes.

DEVELOPING READER BENEFITS

A second way to create a tone of goodwill in your message is to emphasize reader benefits. Reader benefits can improve and sustain business relationships with those inside and outside your organization.

© Dirima/Shutterstock.com

Motivation theorists have shown that sources of motivation can be either extrinsic or intrinsic. Extrinsic motivators are external to the person and include tangible rewards like a bonus of $2,000 or a free gift with immediate renewal.

Intrinsic motivators must meet the internal, psychological needs of the person and include:

- stimulating intellectual curiosity by explaining the importance of an action or task

- being aware of your audience's ego needs; giving informal verbal praise or soliciting suggestions can build feelings of self-worth and enhance self-esteem, making the work challenging or interesting.[33]

Identifying reader benefits helps you determine what points to emphasize in your message. First determine how your policy, product, or service will meet your reader's needs. Second, using both intrinsic and extrinsic motivators, determine what will motivate your reader to become interested in your project. Third, choose one or two benefits that will most likely motivate your reader to take action and emphasize them in your supporting points.[34]

EMPHASIZING THE POSITIVE

Another way to create a tone of goodwill is to emphasize the positive rather than the negative. Emphasize what you or your organization can do rather than what you cannot do. In the following examples, the negative and abrupt tone in the first sentence is changed to a positive tone in the second. Words such as *no, do not, cannot, should not, failed*, and *ruined* have no power to change the situation for the better. Whenever possible, then, choose positive language that motivates your audience to new ways of thinking and new courses of action. In the following examples notice how the change from negative to positive changes your attitude about the writer and your motivation to take action.

© StockLite/Shutterstock.com

Negative: *You failed to pay your American Express bill due December 31. Failure to pay this bill by January 10, 20xx will result in your credit rating being negatively affected. You must resolve this matter immediately.*

Positive: *Please check to see whether you have mailed your American Express payment, due December 31. Continuing to pay on time will protect your outstanding credit rating.*

Negative Words	Positive Words
Claim	Appreciate
Blame	Benefit
Cannot	Can
Problem	Pleased
Complaint	Thoughtful reply/request
We cannot	We'll be happy to
We do not	We'll do what we can

Avoid double negatives. Using two or more negatives, like *not, no, except, less than, not less than*, in the same sentence obscures the meaning. Consider the following example from an English newspaper:

It is surely less painful to be unemployed if one is not sober, drug-free, and filled with a desire to work.

The double negative puts a strain on the reader who may give up trying to figure out what's really being said. Put in the positive, the sarcasm behind the message is easier to understand.

It is surely painful to be unemployed if one is sober, drug-free, and filled with a desire to work.

or

It is surely less painful to be unemployed if one is drunk, hooked on drugs, and does not want to work.

This sentence from an insurance policy, "Persons other than the primary beneficiary may not receive these dividends," could easily be rewritten in the positive for clarity: Only the primary beneficiary may receive these dividends.

Use euphemisms with care. To be positive, a writer must sometimes use euphemisms, mild words substituted for words with negative connotations. For example, in the United States you rarely hear someone ask you for directions to the nearest *toilet*. The *restroom, Ladies' or Men's Room,* and *bathroom* are all euphemisms in American culture for *toilet*.

Mild Word	Negative Equivalent
Senior citizen	Elderly
Exfoliate	Wipe off dead skin cells
Bathroom tissue	Toilet paper
Perspiration	Sweat

doublespeak
Language that appears to say something but really does not.

While euphemisms foster positive and polite communication, they also distort the actual meaning of something, making it seem better or worse than it really is. In corporate America the use of euphemisms has been taken to extremes of corporate doublespeak. **Doublespeak** is a language that appears to say something but really does not. It is evasive and misleading. A company that fires half of its workforce may try to hide that fact behind terms like *cost rationalization* and *volume-related production adjustment schedule*, or more recently, to *rightsize*. In doublespeak, *kickbacks* become *rebates* and *financial losses* become *deficit enhancements*. No one gets fired anymore; instead they are *involuntarily terminated*.[35] When you write ethically, you avoid language that misleads your readers. Avoid using words as a way to circumvent the truth. Be precise when you write.

Popular buzzwords also fit into the doublespeak category, like *empowerment, synergy, competitive dynamics*, and *re-engineering*. Although these examples make euphemisms sound like something writers must avoid, usage experts agree that, on the other hand, euphemisms can be used to avoid causing pain or embarrassment. On the whole, though, cut out the meaningless word or phrase and substitute effective, meaningful content.

USING UNBIASED LANGUAGE

As we settle into the 21st century, discrimination lawsuits are everywhere. With universal efforts to end discrimination, businesses have a responsibility to avoid discriminatory slurs. Misuse of terms is perceived as biased and insensitive behavior. Create goodwill by avoiding language that may offend your readers and that may be construed as bias, sexism, or stereotyping.[36]

Use Sex-Neutral Terms to Avoid Sexist Language Would you use the following sentence in your annual Christmas message informing your entire workforce—men and women, alike—of their upcoming Christmas bonuses?

All saleswomen can expect to receive their bonuses on December 23. As usual you have all done a terrific job.

You probably would not say this since it likely excludes half your workforce. Similarly, using language like *salesman, businessman*, and *workman* builds a barrier between you and half your readers, a barrier that diminishes the impact of your message. Replace terms that contain the word *man* with words that represent people of either gender. Use the same label for everyone in a particular group. Avoid referring to a woman as a *chairperson* yet calling a man a *chairman*.

Sex-Specific Words	Sex-Neutral Words
Actress	Actor
Authoress	Author
Chairman, chairwoman	Chair or chairperson
Craftsmen	Craft workers, artisans
Foreman, forelady	Supervisor
Hostess	Host
Man, mankind	Human beings, people, humans
Man-hours	working hours, work hours
Salesman	Sales agent, sales representative
Workman	Worker

Avoid *He* to Refer to Both Men and Women To avoid this, use *he or she* or reword the sentence using the plural form. You can also reword the sentence to leave out the pronoun entirely.

Rather than these:
Each person did **his** job quickly.
The typical accountant … **he**

Write these:
Each person did **his** or **her** job quickly.
The **engineers** did **their** jobs quickly.
The typical accountant … **he or she**
Typical accountants … **they**

Avoid Racial and Ethnic Bias Avoid identifying someone by his or her race or ethnic origin unless it is relevant to the matter being discussed.

Rather than:
Dr. Mendoza is an intelligent and industrious Hispanic.

Write this:
Dr. Mendoza is intelligent and industrious.

Examples of Bias
http://www.writeex-
press.com/bias.html

Rather than these:
James Miller, an African-American accountant, will supervise the audit.
Roderick, the Russian stockbroker, saw red when the market crashed yesterday. (The color "red" implies Russia's Communist past.)

Write these:
James Miller will supervise the audit.
Roderick, the Russian stockbroker, was upset when the market crashed yesterday.

Avoid Age Bias Mention a person's age only when it is relevant, and avoid using adjectives that stereotype the person.

Rather than these:
Jenny Brown, 53 and spry, joined our human resources department yesterday.
Goldie Hawn sure looks great for her age.

Write these:
Jenny Brown joined our human resources department yesterday.
Goldie Hawn sure looks great.

Avoid Disabilities Bias If you must refer to a person's physical, mental, emotional, or sensory impairments, always refer to the whole person first and the disability second. Avoid outdated usages such as *crippled, retarded,* and *handicapped.*

Rather than:
William Robinson, the crippled worker, will start work on Monday.
Please reserve this parking space for disabled customers.

Write this:
William Robinson will start work on Monday.
Please reserve this parking space for customers who are disabled.

The goal of bias-free writing is to concentrate on an individual's unique characteristics, not on stereotypical assumptions about what or who an individual is or what he or she can or cannot do.

Being Polite A third way to create a positive tone in your message is to be civil and polite. Being polite is a way to enhance your *ethos* (your attitude toward your reader). Ethos is the most important factor in persuading an audience. When you are polite, you project a sincere and credible image to your audience.

Business writing demands diplomacy. A recent study revealed that 90 percent of the American public surveyed felt that incivility is a serious problem. While the business world was thought to be one of the last "bastions of civility," it, too, has started to reflect the informality of society at large, as organizations have flattened and gone casual.[37]

As incivility escalates, so do instances of workplace aggression and violence. Since most people want to do business with those who treat them with respect and courtesy, civility is fundamental to the successful operation of any business.

Some supervisors enjoy intimidating employees by treating them rudely because the supervisors fear losing clout; however, according to management experts, being polite increases employees' and clients' respect. Most people respond favorably to being treated with respect and are more willing to go the extra mile for someone who is courteous and acts professionally. In addition, appropriate business behavior directly and indirectly enhances your company's bottom line, since clients and customers are more likely to do repeat business with a company that makes them feel they are being treated fairly and courteously.[38] Therefore, soften your words when pointing out someone else's mistakes or requesting action.

Blunt: Where's my order? I demand a response within the hour!

Better: I placed order #1254 with you last Friday, May 3. Please let us know as soon as possible when we can expect delivery.

Blunt: You can't go near that stupid copier without jamming it. Maybe you better just stop using it.

Better: The copier jams easily when it is overheated. Please run your copies later when it has cooled down.

Blunt: This is second time you've sent out duplicate billings to Mr. Smith. I can't believe you are this unorganized. Can't you learn the system? Mr. Smith is hopping mad!

Better: Why not let me show you again how we handle billings so that we don't send duplicates. Sending duplicates really annoys some clients.

In terms of writing, politeness means using the common conventions of courteous expression:

- I would appreciate it if you could get back to me before 5 today.
- Thank you for your continued business. We appreciate it.
- Please have the report to me by 5 today.

Writing requires more tact than does speaking. When you are speaking face-to-face, your message can be softened by a smile, a twinkle in your eye, your tone of voice, or your inflection. Plus you have the immediate feedback of the other person's nonverbal behavior.

Usually you can tell if you have inadvertently hurt someone's feelings, in which case you can immediately remedy the situation with a quick apology. In contrast, writing does not provide this kind of immediate feedback. You may never know that you hurt a person's feelings with your hasty and tactless message, as in the following example of an e-mail requesting information for a meeting.

Date: Monday, 7 May 201__ 13:30
From: Jack Crumb
To: Linda Jacobs
Subject: Today's Meeting

Linda,

This afternoon you'd better remember to bring those reports on the Deer Lake project with you. I don't want to waste time like we did at the last meeting while you go back to your office and look for them. We just don't have that kind of time around here.

Jack

In the revised example, the writer communicates his message just as effectively without offending the reader.

Date: Monday, 7 May 201__ 13:30
From: Jack Crumb
To: Linda Jacobs
Subject: Today's Meeting

Linda,

This is just to remind you to please bring the reports on the Deer Lake project with you to the meeting this afternoon. We'll need to go over them right after we get started.

Thanks, and see you there.

Jack

Another way to use courtesy effectively when writing messages is to open your message politely. This is especially good advice when writing to those with higher status and power. As a writer, be aware of the differences in status and power between you and your audience. In general, as differences in status or power increase between the writer and the audience, so does the level of courtesy used by the writer toward the more powerful audience.[40] Words and phrases such as *please*, *thank you*, and *I would appreciate it if* … go a long way toward softening an overly direct tone.

Avoid using too many indirect strategies in one sentence since doing so sounds like you are groveling: "I apologize ahead of time for asking this, but please, if at all possible, could you submit your report by Friday?"[41]

DRAFTING WITH ORGANIZATION IN MIND: BUILDING PARAGRAPHS

Paragraphs are chunks of information that support the purpose of your message. In business writing, your main concern is writing so that your reader can easily understand your message. Paragraphs signal a pause between ideas. One way to think about paragraphs is as chunks of information in your document. Each sentence in the chunk relates to the other. In general, business paragraphs are short—no more than three or four sentences—unified, and coherent.

PARAGRAPH UNITY

The *topic* or *lead sentence* is the umbrella that covers all the other sentences in the paragraph. It tells your reader what is in the paragraph. A good topic sentence tells readers what is to follow and enables skimming.

Business contexts call for a variety of expository documents, documents that provide information. You might write a proposal to persuade your boss to update your department's computers, or you might explain a newly acquired computer program to your coworkers. In these cases you could start your paragraphs with *It's easy. … It will save us time. … It's fun. … It's secure. …* or *It will improve profits.* The topic sentences tip off your reader to the information in each paragraph before getting into the nitty-gritty details.[42]

Not all paragraphs in business documents are expository, and not all paragraphs need topic sentences. Instead, they might be narrative or process (how-to) oriented. Narratives tell a story about what happened; process messages tell people what to do. In both cases, organize your details chronologically along a timeline: Process—First, do this, second do this. Narrative—First this happened, next this happened, and so on.

Another time that you do not need a topic sentence is when your topic is too long to cover in three or four sentences. Rather than writing a 10–20 sentence paragraph, break the material into information chunks. Just be sure that each chunk conveys only one idea.[43]

Finally, as writing expert Donald M. Murray points out in *The Craft of Revision*, while you should fulfill reader expectations by making clear the main point of the paragraph, don't sacrifice clarity and content to achieve this goal with a "single, superheroic topic sentence."[44] In other words do not lose sight of your message in an effort to fit the content of your paragraph to the topic sentence.

PARAGRAPH DEVELOPMENT

© Igor S. Srdanovic/Shutterstock.com

Develop the idea in your topic sentence with sentences that illustrate or support it. Once you have written your topic sentence, ask yourself, "Why or how do I know this is true?" Your answer will suggest how to develop the paragraph. Just remember that all the sentences in the paragraph should develop or relate to the paragraph's main idea.

You can develop your idea in a variety of ways. Further, a single paragraph may include more than one development method. Use examples and illustrations, comparison and contrast, cause and effect, process, narration, and problem and solution to develop your paragraphs.

These common methods of development reflect our thinking processes. They are not magic.[45] The main point is to stay focused on developing one idea per paragraph, so that you do not overload your readers' comprehension circuits or confuse them by presenting more than one point without developing every one.

Avoid relying on one- to two-sentence paragraphs. The way you develop a paragraph reflects your thought processes, so you probably would not want to write a document, especially a complex one, with a long series of short, one- to two-sentence paragraphs. This suggests inadequate development, which in turn, reflects a need for more thought.

PARAGRAPH COHERENCE

In any business message, sentences and paragraphs should be coherent, that is, they should flow from one to the next without discernible shifts or gaps in thought. Readers new to the material immediately recognize coherence violations, but writers often do not. Why? Because as you write, you make mental connections between your sentences and paragraphs that you may not put down on paper. When you revise, those mental connections are still there, so once again, you may miss shifts and gaps in thought.

You can improve your coherence by thinking in terms of your readers' expectations. As you write from your readers' point of view, strengthen the ties between what the readers have already read and what they are about to read, what you have written and are about to write, and the old and new material.[46] Three techniques for improving your coherence are (1) repeating key words and phrases, (2) maintaining consistency, and (3) providing transitions.

1. Repeating key words and phrases is one of the most common ways to connect thoughts within paragraphs and documents because repetition helps your reader keep the old information in mind while acquiring new information in the next sentence or paragraph. However, too much repetition can be dull. Therefore, use pronouns that refer to the key word (dogs … they) or synonyms (canines).

2. Maintaining consistency in point of view and verb tense is an important part of writing a coherent document. When the writer shifts back and forth from one point of view to another (*one* to *I* to *you*, or third person to first person to second person) and from one verb tense to another (present to past), the reader becomes confused about who is doing what and when. It is less confusing to pick one point of view—first, second, or third person—and stick with it. Similarly, unless there is a reason to use more than one tense, stay with one tense.

3. Transitions are signposts that point your reader in the right direction. Words and phrases such as *first, second, third, and, although, first, however,* and *in addition* show relationships between your ideas and tell your readers how to connect them. Words and phrases such as *consequently* and *as a result* show cause-and-effect relationships, whereas words such as *similarly* and *likewise* show comparisons. In addition, phrases such as *for example* and *in other words* signal that illustrations of points just made are forthcoming.

Be sure to select the transition that fits the overall tone of your document; for example, *in short* has a perfunctory, formal tone, while *so* could be used in more informal writing such as e-mail.

Finally, to link paragraphs within a document, use the same transitional devices that connect sentences within a paragraph. Repeating a key term, using signposts, and maintaining a consistent point of view and tense help you transition smoothly from one paragraph to the next.

SUMMARY: SECTION 7— DRAFTING WITH ORGANIZATION IN MIND: BUILDING PARAGRAPHS

- Paragraphs are chunks of information that support the purpose of your message.
- A good paragraph should be relatively short—no more than 100 words.
- The lead sentence or topic sentence in an expository paragraph lets the reader know what the paragraph is about.
- A paragraph should develop one main idea.
- Paragraphs need transitional devices to connect ideas.

MANAGING THE DRAFTING PROCESS IN ORGANIZATIONS

The process of drafting documents in an organization can be overwhelming if you are inexperienced at doing so. One way writers handle drafting is by document modeling.

DOCUMENT MODELING

document modeling The process whereby workplace writers use documents or parts of documents already written for a similar situation as a template for their own writing.

model document An existing document written for a similar situation

boilerplate language Text used again and again in similar situations.

One of the key ways workplace writers draft documents is through the process of **document modeling**. Document modeling is a process whereby workplace writers use documents or parts of documents that have already been written for a similar situation as a template for their own writing. Because of the pressure to write quickly, writers use **model documents** and **boilerplate language** (language that has been used in other documents of the same type).[47]

Watch for two common problems when using language from other documents. Inexperienced writers often cut and paste whole sections of other documents into their own without attention to the clash of differing writing styles and tones. In this case, the final document will not sound like a coherent, unified document. Instead, it will read like a hodge-podge of documents by different writers. Create smooth transitions between the boilerplate sections and your own ideas so the gaps do not show.[48]

The writing in the "file-cabinet" models may be outdated, bloated, and unorganized, so choose your models carefully with your readers in mind.[53] Do not allow boilerplating to be an excuse for not thinking through the new situation. A hodge-podge results in a document that does not meet the needs of the new audience or the unique needs of the situation. Selling points that you could emphasize in the new proposal are ignored when you use boilerplating as a crutch that offers a seemingly quick and easy solution to a complex rhetorical problem.[50]

SUMMARY: SECTION 8— MANAGING THE DRAFTING PROCESS IN ORGANIZATIONS

- Document modeling is a technique new writers in organizations use to help them adapt to the organizational writing style and document format.
- Using large sections of boilerplate language from other documents is no excuse for not thinking about the new writing situation and meeting its unique requirements. When you don't think things through, your document suffers.

Notes

1. Donald Samson, "Writing in High-Tech Firms," in *Professional Writing in Context*, eds. J. F. Reynolds, C. B. Matalene, J. N. Magnotto, D. C. Samson, Jr., and L. V. Sadler (Hillsdale, NJ: Lawrence Erlbaum, 1995), 97–127.

2. Pamela A. Angell, *Business Communication Design: Creativity, Strategies, and Solutions*, 2nd ed. (Boston, MA: McGraw Hill Irwin, 2007), 193.

3. J. C. Mathes and Dwight W. Stevenson, *Designing Technical Reports* (Needham Heights, NY: Macmillan, 1991), 107.

4. Ibid, 68.

5. Securities and Exchange Commission, *A Plain English Handbook*, http://www.sec.gov/pdf/handbook.pdf

6. Mathes and Stevenson, 42–43.

7. Ibid.

8. Mary Munter, *A Guide to Managerial Communication* (Upper Saddle River, NJ: Prentice Hall, 2000), 11.

9. Kitty O. Locker, *Business and Administrative Communication* (New York: McGraw Hill, 1999), 60.

10. Munter, 12.

11. Ibid.

12. Ibid., 14.

13. Ibid., 13.

14. Ibid., 11.

15. Janice C. Redish, Robbin M. Battison, and Edward S. Gold, "Making Information Accessible to Readers," in *Writing in Nonacademic Settings*, eds. Lee Odell and Dixie Goswami (New York: The Guilford Press, 1985), 129–53.

16. John S. Fielden and Ron E. Dulek, "How to Use Bottom-Line Writing in Corporate Communication," in *Strategies for Business and Technical Writing*, ed. Kevin J. Harty (Boston: Allyn & Bacon, 1991), 179–88.

17. Alec Appelbaum, "The Evils of E-mail," *CIO Magazine* (December 1, 2000), www.cio.com/archives.

18. John S. Fielden, "What Do You Mean You Don't Like My Style?" *Harvard Business Review* (March–June, 1982): 7.

19. Ibid.

20. Fred Reynolds, "What Adult Work-World Writers Have Taught Me about Work-World Writing," in *Professional Writing in Context* (Hillsdale, NJ: Lawrence Erlbaum, 1995), 19.

21. Ibid.

22. Barry Eckhouse, *Competitive Communication* (New York: Oxford University Press, 1999), 28.

23. Marian M. Extejt, "Teaching Students to Correspond Effectively Electronically," *Business Communication Quarterly* 61, no. 2 (1998): 57–67.

24. Malcolm Forbes, "How to Write a Business Letter," in *Strategies for Business and Technical Writing,*" ed. Kevin J. Harty (Boston: Allyn & Bacon, 1999), 108–11.

25. Peggy Post and Peter Post, *The Etiquette Advantage in Business* (New York: HarperCollins, 1999), 314.

26. Ruth Davidhizar and Sally Erdel, "Send Me a Memo on It; or Better Yet, Don't," *The Health Care Supervisor* 15, no. 4 (June 1997): 42–47.

27. Richard A. Wueste, "Memos on the Loose," *Manager's Notebook* (September/October 1988): 39–40.

28. Davidhizar and Erdel, 3.

29. Wueste, 39.

30. Faye Bradwick, "Writing Skills of New Accounting Hires: The Message Is Mixed," *The Tax Advisor* 28 (August 1997): 518–21.

31. Gary Blake, "Making Insurance Documents Readable and Friendly," *LIMRA's Market Facts* 18, no.1 (January/February 1999): 15–16.

32. Elizabeth B. Brockman and Kelly Belanger, "You-Attitude and Positive Emphasis," *Bulletin of the Association for Business Communication* 56, no. 2 (June 1993): 1–9.

33. W. Huitt, "Motivation," http://chiron.valdosta.edu/whuitt/col/motivation/motivate.html.

34. Locker, 72–73.

35. "William Lutz Talks about How Doublespeak Has Taken Over the Businessworld," *Business News: New Jersey* 11, no. 4 (January 1988): 13.

36. Judy E. Pickens, "Terms of Equality: A Guide to Bias-Free Language," *Personnel Journal* (August 1985), 24.

37. Lynne Andersson and Christine Pearson, "Tit for Tat: The Spiraling Effect of Incivility in the Workplace," *Academy of Management Review* 24, no. 3 (1999): 453.

38. Ibid, 470–75.

39. Kathryn Riley, Kim S. Campbell, Alan Manning, and Frank Parker, *Revising Professional Writing* (Superior, WI: Parley Press, 1999), 97–99.

40. Ibid., 98.

41. John Clayton, "When to Use a Topic Sentence—and When Not To," *Harvard Management Communication Letter* (March 2001): 3.

42. Ibid., 4.

43. Ibid.

44. Diana Hacker, *The Bedford Handbook for Writers* (New York: St. Martin's Press, 1991), 83.

45. Hacker, 99.

46. Mark Mabrito, "From Workplace to Classroom: Teaching Professional Writing," *Business Communication Quarterly* 62, no. 3 (September 1999): 103.

47. Glenn J. Broadhead and Richard C. Freed, *The Variables of Composition: Process and Product in a Business Setting* (Carbondale: Southern Illinois University Press, 1986), 57–58.

48. Lee Clark Johns, "The File Cabinet Has a Sex-Life: Insights of a Professional Writing Consultant," in *Strategies for Business and Technical Writing*, ed. Kevin J. Harty (Boston: Allyn & Bacon, 1999), 145–76.

49. Broadhead and Freed, 57.

REVISING BUSINESS DOCUMENTS

LEARNING OUTCOMES

After reading this chapter, you should be able to:

1. Identify the three stylistic choices for business documents and when to use each.

2. Discuss techniques for revising a document/message's purpose, introduction, and conclusions.

3. Describe ways to revise formatting.

4. Discuss how to revise for tone.

5. Describe several proofreading strategies.

6. Describe how to give and take writing criticism effectively.

© arka38/Shutterstock.com

SELECT KEY TERMS

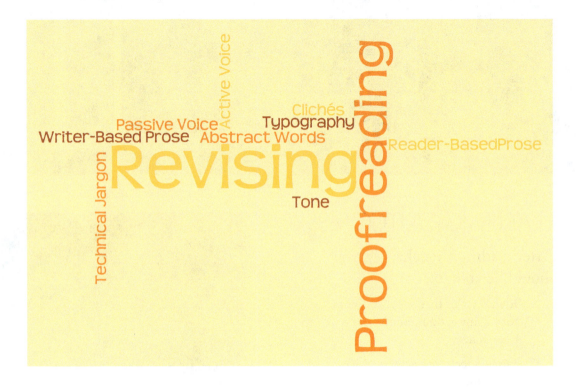

INTRODUCTION

The focus now turns to identifying weaknesses in draft copies of business documents and then making the related revisions. For example, business writers often identify issues pertaining to organization, reader-centered prose, tone, word choice, sentence structure, and/or spelling. By making needed revisions, a business writer typically improves document quality as well as reinforces his or her professional image.

The intent of this chapter is to provide you with information on how to effectively revise draft copies of business documents, including how to manage the revision process in organizations. These goals are realized through discussions of the following topics: stage three of the writing process, revising, revising for organization, revising for your audience: style and tone, proofreading, and managing the revision process in organizations.

STAGE 3 OF THE WRITING PROCESS: REVISING

You have a rough draft of your document, and now it is time to improve its clarity and quality. Doing so involves three steps: editing, revising, and proofreading. **Editing** involves reviewing the rough draft with the purpose of determining where it can be improved. **Revising** involves making written changes/improvements based on what was determined when editing. **Proofreading** involves conducting a final review of the revised document to catch oversights that need correcting such as misspellings. Most writers revise in tandem with editing. In other words, they identify something in need of change and revise it right then before moving on. It is during the revising stage that the greatest potential for quality writing occurs, which is why writing experts agree that writers should spend more time editing, revising, and proofreading documents than they spend on drafting them.

Lastly, give the document a good proofreading with the purpose of identifying and correcting all those oversights you overlooked while editing. It seems that no matter how thorough we are while editing and revising documents, we often overlook one or more silly errors (e.g., spelling errors, grammar errors, transposed words, etc.). This is where a "last-pass round" of proofreading typically saves the day. Proofreading suggestions are shared later in this chapter.

Some businesspeople finish the draft writing stage with one idea in mind—sending the document out then and there.[1] They believe rewriting is a needless, time-consuming activity. Or, they think that editing and revising means simply moving some words around, correcting a few typos, inserting a comma or two, and then sending the document the second they've made the last change.

Unfortunately, many documents are not ready to go anywhere—least of all to your manager or client—at this stage. While the punctuation may be perfect, the ideas may be confused, the tone may be wrong, and the style may be too ornate to be read easily. The reader of this unrevised document is frustrated and puzzled, rather than informed or persuaded.

To avoid bearing the brunt of your manager's frustration or your client's confusion, revise your document carefully before you send it up the chain of command or to an outside audience. Ideally, you should let your rough draft sit for a while after you finish. This helps you gain perspective on it.

editing Reviewing the rough draft with the purpose of determining where it can be improved.

revising Making written changes and/or improvements to a draft copy of a document.

proofreading A final review of a document to catch oversights in need of correction such as misspellings.

Many times at work, however, you do not have time to let it sit for a day, a few hours, or even a few minutes. In that case, reread your message, but from your readers' perspective. Good editing and revising is the act of anticipating how your readers will respond and adjusting the text to get the response you hope for.[2]

A logical approach to the revision process helps you move through it more quickly. One way to approach revision is to work from the general to the specific, concentrating on the global issues first—content and organization—and then moving to local issues, like style and tone, sentence structure and word choice, and grammar and punctuation. Otherwise, you waste time refining sentences and words that you may eventually cut when you make structural changes.

REVISING FOR CONTENT

The first thing to look at is the clarity of your purpose. Is it clear what you want your audience to do or think after reading your document? Have you immediately answered the reader's question: "What's this all about?" or "So what?"

Sometimes your purpose is hiding in the middle or at the end of your document, rather than at the beginning. In that case, cut and paste your purpose into the first paragraph (unless you are using the indirect organizational plan). Here are some revision tips to help the reader figure out why you are writing.[3]

Problem: As you reread, you find a sentence in the final paragraph that says: "This memo was written to document …" or "… "which is why I have written this letter."

Solution: State the purpose of your memo or letter in the first or second line of the document.

Problem: The first paragraph introduces your topic but does not include your intention. For instance, "I am responding to your letter of January 8, 20xx."

Solution: State your reason for writing along with your topic: "In response to your letter of January 8, 20xx, I am writing to clarify the firm's policy on past due accounts."

Problem: You notice that the subject line of your memo conveys only the topic: "Re: Recommendation."

Solution: Rewrite the subject line to specifically reflect your purpose for writing: "Re: Recommendation--Susan Jones."

Problem: Your letter or memo tells a story but makes no clear point or recommendation about why you are telling the story.

Solution: At the beginning of your memo or letter, state your purpose for telling the story: "In light of Ms. Jones' performance record and in light of a recent customer complaint, I recommend that we terminate Ms. Jones."

REVISING THE INTRODUCTION

After making sure your purpose is clear, reread the introduction. Have you gained your audience's attention in addition to clearly stating your purpose? If you are providing your audience with important information, be sure you included that information in the first or second line of your opening. In an instructional document, proposal, or action-oriented message, you may need to entice your readers to keep on reading. In this case, you want to mention the advantages first—what's in it for them to keep reading—before you discuss the action you want them to take. This gives your readers a reason for taking the action recommended.[4]

The following SkillPath Seminars' letter, addressed to managers and supervisors, correctly opens with examples of what their seminars can do for you:

When a worker's behavior or performance is not acceptable, it is important that you step in and get things back on track right away.

The cost of unsatisfactory job performance is staggering—and often comes in ways that are hard to measure. Performance and behavior problems take their toll in terms of lost productivity, inferior products and services, wasted management time and low worker morale.[5]

The letter continues with actions you can take to alleviate these problems, all to be revealed by attending their seminar on dealing with problem employees.

REVISING THE BODY

The body can be anywhere from one to hundreds of pages long. Trying to figure out where to fit in a seemingly ill-fitting but essential point or figuring out when to cut a point that pops up in every other section can be a daunting task.[6] However, if you constructed an outline before you began, go through your document, comparing it point for point against the outline. Check to see if your evidence is strong enough to support the point you have made and if it is accurate.

If you have included irrelevant information or omitted essential information, you should be able to catch it as you move through the document. This is also the time to test your original outline. Perhaps you find additional but essential information since constructing the outline. If so, change the outline as you revise the document itself.[7] The main thing here is to ensure your evidence is logical and convincing, and that it clearly supports your purpose.

REVISING THE CONCLUSION

The document's conclusion is your last chance to inform or to persuade your reader. If your reader has had time to read only your opening and closing, then your closing had better be strong. Do not risk a weak, ineffective ending.

The information in your conclusion depends on the kind of document you are writing. A routine letter or memo may simply end positively with a look to the future: "If you need further explanation or more materials, please contact Betty at ext. 321, between 8 and 5, Monday through Wednesday."

On the other hand, if you are writing a substantial report or proposal, include both a summary section, in which you summarize your main points, and a conclusion, in which you draw conclusions from the points you have made. Here are some techniques to help you make your conclusion get results.[8]

1. Be sure your conclusion eases the reader out of the subject gracefully without an abrupt end that leaves the reader wondering, "Where's the rest of the information?"
2. Especially in longer documents, reinforce the main points in your conclusion (since this is the only chance for the skimmer to get them), and use your conclusion to point to the implications of your main points. For example, a memo that offers solutions to the problem of low employee morale could close with suggestions on how these solutions will improve employee morale, which in turn, would eventually improve the company's bottom line.
3. Create document unity and refer to a theme introduced at the beginning of the document, effectively bringing the reader back to where he or she began.
4. Avoid bringing up new issues in your conclusion.
5. Balance your conclusion with the rest of the document. If you have a 300-word document with a 200-word conclusion, you are belaboring your conclusion. On the other hand, do not end a 5,000-word document with a quick sentence. The goal is to achieve a graceful exit, easing the reader out of the message.
6. Revise for ethical lapses.

FIGURE 10-1: WRITER'S CHECKLIST: ETHICAL WRITING

To avoid ethical problems, ask the following questions as you revise your writing:

- Is the document truthful? Scrutinize findings and conclusions carefully. Make sure the data supports them.
- Am I acting in my employer's best interest? My client's or the public's best interest? My own best long-term interest? Your writing reflects on you and your employer. Review it from the perspective of its intended effect. When possible, ask someone outside your company to review and comment on what you wrote.
- What if everybody acted or communicated in this way? Apply the Golden Rule (Treat others as you would like them to treat you). If you were the intended audience, would the message be acceptable and respectful?
- Am I willing to take responsibility, publicly and privately, for what the document says? Will you stand behind what you have written? To your employer? To your family and friends?
- Does the document violate anyone's rights? Have people from different backgrounds review your writing. Have you considered their perspective?
- Am I ethically consistent in my writing? Only by the consistent application of ethical principles can you meet this standard.

Source: Gerald J. Alred, Charles T. Brusaw, and Walter E. Oliu, The Business Writer's Handbook (New York: St. Martin's Press, 2000), 227.

SUMMARY: SECTION 1—
STAGE 3 OF THE WRITING PROCESS: REVISING

- The revision stage is essential to improving the quality and clarity of your rough draft. Take a logical approach to revising your document, moving from general issues—content and organization—to specific issues—style and tone, sentence structure and word choice, and proofreading.
- When revising, be sure your document is clear about what you want your reader to do or think after reading your document.
- When revising the introduction, be sure it will grab your audience's attention.
- When revising the body of your document, check it against the points on your outline to ensure that you have included all relevant evidence and excluded all that is irrelevant.
- When revising the conclusion of your document, be sure your conclusion eases your reader out of your document without adding new information.

REVISING FOR ORGANIZATION

Revising for organization helps your reader better understand your document.

REVISE WRITER-CENTERED WRITING INTO READER-CENTERED WRITING

First drafts often contain writer-based prose. **Writer-based prose** is writing that focuses on the writer's thinking processes rather than on the readers' questions or needs. One reason first drafts often contain writer-based prose is because that is when writers talk themselves through a problem on paper, exploring their knowledge of the problem, or when writers put their ideas down on paper.[9] The readers' needs are forgotten for the time being. This often happens when writers are uncertain about the topic and are unsure what their readers expect.

One way to spot writer-based prose is to look for loosely connected ideas in narrative form. Sometimes writers record everything they know about the topic or report what they have done rather than what it means, leaving readers to wade through the text looking for the information they need.[10] Or look for places where the writer is trying to answer his or her own question (What will I do?) rather than focusing on the reader's question (What will you do for me?)[11] For example, a new auditor may try to retell the history of an audit rather than offer an analysis of his or her findings. This leaves the busy reader thinking "so what?" or "where's the bottom line?"

Reader-based prose emphasizes the information that the reader needs or expects to find. One way to test your document for a reader-based structure is to check for cues that reveal your plan to your reader. Readers expect to find cues in:

- The introduction, e.g., main idea and preview of points
- The first sentence of each paragraph
- The transition words that you use: *further, finally, nevertheless, to illustrate, first, second, third,* etc.

writer-based prose
Writing that focuses on the writer's thinking processes and needs rather than on the reader's questions or needs.

reader-based prose
Writing that answers the reader's questions and/or emphasizes information the reader needs or expects to find.

- The headings. Readers prefer headings that address the concerns they bring to the document. So rather than "Eligibility Determination" or "Policy Termination," try "Who Is an Eligible Student Borrower?" or "Can This Policy Be Cancelled?"[12]

Another way to test your structure for reader-based prose is to see if you followed through on the promises you made. As you read your text, see that key points are supported with the necessary details.[13]

For example, imagine you are writing an internal report that justifies the expense of an instant messaging service. In paragraph three, you promise to discuss two factors that show how an instant messaging service will save your company money. Check to see if the paragraph does indeed discuss the two factors with the detail necessary to convince even a skeptical audience. If you have not fulfilled your promise to your reader, revise the paragraph, making it reader based.

REVISE THE FORMAT FOR A READER-FRIENDLY DOCUMENT

The format of your document refers to (1) the arrangement of the text on the page—the **layout**—and (2) the visual features of the print—the **typography**. While you do not need to be a graphic artist to put together a visually appealing document, giving attention to several features of your document's design as you revise make it easier for the reader to follow the text's organization.[14]

Page Layout Your document's design not only makes it easier for the reader to follow but also reflects on you as a writer. To design a layout that is internally consistent, reflective of the standard practice in your field, and attractive, observe the following guidelines. These guidelines reflect the standard formatting practices in many organizations. However, if your organization has a style guide of its own, follow those guidelines.

layout
The arrangement of text on a page.

typography
Visual features of the text.

© Alberto Zornetta/Shutterstock.com

- **Margins.** Generally allow a 1–1½-inch margin around your text. Page numbers are placed within the margin, usually in the bottom center or upper outside corner. Header and footer areas are for material that appears on every page in the top or bottom margin, such as chapter titles.

- **Line Spacing.** Most business documents are single-spaced with double-spacing between paragraphs. Extra space is used before and after headings to help the reader follow your organization.

  Sometimes single lines of paragraphs can be "widowed" or "orphaned" at the bottom or top of a page. To eliminate these one-liners, check your word processing program's formatting help for "Widow and Orphan Protection." This protective device groups the outcast line with the rest of the paragraph.

- **White Space.** As with margins and line spacing, careful use of white space improves your text's readability. **White space** refers to areas in documents that do not contain text, numbers, figures, tables, graphs, and/or images. Margins are good examples of white space. White space is especially effective in setting off vertical lists of items from the surrounding text. This way the information is highlighted for the reader. Use white space to highlight and group details as a unit.

- **Indentation.** Like white space, use indentation to highlight important information, such as long quotations or lists of important details.

- **Justification. Justified text** means that the text is aligned along a vertical margin. Usually text is either full-justified—aligned along both the left and right margins— or left-justified—aligned along the left margin with a ragged right margin.

  The advantage of full justification is that it presents a formal-looking document, but full justification has three drawbacks. (1) If used with a font that has nonproportional spacing, such as Courier or Letter Gothic, it creates distracting gaps between words. (2) Full justification makes corrections difficult since adding or deleting even a few words creates the need to reformat the entire document. (3) Full justification is difficult to read for long periods. The ragged edges of left-justified text are easier on the eyes.

Typographical Effects Once you have revised the layout of your document, create a unified, professional-looking document by using effective typography.

- **Typeface.** The two kinds of typefaces are serif and sans serif. A **serif typeface** has tiny extenders on the ends of the letters. A typical serif typeface known as Times New Roman is available on most computers.

  In contrast, a **sans serif typeface** has no extenders. A sans serif typeface known as Arial is available on most computers.

  In general, a serif typeface is easier to read on hard copy, so it is good for extensive prose documents, such as business reports. Sans serif is good for headings or other short elements in documents. Online documents, however, are easier to read if you use a sans serif typeface for both headings and prose.

- **Type Size.** Most business documents use a 10- or 12-point type. Larger type sizes are often used to unify major headings and titles. This unity helps the reader mentally organize the material.

- **Capital Letters.** A text written in all capital letters is hard to read. Reserve all capitals (uppercase type) for headings or short phrases that need particular emphasis.

- **Boldface.** Boldface provides extra emphasis to particular elements in a text. It is often used to unify headings and can even be used to highlight a particular word, phrase, or sentence. The trick with boldface is to be consistent with its use. Putting too much text in bold eliminates the reason for its use—emphasis—and confuses the reader.

white space
Areas in documents that do not contain text, numbers, figures, tables, graphs, and/or images.

justified text
Text that is aligned along a vertical margin. Usually this means text is aligned along both the left and right margins.

serif typeface
Font with tiny extenders on the ends of the letters.

sans serif typeface
Font having no extenders on the ends of the letters.

- **Underlining.** Like boldface, underlining emphasizes and unifies parts of the text, such as second-level headings, which are often underlined rather than capitalized to distinguish them. However, if you are using underlining for emphasis, rather than **boldface**, do not underline technical or foreign terms; instead use *italics* to identify these words: *habeas corpus*. Use underlining sparingly in hard copy documents. Avoid underlining in online text and in professionally produced documents of any type.
- **Headings.** Descriptive headings help readers move through documents quickly. Descriptive headings help the reader follow your ideas more easily. However, to keep your material unified, always use the same typographical features in each heading at each level. For example, use all capital letters (caps) and boldface for first-level headings, use standard capitalization and boldface for second-level headings, and use standard capitalization and italics for third-level headings. You may also want to use a larger typeface for first- and second-level headings. Be consistent throughout the text. Headings are discussed in detail in Chapter 11 on business reports.

FIRST-LEVEL HEADING
Text text text text text text text text text text text text text text text text text text text text text text text text text text text text text text text text text text text text

Second-Level Heading
Text text text text text text text text text text text text text text text text text text text text text text text text text text text text text text text text text text text text

Third-Level Heading.
Text text text text text text text text text text text text text text text text text text text text text text text text text text text text text text text text text text text text

- **Lists.** Lists emphasize items within the text or in a stacked (vertical) list. A list can be numbered within a sentence like this: The advantages of e-mail include (1) speed, (2) reliability, and (3) anonymity. You can use symbols like a dash (-) or bullet (·) to create a vertical list. These symbols, however, are not effective for showing chronology or order of importance.

Know when not to use lists. When a report or letter has bullets everywhere, it quickly loses its effectiveness and looks as though you were unable to develop a paragraph of complete sentences. Remember that the two best reasons for using lists are to organize many numerical facts and to emphasize important recommendations.[15]

A Final Word on Formatting. As with most special effects today, word processing programs make creating effects easier than ever before. That's why you should be wary of overdoing it. Overdoing it results in a cluttered and unprofessional appearance, rather than a unified and polished one, and you lose credibility with your readers.

Choose one way to emphasize words, either boldface or italicize (underline only when you do not have a better alternative). Do not use all three. After you make your choice, use it consistently throughout your document. A document that changes typefaces frequently looks unpolished and chaotic.

REVISING FOR YOUR AUDIENCE: STYLE AND TONE

Writing style refers to the strategies we develop for using words or sentences in a particular way. John Fielden defines *style* in business writing as "that choice of words, sentences, and paragraph format which by virtue of being appropriate to the situation and to the power positions of both writer and reader produces the desired reaction and result."[16]

We make many stylistic choices every time we sit down to write. We may decide to use a technical term rather than an ordinary word; we may use active rather than passive verbs; or we may choose to use a series of short sentences rather than one long, cumbersome, complex sentence.

Tone refers to the writer's attitude toward the reader and to the subject matter. Your tone could be sarcastic or straightforward, pompous or accessible, condescending or respectful, impersonal or personal. In general, good business writing should have a confident, conversational, courteous, and sincere tone.

While we are sensitive to the harsh, cold, pompous tone of other people's business writing, we are usually not as alert to our own. Just as their tone offends us and perhaps even costs them our business, our tone can offend them and cost us their business.

Our specific stylistic choices influence a wide range of reader responses, from the reader's willingness to read the document to his or her acceptance of our ideas.[17] CEOs and managers know that clear, simple, and accurate letters and reports save the reader time, translating into increased productivity and higher profits.

Clear language has become a business necessity in the information economy where human attention is a scarce resource.[18] Drowning in information, we attend to the piles of letters, memos, e-mails, text messages, and reports for a few seconds at most.

In such an economy, revising your prose to catch the busy reader's short attention span takes on a new urgency. It becomes essential, since the cost exacted by an unreadable, unorganized, impenetrable document can be estimated in lost business, personal reputation, etc.

Revising for style and tone, then, makes good business sense and can be thought of as strategy building. The next section guides you in making judicious stylistic choices among the available options. Stylistic and tone questions are not about right or wrong; they are about good, better, best.[19]

Revising for Style The three broad styles available to business writers are described below. To be an effective communicator, evaluate your style strategy carefully. Adjust your style to suit the writing circumstances. If you lack a clear sense of the best style, ask yourself what effect you want to produce in your readers, then go with the style that best supports that goal. The answer will help you determine which style is appropriate for your writing situation.

The Impersonal Style. The impersonal style is characterized by a(n):

- Passive voice
- Official, bureaucratic tone
- Excessive nominalization (turning an action verb into a noun)
- Long, convoluted sentence structure
- Superfluous, outdated, and redundant language
- Business and legal jargon
- Abstract words

Although generalizations about when to use a particular style are tricky, a passive style can be appropriate in negative situations and in situations where the writer is in a lower position than the reader.[20] However, because this style is difficult to read and slows down the reader's comprehension, save it for sensitive situations.

The Modern Business Style. The modern business style is characterized by a(n):

- Active voice
- Confident, conversational, courteous, and sincere tone
- Strong verbs
- Parallel structure
- Short sentences
- Everyday words
- Concrete words
- Precise words

This style is appropriate for most business documents, from internal memos to external reports, because it is easy to read and understand. Writers who use this style follow the rules of Plain English. See Figure 10-3 for an explanation of Plain English.

© PePI/Shutterstock.com

The Informal/Colorful Style. The informal/colorful style is characterized by a(n):

- Active voice
- Personal, conversational tone
- Strong verbs
- Colorful use of adjectives and adverbs
- Parallel structure
- Short sentences
- Everyday words
- Concrete words
- Precise words

This style is good for situations where you are familiar with the reader. This style is also effective for delivering good news and in some persuasive action-request situations. Sales letters and advertisements often use a colorful style to capture the reader's attention.

FIGURE 10-2: EXAMPLES OF LETTERS IN THREE WRITING STYLES

1. **Passive and Impersonal Style.** Filled with **jargon** and difficult to read. Ineffective for routine correspondence as in the following example.

Dear Mr. Smith:

Per your letter of April 7, 20xx, enclosed please find the information in reference to our company that will help in optimizing your choices to build a website. Prices charged are in line with other designers of similar background and experience.

The company objective is to develop end-to-end robust solutions through continued focus on core competencies: Website development, hosting, and maintenance; full access to PHP and CGI; and, of course, SSL encryption. It is believed that the customer deserves the highest quality products and services possible. Through continued expansion of the company's staff and through application of corporate quality programs, such as benchmarking, our establishment of superior processes in each of the core competencies excels over our competitors.

Continued expansion into new, profitable markets will enable the company to provide clients with value-added services and turnkey solutions that will translate into client satisfaction.

Please find herein the company's packages that will endeavor to help the client learn more about the company's superior capabilities and its motivated professional team.

If you have any questions or concerns regarding the above, please feel free to contact Joanne Jones, at 800-543-6677, ext. 213. It is toll free for your convenience.

Very truly and obediently yours,

jargon (buzzwords) Words peculiar to a particular profession that do not necessarily make sense to others outside of that profession.

FIGURE 10-2: EXAMPLES OF LETTERS IN THREE WRITING STYLES

2. **Modern Business Style.** Uses active voice, strong verbs, short sentences.

Dear Mr. Smith:

Thank you for inquiring about our Web services. Our company specializes in creating websites. Your satisfaction is our priority. We work on projects of any size from large to small. Our prices range from $60 an hour for basic logo design to $100 an hour for designing and implementing a full-featured website.

Our staff includes seven Web designers who will turn your image of a perfect website into reality. We can fulfill any of your Web design needs from developing high-end graphics and animation to incorporating video and sound. We realize that your organization may not yet be clear on what your Web needs are. Our talented staff will work with you to guide you in the right direction.

I have enclosed a brochure that explains the four website design packages we offer. Choose the one that is right for your needs, then give us a toll-free call any time at 800-543-6677. We will be glad to set up a free consultation.

Sincerely,

3. **Informal/Colorful Style.** Good for communicating with people you know well or for communicating good news to those you are familiar with.

Dear Jack,

Thanks for asking about our Web design services. We have a full range of services and can provide you with just about anything you want in the way of website design. Our prices are competitive. We charge $60 an hour for basic logo design and up to $100 an hour to design and get your site up and running.

As you know, we have seven talented designers who work on all projects. I have included a brochure that explains the various website design packages we offer. If you have a clear idea of what you want on your site, shoot your ideas over via e-mail to bwo@clear.com or give me a call at 800-657-8000. If you're not sure exactly what you want from a website, just give me a call, and we can set up a consult.

It's great to hear from you, and I look forward to working with you again.

Sincerely,

As you can see from the letters in Figure 10-2, the three styles are not mutually exclusive. For example, the modern business style is more personal than impersonal and can be colorful as well. Nevertheless, these general distinctions allow us to learn how to appropriately apply a style and its elements to each writing situation.

Since most business writing situations call for using the modern business style, when you revise your documents, follow the guidelines outlined next to revise for tone, sentence structure, and word choice. Then use your knowledge of each stylistic characteristic to achieve the style that best suits your purpose.

Revising for Tone The right tone for your business document depends on your audience and your purpose. In general, strive for a tone that is confident, but not arrogant; conversational, but not too personal; courteous and sincere, but not condescending. Revising the tone of your writing can be as simple as changing a sentence or choosing a different word. Improving your tone also improves other sentence structure problems, like wordiness or awkward syntax.

1. **Identify the Problem.** I'm confident that our Web design capabilities are far beyond what you could ever imagine and will more than exceed any needs that you could possibly have.
   Problem: Over-confident and arrogant
   Correction: After you read our proposal, I believe you will agree that our Web design capabilities will meet your needs.

2. **Identify the Problem.** Just between you and me, I know you will love our Web design capabilities. Plus I'm a single mom, and I could really use your business.
   Problem: Too personal and unprofessional
   Correction: After you read through the Web design packages we offer, I believe you will find one that meets your company's needs.

3. **Identify the Problem.** Our clothes are made of the finest material. You ruined the material by washing the garment rather than having it dry cleaned. Next time, try ordering clothes that are machine washable.
   Problem: Condescending, rude, and preachy
   Correction: Our clothes are made of the finest material. To maintain their good looks, they need to be dry cleaned.

4. **Identify the problem.** If you have questions or concerns, please feel free to contact us. We look forward to hearing from you.
   Problem: Tired conclusions sound anything but sincere.
   Correction: You may have questions about the restructuring process. We would be glad to clarify your concerns.

REVISING YOUR SENTENCE STRUCTURE

Use Active Voice When writing in the modern business style, use the active voice most of the time rather than the passive voice. **Active voice** means that the subject or agent of the sentence performs the action. This kind of sentence is easy to understand because it mirrors our thinking processes: Subject/Verb/Object is the standard sentence order in English. "Still, we incurred no debt in making these purchases, and our shares outstanding have increased only 1/3 of 1%" (Buffett, 2000).[21]

The **passive voice** is the normal action backward. The subject or agent is acted upon. The person or thing doing the action can be found in the "by" clause at the end of the sentence. Using the passive voice forces the reader to take extra time to mentally convert passive voice into the active voice.

active voice
A sentence in which the subject performs the action; opposite of passive voice.

passive voice
A sentence in which the subject or agent is acted upon; opposite of active voice.

Here are three sentences written in the passive voice.

1. Still, no debt was incurred **by us** in making these purchases, and an increase of only 1/3 of 1% was experienced **by our shares outstanding**. (Here the agent is deleted altogether.)
2. The decision to lay off 50% of the workforce was made yesterday. (Who made the decision?)
3. The proxies solicited hereby for the Heartland Meeting may be revoked, subject to the procedures described herein, at any time up to and including the date of the Heartland meeting. (Who may revoke the proxies?)[22]

Here are these same sentences revised using the active voice.

1. Still, **we incurred** no debt in making these purchases, and **our shares outstanding increased** only 1/3 of 1%.
2. Yesterday, **top management** made the decision to lay off 50% of the workforce.
3. By following the directions on page 10, **you** may revoke your proxy and reclaim your right to vote up to and including the day of the meeting.

In example B, the active version tells you who decided to lay off the employees, which shows management's willingness to take the responsibility.

Example C makes clear who may revoke a proxy. The revised version also replaces the wordy *described herein* with the clear *page 10*. The second examples show how the active voice transforms sentences, making them less wordy and easier to understand.

Sometimes using the passive voice makes sense; for example, when you do not want to blame someone or when the agent is less important than the action. Look at the following three examples. These are appropriate uses of the passive voice.

1. **When you do not want to take responsibility for the action:** Your order was lost but will be immediately replaced and shipped by overnight mail. You will receive it tomorrow, December 1, by 10:30 a.m.
2. **When you do not want to directly blame or accuse the person who acted:** The credit card number for payment was not included.
3. **When the subject or agent who performed the action is not important:** Your order will be shipped overnight mail.

FIGURE 10-3: PLAIN ENGLISH VS. THE BUREAUCRATIC STYLE

Plain English means writing in a style that readers can easily understand. Its original aim was to make formal documents, such as insurance policies, leases, warranties, stock prospectuses, and tax forms published by corporations and government agencies understandable to consumers. In 1998, the Securities and Exchange Commission (SEC) made Plain English official when it released the "Plain English Rule," requiring the issuers of stock prospectuses to write them in a clear and understandable (accessible) manner. The SEC also published *A Plain English Handbook* to assist puzzled corporate writers. You can download a copy of the handbook at www.sec.gov/pdf/handbook.pdf.

Today, many organizations such as Texaco, MBNA American Bank, Procter & Gamble, Ford, General Electric, and governmental agencies have adopted the Plain English style.

FIGURE 10-3: PLAIN ENGLISH VS. THE BUREAUCRATIC STYLE

© auremar/Shutterstock.com

In contrast to the Plain English style, the bureaucratic style is impersonal, wordy, cumbersome, and often passive. It has an "official" sound, however, that some writers prefer because they believe the style lends their writing an authoritative voice.

One of the earliest cases reported under the New York State Plain English law on contracts involved the Lincoln Savings Bank's customer agreement on safe-deposit boxes. State attorney general Robert Abrams sued the bank, demanding that it simplify the following agreement, saying, "I defy anyone, lawyer or lay person, to understand or explain what that means." Here is the 121-word sentence that puzzled Abrams.

The liability of the bank is expressly limited to the exercise of ordinary diligence and care to prevent the opening of the within-mentioned safe deposit box during the within-mentioned term, or any extension or renewal thereof, by any person other than the lessee or his duly authorized representative and failure to exercise such diligence or care shall not be inferable from any alleged loss, absence or disappearance of any of its contents, not shall the bank be liable for permitting a colessee or an attorney in fact of the lessee to have access to and remove contents of said safe deposit box after the lessee's death or disability and before the bank has written knowledge of such death or disability.[23]

The lawsuit ended when the bank settled and changed the passage to the following: "Our liability with respect to property deposited in the box is limited to ordinary care by our employees in the performance of their duties in preventing the opening of the box during the term of the lease by anyone other than you, persons authorized by you or persons authorized by the law."

The revised version is more direct and readable. It uses active voice and the personal pronoun "you" to replace the cumbersome passive voice and the impersonal legalese, such as colessee and lessee. In addition, the second passage eliminates meaningless legal phrases like *renewal thereof, duly authorized representative*, and *within mentioned term*, to name a few. Once pared to its essential meaning, the sentence is much easier to read and understand.

Avoid Nominalizations (Nouns That Hide Verbs) Nouns that end in -ion, -ment, -ship, and -ize hide strong verbs. When released, these strong verbs make your sentence less abstract and more vigorous. So get busy and spring those hidden verbs. Make your sentences vivid and powerful.

Before: The attainment of our goals will be possible this year.
After: We will attain our goals this year.
Before: Company B will have no stock ownership of the company.
After: Company B will not own the company's stock.
Before: We made a determination that Ms. Woods should be hired.
After: We determined that we should hire Ms. Woods.

parallel structure
Two or more sentences are worded such that they have similar grammatical structures.

Use Parallel Structure **Parallel structure** means two or more sentences are worded such that they have similar grammatical structures. Make constructions in a sentence parallel—balanced—by matching phrase with phrase, clause with clause, verb with verb, and so on. Parallel structure provides a rhythm and clarity to your writing that makes it sound polished and easy to read. Items in a series should be parallel, as should the connecting words or phrases (and, but, or, for, nor; either or, neither nor, not only but also, both and).

Here is an example of parallel structure.

The writing team wrote the draft copy, revised the draft copy, and proofread the draft copy.

Keep Sentences Short Short sentences are easier to read than long ones. The average sentence length in business documents should be no more than 20–22 words. A sentence should convey one main idea or two closely related ideas. Here are three sentence types and when to use them.

1. The **simple sentence** is short, direct, and clear. Its form is subject/verb/object.
    Example: Profits collapsed this quarter.
    Use short sentences to add punch to your prose. They are especially useful to emphasize an idea in conclusions or after several complex sentences. However, watch overuse of the short, punchy sentences since they can make your prose sound choppy and monotonous when used again and again.

2. The **compound sentence** comprises two sentences connected by a coordinating conjunction: *and, but, or, for, yet, nor*, and *so*. The subjects or ideas of these sentences should be closely related.
    Example: During the Internet bubble, stocks such as Yahoo, Spyglass, Cyber-Cash, E-Pay, and E-Fax commanded huge sums of money, but the soaring prices of these same stocks collapsed two years later when the speculative bubble burst.

dependent clause
An incomplete sentence.

3. The **complex sentence** is composed of one independent clause and one or several dependent clauses. A **dependent clause** is an incomplete sentence. Complex sentences are good for showing the relationships between ideas. In the following sentence, the less important idea appears in the dependent clause, while the sentence's independent clause emphasizes the main idea.
    Example: Although stocks such as Yahoo, Spyglass, and E-pay commanded huge sums of money during the Internet bubble, their soaring prices crashed when the speculative bubble burst two years later.

REVISING FOR WORD CHOICE

Use Everyday Words Using familiar, everyday words helps your readers understand your document. Short, familiar words help you get your points across without slowing down your readers. Some beginning business writers mistakenly think that pompous, bureaucratic jargon impresses their supervisors. This could not be farther from the truth. Supervisors fume as they revise employees' wordy prose, eliminating deadwood and bureaucratic jargon.

© Mascha Tace/Shutterstock.com

In short, do not confuse short words with simple ideas. The trick is to express complex ideas in words your readers can easily understand. Revise your sentences to eliminate the deadwood of business and bureaucratic jargon, legalese, trite expressions, and clichés. **Clichés** are overused, worn-out words or expressions. In addition, know when using technical jargon supports your communication goals and when doing so threatens them.

cliché
Overused, worn-out words or expressions.

Eliminate Business and Bureaucratic Deadwood Substitute shorter, more direct words in place of long-winded words.

Instead of	Use
Terminate	End
Elucidate	Explain
Utilize	Use
Ascertain	Learn
Endeavor	Try
Impact	Affect, influence
Necessitate	Require
Input	Views, comments
Throughput	Material
Prioritize	Rank
Peruse	Review
Remunerate	Pay
Strategize	Plan

Another perpetrator of wordiness is trite expressions, which, like clichés, are words and phrases that have been used for so long they have lost their meaning and punch. Many of the trite phrases remaining in business writing are holdovers from a time when business correspondence followed strict and formal conventions. When you use trite expressions in your letters, memos, and reports, you sound hollow and stuffy. Eliminate the following trite phrases completely or replace each with more up-to-date phrases.

Avoid	Use Instead
Per your request	As you requested
Under separate cover	By overnight mail
Pursuant to your request	As you requested
Enclosed please find	Enclosed
The undersigned	I or me
Permit me to say	Just say it!
At your earliest convenience	Specify a date
Set forth herein	In this agreement

Avoid the following clichés whenever possible. Substitute with meaningful words or fresh metaphors:

grandstand play
hit the nail on the head
worth its weight in gold
solid as a rock
in the ballpark

Every year since 1976, Lake Superior State University has added several words and expressions to its archive of what they refer to as banished words. Since the tradition's inception, words and expressions such as *selfie, perfectly candid, my bad, hunker down, sexting, teachable moment, bromance, a-ha moment, man up, chillaxin, thanking you in advance,* and *ginormous* have made their list along with many others. Unlike most clichés, most of the words and expressions that make Lake Superior State University's banished words list have not been around for a long period of time. Whether we call such words and expressions banished words or clichés, they have apparently overstayed their welcome.

technical jargon
Terms that allow experts within a discipline to speak and write to one another in a technical shorthand that is not necessarily understood by non-experts.

Use Technical Jargon Cautiously Technical jargon allows experts within a discipline—accountants, doctors, lawyers, stockbrokers, information technology specialists—to speak and write to one another in a technical shorthand. Technical jargon refers to terms that allow experts within a discipline to speak and write to one another in a technical shorthand that is not necessarily understood by non-experts. However, the SEC's *Plain English Handbook* recommends we eliminate jargon and legalese in business documents.[24] Why? Because technical jargon, when used in a document to be read by people who do not share knowledge of the jargon, inevitably causes frustration and misunderstandings (see Figure 10-4). Therefore, when writing business documents, avoid technical jargon unless you know your reader understands it.

Here is an example of technical jargon in a letter to a customer: "The account was never reported as a repossession, but was reported as a charge off." Translated into layperson's terms, this means: "Your account was cleared."

Technical jargon may be a natural part of your vocabulary. That's understandable. However, not everyone you communicate with understands such terms. The trick is to determine who would be confused and frustrated by technical jargon, then replace the words you know he or she will not understand.

Use Concrete Rather Than Abstract Words Choose words that are as specific and concrete as your context requires. Concrete terms, such as *cheeseburgers* and *French fries*, help your readers visualize what you say. The more abstract word *meal* would not prompt the *cheeseburger and French fries* image in most readers' minds. When you write, you want the pictures in their minds to match your image. Complex concepts are more comprehensible when readers can form a mental picture.

Avoid Using Abstract Words Abstract words refer to language that is often unclear and subject to different interpretations. When you use abstract words—*asset, freedom, love, integrity, liberty, capital appreciation value, zero coupon bond*—you risk reader misunderstanding. To make abstract concepts more comprehensible to your reader (1) use as many concrete terms as you can, and (2) create a hypothetical scenario in which people perform actions.

> **abstract words**
> Language that is often unclear and is subject to differing interpretations.

Here is an example from the SEC *Plain English Handbook*.[25]

Before: Sandyhill Basic Value Fund, Inc. (the "Fund") seeks capital appreciation and, secondarily, income by investing in securities, primarily equities, that management of the Fund believes are undervalued and therefore represent basic investment value.

© auremar/Shutterstock.com

After: At the Sandyhill Basic Value Fund, we will strive to increase the value of your shares (capital appreciation) and, to a lesser extent, to provide income (dividends). We will invest primarily in undervalued stocks, meaning those selling for low prices given the financial strength of the companies.

Make your references clear. Words like *this, that, thing,* and *they* can confuse your readers because the words are vague and imprecise. Substitute vague references with precise equivalents.

Finally, quantify what you mean whenever possible. Words like *few, several, good, interesting, more, small,* and so on have different meanings to you and to your reader. Replace the vague words with specific words, like *two dollars, 200 people, had an intricate plot,* and *two inches tall.*

readability
A reader's ability to read and understand a document.

FIGURE 10-4: EVALUATE YOUR DOCUMENT'S READABILITY

A document's **readability** refers to the readers' ability to read and understand your document easily. They may even find it interesting. Two key elements of readability are (1) the complexity of the sentence structure and (2) the complexity of the vocabulary. Readability formulas, such as the Fog index and the Flesch-Kincaid Scale, measure the number of words in a sentence and syllables in each word to measure textual difficulty. Each scale makes its determination in terms of grade level.

For the Flesch-Kincaid Scale, you want your text to be somewhere below grade 12, preferably in the single digits. Most routine business documents should score between grades 7–9. Business publications such as the *Wall Street Journal* and *Fortune* rate between 9–11, and technical documents score between 12–14.

Do not get the idea that you want to write at a grade 15 level to reflect your education. Rudolf Flesch, a pioneer in the Plain English movement, developed formulas to predict readability for businesspeople but kept the term *grade level* from his earlier work with grade school students. Do not let the term mislead you; the lower your number, the better your writing, the easier it is to read. Your word processing program should include the results of several readability indexes as part of its grammar checker. Test a section of your writing to see how it rates.

Do not rely solely on readability scales to determine your writing's readability. While word difficulty and sentence length are factors in making your document readable, the indexes overlook other important considerations that contribute to the ease of reading, such as sentence structure, paragraph coherence and unity, logical connection and convincing support of your major ideas, and document design. To fully evaluate your document's readability, check its purpose, content, organization, style, and tone.

Use Precise Words When you revise, be sure you use each word precisely. Misuse of one word for another can destroy your document's credibility. For example, the misused words in the following sentences express wrong meanings.

- The real estate mongrel made a fortune before he was 30. (*mogul* is intended)
- The CEO's decision was purely obituary. (*arbitrary* is intended)
- Our manager is a man of great statue. (*stature* is intended)
- Irregardless of his decision, I'm staying with the team. (*irregardless* is not a word; *regardless* is intended)
- The proofreader commentated on my letter. (*commented* is intended; do not make up words because they sound more official)

Besides revising for exact meanings, ensure your words work in context. Make them work for you, not against you. For example, if you are writing a fundraising letter for a cancer research organization, do not use *sick* in your opener: "Are you sick and tired of all the requests asking for your hard-earned money?"

If you are unsure of a word's meaning, look it up in a hardcopy dictionary or a comprehensive online dictionary such as *Merriam-Webster Online, Collins Online Dictionary*, or *Oxford Dictionaries Online*. Or visit www.facstaff.bucknell.edu/rbeard/diction.html where you will find links to online dictionaries in languages ranging from English, German, and French to Spanish, Japanese, and Korean.

Revise for Wordiness Wordiness refers to the fat in your sentences that you could delete to give you sleek, easy-to-read, powerful sentences. Use the following Just-In-Time (JIT) writing tips to check your sentences for extra verbiage.

JIT Tips for Cutting the Fat As you revise for wordiness, check your prose for the following common problems and tighten accordingly.[26]

JIT #1: Watch for the overused impersonal opening. "It is/was," "there is/are." Check your sentences for these wordy beginnings. Cut them out, and replace them with the real subject of the sentence as in the following examples.

It was clear to **the employee** why ... (7 words)
The employee knew why ... (4 words)
There are **five employees** in this division who were late for flying lessons. (13 words)
Five employees were late for flying lessons. (6 words)

JIT #2: Break up stringy sentences. Avoid too many connectors, such as *and* and *but*, that tie loosely related ideas together in one sentence.

Problem. Regardless of their seniority, all employees who hope to become vampires should start their education by enrolling in the special course to be offered at Vampire U., **and** this course will be offered on the next eight Saturdays, beginning on January 24, **but** you could also begin your apprenticeship by taking approved online-after-dark courses selected from a list available in the Un-Human Resources Office, ext. 123.

Revision. Regardless of seniority, all employees who hope to become vampires should take one of the following steps. (1) Enroll in the special Vampire U. course beginning January 24 and continuing for eight Saturdays. (2) Take approved online-after-dark courses from a list available in the Un-Human Resources Office, ext. 123.

JIT #3: Keep the subject and verb of a sentence as close together as possible.
Difficult to read. Webspeak, pervading everything from the *New York Times Manual of Style* to office e-mail and reminding us that putting the English language in the hands of engineers is like putting Vikings in charge of neurosurgery, **makes** business communication even more vague and stilted.
Unites the subject and verb. Webspeak makes business communication even more vague and stilted, pervading everything from the *New York Times Manual of Style* to office e-mail. The pervasiveness of webspeak reminds us that the English language is now in the hands of computer engineers, something akin to putting Viking marauders in charge of neurosurgery.

JIT #4: Eliminate unneeded prepositions.
I am writing **in order to** list the potential issues **in regard to** the Russell account **in advance of** the client visit. (22 words)
I am writing **about** the Russell account **to** list the potential issues before the client visit. (16 words)

JIT #5: Eliminate Superfluous Words. **Superfluous words** are unnecessary words that can be eliminated or reduced. Correcting them supports clarity and concision. For example, replace the phrase in column one with the word(s) in column two:

Drop this	In favor of this
In order to	To
In the event that	If
Subsequent to	After
Prior to	Before
Despite the fact that	Although
Because of the fact that	because, since
In light of	because, since
Owing to the fact that	because, since
Take into consideration	Consider
Very good	Good
In reference to	About

JIT #6: Eliminate Redundancies. **Redundancies** are words that repeat the same idea in a different word(s). Correcting for them not only eliminates necessary text, but also supports clarity and conciseness. For example, replace the phrase in column one with the word in column two:

Drop this	In favor of this
Absolutely free	Free
Reduce down	Reduce
Cancel out	Cancel
True facts	Facts
Past experience	Experience

SUMMARY: SECTION 3—
REVISING FOR YOUR AUDIENCE

- Our stylistic choices influence the way our reader responds to our document, from a willingness to read it to accepting our ideas. As business writers, we have three broad styles to choose from: (1) the passive/impersonal style, (2) the modern business style, and (3) the informal/colorful style. While you should evaluate your purpose and audience before you choose a style, in most cases, the modern business style is the most effective for business documents.
- When we revise for tone, we evaluate how close we have come to having a confident, conversational, courteous, and sincere tone. Improving your tone can be a simple matter of revising a sentence or two and correcting word choices.
- Revising for sentence structure involves looking at the sentence structures that produce the modern business style: active voice, strong verbs, parallel words and phrases, short sentences, and everyday words.

PROOFREADING

After carefully revising your document for tone, organization, sentence structure, and word choice, take the time before sending it out to proofread. **Proofreading** refers to conducting a final review of a document to catch oversights in need of correction such as misspellings. Your focus here will be on looking for grammar, punctuation, spelling, and typographical errors you didn't notice while revising. In addition, double check all figures (e.g., dates, dollar amounts, etc.) and names for correctness, using the original source if possible.

If you think you can get by without this final pass, think again. Being 99 percent correct is not good enough. For example, the need to proofread thoroughly comes to the forefront

proofreading
A final review of a document to catch oversights in need of correction such as misspellings.

© B Calkins/Shutterstock.com

when asked how many spelling errors are too many in a résumé. The typical answer is one! Well, that is also true of other business documents.

At the proofreading stage, you could pull in a proofreading buddy to help you out. A buddy system lets you receive and give help. One way to use a proofreading buddy is to ask the person to read aloud the final draft while you follow along on the recipient's copy. Reading aloud is a powerful proofreading tool because you catch problems in tone as well as sentence structure and word choice problems.

If you do not have a partner, read the material backward, starting from the last word and reading from right to left. This keeps you from getting caught up in the sense of the document so that you do not overlook errors. Look especially for those spelling errors that your spell checker does not catch: to/too/two; their/there; etc.

As you look over your document for formatting, be sure that you have properly located and identified graphics and that your headings at each level match. See Figure 10-5 for more proofreading tips.

FIGURE 10–5: PROOFREADING TIPS

- Always double check the spelling of every proper name—especially those you think you know by heart. One mistake can mean doing the entire job over again, which can easily be a six-figure blooper.

- Always call every phone number that appears in your document.
- Double check little words: *or* and *of*; *it* and *is* are not interchangeable.
- Do not proof for every type of mistake at once—do one proof for spelling, another for spaces, consistency of word usage, font sizes, etc.
- Have other people read the document.
- Keep a list of your (or the writer's you are proofing) most common errors and proof for those in separate passes.
- Double check boilerplate text like the company letterhead. Just because it is frequently used, does not mean it has been carefully checked.
- Double check whenever you are sure something is right—certainty is dangerous.
- Lay document pages side by side to check for formatting consistency. If your paragraphs look like a Rorschach Inkblot Test, you need some formatting revision.

Source: Adapted from Carl T. Hagberg and Associates, The 1998 Annual Meeting Planner (1998).

GIVING AND TAKING CRITICISM EFFECTIVELY

Criticizing someone else's writing is a tricky business. Many writers take criticism of their writing personally. To avoid hurting someone's feelings, while still making helpful comments, follow these guidelines.

- Preface your comments with *The reader* as in "The reader is confused here." Avoid using *you* or *I*, which personalizes your comments.
- Try to meet face-to-face with the writer to review your comments. This softens the impact of your marks on the page.
- When you edit for content concerns, make your comments specific. For example, if the writer has not answered the reader's questions, point out which ones were unanswered.
- When editing for style and tone, be specific. Writing *wrong tone* is not helpful.
- When you edit for grammar and punctuation, remember that these are usually the last things on the writer's mind. Do not belittle the writer. Point out these mistakes with empathy. Otherwise, you only arouse anger and defensiveness in the writer.

Just as criticizing writing is tricky, taking and digesting criticism is also a tricky business. To avoid getting defensive and feeling that you are now a worthless worm of a human, follow these guidelines as you read through the critical comments and make your changes.

- Do not view criticism as a personal attack on you and your judgment.
- Do not base your self-worth as a writer on negative criticism.
- Ask for examples that illustrate the criticism.
- If you truly believe a critical comment is wrong, talk it over with the editor or proofreader before you make or ignore the suggested change.
- Remember that editors and proofreaders put effort into their reviews to help you improve your documents. Thank them for it.

MANAGING THE REVISION PROCESS IN ORGANIZATIONS

In a typical organization, documents cycle through many layers of management; each manager adding, deleting, or re-organizing until the top executive signs off, usually as "lead" writer. The final document may not resemble in the least the original written by the junior staff member. However, as each writer leaves his or her stamp on it, the document finally reflects the company's persona, the "accepted" look and feel of the organization's documents.[27]

Although supervisors revise to ensure uniformity in documents that their departments or groups produce, they also bring an understanding of the corporate politics that entry-level employees may be unaware of.

Document cycling is another form of collaborative writing within organizations. Indeed, it is an integral part of organizational writing. **Document cycling** basically involves sending a document to a fellow employee who makes suggestions and then passes the document on to another fellow employee who follows the same process. According to Susan Kleimann at the U.S. General Accounting Office, the review process is what transforms individual products into institutional products.[28] Many staff-level employees see the review process as having a single function—approval of their work—and are frustrated by the document cycling process. Understanding the organization's review process helps you be prepared for its complexities.

document cycling
Involves sending a document to a fellow employee who makes suggestions and then passes the document on to another fellow employee who follows the same process.

In the basic review unit, a staff member sends a completed document to a supervisor, who sends it to a manager, who then sends it back to the employee with notes for revisions to incorporate into the final document. This one-cycle review may turn into several as the employee makes the requested changes and resubmits, only to find the document returned once again for revision. Usually this cycle is not repeated more than three times.[29]

© OtnaYdur/Shutterstock.com

This constant appearance of disapproval can be frustrating to the staff member; the process itself is time consuming. However, supervisors and managers have other reasons besides approval for recycling documents. After years of writing documents that are purposeful, audience sensitive, and politically savvy, the experienced manager revises a subordinate's writing according to the organization's changing needs and the political climate. In these instances, revision requests become a primary means of transmitting corporate values and culture, and the requests play a key role in making the individual's work advance the organization's objectives.[30]

Two factors complicate the review practice in the workplace:

1. The importance of the document to the organization.
2. The presence of multiple internal and external reviewers.[31]

A document with high impact on an organization, such as an executive letter for an annual report or a mission statement, will go through multiple layers of extensive review to assure that the document reflects the company viewpoint and to guard against liability concerns.

In flatter, less hierarchical organizations, where responsibilities and expertise are often fragmented, many readers review a document to ensure that all areas of expertise are represented. A document is reviewed for legality, methodology, content, regulatory compliance, and many other concerns.[32] In addition, many of these reviewers will see a document twice, once as an initial draft on which they make their comments, and again as a final draft that incorporates the comments. The document may also be circulated to external readers with interests in the final draft, such as clients and attorneys.

Although the review process can be overwhelming to the novice writer, as Kleimann's study points out, document cycling serves two important purposes in organizations:

1. To ensure better-written products through the process of vertical review.
2. To provide a form of feedback that works; therefore, the writers improve over time.[33]

Since these documents are not only recycled during the review process but may also become part of other documents over time, the review cycle is one that enhances the final product and sharpens the writer's expertise.

SUMMARY: SECTION 4— PROOFREADING, GIVING AND TAKING WRITING CRITICISM, AND MANAGING THE REVISION PROCESS IN ORGANIZATIONS

- After revising, proofreading is the last pass at your document. Proofreading is intended to catch spelling, grammar, and punctuation oversights as well as typographical errors.
- Knowing how to give and receive writing criticism is important for two reasons: to help others improve their writing and to help you improve your own.
- The revision process varies across organizations. Once you are on the job, become familiar with how your organization manages the revision process.

Notes

1. Susan Benjamin, *Words at Work* (Reading, MA: Addison-Wesley, 1997), 71.
2. Linda Flower and John Ackerman, "Evaluating and Testing as You Revise," in *Strategies for Business and Technical Writing*, ed. Kevin J. Harty (Boston: Allyn & Bacon, 1999), 24.
3. Elizabeth A. Powell, "A Note on Purpose, Voice, and Style in Business Writing" (University of Virginia: Darden School Foundation, Charlottesville, UVA-BC-0113, 1995), 2.
4. Benjamin, 91.
5. *Dealing Effectively with Unacceptable Employee Behavior*, SkillPath Seminars, 1997. Brochure.
6. Benjamin, 94.
7. Ibid., 95.
8. Guidelines for writing conclusions adapted from Richard Bierck, "How to Begin to Write, When to End," *Harvard Management Communication Letter*. Collected in *The Manager's Guide to Effective Business Writing* (Cambridge, MA: Harvard Business School Publishing, 2000).
9. Flower and Ackerman, 24.
10. Ibid., 24–25.
11. Glenn J. Broadhead and Richard C. Freed, *The Variables of Composition: Process and Product in a Business Setting* (Carbondale: Southern Illinois University Press, 1986), 59.
12. John Clayton, "Writing in Scenarios," *Harvard Management Communication Letter* (January 2001): 3.

13. Flower and Ackerman, 33–34.

14. Guidelines for revising document format and typography adapted from Kathryn Riley, Kim S. Campbell, Alan Manning, and Frank Parker, *Revising Professional Writing* (Superior, WI: Parley Press, 1999), 59–64.

15. Bruce Ross-Larson, *Effective Writing* (New York: W.W. Norton, 1999), 137.

16. John Fielden, "What Do You Mean You Don't Like My Style?" *Harvard Business Review* (May/June 1982): 3.

17. Edward P. J. Corbett and Sheryl L. Finkle, *The Little English Handbook* (New York: Longman, 1998), 55–56.

18. Richard Lanham, *Revising Business Prose* (Boston: Allyn & Bacon, 2000), 89.

19. Corbett and Finkle, 56.

20. Fielden, 7.

21. Warren Buffet, *Annual Report* (Omaha: Berkshire-Hathaway, 2000), 3.

22. Securities and Exchange Commission (SEC), *A Plain English Handbook* (Washington, DC: (2001), 20, www.sec.gov/pdf/handbook.pdf.

23. Robert Abrams, "What They Said," *ABA Journal*, 66 (August 1980): 950.

24. SEC, 30.

25. SEC, 30.

26. Just-In-Time (JIT) Tip Sheets idea adapted from Lynn Veach Sadler, "Preparing for the White Rabbit and Taking It on the Neck: Tales of the Workplace and Writingplace," in *Professional Writing in Context*, ed. J. F. Reynolds C. B. Matalene, J. N. Magnotto, D. C. Samson, Jr., and L. V. Sadlert, (Hillsdale, NJ: Lawrence Erlbaum, 1995), 129–178.

27. Susan D. Kleimann, "The Complexity of Workplace Review," *Technical Communication*, Fourth Quarter (1991): 520–526.

28. Ibid., 521.

29. Ibid.

30. Ibid.

31. Ibid., 522.

32. Ibid., 524–525.

33. Ibid., 526.

11

BUSINESS LETTERS AND MEMOS

LEARNING OUTCOMES

After reading this chapter, you should be able to:

1. Identify the various forms of written business communication.

2. Discuss the roles of formality and informality in selecting the best form for each writing situation.

3. Describe key writing principles that affect business letters and memos.

4. Discuss the role of business letters.

5. Describe the three business letter styles.

6. Discuss the role of business memos.

© korrr/Shutterstock.com

SELECT KEY TERMS

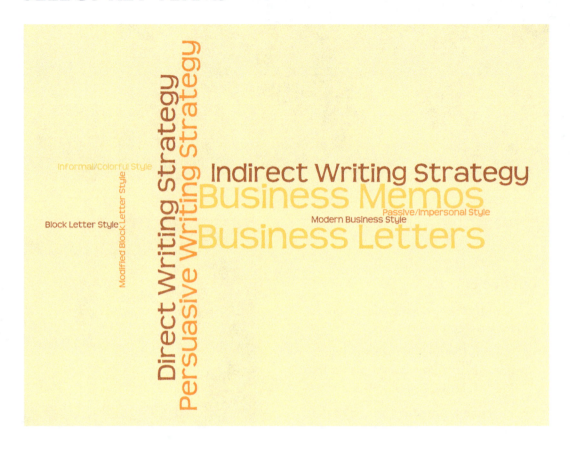

INTRODUCTION

Business letters are formal documents that convey information predominately to external stakeholders. The most common business letter styles are the block style and modified block style. The three business letter strategies are the direct strategy, indirect strategy, and persuasive strategy. The direct strategy is recommended for neutral-news and good-news letters. The indirect strategy is recommended for negative-news letters, and the persuasive strategy is recommended for persuasive letters.

Business memos are relatively short, informal and semi-formal documents used to exchange information among people within organizations. Business memos are often sent as e-mail messages, and some refer to these as e-memos.

The intent of this chapter is to provide you with information about how to write effective business letters and memos. The goals of this chapter are realized through discussions on the following topics: written communication in organizations, the roles of letters and memos in organizations, impact of writing basics on letter and memo quality, business letters, business letter styles, business letter components, writing strategies, writing styles, and business memos.

WRITTEN COMMUNICATION IN ORGANIZATIONS

Written communication is developed and transmitted in many ways in organizations. Common forms of written communication in today's workplace include e-mail messages, text messages, instant messages, letters, memos, and reports. In addition, organizations routinely post written information on company websites and social media sites.

The focus in this chapter is on *letters* and *memos*. The other forms of written communication mentioned above are addressed elsewhere in the book.

Formality plays an important role in selecting the best form of written communication for each writing situation. Written documents and messages are frequently viewed as being formal, informal, or semiformal. For example, letters are considered to be formal documents. Most documents and messages that are developed and/or transmitted electronically (e.g., e-mail messages, text messages, tweets) are considered to be informal. Awareness of such differences in perceptions is important because readers' formality expectations vary and should be taken into consideration. For example, if you need to send an important message to a client, a formal document is typically expected. In this case, you would send a hardcopy letter. In contrast, if you need to send a brief message containing routine, straightforward information to a subordinate within the company, an informal written medium such as e-mail would be a good choice. Or, if you and a fellow worker, who are on the same job level, need to discuss some points pertaining to a routine, noncontroversial matter, instant messaging would be a good choice. Before moving on, let's look at one more example that would land you midstream on the formality spectrum. If you need to send a message regarding changes in procedures internally to subordinates, a semiformal document such as a memo would be a good choice.

THE ROLES OF LETTERS AND MEMOS IN ORGANIZATIONS

THE ROLE OF BUSINESS LETTERS

A substantial portion of communication that occurs in the business place is accomplished via letters. Letters are formal documents that convey information mostly to communication partners outside the organization. Examples include customers, clients, investors, suppliers, and government officials. In addition, some **business letters** are sent internally, most often to superiors. Business letters contain messages ranging from routine, informational matters to complex, controversial matters. The goal is typically to share neutral, good, or negative news or persuade readers to take a specific course of action. There are several types of business letters ranging from sales and inquiry letters to adjustment and follow-up letters.

© Zoltan Zempleni/Shutterstock.com

THE ROLE OF BUSINESS MEMOS

*Memo Examples
http://business.
lovetoknow.com/wiki/
Memo_Examples*

A substantial portion of internal communication in the business place is accomplished via memos. Memos most frequently contain routine information. Like letters, the goals of memos range from sharing neutral, good, and negative news to persuading readers to take a specific course of action.

Today's memos come in one of two forms—hardcopy memos and e-memos. On the surface one might think that all memos should take the form of e-memos due to e-mail's efficiencies. Despite the convenience and ease of developing and sending e-memos, they have their shortcomings ranging from general writing quality to privacy concerns. Such shortcomings are discussed in detail in this chapter.

© Tatchaphol/Shutterstock.com

IMPACT OF WRITING BASICS ON BUSINESS LETTER AND MEMO QUALITY

No doubt about it, appropriate writing strategies and well-ordered, message-appropriate content are central to effective business letters and memos. However, these features alone do not typically get the job done. Well-written letters and memos are grounded in writing basics. They depend on the writer's mastery of the three-stage writing process (planning, drafting, revising) and the ability to apply appropriate business writing principles and writing mechanics, such as grammar and punctuation.

Think of business writing basics like the bricks-and-mortar analogy. As it relates to writing, our words and thoughts are the bricks, and writing principles and mechanics are the mortar. Much as mortar forms a strong bond with bricks when properly mixed and applied, writing principles and mechanics form a strong bond that unites our words and thoughts in business letters. Will your letters and memos be strong like a well-constructed brick structure, or will they be weak and crumble, resulting in miscommunication and other problems?

Select writing principles that are especially important to developing effective business letters are discussed below. These writing principles are addressed in detail in the "writing process" overview in this chapter and the next.

KEY WRITING PRINCIPLES THAT AFFECT BUSINESS LETTERS AND MEMOS

While all writing principles are important to the development of effective letters and memos, some are especially effective in helping writers achieve their objectives. These particular writing principles are the writer's tone of goodwill, using the you-attitude, emphasizing reader benefits, emphasizing the positive, using unbiased language, and being polite, These writing principles are discussed in detail, along with others, in Chapters 8 and 9. Additional writing principles important to the development of letters and memos are: word choice, emphasis and de-emphasis, and writing concisely while including enough detail to support message clarity and purpose. These are discussed below.

Word Choice Appropriate word choice contributes to clear, effective letters and memos. Careless word choice can lead to confusing messages that result in frustration, miscommunication, and other problems. Obviously, you are challenged to take care in your word choice.

Familiar, everyday words help your reader grasp your message. Short, familiar words help you get your points across without slowing down your reader. Some business writers mistakenly think that pompous, bureaucratic jargon impresses their supervisors. This could not be farther from the truth. Supervisors fume as they revise employees' wordy prose, eliminating deadwood and bureaucratic jargon. In short, do not confuse short words with simple ideas. The trick is to express complex ideas with words that your readers understand. Therefore, revise your sentences to eliminate the deadwood of business and bureaucratic jargon, legalese, trite expressions, clichés, and technical jargon.

Emphasis and De-emphasis Techniques   The ability and willingness to use emphasis and de-emphasis techniques can make the difference between average and exceptional letters and memos. For example, in a sales letter you would use emphasis techniques to highlight your central selling point. If your central selling point is some feature other than price, then you would use de-emphasis techniques to downplay your price. There are many opportunities in letters and memos to emphasize and de-emphasize information.

Common emphasis techniques include italicizing and boldfacing words, phrases, and sentences. Other examples include placing material you want to emphasize in emphasis positions in short sentences within short paragraphs. (*Emphasis positions* are near the beginning and end of sentences and paragraphs.) Still other examples include writing extensively about something and placing material you want emphasized in *active voice* sentences.

Common de-emphasis techniques include not italicizing and boldfacing words, phrases, or sentences. Other examples include placing material you want to de-emphasize near the center of long sentences in long paragraphs. Still other examples include writing briefly about the material you want to de-emphasize and placing it in a *passive voice* sentence.

Writing Concisely   In today's business place, employees who write concisely and clearly are valued. So be careful not to include unnecessary details. Know the depth of detail your reader needs. In addition, use short words instead of long words when short words can get the message across. If necessary, challenge yourself to write a greater number of short sentences. Finally, avoid using surplus words and phrases. *Surplus words and phrases* are those that do not affect message clarity when deleted or substituted with a shorter replacement.

Well-written, concise messages promote clarity and save people time. However, in your quest to write concise messages, be careful not to leave out details necessary for message clarity. Message clarity is always more important than conciseness!

SUMMARY: SECTION 1— THE FOUNDATIONS OF EFFECTIVE BUSINESS LETTERS AND MEMOS

- Decisions regarding formality expectations are crucial to selecting the best form of communication for writing situations.
- Business letters and memos are formal documents typically sent to external communication partners, but may also be sent internally to people within your organization.
- Business memos are semiformal documents that convey information to readers within the organization.
- Writing basics—grammar, punctuation, and spelling—impact the effectiveness of business letters.
- Key writing principles, such as appropriate word choice, emphasis and de-emphasis techniques, and concise writing, are critical to writing effective business letters and memos.

BUSINESS LETTERS

As mentioned before, letters are formal documents that are typically used to convey information to communication partners outside the organization. The goal most often is to either share neutral, good, or negative news or to persuade readers to a specific course of action.

Most letters are hardcopy documents sent to readers on company letterhead. Most are one page in length, although two- to three-page letters are not uncommon.

Some letters are developed and sent as e-mail letters, and some are sent as attachments to e-mail messages. Still others are transmitted through fax machines. Keep in mind, however, that sending hardcopy letters on company letterhead is the preferred approach, whether you are communicating with external or internal audiences. Some of this has to do with tradition, some with the formal statement that letters make, and some with the realization that e-mail can be easily hacked, raising privacy and security concerns.

© timquo/Shutterstock.com

FIGURE 11–1: FORM LETTERS

Some letters are sent to many people. This is especially true of sales letters or, for example, debt collection letters. In such situations writing separate, customized letters for each recipient would not be possible or necessary. Such letters are typically referred to as *form letters*. Form letters provide a cost-effective alternative in these letter-writing situations, whether the letter is sent in its entirety to numerous recipients or boilerplate text is inserted.

When the importance of the message escalates and the situation is non-routine, a form letter is the incorrect choice, in large part because it is often seen as too general, unpersuasive, and impersonal. A customized letter is required. A job application cover letter is such a situation. Since no two employers are exactly the same, it would be foolish to send a form cover letter to several recruiters. Cover letters should be customized for each employer and available position. If it is well written, such a letter is specific to the potential employer, persuasive, and personal. To send out form cover letters is like rolling dice—the odds are against you.

BUSINESS LETTER STYLES

The two most common letter styles are the block style and the modified block style. The **block style** is the more efficient of the two styles because all lines begin on the left margin, eliminating the need to set tabs and indent lines. With the block letter style you do not have to worry about forgetting to indent a line, whether it is the first line of a paragraph or another letter component. The **modified block letter style** is the more traditional style. Each style is presented below followed by a brief description of each component.

block letter style
Format for a business letter in which all lines, with the exception of the letterhead, begin at the left margin.

modified block letter style
Format for a business letter in which the date, complimentary closing, written signature, and keyboarded name start at the horizontal center point and the first line of each paragraph is indented one-half inch.

Block Letter Style The block letter style has gained popularity over the years due to its efficiencies. This style rightfully earns its name because every line of every letter component, with the exception of the company letterhead, starts at the left margin. The company letterhead is typically centered horizontally about one inch from the top of the page, whether keyboarded or preprinted. Standard top, bottom, and side margins are one inch.

The block style does not necessarily mean full justification. For many reasons, there is usually no attempt to have each line end evenly on the right margin. Figure 11-2 contains the block style letter contents.

FIGURE 11-2: BLOCK LETTER STYLE COMPONENTS

Company Letterhead

Return Address – If company letterhead is not used
Current Date
Inside Address – Person to whom you are writing
Attention Line – ATTENTION: Person's Name
Salutation:
Body Paragraphs – Do not indent the first line of each paragraph. Single space the paragraphs. Double space before the first paragraph, between paragraphs, and after the last paragraph.
Complimentary Close, – Followed by three blank lines for the written signature
Written Signature
Keyboarded Name
Sender's Title
Writer/Typist Initials – RW/gt
Enclosure Notation – Enclosed: Photos of new building
Copy Notation – Name(s) of people who also received the letter

Modified Block Letter Style The modified block letter style is a traditional style still used in some businesses. It differs from the block style in that the current date, complimentary closing, written signature, and keyboarded name/title start at the horizontal center point. The first line of each paragraph may start at the left margin as in the block style or may be indented one-half inch. With this style, the company letterhead is typically centered horizontally about one inch from the top of the page, whether keyboarded or preprinted. Standard top, bottom, and side margins are one inch.

As with the block style, there is usually no attempt at full justification. Figure 11-3 shows the modified block style letter contents.

FIGURE 11–3: MODIFIED BLOCK LETTER STYLE COMPONENTS

Company Letterhead

Current Date

Return Address – If company letterhead is not used

Inside Address – Person to whom you are writing

Attention Line – ATTENTION: Person's Name

Salutation:

Body Paragraphs – Do not indent the first line of each paragraph. Single space the paragraphs. Double space before the first paragraph, between paragraphs, and after the last paragraph.

Complimentary Close, – Followed by three blank lines for the written signature

Written Signature

Keyboarded Name

Title

Writer/Typist Initials – RW/gt

Enclosure Notation – Enclosed: Photos of new building

Copy Notation – Name(s) of people who also received the letter

© Lichtmeister/Shutterstock.com

SECOND-PAGE LETTER HEADINGS

When you write business letters that exceed one page, include a standard heading on succeeding pages. This way if the pages get separated or mixed up, they can be easily reordered.

The three components you should include in a standard second-page heading are the name of the person or company you are writing to, the page number, and the letter date. The most common second-page headings are the *vertical heading* and the *horizontal heading*.

Vertical Second-Page Heading This heading should start one inch from the top of the page on blank paper (or second-page stationery if your company uses it). Each heading component should begin at the left margin in a block format and should be single spaced. Triple space after the third line (current date), then continue with the body of the letter. Figure 11-4 contains an example of a vertical second-page heading.

FIGURE 11–4: VERTICAL SECOND-PAGE HEADING

Name of Recipient
Page # –Page 2
Current Date

Horizontal Second-Page Heading This heading should also start one inch from the top of the page on blank paper (or second-page stationery if your company uses it). With this heading style, all three heading components are on the same line. The name starts at the left margin, the page number is centered horizontally, and the current date is positioned so that it ends at the right margin. Triple space after that line, then continue with the body of the letter. Figure 11-5 contains an example of a horizontal second-page heading.

FIGURE 11–5: HORIZONTAL SECOND-PAGE HEADING

Name of Recipient	**2**	**Current Date**

BUSINESS LETTER COMPONENTS

The typical business letter contains the following standard components: *company letterhead, current date, inside address,* **salutation**, *body,* **complimentary close**, *written signature,* and *keyboarded name/title*. Each is described below. In addition, some business letters contain one or more other components. Common among these are **attention line**, **subject line**, *enclosure notation, copy notation,* and *postscript*. Each of these is also described below.

© Vectomart/Shutterstock.com

Company Letterhead This is typically preprinted on company stationery and contains information such as company logo, company name, post office box address, physical address, e-mail address, telephone number, and fax number.

Current Date This sounds simple enough, but certain standards should be adhered to. When writing letters to U.S. communication partners, spell out the month followed by the date and year (June 5, 2014). Do not use the digital version (06-05-14 or 6-5-14 or

6-5-2014). When writing letters to international communication partners, it is more typical to start with day followed by the month and year (5 June 2014).

Inside Address The inside address (or letter address) contains the name and mailing address of the person or company the letter is being sent to.

Salutation This is the greeting to the reader. If you are writing to a specific individual, the typical salutation is the word *Dear* followed by the receiver's title (Ms., Mr., Dr., etc.) and surname followed by a colon, for example, Dear Ms. Garcia:. If you are writing to a company and do not have a specific individual's name, use a salutation such as Human Resources Department or To Whom It May Concern.

Body This is the message. Most business letters contain three parts: an *opening paragraph*, one or more *body paragraphs*, and a *closing paragraph*. Each of these parts is discussed at some length in the Writing Strategies section.

Complimentary Close As the term suggests, this closes the letter. It is typically a word or phrase followed by a comma. Examples of popular complimentary closes include *Sincerely* and *Respectfully*. Although they are less widely used, complimentary closings such as *Sincerely yours* and *Very truly yours* are still used by some.

Written Signature This is the writer's written signature. It is typical to leave three blank lines between the complimentary close and keyboarded name components for the writer's written signature.

Keyboarded Name/Title At minimum, this component contains the keyboarded name of the writer. In addition, the writer's job title should follow his or her name either to the right of it (e.g., William G. Rogers, Project Director) or below it. If your title appears on the line below, omit the comma after your name on the line above.

OTHER BUSINESS LETTER COMPONENTS

Attention Line Use this when you will send your letter to a company, but want to direct it to a specific person (Attention: Mr. Kuo), position (Attention: Marketing Director), or a department within the company (Attention: Information Systems Department). It is the second line of the inside address.

Subject Line As the term implies, the subject line tells the reader, in brief, the nature of the letter. It starts with the word *Subject*: followed by colon, then a five- or six-word message description. The subject line is located between the salutation and the first paragraph of the body.

Enclosure Notation This notation indicates to the reader that you have sent along one or more items with the letter. If you enclose one item, either type Enclosure (the word only) or type Enclosure followed by a colon and the item enclosed (Enclosure: Sale Flyer). If you enclose two or more items, type Enclosures followed by a colon and the number of enclosures (Enclosure: 2). The enclosure notation is located one blank line below the keyboarded name/title component.

Copy Notation This tells the reader the name(s) of others the letter was sent to. Here are some examples: cc: Tamara Jones, cc: Tamara Jones & Jennifer Maxwell. The copy notation is located one blank line below the enclosure notation. If there is no enclosure, the copy notation is located one blank line below the keyboarded name/title component.

Postscript The postscript typically contains an afterthought or a brief reminder of information that the writer wants to emphasize. Type PS followed by the entry. The

salutation
The letter's greeting (e.g., Dear
_____).

complimentary closing
The letter's closing (e.g., Sincerely).

attention line
In the address block, drawing attention to a specific person or position.

subject line
Brief statement that specifies the letter's subject.

postscript is located one blank line below the copy notation. If there is no copy notation, the postscript is located one blank line below the enclosure notation. If there is no enclosure notation or copy notation, the postscript comes one blank line below the keyboarded name/ title component.

SUMMARY: SECTION 2— BUSINESS LETTERS

- The two major business letter styles are the block and modified block.
- In business letters that exceed one page, include a standardized heading on each page beyond the first page.
- Business letter components include company letterhead, current date, inside address, salutation, body, complimentary close, written signature, keyboarded name/title, attention line, subject line, enclosure notation, copy notation, and postscript.

WRITING STRATEGIES

Business letters and memos typically have one of three purposes. The purpose may be to (1) share neutral or good news, (2) share negative news, or (3) persuade the reader to take some action. Each letter-writing strategy is discussed and presented in detail.

But first, a practical reminder is in order. Even if a specific letter-writing strategy is the clear and logical choice for a message, do not use that strategy if you know your

© YanLev/Shutterstock.com

communication partner wants the message structured differently. For example, when conveying negative news, writers typically avoid sharing the bad news until later in the letter for reasons that are explained shortly. However, if you know your communication partner (reader) wants you to get to the main point early in the letter, then overlook the dictates of the preferred writing strategy. While letter-writing strategies are both logical and effective, reader expectations and desires must also be taken into consideration.

Now, let's look at the recommended letter-writing strategies for the three business letter categories—neutral or good news, negative news, and persuasive messages. When properly integrated, these strategies typically improve your ability to accomplish your message objective. The three strategies are most frequently referred to as the *direct strategy*, the *indirect strategy*, and the *persuasive strategy*. Before doing so, however, it is especially helpful to remind you of the roles de-emphasis and emphasis techniques play in the development of effective business letters. This is especially true of indirect strategy (negative news) and persuasive strategy (persuasive) business letters. Figure 11-6 contains several de-emphasis and emphasis techniques.

FIGURE 11–6: DE-EMPHASIS AND EMPHASIS TECHNIQUES

De-emphasis Techniques

In regard to indirect strategy (negative news) business letters, writers are challenged to not only share the negative news with the reader, but to do so in such a way that the reader won't take their business elsewhere permanently. Appropriate letter-writing strategy and tone are critical to achieving this goal. Appropriate use of de-emphasis techniques plays an important role also. Business writers obviously need to state the negative news in such letters, but they do not have to put the spotlight on it, which many readers would find annoying. Instead, they should use de-emphasis techniques that lower the spotlight. Here are some de-emphasis techniques that will help you do so when you are writing indirect strategy business letters.

- State the negative news in a paragraph located near the middle of the letter
- State the negative news in the middle of a paragraph
- State the negative news in the middle of a reasonably long sentence
- State the negative news using the passive voice
- Avoid repeating/restating the negative news
- Avoid using emphasis techniques such as boldfacing and italicizing

Emphasis Techniques

In regard to persuasive-strategy (persuasive) business letters, writers are challenged to persuade readers to buy, do, or support something. Creating reader desire is the central goal when writing these letters and using appropriate emphasis techniques will help you achieve it. Essentially, you would use emphasis techniques in persuasive-strategy business letters to emphasis (put the spotlight on) qualities that will build reader desire (e.g., *central selling point in a sales letter*) Here are some emphasis techniques that will help you do so when you are writing persuasive-strategy business letters.

- State desire-building qualities near the beginning and/or end of paragraphs
- State the desire-building qualities in short sentences
- State the desire-building qualities using the active voice
- Restate the desire-building qualities where appropriate
- Use emphasis techniques where appropriate (e.g., *boldfacing, underscoring, italicizing*)

DIRECT STRATEGY

The **direct strategy** works well with business letters meant to share neutral or good news. Neutral- and good-news letters include a wide range of letter types, including letters providing or requesting routine information and responding favorably to requests for action. Examples range from claim letters, thank-you letters, and job-offer letters to letters providing credit information, letters of appreciation, and letters of condolence.

direct strategy
Letter-writing style used for positive or neutral news in which the main idea is presented at the beginning of the letter.

This is the easiest strategy and message type to write because you are satisfying your reader's needs and, in the case of good-news messages, putting him or her in a good mood. Believe it or not, it is possible to write ineffective neutral- and good-news letters by careless handling of writing strategy, tone, clarity, grammar, and/or punctuation. This is unfortunate when it happens because writing these letters effectively is not difficult.

Central to the direct strategy is sharing the neutral or good news in the first paragraph, thus placing the reader in a positive frame of mind. This vastly increases the likelihood that the reader's interest and attention will be maintained to the end of the letter. The direct strategy is outlined below.

Direct Strategy Outline

- **Opening Paragraph.** Present the main idea—the neutral or good news—and develop a friendly tone.

Specifically, state the news in the first sentence of the opening paragraph so you can capture the reader's interest from the outset.

- **Body Paragraph(s).** Present the supporting information and maintain a friendly tone.

The central purpose of the body is to logically and clearly present information that supports the main idea (the neutral or good news).

- **Closing Paragraph.** Maintain a friendly tone and include some forward-looking talk when applicable. End the letter positively.

The tone in neutral-news and good-news letters should be positive, sincere, and conversational. It should be devoid of negative words.

Now, let's look at a poorly written, direct strategy, good-news letter (Figure 11-7). The letter makes a job offer to a candidate following his interview. Sounds like an easy letter to write—right? They are easy letters to write if we know how to write them and care about doing a good job.

FIGURE 11-7: DIRECT STRATEGY, GOOD-NEWS LETTER (POORLY WRITTEN VERSION)

22 Harris Drive
Houston, TX 77003
(713) 436-9102

April 2, 2021

1078 First St.
Austin, TX 78702

Dear Chao:

It was a pleasure visiting with you on March 15. Advanced Energies is a leader in the energy industry, and I am certain you were impressed with all you learned about us during your visit. While Advanced Energies has focused predominately on oil and natural gas exploration in the past, we are currently entering the solar energy market with plans for expansion. With all this growth and diversity, we are adding to our ranks of employees and that's where you come in. We would like you to come to work for us.

We will start you out with a two-day orientation next month. Then, we will place you in one of the areas where we have the most need of help. I hope you are flexible in regard to the type of work you do. During your orientation we will discuss your starting pay rate and benefits package.

See you in May.

Very truly yours,

Juan Lopez
Legal Department

Enclosures: 3

Before reading further, take a few minutes to identify the weaknesses in the poorly written letter above. You should be able to identify a number of weaknesses in all three letter parts.

Now, let's look at some of some of letter's weaknesses.

Opening Paragraph. While the tone is friendly, there are three noticeable weaknesses. (1) The good news should have been shared in the first sentence, not the last. The reader may have tossed the letter before getting to the last sentence, assuming a rejection was forthcoming. (2) All the hype about the company in sentences 2 and 3 is unnecessary, making the letter longer than necessary. (3) The you-attitude is weak. The opening is writer centered instead of reader centered and is reinforced by the inclusion of several *I's*, *we's*, and *our's*.

Body Paragraph. There are three noticeable weaknesses. (1) The tone is semifriendly at best. (2) The you-attitude is weak. (3) Many details are missing, thus leaving questions. When will the orientation take place? Where will the orientation take place? What type of work will the reader do? What is the starting pay? What are the starting benefits?

Closing Paragraph. There are three noticeable weaknesses. (1) The tone is not friendly. (2) The closing is writer centered. A you-attitude is nowhere to be found. (3) There is no

"We look forward to …" statement at the end. In addition, the complimentary closing *Very truly yours* is outdated. *Sincerely* is a friendly close that is appropriate for this letter.

Now let's look at an improved version of the letter (Figure 11–8).

FIGURE 11–8: DIRECT STRATEGY, GOOD-NEWS LETTER (IMPROVED VERSION)

22 Harris Drive
Houston, TX 77003
(713) 436-9102

April 2, 2021

Mr. Chao Yung
1078 First St.
Austin, TX 78702

Dear Chao:

We are pleased to offer you the position of Research Director in the Legal Department at Advanced Energies. You have the exact qualifications and personality we hoping to find in a candidate for this position and believe we are a good fit for you also.

As mentioned during our March 24 interview, orientation will take place on April 17–18. Plan to arrive at my office (2024B, second floor, Progressive Tower) at 9 a.m. on April 17. We have much information to share with you, and know you will have questions. Please develop a list of questions you have and e-mail it to me by April 16 so I have time to review it prior to meeting with you. In addition, please review the attached benefits information and be prepared to make selections from the benefits options. Finally, please review the Legal Department's policy handbook, which can be found at AEpolicies@lgldept.com prior to April 17.

We are excited about having you as a member of the Advanced Energies team. During the upcoming days, please contact me at (713) 436-9102, ext. 32 or at juan.lopez27@AE.org. See you on the 17th.

Sincerely,

Juan Lopez
Legal Department

Enclosures: 3

Before reading further, take a few minutes to identify the strengths of this improved version.

Now, let me share some of the strengths in the improved letter.

Four strengths are particularly noticeable in this improved version of the opening paragraph. (1) The good news is shared in the first sentence, placing the reader in a good frame of mind. He will read more! (2) There is a strong you-attitude. The opening is reader centered, as it should be. (3) The writer compliments the reader. (4) The tone is friendly.

Body Paragraph. Three strengths are evident in this improved body paragraph. (1) The you-attitude is strong. (2) Supporting information is included, which removes guessing and frustration from the equation. (3) The tone is friendly.

Closing Paragraph. Four strengths should jump out in the closing paragraph of this improved version. (1) The you-attitude is strong. (2) The tone is friendly. (3) Practical, forward-looking talk is included. (4) Contacting the company is made clear and easy.

In addition, using *Sincerely* for the complimentary closing was the right choice. It is friendly and right on the mark.

Now let's look at another poorly written, direct strategy, good-news letter (Figure 11-9). The situation the letter is based on grows out of a farmer's request to a farm equipment distributor for a line of credit so he can purchase global positioning systems for his combine and tractors. The equipment distributor decided to grant the farmer's request and is writing to inform him of the good news. Sounds like a simple letter to write—right? The poorly written sample below reminds us that, when we are careless, we can weaken even an easy letter!

© PathDoc/Shutterstock.com

FIGURE 11-9: DIRECT STRATEGY, GOOD-NEWS LETTER (POORLY WRITTEN VERSION)

213 Lima Avenue
Findlay, OH 45840
(419) 724-6153

June 12, 2021

Mr. Robert G. Conway
CR347
Arcadia, OH 44804

Dear Mr. Conway:

We are pleased with your interest in the Global Star global positioning system. Our Global Star global positioning system is revolutionizing the farming industry! Our global positioning system can save users enough money to pay it off quickly with increased profits. This is why we are happy to grant you credit to purchase the equipment you expressed interest in.

Our field representative, Tom Holman, will call you soon to get you on his installation schedule. Following this initial meeting, contact Tom any time you have questions.

Thanks for giving us your business.

Cordially,

Sharon Tyler
Accounts Manager

Before reading further, take a few minutes to identify the weaknesses in the poorly written letter. You should be able to identify a number of weaknesses in all three letter parts.

Now, let me share some of the letter's weaknesses.

Opening Paragraph. While the tone is friendly, there are four noticeable weaknesses. (1) The good news should have been shared in the first sentence, not the last. The reader may have tossed the letter before getting to the last sentence, assuming a rejection was forthcoming. (2) All the unnecessary sales talk leading up to the good news makes the letter longer than necessary. (3) The you-attitude is weak. The writer-centered opening (instead of being reader centered) is reinforced by the inclusion of several *we's* and *our's*. (4) More detail is needed in the last sentence. Credit is being granted, but the amount is not specified. This farmer could be left guessing and wondering if he received the full amount he applied for or less or more.

Body Paragraph. While the tone is friendly and a you-attitude is evident, there are two noticeable problems. (1) The word *soon* is vague and can be improved by being specific. Farmers often live by tight schedules, especially around planting and harvest times. They need specifics. (2) Lots of details are missing, thus leaving questions. How long will the installation take? Will time be set aside for training and, if so, how long will it take? What is the preferred way to contact Tom?

Closing Paragraph. While the tone sounds friendly on the surface, there are two major problems. (1) The closing is writer centered. A you-attitude is nowhere in sight! (2) There is no attempt to offer some forward-looking talk. This situation is ripe for forward-looking talk. For example, the writer could mention future increases in the farmer's credit line or include a brochure describing other equipment the farmer might find of interest. In addition, the writer could offer the farmer discounts on future purchases based on referred customers (fellow farmers). Oh, the missed opportunities!

The complimentary closing *Cordially* is cold. *Sincerely* is a friendlier close, and a friendly close is appropriate for this letter.

Now, let's look at an improved version of the letter (Figure 11-10).

FIGURE 11–10: DIRECT STRATEGY, GOOD-NEWS
LETTER (IMPROVED VERSION)

213 Lima Avenue
Findlay, OH 45840
(419) 724-6153

June 12, 2021

Mr. Robert G. Conway
CR347
Arcadia, OH 44804

Dear Mr. Conway:

Your request for a $20,000 line of credit toward farm equipment purchases has been approved. This clears the way for you to move ahead and purchase the global positioning systems for your combine and tractors and get them installed before it's time to harvest your wheat crop next month.

Our field representative, Tom Holman, will call you on June 16 to schedule a day and time convenient for you to install your new systems. If you have questions regarding the credit conditions, equipment, installation, or training that you want to ask Tom about before he calls you on the 16th, please contact him at (419) 724-6153, ext. 5 or at tholman@globalstar.org. It will take approximately four hours to install the systems and approximately one hour to train you on them.

We really appreciate that you came to us with your equipment needs, and we trust that the global positioning systems will exceed your expectations! The $20,000 credit line will easily cover the cost of the equipment you expressed interest in; leaving you an extra $5,000 for future purchases. With this in mind, consider visiting our website to learn about other farm equipment products you may find useful. If you have questions or want to explore your next equipment purchase, stop by our store in Findlay or call me at (419) 724-6153, ext. 2.

Sincerely,

Sharon Tyler
Accounts Manager

Before reading further, take a few minutes to identify the strengths in this improved version.

Now, let me share some of the strengths in the improved letter.

Opening Paragraph. Four strengths are noticeable in this improved version of the opening paragraph. (1) The good news was shared in the first sentence, placing the farmer in a good frame of mind. He will read on! (2) There is a strong you-attitude. The opening is reader centered, as it should be. (3) The specific amount of credit approved is stated, leaving no room for confusion or frustration. (4) The tone is friendly.

Body Paragraph. Four strengths should be evident in this improved version of the body paragraphs. (1) The you-attitude is strong. (2) Vague words such as *soon* have been omitted. (3) Supporting information is included, which removes guessing and frustration from the equation. (4) The tone is friendly.

Closing Paragraph. Three strengths should jump out in the closing paragraph of this improved version. (1) The you-attitude is strong. (2) The tone is friendly. (3) Practical, forward-looking talk is included that ranges from mention of the excess available credit to the invitation to explore other product lines online.

Using *Sincerely* for the complimentary closing was the right choice. It is a friendly complimentary close and right on the mark.

INDIRECT STRATEGY

indirect strategy
Letter-writing style used for negative news in which the main idea is presented after the reasons building to the bad news have been presented.

The **indirect strategy** works well with negative-news business letters. Examples of negative-news letters include request refusals, claim refusals, credit refusals, job rejection letters, and a host of other situations requiring a negative response.

For many, this is the most difficult strategy and message type to write because you are sharing information that your reader does not want to see, all the while doing your best to maintain goodwill. This is no small challenge! These letters require special attention to writing strategy and tone.

Central to the indirect strategy is delaying the mention of the negative news until after you have laid out the reasons supporting the negative outcome. The attempt here is to set a logical base for the decision that the reader can understand. The reader may not be pleased with your negative decision, but should understand on a logical level why the decision had to be made as it was.

Indirect Strategy Outline

- **Opening Paragraph.** Present neutral, on-topic talk and develop a friendly tone.

Key to this strategy is not stating or hinting at the negative news in the opening paragraph. Not hinting that the outcome is good news is also equally important. To state or hint at the negative news in the opening paragraph turns off your reader to the rest of the letter. To hint at good news would only result in a harder fall for the reader when he or she reads the negative news later. Remain neutral and friendly and do not hint!

- **Body Paragraph(s).** Present reasons supporting the negative news, state the negative news, offer alternative(s) to the original request where applicable, and maintain a friendly tone.

This is the section where most of the work is accomplished in this type of letter. Start this section with the reasons leading up to the negative-news decision, all the while not giving away the negative news. That is a tough job! Then state the negative news clearly and tactfully. However, do not end the body at that point if possible. When applicable, follow up the negative news with one or more alternatives. Alternatives tell readers you care and give them choices in an otherwise uncontrollable situation.

- **Closing Paragraph.** Maintain a friendly tone and include some forward-looking talk when applicable.

Your goal here is to ease your reader in a forward-looking direction. This means you do not apologize and do not repeat the negative news. After all, you stated and explained the negative news clearly and tactfully in the body paragraph(s) and started easing the disappointment with offers of alternatives. Why would you now in the closing paragraph want to circumvent all that good effort by reminding the reader of the negative news? Finally, end the paragraph with a friendly tone and some forward-looking talk.

As previously mentioned, your tone in negative-news letters is crucial. Keep the tone positive, sincere, and tactful. Avoid using negative words or coming across as preachy, cold, defensive, condescending, patronizing, or arrogant.

Now let's look at a poorly written, indirect strategy, negative-news letter (Figure 11-11). The situation involves a ski resort and a job applicant. The ski resort has received below-average snowfall going into December, which has reduced customer traffic. As a result, it is unable to hire this job applicant at this time. Thus, we are looking at an employment rejection letter.

FIGURE 11–11: INDIRECT STRATEGY, NEGATIVE-NEWS LETTER (POORLY WRITTEN VERSION)

14 Timberlane Rd.
Sante Fe, NM 87594
(505) 331-2424

December 2, 2021

Mr. Nicholas P. Brunsell
2400 Brumly St., Apt. 27
Santa Fe, NM 87504

Dear Nick:

The weather sure hasn't been very cooperative this fall. Here we are in early December, and we've had only one decent snowfall. It dropped enough snow for us to open a few runs, but we are nowhere close to full operation. We are really hurting because of this situation. This is not what you want to hear because the situation has caused us to initiate a hiring freeze.

Conditions will change if we get some more snow soon, but I am not holding out much hope with all this talk about global warming. If by some miracle we do get two or more significant snowfalls soon, everything will be good for us, and we will consider hiring additional help. I guess we will see what happens.

Sorry to have to share bad news. Thanks for your interest in working for the Sunny Valley Resort.

Sincerely,

Ron Baker
Operating Manager

Before reading further, take a few minutes to identify the weaknesses in the poorly written letter. You should be able to identify a number of weaknesses in all three letter parts.

Now, let me share some of the weaknesses in the letter.

Opening Paragraph. Very little positive can be said about this opening paragraph except that the grammar, punctuation, and spelling are in pretty good shape. Otherwise, it is loaded with weaknesses. Three main weaknesses come to mind. (1) The writer uses the direct strategy instead of the indirect strategy, giving away the bad news in the opening paragraph. (2) There is too much detail in the first two sentences, contributing to unnecessary wordiness. (3) The you-attitude is weak.

Body Paragraph. As was the case with the opening paragraph, little positive can be said about it. The paragraph contains numerous weaknesses. (1) It opens with pessimistic news. (2) The you-attitude is nonexistent. (3) The writer does not offer any tangible alternatives.

Closing Paragraph. The closing paragraph also contains several weaknesses. Four are evident. (1) The writer reminds the reader of the negative news from the first paragraph. (2) The writer apologizes to the reader. (3) The closing is not especially friendly. (4) There is no forward-looking talk.

Now, let's look at an improved version of the same letter (Figure 11-12).

FIGURE 11–12: INDIRECT STRATEGY, NEGATIVE-NEWS LETTER (IMPROVED VERSION)

14 Timberlane Rd.
Sante Fe, NM 87594
(505) 331-2424

December 2, 2021

Mr. Nicholas X. Jackson
2400 Brumly St., Apt. 27
Santa Fe, New Mexico 87504

Dear Nick:

We have finally been blessed with a long-overdue snowfall. For snowboarding enthusiasts, such as yourself, this is certainly good news.

We plan to open approximately half of our beginner and intermediate runs and one-quarter of our advanced runs this coming Saturday, with the hope that there will be enough new snowfall during the next three weeks to open the remaining runs by Christmas. In the meantime, we plan to supplement as much as possible with man-made powder. Even then, at least one significant snowfall will be needed to ready the remaining runs. At the time that we are able to open at least 80 percent of the runs, we will be able to hire on additional help. Until then, the volume of business will not support hiring additional seasonal staff. Despite this temporary setback, if you are still interested in working at the Sunny Valley Resort this winter, please e-mail me at Ron-Baker12@sunnyvalley.org. As soon as snow conditions are right to support opening most of the remaining runs, we will bring you onboard. If for some reason this doesn't occur, we would like you to consider joining our summer whitewater rafting staff. Doing so would then secure you a guaranteed position with us for next winter.

I believe you will be a valuable member of Sunny Valley team and look forward to working with you. Please stay in touch.

Sincerely,

Ron Baker
Operating Manager

Before reading further, take a few minutes to identify the strengths in the improved version.

Now, let's look at some strengths in the improved letter.

Opening Paragraph. Five strengths are particularly noticeable in this improved version of the opening paragraph of the letter. (1) The negative news is not stated in the opening paragraph. (2) There is no hint of negative or positive news in the opening paragraph. The writer remains neutral. (3) There is a strong you-attitude. (4) The subject matter is on topic. (5) The tone is friendly.

Body Paragraph. Five strengths are particularly evident in this improved version of the body paragraph of the letter. (1) The you-attitude is strong. (2) Reasons supporting the negative news are presented in appropriate order and stated clearly. (3) The negative news is stated clearly, yet tactfully. (4) Alternatives are presented following the negative news, thus de-emphasizing the negative news. (5) The tone is friendly.

Closing Paragraph. Five strengths should jump out in the closing paragraph of this improved version of the letter. (1) The reader is not reminded of the negative news nor did the writer apologize in the closing paragraph. (2) The you-attitude is strong. (3) The tone is friendly. (4) The writer compliments the reader and expresses interest in working with him. (5) Forward-looking talk is included in such a way that the writer can be easily contacted.

Using *Sincerely* for the complimentary closing is the right choice. It is friendly and right on the mark.

Now let's look at another poorly written, indirect strategy, negative-news letter (Figure 11-13). The letter situation grows out of a researcher's request to access some of a company's data for a research project. The company has decided not to grant the researcher's request. Thus, the letter is a negative-news letter informing the researcher that she cannot access the desired company data. The poorly written sample below reminds us of the damage to goodwill that can result from a carelessly written, negative-news letter.

10 Franklin Avenue
Boston, MA 02103
(617) 558-9867

February 16, 2021

Ms. Nancee L. Reid
457 Hartford Lane
Boston, MA 02105

Dear Ms. Reid:

This letter is being written to inform you that DD&D Corporation has no interest in taking part in your corporate sales projections research project. We will not grant you permission to access our sales projections figures.

In fact, our company has a policy that prohibits its participation in external research projects such as yours. If we were to provide sales projection figures to you for your proposed project, it would cause us numerous problems because other researchers would then expect the same treatment!

We are sorry we couldn't meet your request. However, if we can help you in any other way, please let us know.

Cordially,

Jeff Oliver
Public Relations Manager

Before reading further, take a few minutes to identify the weaknesses in the poorly written letter. You should be able to identify a number of weaknesses in all three letter parts.

Now, let me share some of the weaknesses in the above letter.

Opening Paragraph. Very little positive can be said about this opening paragraph except that the grammar, punctuation, and spelling are in pretty good shape. Otherwise, it is loaded with weaknesses. Five weaknesses come to mind. (1) The writer uses the direct strategy instead of the indirect strategy, giving away the bad news in the opening paragraph. (2) The second sentence is unnecessary, contributing to unnecessary wordiness. (3) The tone is unnecessarily negative, abrupt, and unfriendly. (4) The writer implies that the researcher's project is unimportant. (5) The you-attitude is nonexistent.

Body Paragraph. As is the case with the opening paragraph, little positive can be said about the body paragraph. It also contains numerous weaknesses. Four weaknesses come to mind. (1) The opening phrase, *In fact*, rubs salt into the wounds already opened in the first paragraph and is a continuation of an unwarranted negative tone. (2) The you-attitude is nonexistent. (3) The writer does not provide the reader much to base the denial on. (4) The writer hides behind a company policy he doesn't explain.

Closing Paragraph. The closing paragraph also contains several weaknesses. (1) The writer reminds the reader of the negative news in the closing paragraph. (2) The writer apologizes to the reader in the closing paragraph. (3) Attempts at being friendly and the brief forward-looking talk come off as insincere in light of the unnecessarily negative tone throughout the opening and body paragraphs.

Cordially is a cold closing. *Sincerely* is a friendlier close, and a friendly close is more appropriate for this letter.

Now, let's look at an improved version of the same letter (Figure 11-14).

FIGURE 11–14: INDIRECT STRATEGY, NEGATIVE-NEWS LETTER (IMPROVED VERSION)

10 Franklin Avenue
Boston, MA 02103
(617) 558-9867

February 16, 2021

Ms. Nancee L. Reid
457 Hartford Lane
Boston, Massachusetts 02105

Dear Ms. Reid:

We appreciate your interest in using DD&D Corporation data in your corporate sales projections research project. The project sounds very interesting.

Each year we receive several requests asking for our assistance with research projects similar to yours. As a result, we established guidelines to determine which requests we can honor and which we cannot. One such guideline is that we only permit sales projections figures to leave corporate headquarters after they are announced publicly through press releases. The timing of your request is such that the sales projections figures you are requesting will not be released until April 15. Thus, we are unable to grant your request at this time. However, if you can wait for another two months, we should be able to grant your request then.

Your project has piqued my interest, and I look forward to seeing your findings once you finish. Please contact me at oliver@dd&dcorp.org if you have questions or other research needs.

Sincerely,

Jeff Oliver
Public Relations Manager

© Elnur/Shutterstock.com

Before reading further, take a few minutes to identify the strengths in the improved version.

Now, let's look at some strengths in the improved letter.

Opening Paragraph. Five strengths are particularly noticeable in this improved version of the letter's opening paragraph. (1) The negative news is not stated in the opening paragraph. (2) There is no hint of negative or positive news in the opening paragraph. The writer remains neutral. (3) There is a strong you-attitude. (4) The subject matter is on topic. (5) The tone is friendly.

Body Paragraph. Five strengths are evident in this improved version of the body paragraph. (1) The you-attitude is strong. (2) Reasons supporting the negative news are presented in appropriate order and stated clearly. (3) The negative news is stated clearly, yet tactfully. (4) An alternative is offered following the negative news, thus de-emphasizing the negative news. (5) The tone is friendly.

Closing Paragraph. Five strengths should jump out in the closing paragraph of this improved version. (1) The reader is not reminded of the negative news nor does the writer apologize in the closing paragraph. (2) The you-attitude is strong. (3) The tone is friendly. (4) The writer makes a complimentary statement about the research project and expresses interest in seeing the findings. (5) Forward-looking talk is included in such a way that the writer can be easily contacted.

Using *Sincerely* for the complimentary closing is the right choice. It is friendly and right on the mark.

PERSUASIVE STRATEGY

persuasive strategy
Letter-writing style used for persuasive letters in which the request is made after the reason(s) have been presented.

The **persuasive strategy** works well with business letters that are meant to persuade the reader to take a specific course of action. Examples of persuasive business letters include sales letters, collection letters, recommendation letters, job offer letters, and letters ranging from requesting a favor to requesting some form of support. The persuasive letter-writing strategy is similar to the indirect strategy in that the request is made later in the letter, just as the negative news is stated later in the negative-news letter.

Many find writing persuasively a challenging strategy and a difficult message approach to write because persuading others to a course of action is not easy. Writing persuasively is no small challenge! These letters require special attention to writing strategy and tone.

Central to the persuasive strategy is delaying the request until after you have laid out reader benefits. This involves not only capturing the reader's attention, but also building his or her interest and, ultimately, desire before making the request. Using the persuasive strategy properly increases the odds that your reader will act on your request in the desired fashion. The persuasive strategy is outlined below.

Persuasive Strategy Outline

- **Opening Paragraph.** Gain the reader's attention and develop a friendly tone.

Key to the persuasive strategy is not making the request in the opening paragraph. To state the request here would likely turn your reader off to your objective. It is also important that you capture your reader's attention in the opening paragraph so he or she will want to read on. A question is a good sentence structure for capturing readers' attention. Here is an example that I bet will catch your attention: How would you like to reduce your costs?

- **Body Paragraph(s).** Build the reader's interest, then their desire. Next, state your request.

The body paragraph is an important section in persuasive letters. Here you start by building reader interest and ultimately desire before stating your request. Building interest and desire are at the heart of your ability to persuade your reader to respond positively to your request. Essentially, you are challenged to determine one or more ways to appeal to your reader, realizing that different situations and people are persuaded by different appeals. Common appeal categories include *direct gain*, *prestige*, and *altruism*. Specific examples of appeals include profit, recognition, pride, usefulness, and savings. As you might guess, the list of appeals is long. Once you have built desire, state your request clearly and make sure you make it easy for the reader to respond.

- **Closing Paragraph.** Restate your request or make the request if you didn't do so in the body. Make it easy for your reader to respond and include some forward-looking talk when applicable. Maintain a friendly tone.

The closing paragraph of a persuasive letter is more involved than the closing paragraph of direct and indirect strategy letters. For example, you would start the closing paragraph in a persuasive letter by stating the request if you did not do so in the body. Or, you might choose to open the closing paragraph with a restatement of the request if you made it in the body section. Make it easy for the reader to respond. End with a friendly tone and forward-looking talk.

As previously mentioned, your tone in persuasive request letters is important. Keep it positive, sincere, and tactful. Avoid negative words and do not come across as patronizing, condescending, arrogant, or pushy.

Let's look at a poorly written persuasive letter (Figure 11-15). This is a basic sales letter written with the goal of persuading the reader to choose Shooting Star Airlines the next time he or she takes a commercial flight. The poorly written sample will likely do little to convince the reader to fly Shooting Star Airlines.

AIDA: Attention-Interest-Desire-Action
http://www.mindtools.com/pages/article/AIDA.htm

FIGURE 11–15: PERSUASIVE STRATEGY LETTER (POORLY WRITTEN VERSION)

217 North State Street
Chicago, IL 60604
(312) 852-6311

August 18, 2021

Ms. Leslie Koval Tanner
319 Bradford Lane
St. Louis, MO 63105

Dear Ms. Koval Tanner:

Tired of all the hassle and expense involved in flying commercial? We are here to offer you a much more pleasant and affordable travel experience. We want you to fly Shooting Star Airlines.

Shooting Star doesn't nickel and dime you to death with all those fees like most of the other commercial airlines, with the exception of luggage. Luggage is something that we can't even avoid charging you extra for. While we are disappointed that we have to charge for luggage, we trust you understand our position.

We know you are going to want to fly Shooting Star Airlines when you hear about our food and beverage offering. Unlike our competitors, on Shooting Star flights you will receive a free refill on soft drinks, tea, and coffee and an extra bag of peanuts or pretzels. We even let you use a small blanket for free when you get cold, which is typical on those northern routes. One of the ways we are able to offer so many extras, free of charge, is that all our flights have stopovers at two or more small, regional airports where we pick up additional passengers. Each of these stops will provide you with an opportunity to stretch your legs and, in some cases, buy a snack in the airport lobby. And if all that is not enough to impress you, every passenger on our flights can use the restroom at the front of the plane. There is no discrimination against passengers who fly coach!

Are you ready to fly Shooting Star Airlines? I bet you are, and we are ready to book your next flight. Just go online and look us up. Our service agents are standing by. Have your credit card ready, and thanks for the business!

Sincerely,

Miranda Krause
CEO & President

Before reading further, take a few minutes to identify the weaknesses in the poorly written persuasive letter above. You should be able to identify a number of weaknesses in all three parts.

Now, let's look at some weaknesses in the poorly written letter.

Opening Paragraph. There are three major weaknesses in the opening paragraph. (1) The writer follows a direct strategy by making the request in the opening paragraph instead of the less direct persuasive strategy. (2) The tone is neutral. (3) The you-attitude is weak at best.

Body Paragraphs. There are two problems with the body paragraphs. (1) While the writer builds interest, she did not build desire. For example, stating that there is a luggage fee and two or more stops at regional airports is a turnoff to most. (2) The request is not stated in the body as the persuasive strategy dictates.

Closing Paragraph. The closing paragraph contains three major weaknesses. (1) The you-attitude is weak. (2) The tone is cheesy and sounds like a cheap radio or TV commercial. (3) Contact information is not provided.

Now look at an improved version of the same letter (Figure 11-16).

FIGURE 11-16: PERSUASIVE STRATEGY LETTER (IMPROVED VERSION)

217 North State Street
Chicago, IL 60604
(312) 852-6311

August 18, 2021

Ms. Leslie Koval Tanner
319 Bradford Lane
St. Louis, MO 63105

Dear Ms. Koval Tanner:

Do you remember the last time you enjoyed a commercial airline flight? It has probably been several years since you used words such as *enjoyable* and *pleasant* to describe your flying experience. Fortunately, enjoyable, pleasant commercial flights have not been lost to the past!

You may have heard about Shooting Star Airlines. We are "the new kids on the block" in the commercial airline industry, having provided service for slightly more than six months. Shooting Star Airlines currently flies routes to all major metropolitan airports and select regional airports in the United States and leads the industry in on-time flight arrivals and customer satisfaction.

From the outset, Shooting Star Airlines set a goal to be noticeably different than its competitors. Specifically, we set out to put the fun back into flying by making it a more enjoyable and pleasant experience so people would look forward to flying. The first step was to hire positive people who have a strong desire to serve customers. Next, we built more comfort into our airplanes, resulting in more legroom and bigger seats than our competitors. Shooting Star didn't stop there. We also provide flat screen monitors at each seat, along with headphones. We provide electrical outlets at each seat for your convenience, and the restroom at the front of each airplane is not off limits to coach passengers. Shooting Star Airlines also offers free blankets and pillows to passengers and serves free sandwiches, cookies, and non-alcoholic beverages on all flights.

The combination of above-average services and amenities, combined with friendly, helpful flight attendants, removes much of the drudgery from 21st-century flying and puts fun back into the experience. Learn more about Shooting Star Airlines by visiting our website at ShootingStarAirlines@fun.org. And the next time you are going to fly a U.S. route, consider giving us a try. We think you will be pleasantly surprised, and we guarantee that you will arrive at your destination relaxed.

Sincerely,

Miranda Krause
CEO & President

Before reading further, take a few minutes to identify the strengths of the improved letter.

Now, let's look at some strengths in the improved letter.

Opening Paragraph. Four strengths are noticeable in this improved version of the opening paragraph. (1) Appropriately, the request is not made in the opening paragraph. (2) The tone is friendly. (3) The you-attitude is strong. (4) The writer does a good job of gaining the reader's attention (e.g., opens with a question, piques the reader's interest with talk about enjoyable, pleasant commercial flights).

Body Paragraphs. Four strengths should be evident in this improved version of the body paragraphs. (1) The you-attitude is strong. (2) The tone is friendly. (3) The body paragraphs contain several statements that build interest and desire (e.g., free sandwiches and cookies, flat screen monitors at each seat). (4) Sufficient details are included.

Closing Paragraph. Three strengths should jump out in the closing paragraph of this improved version. (1) The request is clearly stated. (2) The tone is friendly. (3) Sufficient contact information is included so the reader can make contact easily.

Using *Sincerely* for the complimentary closing is the right choice. It is friendly and right on the mark.

Now, let's look at another poorly written persuasive strategy letter (Figure 11-17). In this letter the conference chairperson asks an expert in the real estate appraisal field to be the keynote speaker at an annual conference. The poorly written sample below will likely do little to convince the reader to say yes to the request.

FIGURE 11–17: PERSUASIVE STRATEGY LETTER (POORLY WRITTEN VERSION)

1405 Wilson Dr.
Portland, OR 97205
(503) 784-3288

February 20, 2021

Dr. Kobe B. Evans
576 Vista Lane
Reno, Nevada 89503

Dear Dr. Evans:

We would like you to speak at the annual conference of The Society of Real Estate Appraisers. The conference will be held on August 13–15, and we would like you to join us and be this year's keynote speaker.

We hate to bother you because we know an important, busy person like you has many commitments. This is why we are contacting you well in advance of the conference—approximately six months. We're not picky about the topic of your talk. Pick one of interest to you. In addition, audience members take well to handouts, so make sure to bring plenty.

Please send your confirmation and the topic of your talk promptly so we can get the information printed on the conference flyers.

Cordially,

Yolanda Jordan
Conference Chairperson

Before reading further, take a few minutes to identify the weaknesses in the poorly written letter. You should be able to identify a number of them in all three paragraphs.

Now, let's look at some weaknesses in the above letter.

Opening Paragraph. There are four weaknesses in the opening paragraph. (1) The writer follows a direct strategy by making the request in the opening paragraph instead of the less direct persuasive strategy. (2) The tone is rather vanilla. It is not negative, but it's not overly friendly, either. (3) The you-attitude is nonexistent. (4) The opening does little to gain the reader's attention.

Body Paragraph. There are several problems with the letter's body paragraph. (1) At the heart of the problem, the writer does not build reader interest at the outset, then does nothing to build desire. (2) The request is not stated in the body as the persuasive strategy dictates. (3) Opening statements give the reader an out. (4) Details are scarce, for example, the talk topic and length.

Closing Paragraph. The closing paragraph contains several weaknesses. (1) The you-attitude is weak. (2) The tone is neutral. (3) Contact information to send along acceptance or denial is not provided.

Now, let's look at an improved version of the same letter (Figure 11-18).

FIGURE 11-18: PERSUASIVE STRATEGY LETTER (IMPROVED VERSION)

1405 Wilson Dr.
Portland, OR 97205
(503) 784-3288

February 20, 2021

Dr. Kobe B. Evans
576 Vista Lane
Reno, Nevada 89503

Dear Dr. Evans:

Your recent article "Are Appraisers Talking to Themselves?" in the *Appraisal Journal* has drawn many favorable comments from local real estate appraisers. Congratulations on your publication.

The Society of Real Estate Appraisers wants to share with its members more information about appraisal report writing from the point of view of a specialist in real estate education and hopes to do so at the President's Dinner Session during the upcoming Annual Conference in Phoenix on August 13–15. Approximately 400 members will attend the dinner meeting, and we know they would be especially interested in hearing your thoughts and experiences regarding appraisal report writing. With this in mind, we extend to you an invitation to be our keynote speaker at the President's Dinner Session. This would be a wonderful opportunity for you to meet several members of the society and expand your professional network. In addition to covering your travel expenses, we will pay you an honorarium of $10,000.

The post-dinner meeting will be held from 7–9 p.m. at the McGallister Hotel in Phoenix on Thursday, August 14, with your talk running from 7:45 to 8:15 followed by 15 minutes of audience questions. We can promise you a pleasant evening and a receptive audience.

Along with your acceptance, we would like to have a photograph of you for display purposes. Please send your acceptance and photo to me by March 15 at yjordan@scsrea.org. I look forward to hearing from you.

Sincerely,

Yolanda Jordan
Conference Chairperson

Before reading further, take a few minutes to identify the strengths in the improved letter.

Now, let's look at some strengths in the improved letter.

Opening Paragraph. Four strengths are particularly noticeable in this improved version of the opening paragraph. (1) Appropriately, the request does not come in the opening paragraph. (2) The tone is friendly. (3) The you-attitude is strong. (4) The writer did a nice job of gaining the reader's attention (e.g., publication, favorable comments).

Body Paragraphs. Four strengths should be evident in this improved version of the letter's body paragraph. (1) The you-attitude is strong. (2) The tone is friendly. (3) The body paragraphs contain several statements that build interest and desire (e.g., audience size, networking opportunities, honorarium). (4) Sufficient details are included.

Closing Paragraph. Three strengths should jump out in the closing paragraph of this improved version. (1) The acceptance is restated. (2) The tone is friendly. (3) Sufficient contact information is included to make it easy for the reader to respond.

Using *Sincerely* for the complimentary closing was the right choice. It is friendly and right on the mark.

A FINAL LETTER-WRITING STRATEGIES REMINDER

Now that we have reviewed the three letter-writing strategies, you are reminded that exceptions to these strategies are made at times and for logical reasons. The most common exception occurs when a writer knows with certainty that his or her reader wants the information presented directly (get to the point), even if the message contains negative news or if its goal is persuasion.

FIGURE 11-19: EMOTICONS AND EMOJIS IN BUSINESS LETTERS

Emoticons and *emojis* are visual images of facial expressions and objects. Emoticons and emojis are common in some e-mails, which is not to suggest that they are always welcome there. For example, including emoticons and emojis in personal e-mails is generally accepted; however, including emoticons and emojis in business e-mails is discouraged.

The general rule is that when you are writing business letters, do not include them. Otherwise, you may leave your reader with one or more negative perceptions about you and the organization you represent. You and your organization will be perceived by some as being unprofessional. Some readers will be distracted by them, while others will question your maturity.

WRITING STYLES

Writing style is often dictated by company policy or personal preference. Some styles are effective; others are not. Some styles target specific audiences (readers). Do you have a writing style? If so, can you describe and/or identify it? Is it an effective style? Are you open minded enough and skilled enough to switch writing styles when necessary to enhance your written communication?

Examples of letters written in three writing styles are presented here.

Passive/Impersonal Style This style is filled with jargon and clichés and is difficult to read. This style is ineffective for routine correspondence as you can see in the example in Figure 11-20. This is an outdated style that not only invites miscommunication, but results in unnecessarily long messages. See if you can identify the jargon and clichés in the sample letter.

passive/impersonal style
Language characterized by official, bureaucratic tone; passive voice; excessive nominalization; convoluted sentence structure; superfluous, outdated, and redundant language; business and legal jargon; and abstract words.

FIGURE 11–20: SAMPLE PASSIVE/IMPERSONAL STYLE BUSINESS LETTER

12 Second Ave.
Birmingham, AL 35203
(205) 222-4993

May 4, 2021

To Whom It May Concern:

As per your request, enclosed please find the information in reference to our company that will help in optimizing your choices to build a website. Prices charged are in line with other designers of similar background and experience.

The company's objective is to develop end-to-end robust solutions through continued focus on core competencies: website development, hosting and maintenance, full access to PHP and CGI, and of course, SSL encryption. It is believed that the customer deserves the highest quality products and services possible. Through continued expansion of the company's staff and through application of corporate quality programs, such as benchmarking, our establishment of superior processes in each of the core competencies excels over our competitors.

Continued expansion into new, profitable markets will enable the company to provide clients with value-added services and turnkey solutions that will translate into client satisfaction.

Please find herein the company's packages that will endeavor to help the client learn more about the company's superior capabilities and its motivated professional team.

If you have any questions or concerns regarding the above, please feel free to contact Joanne Jones, at ext. 213, 1-800-543-6677. The number is toll free for your convenience.

Sincerely,

Scott Davis, President

© slava17/Shutterstock.com

Modern Business Style This style uses the active voice, strong verbs, and short sentences. This style typically results in concise messages that are clear and professional. It is a good style and works well with external audiences (readers) and others you are unacquainted with. The letter in Figure 11-21 is an example of a modern business-style letter.

FIGURE 11-21: SAMPLE MODERN BUSINESS STYLE LETTER

24 Sea Side Drive
Fort Lauderdale, FL 33302
(954) 515-3276

January 20, 2021

Mr. Marshall M. Smith
Mass Spectrum Plastics
142 South Seabay Drive
Sea Island, FL 33617

Dear Mr. Smith:

Thank you for inquiring about our Web services. Carter Web Design specializes in creating websites. Your satisfaction is our priority. We work on projects of any size from large to small. Our prices range from $75 an hour to design a basic logo to $150 an hour to design and implement a fully featured website.

Our staff includes seven Web designers who will help you turn your image of a perfect website into reality. We can fulfill any of your Web design needs, from developing high-end graphics and animation to incorporating video and sound.

We realize that your organization may not be clear on what your Web needs are. Our talented, insightful staff will work with you to develop a vision and implement your strategy.

I have enclosed a brochure that explains the four website design packages we offer. Choose the one that is right for your needs and give us a call anytime at 1-800-543-6677. We will be glad to set up a free consultation.

Sincerely,

Sarah Carter, President

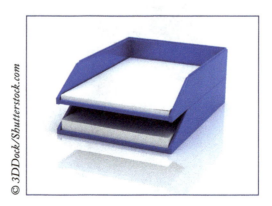
© 3DDock/Shutterstock.com

Informal/Colorful Style This style is good for communicating with people you know well or for communicating good news to those you are familiar with. The letter in Figure 11-22 is an example of an informal/colorful style letter.

As you can see, these three styles are not mutually exclusive. For example, the modern business style is likely to be more personal than impersonal and can be colorful. Nevertheless, the three general categories let us learn how to appropriately apply a style and its elements to each writing situation.

informal/colorful style Language characterized by personal, conversational tone; active voice; strong verbs; colorful adjectives and adverbs; parallel structure; short sentences; everyday, concrete, and precise words.

FIGURE 11–23: CARELESS WRITING STYLES AND BUSINESS LETTERS

Let's first establish what careless writing means. On its simplest level, *careless writing* speaks to a disregard for the rules of grammar and spelling. Careless writing can also result in inclusion of too little information or too few details, leading to confusion or misunderstandings. Careless writing can also take the form of a poorly structured letter in which the message does not flow logically.

In regard to business letters, careless writing is not appreciated. Business letters are formal documents, and there is an expectation that they be written with care. In contrast, carelessly written business letters often result in miscommunication and all the related problems they cause, as well as the negative perceptions about their writers and the organizations they represent.

Why do some people have careless writing styles? For some, it is because they never learned to write properly. For others, it is because they do not value or feel the need for such a level of care. Some people are probably too lazy to put forth the effort. Still others have been influenced by other writing methods that did not call directly for careful writing. For example, some people have so much experience at writing e-mails, IMs, and tweets that these experiences have negatively influenced how they write other messages such as letters. In other words, they have become so accustomed to writing messages that comprise incomplete sentences, single-paragraph messages, nonstandard abbreviations, and punctuation and capitalization errors that they appear to know no better or don't care when it is time to write a business letter. They write on autopilot, based on their past writing experiences. The result includes letters that are difficult to read, hard to understand, and frustrating. And, their readers are left not appreciating their communication partner's careless writing style and not feeling positive toward the writer's employer.

© Jennifer Nicole Buchanan/Shutterstock.com

BUSINESS MEMOS

As mentioned earlier, hardcopy memos and e-memos are commonplace written documents in the U.S. business place. Memos are semiformal documents used to exchange information among people within an organization. Memos most frequently contain routine information. Much like letters, the goal of memos also ranges from sharing neutral, good, or negative news to persuading readers to take a specific course of action.

business memo
Informal document used to exchange information among people within an organization.

© marekuliasz/Shutterstock.com

Memos
http://writingcommons.org/index.php/open-text/genres/professional-business-and-technical-writing/memos

Joe LoCicero offers good examples of when to use memos. He states, "Internally, memos may inform their recipients of:

- Announcements for such diverse happenings as hirings or holidays.
- Changes in such aspects as policies, procedures, and prices.
- Confirmations of verbal discussions, decisions, and meeting times.
- Documents to follow, such as reports, gathered research, and survey results.
- Recommendations for action.
- Requests for further information, further research, or reports.
- Solicitation[s] for opinions."[3]

Electronic memos, sent via e-mail, are commonplace in many organizations and are most commonly referred to as *e-memos*. Despite the convenience and ease of developing and sending e-memos, be cautious! They have several shortcomings typically not associated with hardcopy memos. Some of these shortcomings are listed here.

- Receivers are more likely to read hardcopy memos than e-memos because e-memos can be so easily filtered out or deleted before receivers get past the subject line.
- E-memos are often poorly written, with problems ranging from including too little detail, careless tone, and misspelled words to grammatical mistakes and lack of clarity.
- E-memos can be easily hacked, thus raising privacy and security concerns. After all, even deleted e-memos (e-mail) can be resurrected! For example, if you need to relay information regarding a sensitive or private matter (e.g., health conditions, salary), do not do so in an e-memo. Instead, send a hardcopy memo.

FEATURES OF MEMOS

When you look at the features listed below, notice that in some ways the features of both memos and letters are identical. However, you will also notice that other memo features differ from those of letters.

Memos are typically:

- Written in a less formal style than letters. (E-memos are more conversational and there is greater use of first-person pronouns.)
- Written more often using a direct strategy. (Memos can be and still are developed using the indirect and persuasive writing strategies.)
- Tone should be courteous no matter what the receiver's level in the organization.
- Conciseness is desired more so than in letters.
- Clarity is as important in memos as in letters.
- Message completeness is as important in memos as in letters. Degree of completeness directly impacts clarity.
- Message correctness is as important in memos as in letters. In other words, are facts, dates, names, etc., correct? If not, we cause confusion, misunderstandings, and mistakes.
- Subheadings are more prevalent in memos than in letters.
- Lists are more common in memos than in letters.
- Writing mechanics (e.g., grammar, punctuation, spelling) are just as important in memos as in letters.

MEMO FORMAT

From a formatting standpoint, memos look noticeably different than letters. Here are some memo format observations.

- Some are produced on standard, full-size pieces of paper (8½ x 11 inches).
- Some are produced on half-size paper (8½ inches wide x 5½ inches long).
- They may have a preprinted, standardized, company, department, or division header, but this is not as typical as the preprinted company letterhead found on company letter stationery.
- Top and side margins are typically one inch.
- There is a pre-printed, standardized routing header to expedite internal routing. Here is an example of a typical routing header:

MEMORANDUM or **MEMO**
(centered horizontally)
Date: (starts at left margin)
To: (starts at left margin)
From: (starts at left margin)
Subject: or **Re:** (starts at left margin)

Of course, paper size, margins, and routing headers vary based on companies' preferences.

- As with letters, you can include a copy notation following the message.
- In place of the enclosure notation used with letters, an attachment notation (Attachment:) often follows the message.

SAMPLE MEMOS

The following memo (Figure 11-24) was written by the president of Right Ideas, Inc. to the company's employees to announce a policy banning tobacco use on company grounds. The purpose of the message is to share the policy's main points. Since most employees do not use tobacco products, this message will be perceived by most to be good news; thus, it follows the direct writing strategy.

FIGURE 11-24: SAMPLE DIRECT WRITING STRATEGY, GOOD-NEWS MEMO

MEMORANDUM

Date: October 2, 2021
To: Right Ideas, Inc. Personnel
From: Mac Steiner, President
Subject: Tobacco Use Policy

Starting January 1, 201X a companywide ban on the use of tobacco products will go into effect. The intent of the policy is to promote a healthy workforce and work environment.

Employees and visitors will not be allowed to use cigarettes, cigars, pipes, or smokeless tobacco products anywhere on company grounds, including the parking lots and parking garage. In addition, tobacco use will not be allowed in company vehicles or in personal vehicles parked on company grounds. Electronic cigarettes are prohibited inside company buildings, but may be used outside of the buildings on company grounds, as long as they are used 30 feet or more from building entrances.

The detailed tobacco use policy (policy #107b) can be found in the policies folder at the company website. Please contact Lillian Cole in Human Resources if you have questions regarding this policy. Lillian's telephone extension is 327. You can also contact her at lilliancole@rightideas.org.

The following memo (Figure 11-25) was written by the director of the Human Resources department at Graham and Rudley, a Midwest food distributor, to associate recruiters in the employment division about an upcoming series of training sessions on interviewing skills. This is a direct strategy, neutral-news message.

FIGURE 11–25: SAMPLE DIRECT-STRATEGY, GOOD-NEWS MEMO – INTERVIEW SKILLS TRAINING

MEMORANDUM

Date: September 16, 2021
To: Graham and Rudley Associate Recruiters
From: Jan Bishop, HR Director
Subject: Interviewing Skills Training

On October 1 the first of three interviewing skills training sessions will be held from 1–4 p.m. in the training room. The remaining two training sessions will be held in the same location from 1–4 p.m. on October 3 and October 10.

The training sessions are designed to enhance your interviewing skills and to gain a greater awareness of job candidates' expectations. In addition, existing and new employment laws relating to job interviews will be discussed. In addition to the session trainer, our veteran recruiters will join in on some of the discussions and share some sage advice.

The training sessions are mandatory, so mark your calendars accordingly. We scheduled the sessions between the traditional summer vacation period and the busy winter holiday season to avoid schedule conflicts. If you have questions, contact me at extension 554 or at janbishop@gr.org.

Much like e-mails, memos are typically short, but not to the extent that text messages and tweets are. In your quest to write short memos, include enough detail to clearly transmit the message you set out to communicate.

SUMMARY: SECTION 3— WRITING STRATEGIES AND STYLES

- The direct writing strategy works well with neutral-news and good-news business letters and memos.
- The indirect writing strategy works well with negative-news business letters and memos.
- The persuasive writing strategy works well with persuasive business letters and memos.
- Business letter and memo styles include the passive/impersonal style, the modern business style, and the informal/colorful style.

Notes

1. H. J. Leavitt, *Managerial Psychology* (Chicago: University of Chicago Press, 1978), 122.

2. Robert Kreitner and Angelo Kinicki, *Organizational Behavior*, 5th ed. (Boston: Irwin McGraw-Hill, 2000), 486.

3. Joe LoCicero, *Business Communication: Deliver Your Message with Clarity and Efficiency* (Avon, MA: Adams Media, 2007), 93–94.

BUSINESS REPORTS AND PROPOSALS

12

LEARNING OUTCOMES

After reading this chapter, you should be able to:

1. Describe what a business report is.

2. Discuss the role of business reports in organizations.

3. Discuss the importance of using reliable, valid data and information when writing business reports.

4. Discuss the purpose of business proposals.

5. Describe the key components of long, formal business reports.

6. Describe a number of electronic tools that support business report development.

© Dragance137/Shutterstock.com

SELECT KEY TERMS

INTRODUCTION

A **business report** is a document containing information designed to assist others in making an informed decision. Within organizations, business reports travel upwardly, laterally, and downwardly. In addition, some travel to external sources. Some business reports are only a few pages in length whereas others are significantly longer. Electronic tools such as mindmaps, *Qualtrics, and RefWorks* hold the potential of helping business report writers develop reports more effectively and efficiently.

Business report categories include informational reports, analytical reports, and persuasive reports. The two major types of business reports are periodic reports and non-periodic reports. Periodic reports are reports that are submitted at regular intervals such as annual reports, sales reports, and financial reports. Non-periodic reports are not submitted on regular intervals, but instead are developed and submitted when needed. Business proposals are non-periodic reports.

The intent of this chapter is to provide you with instruction on how to write effective business reports. The goal of this chapter is realized through discussions of the following topics: description of business reports, the role of business reports in organizations, characteristics of business reports, conducting research for business writing purposes, business report categories and types, the key components of formal business reports, business report coherence, and electronic tools that support business report development.

business report
A business document containing information designed to assist others in making an informed decision.

WHAT IS A BUSINESS REPORT?

Business reports represent a class of business documents that are developed for the purpose of assisting others in making informed decisions. Business reports contain relevant, factual information that is organized so that it is relatively easy for readers to move about within them and comprehend the data and information presented.

THE ROLE OF BUSINESS REPORTS IN ORGANIZATIONS

In short, reports are vital to organizations. They help businesspeople make informed decisions when planning, organizing, and controlling their operations.

© Pressmaster/Shutterstock.com

How to Write a Business Report
https://www.wikihow.com/Write-a-Business-Report

REPORT REQUESTERS' EXPECTATIONS

There are five things those who request reports want report writers to do. Report writers are expected to: (1) gather reliable, on-topic data and/or information; (2) reduce the data/information collected to a practical quantity so it can be presented concisely without compromising clarity; (3) use structural techniques (e.g., table of contents, headings) that enable the readers to move within the report easily and quickly; (4) analyze and interpret the data and information logically if asked to do so; and (5) complete and submit reports on time. Since report writers are often subordinate to those requesting the report, writers are wise from both job stability and career growth standpoints to meet the above-mentioned expectations.

INTERNAL FLOW OF REPORTS

While some reports are developed for external audiences, many reports circulate within organizations. Internal reports typically travel in three directions—upward, laterally, or downward. Predictably, the specific purposes they serve vary. These purposes often vary based on their directional flow. For example:

- **Reports Moving Upwardly.** These reports typically contain information that assists higher-level decision makers.
- **Reports Moving Laterally.** These typically contain information that assists in the coordination of work activities.
- **Reports Moving Downwardly.** These reports typically contain policies and instructions concerning how to implement them.

EXTERNAL FLOW OF REPORTS

Some reports are developed for external audiences. A company's annual report to stockholders is an example, as are business proposals. Characteristics of Business Reports

---

SUMMARY: SECTION 1— THE ROLE OF BUSINESS REPORTS IN ORGANIZATIONS

- Business reports are written to serve a business purpose.
- Business reports should be relevant, factual, and organized.
- There are five specific things end users expect writers to do when writing reports.
- Business reports flow both externally and internally. Internally they move in an upward, lateral, or downward direction.

CHARACTERISTICS OF BUSINESS REPORTS

There are several characteristics that distinguish business reports from other business documents. Five of these characteristics are discussed below—report length, level of formality, listings, headings, and visual aids.

REPORT LENGTH

Business reports are often classified by length. They are typically considered to be either short reports or long reports.

Short reports are 1–9 pages long and are typically based on routine matters. They are frequently memo and letter reports that are often informal, usually without prefatory or appended components.

Long reports are 10 pages or more. Some long reports can be hundreds of pages in length or longer. Long reports are typically based on non-routine, special matters. They are often formal, **analytical reports** having several prefatory and appended components.

The general rule is, the longer the report, the greater the number of prefatory components (e.g., executive summary) and appended components (e.g., index) that should be included to aid the reader. The prefatory and appended components serve useful and important purposes. They help writers present a more organized and thorough reporting of data and information than they might otherwise do. They also provide efficient and effective guidance to readers as they navigate the report. This latter point is important given how most people use/read long reports. Essentially, the longer the report, the more likely the reader will not read it in its entirety from start to finish as one would read a novel. For example, a reader may only read the Executive Summary or specific sections that are of interest to him or her. In addition, readers will often move in and out of prefatory or appended components, such as the Table of Contents and Indexes that help him or her to locate specific portions of interest.

> **short reports**
> Reports of 1–9 pages; typically presenting routine matters.
>
> **long reports**
> Reports of 10 or more pages.
>
> **analytical report**
> A document identifying an issue or problem, presenting the relevant information, and interpreting that information.

LEVEL OF FORMALITY

Another characteristic of business reports is their level of formality. Business reports are often categorized into one of two general levels of formality—informal reports and formal reports.

Informal reports are usually short, informational reports. If your end user prefers informality in documents, write them accordingly with regard to report structure, word choice, etc. Sales reports and quarterly financial reports are examples of informal reports.

Formal reports contain less conversational language and more structural elements designed to reinforce clarity and guide the reader (e.g., headings, summaries). Formal reports can be either informational or analytical. The main features that define a business report as formal include length, number of topics and subtopics addressed, information complexity and/or data shared, and data interpretation content. For example, if you send a report to a high-ranking decision maker in the organization or an external business partner or stakeholder, you would probably write a formal report.

A good general rule regarding informality and formality is "when in doubt, write a formal report." Unnecessary formality features are rarely viewed negatively, whereas unwanted informality can result in poor perceptions about the writer, his or her company, and the report.

> **informal reports**
> Short, informational reports employing conversational language.
>
> **formal reports**
> Informational or analytical reports employing formal language.

LISTINGS

Another characteristic of business reports is the use of lists. However, do not develop reports that are predominately lists. Doing so is unprofessional. Furthermore, most topics and data cannot be reduced to bulleted lists. Lists would contain too little detail and compromise clarity.

HEADINGS

Another characteristic of business reports is the use of headings, which serve as efficient guides for report readers and writers, alike. The two major types of headings are topic caption headings and talking caption headings.

Topic caption headings identify the topic of discussion. Topic caption headings are typically 1–4 words long. For example:

Store Locations

Talking caption headings identify the specific topic of discussion. They are typically longer than topic caption headings. For example:

Sales Figures Are Typically Correlated with Store Location

As mentioned before, headings help report readers and report writers locate a page or specific information they are interested in. Report writers also benefit from report headings during the organization phase, which is especially important with longer reports addressing numerous topics. Headings here provide the basic outline for the report. By developing an outline composed predominately of headings, the report writer is more assured of the logic of the report's structure. Having headings in place, in turn, offers one more assurance that the writer will not omit necessary sections and information.

topic caption headings Headings that identify the topic of discussion in a report; typically 1–4 words long.

talking caption headings Headings that identify the specific topic of discussion in a report; headings are typically longer than topic caption headings.

General Rules for
APA Format
http://psychology.about.
com/od/apastyle/a/
apageneral.htm

FIGURE 12–1: WRITING STYLES

Writing styles such as the APA style and the MLA style provide guidelines that writeers often find helpful when developing business reports. Each of these styles is described below.

APA (American Psychological Association) style guidelines were developed to assist reading comprehension in the social and behavioral sciences, for clarity of communication, and for word choice that best reduces bias in language. The sample APA style article at the website in the side margin contains a number of APA guidelines as well as links to additional APA style articles.

MLA (Modern Language Association) style guidelines focus on writing and documentation in the humanities. Sample websites containing a number of MLA style guidelines are located in the side margin. The sample MLA style article at the website in the side margin contains a number of MLA guidelines.

The American Psychological Association and the Modern Language Association both publish style manuals. The American Psychological Association's manual is titled *Publication Manual of the American Psychological Association*, and you can learn more about it by visiting the following website: https://en.wikipedia.org/wiki/APA style. The Modern Language Association's manual is titled *The MLA Style Manual*, and you can learn more about it by visiting the following website: https://en.wikipedia.org/wiki/MLA_Style_Manual. You should be able to access both of these manuals at your your university, community college, or junior college library and writing assistance center.

Source: *APA style.* https://en.wikipedia.org/wiki/APA_style
Source: *MLA Style Manual. https://en.wikipedia.org/wiki/MLA_Style_Manual*

VISUAL AIDS

Yet another characteristic of business reports is the regular and extensive (when appropriate) use of visual aids. The good news is that there has never been a time when it has been as easy and fast for writers to develop visual aids for business reports, thanks to the availability of computers, scanners, and graphics software. On the downside, there has never been a time when report readers have had such high expectations of the professional quality of visual aids in terms of appearance and communication accuracy. This means report writers are expected to know how to develop professional-quality visual aids and be willing to do so.

Why do writers include visual aids in business reports? Visual aids serve a number of purposes, such as:

- Sharing messages that are communicated more clearly visually than they are verbally.
- Capturing report readers' attention.
- Helping readers form quick mental images of the data through visual images, charts, tables, diagrams, etc. (See Figure 12-2.)
- Presenting complex information visually to enable quick comprehension.
- Providing an interesting and appealing break for readers from the ongoing drudgery of sentence after sentence and page after page of text.
- Efficient presentation of quantitative data via tables versus paragraphs of text explanation.

FIGURE 12–2: TABLE

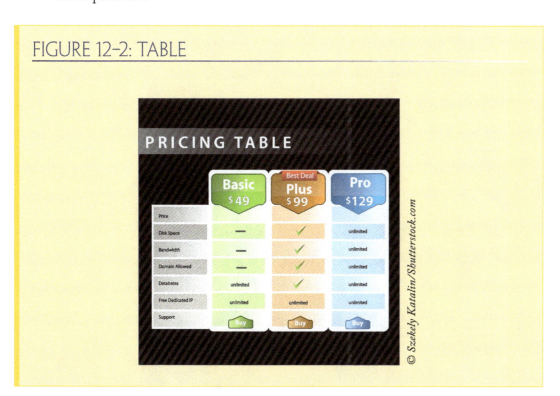

- Showing comparisons with bar charts. (See Figures 12-3 & 12-4.)

FIGURE 12–3: BAR CHART

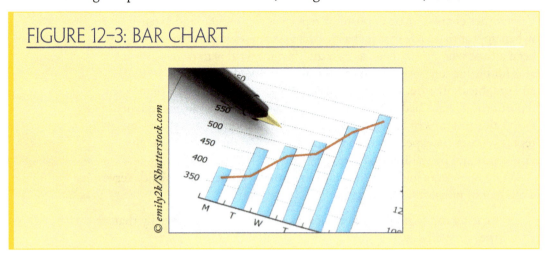

FIGURE 12–4: BAR CHART

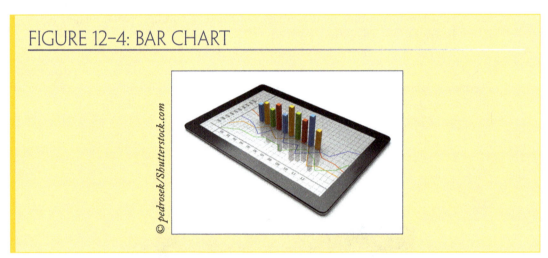

- Showing relationships of the parts to the whole with pie charts. (See Figure 12-5.)

FIGURE 12–5: PIE CHART

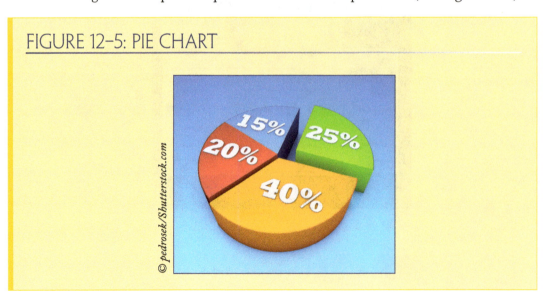

- Showing trends with line charts. (See Figure 12-6.)

FIGURE 12–6: LINE CHART

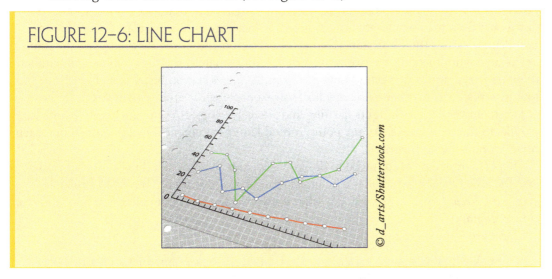

© d_arts/Shutterstock.com

Visual aids included in business reports should never be mere add-ons or afterthoughts, inserted randomly to appease readers' expectations. Each visual aid should serve one or more specific purposes and be an integral, logical component of the report.

Effective business reports are not composed predominately of visual aids strung together with a minimal amount of text. Some novice business report writers who know how to develop visual aids fall into this trap. Be careful!

So, what techniques help writers develop effective visual aids for business reports? Here are several good tips to consider:

- Include a visual aid only if it serves a purpose.
- Strive for clarity in your visual aids so as not to cause confusion, frustration, and misunderstandings.
- Give each visual aid a title, not only a chart or figure number (e.g., Chart 1. Retail Sales by Quarters, 2016–2017).
- Introduce each visual aid in the report text.
- When appropriate and natural, follow up on visual aids with a brief summary in the text.
- Avoid developing visual aids that are too busy. In other words, don't include too much information or show too many comparisons on a single visual aid. Today's technology makes it easy to include far too much information on a single visual aid, or throw in a number of audio and video features simultaneously, all of which can contribute to miscommunication.

© Borodaev/Shutterstock.com

A good analogy for visual aids that are too busy can be drawn from the film *Unstoppable*. The story is about an unmanned, runaway freight train that gains speed as it barrels down on a tight turn on elevated tracks above refinery tanks in a populated area of Stanton, Pennsylvania. The film's stars, Denzel Washington and Chris Pine, stopped the train before an environmental catastrophe occurred. Unfortunately, the film contained a number of unnecessary, annoying distractions. For example, news station helicopters flying too low crisscrossed each other over crowds of townspeople while an incessant stream of law enforcement vehicles with lights flashing and sirens blaring drove up and down the roads parallel to the train tracks. At one point, several law enforcement vehicles crashed into each other for no apparent reason.

Report writers are encouraged to design visual aids in ways that do not distract readers. The KISS Principle provides a practical reminder of this point. The *KISS* Principle stands for *Keep it short and simple*. For what it's worth, the less polite interpretation is *Keep it simple, stupid*.

Here are some more tips:

- Stick with one font style in a visual aid. In fact, use the same font style in all the visual aids you include in a business report. Otherwise, readers may be distracted from your message or purpose.
- Change type size in visual aids as needed. For example, the type size for table headings should be 1–2 points larger than the type size used for table body contents.
- Be careful when presenting visual aids that are produced in a 3-dimensional image. While the 3-D feature produces attractive, attention-grabbing visuals, they can be difficult to interpret accurately and quickly. Make sure the image does not interfere with your reader's ability to accurately interpret the information or data.
- When possible, include color in your visual aids. Business report readers like to see color. Color captures most readers' attention and assists in building reader interest and comprehension. However, don't overdo it! For example, you are less likely to distract readers from your message or purpose if you use five or fewer colors in any one visual. Remember that while color is desirable, you should avoid visual aids that are colorfully chaotic!

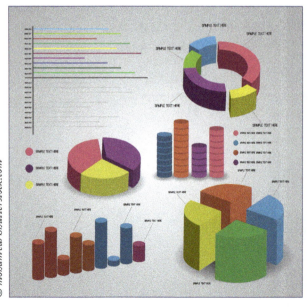

There is so much more to know about visual aids (such as tables, graphs, diagrams, charts, illustrations, maps, etc.) that is beyond the scope of this book. If you have the interest and time, there are two excellent visual aids books you should consider. The first of these is *Information Graphics: A Comprehensive Illustrated Reference—Visual Tools for Analyzing, Managing, and Communicating* by Robert L. Harris. This book contains numerous examples and descriptions of charts, graphics, maps, diagrams, and tables. The other book is *The Visual Display of Quantitative Information* by Edward R. Tufte. The focus of Tufte's book is on displaying quantitative information in ways that do not compromise and/or distort the data. These two books contain a wealth of sound information about visual aids. If you are planning a business career, you are strongly encouraged to read these books.

One closing thought and it's a big one. Long gone are the days when report writers' visual aids were limited to tables, graphs, diagrams, charts, and basic illustrations. Today's technologies, combined with the Internet, have unleashed an ever-growing number of electronics-based visual aids options. Many of these options are discussed later in this chapter in the section on Electronic Tools That Support Report Development. They range from **Prezi** and **Mindmaps** (e.g., **Mindomo**) to **Wordle** and **GoAnimate,** to mention a few. Examples of several of these are included in that section of the chapter. Such programs challenge us to rethink how we integrate and display visual information in reports.

Prezi
Cloud-based presentation software program for exploring and sharing ideas on a virtual canvas.

mindmaps (e.g., Mindomo)
Diagramming software for organizing projects visually.

Wordle
Visually appealing word clouds.

GoAnimate
Software that enables creators to develop short, animated videos and visual aids.

SUMMARY: SECTION 2— CHARACTERISTICS OF BUSINESS REPORTS

- Business reports vary in length from short (1–9 pages) to long (10+ pages).
- Business reports are typically informational, analytical, or persuasive.
- Business reports are informal or formal.
- Bulleted lists are used frequently in business reports.
- Headings and subheadings are used frequently in business reports.
- Visual aids are expected, integral components of business reports.

CONDUCTING RESEARCH FOR REPORT-WRITING PURPOSES

Most report writers must conduct research prior to writing reports. Data and information are typically collected either through primary sources or secondary sources or some combination thereof. *Primary sources,* such as interviews, focus groups, and surveys, are used to obtain firsthand accounts regarding research topics. *Secondary sources,* such as journals and books, are used to obtain secondhand data or information that was originally presented elsewhere.

University and college business librarians are great resources for research guidance and suggestions. In addition, your university may have a media center or media library that has useful business information. There are numerous business research sources and much to know. Do not be shy! Contact your business librarian or media center staff and get on with your research.

As mentioned earlier, decision makers rely on reports when making some of their decisions. They must be able to trust the reliability (trustworthiness) of the data and information they are presented with. They also must be able to trust the validity (soundness) of report writers' conclusions and recommendations. Here are several ways to ensure the reliability of data and information you collect during your research phase.

- Consider the date of publication, scope of information, the author, and publisher. Double-check citations, footnotes, appendices, and other sources to be confident the information is from a recognized authority.
- Use Internet sources cautiously. Remember, anyone can put anything on a website. There may be no editor, publisher, or other means of quality control.
- Determine how search engines such as Google and Yahoo prioritize displayed information. Some Internet search engines "sell" top billing to advertisers.
- Do not assume that an Internet search engine retrieves and evaluates information the same way librarians do.

- Examine how often the search engine updates its information.
- Look for information describing the methodologies used to gather data and information presented on the Internet.
- Seek out the sources or links within the bibliography to the actual documents to ensure accuracy.
- Paid subscriptions to databases are often used by researchers and libraries because of their up-to-date and valid information. One such source is Lexis-Nexis (www.lexisnexis.com).[1]

Fortunately, a wealth of data and information is available. The challenge, however, is knowing how to access the specific information you need. That is where the information presented in this section comes into play.

Before presenting a list of potential business research sources by category (e.g., journals, databases, etc.), here are some specific sources. If you want to locate:

- Industry codes, access SIC code (Standard Industrial Classification) and NAICS code (North American Industry Classification System).
- Benchmark industry ratios, access the Almanac of Business & Financial Ratios, Dun & Bradstreet (D&B), Industry Norms & Key Business Ratios, and RMA (Risk Management Association) Annual Statement Studies.
- Company numbers, access Business & Company Resource Center, Hoover's Online (click on SEC filings), LexisNexis Academic (click on Companies, then click on SEC Filings), Morningstar Document Research, and SEC Edgar Database.
- Industry information, access Business & Company Resource Center, Hoover's Online, and NetAdvantage – Standard and Poor's.
- Articles about companies and industries, access ABI Inform, Business & Company Resource Center, Business Source Complete, and Predicast's PROMT – Predicast's Overview of Markets and Technology.

The following section lists potential business research sources by category—journals, periodicals, books, databases, websites, and other sources.

JOURNALS

Hundreds of journals contain articles on a wide variety of business topics. Here is a sampling.

- *Journal of Management*
- *American Business Review*
- *Business Horizons*
- *Harvard Business Review*

Then, there are journals that frequently contain an international forum section or publish articles pertaining to international business issues. Examples include:

- *The International Executive*
- *International Journal of Intercultural Relations*
- *International Journal of Public Relations*
- *International Journal of Research and Marketing*
- *Foreign Language Annals*
- *Journal of International Studies.*

Thanks to the widespread availability of the Internet, WiFi, and affordable computers and tablets, conducting searches for journal articles is fairly painless!

PERIODICALS AND NEWSPAPERS

Newsstand periodicals, such as *Forbes, BusinessWeek, Fortune, and Newsweek*, and newspapers such as *The Wall Street Journal*, contain articles on a wide variety of business topics. Most of these periodicals and their articles can also be accessed over the Internet.

One of the major advantages periodicals and newspapers have over books is the currency of the information reported. Given how rapidly economic and political conditions change in some countries and regions of the world, this is an important consideration.

BOOKS

Books offer yet another business research source. Fortunately there is no shortage of these book titles pertaining to business. Some are specialized, while others are more general. Examples of these include:

- *The Standard Industrial Classification Manual*
- *NAICS Manual*
- *Business Plans Handbook*
- *RMA* (Risk Management Association) *Annual Statement Studies*
- *Industry Norms and Key Business Ratios* (D&B)
- *Almanac of Business and Industrial Financial Ratios*
- *Craighead's International Business, Travel, and Relocation Guide to* ... various countries
- *Mergent International Manual*
- *Kiss, Bow, or Shake Hands: Sales and Marketing* by Terri Morrison and Wayne A. Conaway (McGraw-Hill).
- *Kiss, Bow, or Shake Hands* by Terri Morrison, Wayne A. Conaway, and George A. Borden (Adams Media Corporation).

Just keep in mind that such books become dated as circumstances and customs change. Of course, this is not always the case, but it is a consideration to keep in mind.

DATABASES

Many databases contain information on business topics. A sampling of such databases is listed below.

- ABI/Inform
- Business & Company Resource Center
- Business Source Complete
- EBSCOhost
- EconLit
- Emerald FullText
- Hoover's Online
- IMF Publications
- LexisNexis Academic
- PAIS International
- Plunket Research
- Predicast's PROMT

- Reference USA
- STAT-USA
- World-Newspapers.com

Databases provide an efficient information-gathering option. We are fortunate to have databases so readily available as well as the computing power to access them. Gathering information has not always been so fast and efficient.

WEBSITES

As can be expected, a number of websites contain information pertaining to business topics. Here are some examples.

- **DoingBusiness.org (World Bank) www.doingbusiness.org**. This site is sponsored by the World Bank. This site provides objective measures of business regulations of individual countries and their enforcement. Indicators cover topics such as starting a business, employing workers, paying taxes, getting credit, etc.
- **Import/Export Guide (Business.gov) business.usa.gov.** Contents include getting started in exporting, how to obtain export financing, importing goods, trade agreements, business travel, and importing/exporting specific products.
- **Business & Company Resource Center.** It has a very long URL. The best way to get to it is by Googling it. This site provides full abstracts and full-text articles from journals, periodicals, and newspapers covering a wide range of business and industry topics. It also provides company and industry information for more than 300,000 companies.
- **Yahoo! Finance finance.yahoo.com.** The site contains quotes, financial news, stock market statistics, and more.
- **Reuters.com reuters.com/finance/stocks.** This site provides financial ratios of industries in addition to market news and company and industry figures.

As the Internet continues to grow, we can anticipate that even more such websites will become available. Locating information pertaining to business topics should not be a problem as long as you know where to look. In addition, many companies have their own websites with information that may meet your needs.

OTHER SOURCES

There are several other ways to locate information on intercultural communication and international business topics. Here are some examples:

- *Quick Study Reference Guide* titled *Business Research,* BarCharts Publishing, Inc., www.quickstudy.com.
- Standard & Poor's Industry Surveys
- *Encyclopedia of American Industries*
- Company websites and annual reports
- SEC filings
- *Standard & Poor's 500 Guide*
- Moody's Manual
- *Who's Who in Finance and Industry*
- *Who's Who in Finance and Business*
- *Financial Yellow Book*

- Standard Industrial Classifications manuals
- *Encyclopedia of Associations*
- Statistical Census information
- *Thomas Register of American Manufacturers*
- Business.com
- Wall Street Executive Library
- D&B Small Business Solutions
- CEO Express

You now have quite a number of sources to start with when you need data and information on business topics.

FIGURE 12–7: WHY SOME REPORT WRITERS PLAGIARIZE

Plagiarism is theft of another person's ideas or writings. It occurs when a person passes off another person's ideas or writings as his or her own. Here's a list of the common reasons why plagiarism occurs.

© marekuliasz/Shutterstock.com

- Some writers procrastinate to the point that they have too little time to handle citations properly.
- Some writers are too lazy to cite when required.
- Some writers are too careless to cite or cite properly when required.
- Some writers are unscrupulous and plagiarize knowingly.
- Some writers think they do not have to cite information they find on the Internet.
- Some writers simply do not understand when they are plagiarizing. For example, they do not understand what a paraphrase is, so they are unable to identify one. If you are confused about what quotations and paraphrases are, read these descriptions.

Quotation To quote an author means you used his or her exact words. A writer typically quotes an author when the writer feels that the author has stated the idea most effectively or clearly. A writer also quotes another person when the writer feels the quote will strongly or clearly emphasize a point or because that person is a respected expert in his or her field.

Paraphrase To paraphrase an author is to restate the meaning or substance of that person's ideas and words. A writer typically paraphrases an author when the writer believes that by restating what the author has said, the writer's document can achieve greater clarity. The writer knows that even when not using the author's exact words, the writer is using enough of the author's ideas and thoughts to warrant giving the author credit by citing his or her work. Identifying a paraphrase is not as easy as identifying a quotation. A safe bet is to cite when you are unsure whether something is or is not a paraphrase. In such situations, it is better to err on the side of caution than to gamble.

One of the best ways to avoid plagiarizing is to be familiar with the common reasons some people plagiarize and then don't repeat their actions.

SUMMARY: SECTION 3— CONDUCTING RESEARCH FOR REPORT-WRITING PURPOSES

- Business reports should be based on reliable and valid data and information.
- Business research should come from reliable and valid sources.
- Business research comes from primary and secondary sources.
- Conducting business research increasingly involves databases and online sources.

BUSINESS REPORT CATEGORIES AND TYPES

BUSINESS REPORT CATEGORIES

Generally speaking business reports fall into the following three categories: informational, analytical, and persuasive.

informational report A document presenting facts, observations, and/or experiences only.

Informational Reports   These reports present facts, observations, and/or experiences only. The report writer makes no attempt to interpret the data by drawing conclusions or offering recommendations. Sales reports and quarterly financial reports are good examples of informational reports. Some are form reports that only require the report writer to fill in blanks.

analytical report A document identifying an issue or problem, presenting the relevant information, and interpreting that information.

Analytical Reports   These reports identify an issue or problem, present relevant information, analyze that information, and interpret it. The interpretation results in conclusions and recommendations for action. Conclusions are drawn from report findings, and recommendations are based on report conclusions. A performance review report is an example of an analytical report.

© banss/Shutterstock.com

Persuasive Reports These reports aim to move their readers to some desired action. A logical presentation of information is central to these reports. People who write **persuasive reports** must capture their readers' attention and then convert it to interest and ultimately desire. A business **proposal** is an example of a persuasive report.

BUSINESS REPORT TYPES

There are two major types of reports—**periodic reports** and non-periodic reports. Each is described below.

Periodic Reports These are reports that are submitted at regular intervals (e.g., monthly, annually). Examples of periodic reports include annual reports, sales reports, and financial reports.

- **Annual reports** are distributed to a number of stakeholders ranging from stockholders to regulatory agencies. Essentially these reports inform corporate constituencies as to how the business is doing, anticipated changes, and potential problems and opportunities in the offing. Annual reports typically include items such as a balance sheet, profit and loss sheet, cash flow statement, board of directors' statement, and auditors' report.

© maxuser/Shutterstock.com

- **Sales reports** are typically developed for managers. Basically they contain sales figures for a past, specified time period, which could be the past week, month, or quarter. In addition, they often contain comparison sales figures for a previous, equivalent time period(s). Client/customer contact histories are typically included, as well as data on marketing costs. Sales reports help managers determine if adjustments ranging from changes to sales personnel to changes to service or product lines and prices need to be made to meet company objectives and goals.

© nasikhan/Shutterstock.com

persuasive reports A document intended to move the reader(s) to a desired action.

proposal Type of business report that proposes (recommends) ways specific needs can be met and problems can be solved.

periodic report Routine report.

sales report Report addressing sales figures and trends.

How to Write a Weekly Sales Report
http://smallbusiness.chron.com/write-weekly-sales-report-42969.html

• **Financial reports** are distributed to a number of stakeholders ranging from stockholders and potential investors to government agencies, including the SEC and IRS. Essentially, they inform these constituencies about the financial condition of the company during a specific period (e.g., quarter, year).

© leungchopan/Shutterstock.com

Non-periodic Reports These are reports that, unlike periodic reports, are not submitted on regular intervals. Instead, non-periodic reports are developed and submitted when needed. They contain data or information that decision makers need to address special situations. Proposals and special-situation reports are examples of non-periodic reports.

• **Proposals** are reports that propose (recommend) ways specific needs can be met or problems can be solved. Proposals are commonplace in both the private and public sectors. For example, in the business sector, one might submit a proposal that addresses ways employee use of electronic communication devices for personal reasons at work can be reduced. In the public sector, proposals are often written when government agencies issue RFPs (requests for proposals) for grants targeted at solving problems. When developing a grant proposal, be especially diligent about following instructions. To do otherwise typically results in a denial of your grant request.

© JohnKwan/Shutterstock.com

Successful proposals meet a need or solve a problem. They contain a clearly stated purpose and are honest, factual, realistic, and objective. Successful proposals are written at a formality level appropriate to their audience and are professional. They are clear and incorporate headings to assist in the proposal's clarity and ease of use. Successful proposals are convincing, in part, because they demonstrate how benefits can outweigh costs. Well-written proposals contain a timetable and appropriate illustrations and visual aids.

Here are some additional important points to keep in mind when writing proposals.

- Use persuasive communication techniques. After all, your goal is to persuade your readers. For example, emphasize reader benefits while de-emphasizing cost.
- Write concisely. This means developing a proposal that is no longer than necessary.
- Eliminate errors ranging from grammar and punctuation to typos and misspellings. Ask someone to proofread your proposal.

FIGURE 12-8: SAMPLE BUSINESS PROPOSAL

Customer Service Assessment: Great Toppings Pizza

Proposal by Todd Shaner, Shaner Consulting Group
www.ShanerConsultingGroup.com
719-378-5682
July 8, 201X

Congratulations on the growth Great Toppings Pizza has experienced this past year. This is certainly a testimonial to the fine pizza you serve and to your employees also. Despite strong competition, your sales continue to grow. However, now is not the time to become complacent. Great Toppings needs to continue to do all it can to remain competitive and grow. That is where Shaner Consulting Group can help.

Opportunity

Great Toppings Pizza currently operates 112 stores across the western half of the United States. Like most businesses that operate many outlets over a wide geographic area, some of Great Toppings Pizza's outlets are more profitable than others. Increasing sales in your less-profitable outlets is certainly important.

Shaner Consulting Group is prepared to help you make Great Toppings Pizza's less-profitable stores more profitable. Our company specializes in all matters to do with customer service. We propose to determine whether customer service shortcomings in your company's less-profitable outlets are directly correlated with sales. We realize that other factors such as store location, local economic conditions, and tax rates also influence sales. While factors such as local economic conditions and tax rates are not easily controlled, Great Toppings Pizza can exercise control over customer service.

Procedures

Given the opportunity, Shaner Consulting Group (SCG) will assess Great Toppings Pizza's customer service situation as follows.

1. SCG will conduct assessments in 25 percent of Great Toppings Pizza's outlets that have been identified as being sufficiently profitable with the purpose of identifying outstanding customer service behaviors that are relatively consistent across these outlets. These assessments will be accomplished through (1) anonymous in-store observations; (2) focus group sessions with current customers, outlet employees, and outlet managers; and (3) questionnaires sent to current and potential customers, outlet employees, and outlet managers.

FIGURE 12-8: SAMPLE BUSINESS PROPOSAL

2. SCG will conduct assessments in all Great Toppings Pizza outlets that have consistently reported substandard sales figures with the purpose of identifying poor customer service behaviors. SCG will also identify best practices that were identified in the profitable outlets that are not apparent in the unprofitable outlets. These assessments will be accomplished through (1) anonymous in-store observations; (2) focus group sessions with current customers, outlet employees, and outlet managers; and (3) questionnaires sent to current and potential customers, outlet employees, and outlet managers.

Proposed Timeline

SCG will complete all the above-mentioned assessments by November 30, 201X and report our findings to you via a written report and presentation by December 15, 201X.

Benefits of Proposed Actions

Great Toppings should realize the following benefits if it implements the proposed actions.

1. SCG findings should ultimately contribute to increased sales and profits for Great Toppings Pizza, assuming steps are taken to improve the quality of customer service in stores currently reporting substandard sales.
2. Great Toppings Pizza will be able to direct its attention to other matters important to the company such as expansion into new markets.

Costs

These are open for discussion and negotiation based on the extent of the investigation Great Toppings Pizza is interested in pursuing.

Shaner Consulting Group opened its doors for business in Pueblo, Colorado in 1987. Since then, we have served numerous businesses of all types and sizes by helping them improve customer service. We look forward to also meeting Great Toppings Pizza's existing customer service needs. If you are interested in seeing a sampling of companies we have served, as well as comments submitted by prior clients, please visit us at www.ShanerConsultingGroup.com.

I look forward to visiting with you.

Sincerely,

Todd Shaner, President
Shaner Consulting Group

- **Special-situation** reports are reports that address decision makers' data or information needs that are not met via proposals and periodic reports. Here, the report writer is not asked to attempt to persuade the reader, but instead to provide relevant data and/or information.

Some special-situation reports are true informational reports in that their purpose is to present facts, observations, and/or experiences only and not to interpret the data or information, draw conclusions, or make recommendations. Other special-situation reports are analytical reports that identify an issue or problem, present relevant data or information, analyze the data or information, and interpret it. The interpretation stage requires the writer to draw conclusions and make recommendations for a specific course of action.

SUMMARY: SECTION 4— BUSINESS REPORT CATEGORIES AND TYPES

- Business report categories include informational, analytical, and persuasive reports.
- Business report types include periodic reports and nonperiodic reports.
- Proposals and special-situation reports are examples of nonperiodic reports.

This chapter's next section describes the components of a long, formal business report, along with an example of each component based on a common business situation. As you piece together the example, you will see a special-situation, analytical report unfolding. This sample report could easily be converted into an informational report by removing the analysis and interpretation components. To do so, remove any mention of key findings, conclusions, and recommendations from the Executive Summary; remove the Summary Paragraphs at the end of each Topic Chapter; and remove the Report Summary chapter.

FORMAL BUSINESS REPORTS

Formal business reports typically contain numerous components. Some of these components are necessary in order to report the needed data or information (e.g., Executive Summary, Report Body). Other components are included to help readers navigate their way through the report (e.g., Table of Contents, Report Preview, Index). On the surface, some components often found in formal business reports might appear to be unnecessary. However, each has its purpose and the interesting thing about many of these components is that they are beneficial to report writers and report-writing teams, as well as to the readers. For example, the Report Preview benefits readers as they head toward reading the Report Body by telling them what major topics will follow and in what order. The Report Preview is also beneficial to writers because, once it is written, it sets out the Report Body topics and topic order for them. Even if extended periods of time pass between writing sessions, the Report Preview helps the author(s) avoid leaving a topic out or presenting topics out of the intended order. And if multiple writers are working on the Report Body, you can see the need and benefit of having the Report Preview to turn to.

Long, formal report components typically fall into one of three categories—prefatory parts, report proper, and appended parts. Each of these categories and report components are presented Figure 12-9, followed by a description of each component.

How to Write a Formal Business Report video http://www.youtube.com/watch?v=F-c9PRlnPZw

FIGURE 12–9: KEY COMPONENTS OF FORMAL
BUSINESS REPORTS

Prefatory Parts
- Title Page
- Letter of Transmittal
- Table of Contents
- Executive Summary

Report Proper
    Introduction
- Statement of Purpose
- Statement of Problem
- Sources of Information
- Report Preview

Report Body
- Report Topic Chapters
- Report Summary

Notes

Appended Parts
- Glossary
- Index
- Additional Data

KEY COMPONENTS OF A FORMAL BUSINESS REPORT

What follows is a description of each of the formal business report components listed in Figure 12-9. Examples are included for most of the report components. Each example is based on the business scenario presented in Figure 12-10. This scenario portrays an ongoing challenge many businesses face routinely worldwide.

FIGURE 12-10: STORE PROFITABILITY SCENARIO

All Sports, Inc. owns a chain of retail sporting goods stores located throughout the United States. As can be expected, some of the company's stores are less profitable than others. Management wants to determine how to make its less-profitable stores more profitable. They suspect poor customer service is at the heart of the problem, but understand that other factors likely contribute also. Imagine you are a member of a team charged with investigating the situation and developing a formal, analytical report in which you make recommendations to management regarding how to turn their less-profitable stores toward greater profitability.

PREFATORY PARTS

This is the first of the five report categories. This category contains standard prefatory parts, which are the components that precede the report proper section.

Title Page The Title Page typically contains the report title, name of the person requesting the report, name of the writer(s), and date the report is submitted. This is also the typical order of the Title Page contents. Figure 12-11 contains a sample Title Page based on the store profitability scenario.

FIGURE 12-11: SAMPLE TITLE PAGE

Store Profitability: Making Substandard Stores More Profitable

Prepared for
Maria Sanchez, Vice President
All Sports, Inc.

Prepared by
Jonathan Reynolds, Director of Operations
All Sports, Inc.

Date
July 27, 201_

Letter of Transmittal This is a brief letter that serves to transmit the report to the reader by communicating who requested the report, when it was requested, the key findings, and words of appreciation for being asked to develop the report. The Letter of Transmittal is a direct strategy letter. Figure 12-12 contains a sample Letter of Transmittal based on the store profitability scenario.

letter of transmittal Brief letter that transmits a report to its reader(s) by stating who requested the report, when it was requested, the key findings, and words of appreciation for being asked to develop the report.

FIGURE 12-12: SAMPLE LETTER OF TRANSMITTAL

July 27, 201_

Dear Ms. Sanchez:

On January 7, 201X you asked our project team to investigate and report on All Sports, Inc.'s less-profitable stores for the purpose of determining ways to bring these stores to greater profitability.

The key findings growing from our investigation of the matter clearly pointed to several customer service behaviors that need to be addressed. Central to these behaviors is how customers are greeted when they enter the store, store employees' willingness to help customers locate merchandise and answer customers' questions, and store employees' overall level of friendliness.

We would like to thank you for this opportunity to investigate the situation, which is of great importance to our company. Please contact us if clarification or additional information is needed.

Sincerely,

Jonathan Reynolds
Director of Operations

Table of Contents The Table of Contents typically presents the primary and secondary report headings, along with the page numbers to indicate where each section starts. Figure 12-13 contains a sample Table of Contents based on the store profitability scenario.

FIGURE 12–13: SAMPLE TABLE OF CONTENTS

Table of Contents

While the following tables are not included in long, formal business reports as frequently as is the Table of Contents, consider including each when there are three or more such items in the report.

- Table of Tables
- Table of Figures
- Table of Charts
- Table of Illustrations
- Table of Photos

Include these sections in the Table of Contents only when you have placed several tables, figures, charts, illustrations, or photos in your report, and you believe your readers will find the their listings helpful. These additions to the Table of Contents present the numbers, titles, and their page numbers.

Executive Summary The **Executive Summary**, referred to by some as the synopsis, provides a summary of all of the essential report ingredients, including the Statement of Purpose, Statement of Problem, Data Collection Process, Key Findings, Conclusions, and Recommendations. Figure 12-14 contains a sample Executive Summary based on the store profitability scenario.

executive summary
A section of a document providing a summary of a report's essential facts and recommendations. Also known as *synopsis*.

FIGURE 12–14: SAMPLE EXECUTIVE SUMMARY

Executive Summary

The purpose of this study is to determine how to make the company's less-profitable stores more profitable. To do so, we set out to determine which specific customer service behaviors are correlated with greater store profitability. How are customers greeted when they enter the store? How are customers assisted while in the store? What are customers' perceptions of how they are treated while in the store?

Data for this study were gathered from a number of sources. Observations were made at 70 percent of the most-profitable as well as 70 percent of the most-unprofitable stores. We carried out these activities:

- Employee surveys were distributed.
- Employee focus group sessions were conducted.
- Customer satisfaction surveys were distributed.
- Customer focus group sessions were conducted.
- Books and journals that address customer service themes were delved into.

The study resulted in two key findings, which were the basis for two conclusions and two recommendations.

Key Finding #1: Based on store observations, we determined that employees in our most profitable stores greet customers with a smile as they enter the store 96 percent of the time.

Conclusion #1: The willingness of employees in profitable stores to greet customers with a smile appears to contribute, in part, to higher profit levels in these stores.

Recommendation #1: Management should strongly consider encouraging employees in all stores to greet customers with a smile when they enter their stores.

Key Finding #2: Based on store observations, we determined that employees in our least-profitable stores greet customers with a friendly word only 22 percent of the time.

Conclusion #2: The infrequency with which customers are greeted with a friendly word in the least-profitable stores appears to contribute, in part, to low profit levels in these stores.

Recommendation #2: Management should strongly consider encouraging employees in all stores to greet customers with a friendly word when they enter the store.

The purpose of the executive summary is to give report readers an overview of the high points of the report. Some report readers read only the Executive Summary when they do not have the time or feel the need to read the entire report. For obvious reasons, the Executive Summary should be well written!

Even though the Executive Summary is located near the beginning of the report, most of it cannot be written until the Report Body has been completed. A good way to determine whether your Executive Summary is too short or too long is to compare its length to that of the Report Body. The Executive Summary should be approximately 10–15 percent of the length of the report.

REPORT PROPER

This is the second of the five report categories. This category is broken into two subsections—Introduction and Report Body. The Introduction contains the Statement of Problem, Sources of Information, and Report Preview.

statement of purpose
The report's main goal.

Introduction **Statement of Purpose** The **statement of purpose** identifies the main goal of the report. Figure 12-15 contains a sample statement of purpose based on the store profitability scenario.

FIGURE 12–15: SAMPLE STATEMENT OF PURPOSE

To determine how to make the company's less-profitable stores more profitable.

It is obviously important that the writer(s) have a clear understanding of their assignment before moving ahead with their research and writing efforts. Otherwise, the result is likely to be wasted time and effort, followed by a weak report that does not serve the readers/decision makers well.

statement of problem
The report's specific topic(s) or concern(s).

Statement of Problem The **statement of problem** identifies the specific topic(s) or concern(s) linked directly to the statement of purpose. Figure 12-16 contains a sample statement of problem based on the store profitability scenario.

FIGURE 12–16: SAMPLE STATEMENT OF PROBLEM

To determine which specific customer service behaviors are correlated with higher store profitability. Specifically: How are customers greeted when they enter the store? How are customers assisted while in the store? What are customers' perceptions of how they are treated while in the store?

It is equally important that report writers have a clear understanding of the specific concern(s) they are attempting to address before moving forward with their research and writing efforts. Otherwise the result will be wasted time and effort, followed by a weak report that does not serve the readers/decision makers well.

Sources of Information The sources of information section lists the sources you accessed while gathering data and information for the report. The entries in this section do not need to be in full citation form as you would when you cite paraphrases and quotations in the notes section. Readers like to browse the sources of information to determine if the sources you used are reliable, current, and best suited to the report's needs. After all, if your reader is going to make decisions based in large part on your report, then he or she needs to have faith in the sources you used. Figure 12-17 contains two sample sources of information based on the store profitability scenario.

FIGURE 12–17: SAMPLE SOURCES OF INFORMATION

Customer Service Done Right by William Meador (2015)
Satisfied Customers Contribute to the Bottom Line by Geoff Goffield, in the *Journal of Customer Service* (2015)

Do not confuse the sources of information section with the notes section as they have different purposes. The purpose of the notes component is to give credit to those authors you quoted and/or paraphrased in your report. Cite sources in full citation form (e.g., APA style, MLA style) for those sources from which you quoted or paraphrased authors.

Report Preview The report preview briefly lays out the topics presented in the report body in the same order as they appear in the report, followed by some discussion of why they are included. The report preview provides the reader with a brief overview that serves as a topic base, leading to the extensive specifics and details in the report body. The report preview also provides the reader with insights into why a topic was included and why it was addressed in a specific location. This section also helps the report writer. As the writer develops the report body, he or she can use the report preview as a guide, so he or she does not forget to include a topic and includes the topics in the correct order. Figure 12-18 contains a sample report preview based on the store profitability scenario.

report preview
Brief text laying out the topics presented in the report body in the same order that they appear in the report, followed by a discussion of why each topic is included.

FIGURE 12–18: SAMPLE REPORT PREVIEW

Chapter 1, Substandard Stores, identifies company stores that reported substandard profit figures during the past six quarters. Identification of these stores was necessary before we could explore what could be done to make them more profitable. Chapter 2, In-Store Customer Service in Profitable Stores, reports how employees in the company's profitable stores greet customers as they enter the store (e.g., a smile, a friendly word). Chapter 3, In-Store Customer Service in Substandard Stores, reports how employees in the company's substandard stores greet customers as they enter the store (e.g., don't look up at them, don't say anything to them). Etc.

REPORT BODY

This is the third of the five report categories. This category is broken into two subsections—Topic Chapters and Report Summary. The Topic Chapters contain the findings. The Report Summary contains the key findings, conclusions, and recommendations.

Topic Chapters Topic chapters have three parts—Introductory Paragraph, Body, and Summary Paragraph.

Introductory Paragraph You are encouraged to start each topic chapter with an introductory paragraph that tells the reader which specific topics will be discussed in the chapter and the order they will be discussed. This section prepares the reader for what he or she is about to read and also helps the report writer stay organized. As the writer develops each topic chapter, he or she can use the introductory paragraphs as a guide so as not to forget to include a topic and to report on the topics in the order designated in the report preview. For an abbreviated sample introductory paragraph based on the store profitability scenario, see paragraph 1 in Figure 12-19.

Body Here is where you present the data or information you gathered that you believe is pertinent to the report's objective. In doing so, you perform some data (information) analysis. After all, every piece of data or information you collect is not included. You will go through the process of choosing what you think is most pertinent and should be included. The data or information you include is called *findings*. For an abbreviated sample body paragraph based on the store profitability scenario, see paragraph 2 in Figure 12-19.

Summary Paragraph You are encouraged to end each topic chapter with a summary paragraph in which you present the key findings for that chapter. To do so, you must first analyze the findings presented in the body of each topic chapter to identify the key (most important) findings from among all those you presented in each body section. Key findings are what the findings (raw data) reveal when analyzed. For an abbreviated sample summary paragraph based on the store profitability scenario, see paragraph 3 in Figure 12-19.

FIGURE 12–19: ABBREVIATED SAMPLE TOPIC CHAPTER

In this chapter we explore in-store customer service behaviors pertaining to how employees greet customers when they enter the store. Specifically, we explore whether employees greet customers with a smile and a friendly word.

Based on observations, we found that **96 percent** of the time, employees in All Sports, Inc.'s most-profitable stores greet customers with a smile as they enter the store. Based on observations, we found that employees in All Sports, Inc.'s least-profitable stores greet customers with a friendly word only **22 percent** of the time.

Ninety-six percent of the time, employees in All Sports, Inc.'s most profitable stores greet customers as they enter the store with a smile. Only **22 percent** of the time, employees in All Sports, Inc.'s least profitable stores greet customers with a friendly word.

Topic chapter summary paragraphs ultimately provide the starting point for the report summary.

Report Summary The report summary chapter contains three components—key findings, conclusions, and recommendations. Key findings, as you know, come from the summary paragraphs of the topic chapters. Conclusions are an outgrowth of the key findings, and recommendations evolve from conclusions.

Key Findings **Key findings** are what the findings (raw data) reveal when analyzed. When writing the report summary chapter, you do not need to rethink the key findings. After all, you already decided on these when you wrote the summary paragraphs for each topic chapter. For an abbreviated sample of key findings based on the store profitability scenario, see paragraph 1 in Figure 12-19.

Conclusions **Conclusions** are logical inferences based on the key findings. For an abbreviated sample of conclusions based on the store profitability scenario, see paragraph 2 in Figure 12-19.

As you draw conclusions, you move farther from the objectivity associated with key findings and find yourself relying increasingly on your perceptions regarding what the findings mean. Subjectivity enters the process in varying degrees.

Here are some ways you can reduce subjectivity in your conclusions:

- Conclusions should be relevant to the report's statement of purpose and statement of problem.
- Conclusions should be as objective as possible and flow logically from the analysis of the key findings.
- Conclusions should not introduce new material. They must be based on the analysis of the key findings.

report summary
Section of a report containing the key findings, conclusions, and recommendations.

key findings
What the report's data reveal.

conclusions
Logical inferences based on key report findings.

Here are some additional guidelines for writing conclusions:

- Do not assume each key finding will generate one conclusion! One key finding may generate one conclusion or it may generate two or more conclusions. Conversely, several key findings may be needed to generate a single conclusion. Then, too, some key findings do not warrant a single conclusion.
- Number the conclusions so readers can identify and refer to them easily while reading and discussing the report.
- Present conclusions in a meaningful order. For example, most-to-least important, easiest-to-most difficult, or immediate-to-long-term.

Recommendations These are confident statements of proposed actions based on report conclusions. Recommendations propose actions about which the writers are confident. They believe strongly enough in their data collection, analysis, and interpretation to encourage others to act on their recommendations. For an abbreviated sample of recommendations based on the store profitability scenario, see paragraph 3 in Figure 12-20.

As is the case with drawing conclusions, subjectivity is part of the process when making recommendations. When determining recommendations, it is helpful to bring to the process logical thinking, experience, knowledge, and a good dose of common sense. Keep in mind that recommendations must respond to the report's purpose and be appropriate for the audience.

Here are some ways you can reduce subjectivity in your recommendations:

- Recommendations must be relevant to the statement of purpose and the statement of problem.
- Recommendations should be as objective as possible and flow logically from the analysis of the conclusions.
- Do not introduce new material in the recommendations. They must be based on analysis of the conclusions.

Here are some additional guidelines for writing recommendations:

- Do not assume each conclusion will generate one recommendation! One conclusion may generate one recommendation or two or more recommendations. Conversely, several key conclusions may be needed to generate a single recommendation. Then too, some conclusions do not warrant a single recommendation.
- Begin each recommendation with an action verb. For example: Establish an ad hoc committee to determine ways to resolve the problem.
- Number the recommendations so readers can identify and refer to them easily while reading the report and making decisions about their implementation.
- Present recommendations in a meaningful order. For example, most-to-least important, easiest-to-most difficult, or immediate-to-long-term.
- Suggest additional research to investigate unanswered questions that become evident during the report-writing process.

recommendations
Confident statements of proposed actions based on a report's conclusions.

NOTES

This is the fourth of the five report categories. The purpose of the notes section is to give credit to the authors you quoted and or paraphrased in your report. Be sure to give credit where credit is due. Figure 12-6 contains a list of the common reasons some writers plagiarize, including definitions of the terms quotation and paraphrase. None of us should plagiarize intentionally or unintentionally. For an abbreviated sample of the notes section based on the store profitability scenario, see Figure 12-21.

APPENDED PARTS

This is the fifth of the five report categories. The appended parts section of your report may include an Index, a Glossary, or Additional Data/Information that include items such as spreadsheets, financial reports, policies, architectural drawings, maps, or schematics that you chose not to include in the report body, but want to make available to your reader. For an abbreviated sample of the index based on the store profitability scenario, see Figure 12-22.

FIGURE 12-22: ABBREVIATED SAMPLE INDEX

Index

SUMMARY: SECTION 5— FORMAL BUSINESS REPORTS

- Formal business reports are broken into five categories—prefatory parts, report proper, report body, notes, and appended parts.
- Prefatory parts include the title page, letter of transmittal, table of contents, table of tables, table of figures, table of charts, table of illustrations, table of photos, and executive summary.
- The report proper contains an introduction. The introduction section contains the statement of purpose, statement of problem, sources of information, and report preview.
- The report body contains the report presentation and report summary.
- The notes section contains the citations for paraphrases and quotations.
- The appended parts section contains the glossary, index, and additional data/information.

REPORT COHERENCE: TYING IT ALL TOGETHER

Given the length and complexity of many long, formal reports, writers are encouraged to integrate several coherence techniques into the writing process that assist their readers and themselves. Coherence techniques are critical to a document's flow, logic, clarity, and ultimately its overall effectiveness.

Coherence, as discussed here, refers to consistency and logical connections built into a report. Consistency and logical connections help readers see the relationships among the report's sections.

GUIDELINES FOR INCLUDING COHERENCE TECHNIQUES

Writers include coherence techniques in their business reports for a number of reasons. Major factors that guide their decisions to include coherence techniques include:

- **Length of the Report.** The longer the report, the greater the need to include coherence techniques to guide report readers and writers.
- **Number of Topics Addressed in the Report.** The greater the number of topics addressed in a report, the greater the need to include coherence techniques to guide report readers and writers.
- **Difficulty Level of the Information in the Report.** The more difficult the topics addressed in a report, the greater the need to include coherence techniques to guide report readers and writers.

COHERENCE TECHNIQUES

There are several coherence techniques that assist report readers and writers. Here are some of the major coherence techniques used by business report writers.

- **Start With a Strong Outline.** This establishes the report structure for the writer. Ultimately readers benefit from this effort.
- **Include a Report Preview.** This briefly presents the topics discussed in the report, the order in which they are presented, and the reasons they are included.
- **Include Topic Chapters Introductory Paragraphs.** These opening paragraphs present the topics discussed within each topic chapter and indicate the order in which they are presented.
- **Include Topic Chapters Summary Paragraphs.** These closing (summary) paragraphs present the key findings based on the findings presented in the topic chapters' body sections.
- **Use Basic Transitional Tools.** These bridging tools include the use of transition words, repetition of key words, topic sentences, and tie-in sentences, to name a few.

SUMMARY: SECTION 6— REPORT COHERENCE

- Coherence refers to consistency and logical connection throughout a report.
- Major factors that guide report writers' decisions to include coherence techniques are based on report length, the number of topics addressed, and the difficulty level of the information in the report.
- Business report coherence techniques include starting with a strong outline and including a report preview, sectional introductory paragraphs, sectional summary paragraphs, and basic transitional tools.

ELECTRONIC TOOLS THAT SUPPORT REPORT DEVELOPMENT

Every year, creative individuals and companies add to the list of electronic tools that support report development. Electronic tools that you likely use routinely include word processing software and research databases. (Several computer- and Internet-based databases and sources were mentioned earlier in this chapter.) If you have developed quantitative, analytical reports, you have probably used one or more statistical software programs. Here are some other electronic tools you may consider using if you have not already done so.

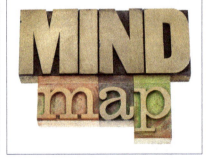

© marekuliasz/Shutterstock.com

FOR PLANNING, OUTLINING, AND ORGANIZING YOUR REPORT

Mindmaps such as *Mindomo* provide a great way to organize your project visually.

Such programs are good for brainstorming the report components, including topics and subtopics, and then determining relationships and connections. If you are on a report-writing team, developing a mindmap on a smartboard is the way to go! (See Figure 12-23.)

FIGURE 12–23: MINDOMO MINDMAP

FOR DEVELOPING AND ADMINISTERING SURVEYS AND QUESTIONNAIRES

Qualtrics is a powerful, user-friendly tool for designing, developing, and administering surveys and questionnaires. This program also has so much more.

FOR CAPTURING, STORING, AND ACCESSING REFERENCE CITATIONS

Programs such as **EndNote** and **RefWorks** are reference management tools. With these programs you either scan the ISBN number of a book or key it into your laptop or tablet. The result is you capture the full citation information digitally without having to write it down. Then you can instruct the program to convert it into your preferred citation style (e.g., APA, MLA) and drop it into your Notes section. How cool is that! These programs help you store and organize your citations and references. They also make it easy for you to share your citations and references.

Qualtrics Powerful software for designing, developing, and administering surveys and questionnaires.

EndNote Bibliographic management system software.

RefWorks Web-based references management software package.

FOR STORING DATA AND INFORMATION

OneNote
Electronic three-ring binder software with tabs for data organization and storage.

To organize and store your information, try **OneNote**. Essentially it is an electronic three-ring binder with tabs. You can easily share the data and information with others if you are on a report-writing team.

FOR DEVELOPING AND DISPLAYING VISUAL AIDS

There are many electronic tools that develop and display static and active visual aids. A good starting point is to discover the tools available on your word processing program. For example, you should have features that let you create and display tables, charts, graphs, and spreadsheets. You can easily import basic *PowerPoint* slides into your reports or liven up the look by developing *Prezi* slides. When appropriate, you could include one or more *YouTube* videos as live links in reports sent digitally. You might even find practical application for *Wordle* visuals, which let you produce word clouds for emphasis. (See Figure 12-24.)

FIGURE 12–24: WORDLE

Certainly, it is easy to import photos into your reports also. You could also insert mind-maps for illustrative purposes. You might even find practical applications for short animated video clips (e.g., *GoAnimate*), and screen capture software that helps you record and overlay audio (e.g., *Camtasia Studio*).

FOR DEVELOPING REPORTS ON WRITING TEAMS

Writing reports with others is not uncommon in the business place. The good news is that there are many electronic tools to aid writing teams in areas ranging from meetings to report writing. For example, programs such as *PBworks SharePoint*, and *Google Drive* are three among many such programs that make it possible for writing team members to share, write, and edit individually and collectively without having to work together in a single location at the same time.

We are fortunate that so many creative, practical electronic tools are available to us, and the cool thing is that most of them are free or reasonably priced. You are encouraged to use the full range of electronic tools available when writing reports and to keep an eye open for new tools that will appear on the scene in the future.

SUMMARY: SECTION 7— ELECTRONIC TOOLS THAT SUPPORT REPORT DEVELOPMENT

- Take advantage of existing electronic tools that support report-writing efforts.
- A number of electronic tools support the following report-writing efforts: planning, organizing, and outlining reports; developing and administering surveys and questionnaires; capturing, storing, and accessing reference citations; organizing and storing data and information; developing and displaying visual aids; and developing reports in writing teams.
- Watch for new electronic tools that support report-writing efforts.

Notes

1. *Quick Study Business: Business Research Guide*, BarCharts, Inc., Boca Raton, February 2002, 1.

SECTION IV

BUSINESS PRESENTATIONS

DEVELOPING BUSINESS PRESENTATIONS

13

LEARNING OUTCOMES

After reading this chapter, you should be able to:

1. Describe common purposes of business presentations.

2. Discuss the types of business presentations you will make in the business place.

3. Describe how organizations, businesspeople, and audiences benefit from effective business presentations.

4. Identify the basic components of effective business presentations.

5. Discuss how to manage and use speaking anxiety while planning and preparing business presentations.

6. Describe the activities involved in planning business presentations.

7. Describe the activities involved in preparing business presentations.

© Dean Drobot/Shutterstock.com

SELECT KEY TERMS

INTRODUCTION

Business presentations are given for purposes ranging from sharing information and persuading others to instructing and making position statements. In turn, your ability to give effective presentations should have a positive influence on your job stability and career growth. Aside from learning effective presentation techniques, it is important that you are able to manage your speaking anxiety effectively. Most of us experience some degree of speaking anxiety predominately due to self-pride, lack of familiarity with our presentation topic, and/or poor preparation. Several practical techniques for managing speaking anxiety while planning and preparing business presentations are shared in this chapter.

Practicing business presentations is very important to the process and is increasingly important when the presentation is a team presentation. In either case, you are strongly advised to make a video/audio recording of your practice sessions in order to better learn from any presentation strengths and weaknesses you notice. In addition, you are encouraged to prepare and practice question-and-answer (Q&A) sessions which typically occur immediately following business presentations.

The intent of this chapter is to provide you with information about planning and preparing effective business presentations. The goal of this chapter is realized through discussions on the following topics: why business presentations are given, why you should develop good presentation skills, benefits of effective presentations, components of effective presentations, your feelings about giving presentations, planning business presentations, and preparing business presentations.

WHY BUSINESS PRESENTATIONS ARE GIVEN

Millions upon millions of business presentations are given each year in organizations worldwide. The purpose for each presentation typically falls into one of four categories: *sharing information, persuading, instructing, and making position statements.*

Some business presentations are given for the purpose of sharing information. For example, a human resources director may give a presentation before the company's employees to convey information and entertain questions about a new benefits policy. Other presentations are given for the purpose of persuading audience members to a course of action. For example, a company representative may give a presentation to employees encouraging them to contribute generously during the upcoming United Way fund drive. Still other presentations are given for the purpose of instructing audience members. For example, an information technology representative may give a presentation to select employees teaching them to navigate a new, online purchasing system. Other presentations are given for the purpose of making official position statements. For example, a company's CEO may give a presentation to employees to announce and explain a merger with another company.

The Main Purpose of Presentations
http://westsidetoastmasters.com/resources/powerspeak/lib0026.html

MAIN TYPES OF BUSINESS PRESENTATIONS

The three main types of business presentations are face-to-face presentations, webcasts, and poster presentations. *Face-to-face* presentations have speakers and their audiences in the same room/space, whereas webcasts are media presentations transmitted over the Internet. *Poster presentations* bring interested audience members together in the same room or space where they discuss the topic addressed on presentation posters. You can develop professional quality poster presentations using programs such as *Adobe Illustrator* and *CorelDraw Graphics Suite*. If you must travel to another location to give a poster presentation, should consider producing a cloth poster instead of a paper stock poster. You can fold it up and transport it easily in your briefcase, computer bag, or suitcase. This is a much more practical option for poster presentations on the go!

WHY YOU SHOULD DEVELOP GOOD PRESENTATION SKILLS

Giving business presentations is not that far off for you. Do not fool yourself into believing that once you are on the job you will not be required to give presentations right away. Some students have the inaccurate perception that new hires in the business place are not required to give presentations. They believe that presentations are given only by middle- and upper-level executives, so their involvement in presentations is several years off. Hence, they are in no rush to develop their presentation skills. What an inaccurate perception! On average, a typical white-collar worker in the United States gives one or two work-related presentations per year for the first several years of his or her business career. These presentations are typically made before relatively small audiences of 30 or fewer people, and the composition of the audience members at any one presentation is often similar (e.g., similar job status, occupations, etc.).

Those individuals whose careers take them past middle-management level typically find themselves giving several presentations per year, and company leaders, such as presidents, CEOs, CIOs, and CFOs, typically make numerous presentations annually. Their audiences often vary in size from very few to several thousand, and the composition is often diverse. Company leaders are also likely to have some of their presentations broadcast to audiences at remote sites. The higher your rank in the company, the greater your audience's expectations are that you are an excellent presenter. So work now at preparing for such a future.

Wise students and businesspeople work continuously on improving their presentations skills. So, how can you grow both your presentation skills and speaking confidence to levels of excellence? Get started now if you are not already doing so. In other words, do not wait until you reach middle management to begin working seriously on your presentation skills. That's too late! Instead, work on them from this point forward. Doing so will serve you well as you move through the early stages and years of your career and will, in turn, prepare you for that point in your career when you will make high-stakes presentations.

ACQUIRING PRESENTATION TRAINING

Unfortunately, just giving one or two presentations each year during the early stages of your career will do little to develop your presentation skills. Most of us need several years of training, practice, and experience to gain sufficient confidence and develop excellent presentation skills. Do not be discouraged. You can develop excellent presentation skills by acquiring training and additional presentation experiences on a regular basis. Consider these suggestions:

- Attend workshops and take speech classes at universities, junior colleges, and private business schools.
- Take Internet-based, distance learning, presentation skills courses.
- Take Internet-based, continuing professional education, presentation skills courses.

- Read presentation skills books. They range from full-coverage books to those that focus on specific elements of the process, such as those that focus on overcoming speaking anxiety.
- Learn from presentation skills audio tapes, videotapes, and online programs.
- Attend **Toastmasters** and **Toastmasters International** meetings and training sessions. The purpose of these organizations is to help people become good speakers.

ACQUIRING PRESENTATION EXPERIENCE

Toastmasters
Well-respected organization that helps members improve their speaking abilities.

Toastmasters International
http://www.toastmasters.org/

- Volunteer to give presentations at work. Since most people do not like to give presentations, your gesture will be welcomed. This approach might even help you earn promotions.
- Speak at professional conferences. Professional conferences provide you with the opportunity to practice in front of both small and mid-sized audiences. Furthermore, you gain valuable experience managing question-and-answer sessions, including an occasional aggressive audience member. For starters, consider presenting at a regional or national conference of the Association for Business Communication (http://businesscommunication.org/).
- Make a presentation before friends or family members. However, instruct them to inform you honestly of your specific shortcomings and strengths. If all they say is "good job," that's not helpful.
- Speak before college, high school, middle school, and elementary school classes. Simply contact the schools and express your interest in speaking. Colleges typically have you talk about your company or career. Schools ranging from elementary schools to high schools may have you speak on the above topics or about your personal interests (e.g., hobbies). Be aware that children at the elementary school level will often interrupt you mid-sentence. This gives you good practice. Of course, adults in your audiences will also interrupt you occasionally. You need to be able to think on your feet, stay on schedule, and pick up on your presentation where you left off at the time of the interruption.
- Speak at senior citizen centers, assisted care facilities, and nursing homes. Your efforts will be greatly appreciated.
- Speak at meetings of public service organizations such as Girl Scouts, Boy Scouts, Kiwanis, Rotary, etc. The audiences are friendly and appreciative of your efforts.
- Speak at personal interest meetings and conferences. For example, each year several people who hold a special interest in studying and analyzing the Battle of the Little Bighorn share their perspectives regarding the battle at meetings and conferences.

There is no great secret to becoming a good presenter. Persistence, hard work, and following the right course of action are the keys to developing the necessary skills and confidence. The good news is that you can become an excellent speaker and actually enjoy giving business presentations!

© Elena11/Shutterstock.com

BENEFITS OF EFFECTIVE PRESENTATIONS

Several parties typically benefit from effective presentations. Among the beneficiaries are organizations, presenters, and presentation audiences. The ways each benefit are presented here.

Organizations Benefit from Effective Presentations Organizations typically benefit from good presentations in three ways. First, organizations benefit when outside speakers give good presentations to their employees. Second, organizations realize benefits when their employees give effective presentations to audiences of fellow employees. Last, organizations benefit when their employees make effective presentations to external audiences on behalf of the organization.

When outside speakers give effective presentations to your employees, your organization typically benefits from the added information, knowledge, and understanding the speakers impart to employees. This occurs, in part, because good speakers capture and keep their audience's attention. As a result, audience members typically focus on the information being presented. The outcome is that the audience members understand, learn, and retain more than they would if they were listening to an inept speaker.

When speakers make good presentations before fellow employees, benefits such as those described above are also typical. With good presentations, organizations benefit from a reduction in miscommunication and the related losses that often result from poor-quality presentations.

When employees give good presentations to external audiences on behalf of their organizations, their organizations stand to benefit. The connection here pertains to the speaker's role as a representative of his or her organization. When organizations allow poor or average speakers to represent them before outside audiences, they risk negative outcomes in terms of poor public relations and lost business. If a speaker has poor or average presentation skills, what impressions do the audience members form about not only the speaker, but also about the speaker's organization? If the speaker is a good presenter, however, the audience members are more likely to be persuaded by the presentation, think well of the speaker's organization, and do business with the speaker's organization in the future.

Speakers Benefit from Giving Effective Presentations Speakers with good presentation skills realize benefits also. Most managers appreciate the impact such employees can have on their organizations. This is why managers place such a high value on presentation skills. In turn, you are encouraged to (1) appreciate the importance the business community places on good presentation skills, (2) develop good presentation skills as early as possible, and (3) continue to develop and refine your presentation skills throughout your career.

One of the times good presentation skills will serve you well is during the job hunting process. It is not uncommon for employers to look for evidence of job applicants' presentation skills on their college transcripts or in their résumés and cover letters. In addition, some recruiters require job applicants to give one or more presentations during the application process to determine the level of their actual presentation skills.

Good speakers also benefit in other ways. For example, organizations often take employees' presentation skills into account when making employment termination, demotion, transfer, pay raise, bonus, and promotion decisions. As can be expected, good speakers often experience higher levels of job security and larger, more-frequent pay raises, performance bonuses, and promotions. There is nothing like a well-delivered, "knock-their-socks-off" presentation to get the attention of those who make the big decisions.

FIGURE 13-1: PRESENTERS' ETHICAL RESPONSIBILITIES

Good speakers understand that adhering to ethical standards is also important. Here are several suggestions on how to be an ethical speaker. Good speakers:

- Avoid sharing inaccurate, misleading, or manipulative information.
- Develop visual aids that avoid distortion of facts and statistics.
- Avoid color and other design techniques that distract audience members' attention from points the speaker wants to gloss over.
- Use visual aids that are visible. Speakers leave the visuals up long enough so the audience has enough time to understand the information, without feeling they are being rushed for less-than-professional reasons.
- Refrain from highly persuasive nonverbal cues, such as gesturing, voice inflection, pauses, and inviting facial expressions, to mask inaccurate, misleading, or manipulative information.
- Avoid using their friendly, inviting personality to mask inaccurate, misleading, or manipulative information.
- Do not use their language in ways that manipulate foreign audiences whose command of the speaker's language is weak.

Individuals with good presentation skills benefit from the increased self-confidence that comes with knowing they have mastered an activity that many people never master. Their self-confidence makes it possible for them to be open to presentation opportunities, address audience questions without hesitation, and enjoy giving presentations. Furthermore, their self-confidence radiates in presentations, making them dynamic speakers.

Audiences Benefit from Effective Presentations How often have you sat through a presentation during which you spent more time looking at your watch or texting than focusing on the speaker? Or you daydreamed, doodled, or did some work. That speaker likely did not have good presentation skills. While we cannot always avoid being subjected to poor speakers, each of us can and should work at not subjecting others to such torment. We owe it to the organizations that provide us with a livelihood, we owe it to our audiences, and we owe it to ourselves.

So how do audiences benefit from effective speakers? They typically learn and retain more information from a good speaker than from one who is less skilled. Audience members may learn how to be better speakers simply by observing the techniques of those who are proficient at their craft. In addition, dynamic, effective speakers are capable of inspiring individual audience members to truly desire to improve their own presentation skills.

Yet another audience benefit is simply the enjoyment factor. Most of us enjoy listening to dynamic, effective speakers. After all, it sure beats the boredom we experience when subjected to a poorly skilled, unenthusiastic speaker. Face it, the topics addressed in business presentations are not always interesting, let alone exciting. With such topics, effective speakers have the ability to help their audiences bridge the gap between disinterest and interest.

BASIC COMPONENTS OF EFFECTIVE PRESENTATIONS

What makes one presentation successful and another mediocre? Is one presentation successful because the speaker effectively covered all of his or her information in the allotted amount of time or was it because he or she was dynamic and interesting? Is another presentation considered mediocre because the speaker appeared disorganized and did not imbue his or her voice and expressions with enthusiasm? Numerous factors contribute to the effectiveness or ineffectiveness of presentations. Each of the basic elements that affect the quality of presentations is presented below.

UNDERSTANDING THE PURPOSE OF THE PRESENTATION

Good speakers have a clear understanding of their purpose before planning and preparing a presentation. Their purpose may be to share routine information or provide some form of instruction to their audience members. Or, the intent of the presentation may be to persuade the audience to make an official position statement.

A good speaker understands that familiarization with the purpose impacts the effectiveness of the planning and preparation as well as the presentation itself. Knowing one's purpose is at the heart of good communication.

Determining Audiences' Information Expectations and Needs Good speakers understand the importance of presenting information that their audiences perceive as useful. When planning and preparing presentations, good speakers take time to determine their audience's information expectations and needs.

Sharing the right information does not preclude the need to be a skilled, dynamic speaker. However, good presentation skills alone are typically not enough to produce an effective presentation. Choosing the right information to share is also important.

Selecting the Right Amount of Information Good speakers understand the importance of selecting the right amount of information. This means they share the information their audiences expect and need. Furthermore, they share this information within the recommended time frame. This implies that they understand their audience's information expectations and needs well enough to make such decisions.[1]

When we do not pay adequate attention to selecting the right amount of information, problems arise. When we select too little information, we do not meet our audience's information expectations and needs. When we select too much information, we compromise our audience's ability to understand and retain information. The key to selecting the right amount of information involves diligent planning, preparation, and practice.

Organizing Information Logically Good speakers understand the need to organize their presentations in ways that help their audiences understand and retain the information shared. It is important that speakers do so because their audiences do not have an opportunity to hear the presentation a second time (unlike a written document that they might read two or more times to achieve understanding and retention). Thus, good speakers organize their presentations so the points they are making are clear and flow logically.

To help their audiences comprehend and retain the information presented, good speakers often share it three times. First, they introduce the presentation topic by giving an overview of the main points to be shared. Second, they present the information in detail. Third, they summarize the main points made.

Choosing the Right Type and Number of Visual Aids Good speakers know that visual aids are expected in business presentations and understand the importance of choosing the right type and number for each presentation. While visual aid types vary significantly (e.g., handouts, PowerPoint slides, mindmaps, graphs, YouTube clips, flip charts), be aware of the growing popularity of professional-quality, colorful visual aids. In a world where we are bombarded by so many visual images (e.g., TV, video games, movies, the Internet), business audiences have come to expect professional-quality, colorful visual aids.

The most common computer-generated presentation tool by far is Microsoft's **PowerPoint**, but it is not the only tool of its kind. **Corel Presentations** and Sun Microsystem's **Apache Open Office Impress** are similar tools. Then there are web-based tools such as Trellix, a program that supports presentations made for the Web, teleconferences, and live electronic presentations. Many freeware programs have been designed to support business presentations. For example, Google has developed a documents and spreadsheets program that lets you share projects online with the general public or specific people.[2]

Be careful not to overdo it with the visual aids. Since computers and presentation software make it easy to produce visual aids, you have time to end up with more visual aids than you can present effectively. Produce only the number needed to communicate and support the points you are making—no more, no less.

Staying on Schedule Make it a point to respect your audience's need to stay on schedule. Plan, prepare, and practice for a designated length; start the presentation on time; keep an eye on your watch; and end on time.

Work to eliminate those obstacles that can cause you to start or end late, such as (1) not planning, preparing, and practicing properly; (2) selecting too much information; (3) developing too many visual aids; (4) arriving at the presentation site late; (5) not understanding how to use the equipment and software; (6) lacking a backup plan to cope with equipment or software that is not working properly; (7) getting away from your notes and rambling; and (8) not controlling question-and-answer sessions.

Presenting Professionally Good speakers understand the importance of good presentation skills. They know that good presentation technique alone does not produce a truly effective presentation. They do know, however, that when good presentation skills are combined with the right content, a good presentation is the result. So, give each of these components sufficient attention, and you will be on the right track.

PowerPoint
A popular presentation software package.

Corel Presentations
Presentation software similar to Microsoft PowerPoint.

Apache Open Office Impress
A presentation program analogous to Microsoft PowerPoint and Apple Keynote. Can export presentations to Adobe Flash (SWF) files, allowing them to be played on any computer with a Flash player installed. Impress lacks ready-made presentation designs but this can be overcome by downloading free templates online.

In all presentation phases—planning, preparing, practicing, presenting, and Q&A sessions—acknowledge and control your presentation anxiety. Most people experience some level of presentation anxiety. If you do, take comfort in knowing that you are not alone! The trick is to learn to control anxiety and use it to your and your audience's advantage. The next section contains information about why most of us experience *presentation anxiety* and some techniques to control it during the planning, preparation, and practicing phases. The benefits of managing and using presentation anxiety are addressed in Chapter 14, along with some techniques to control speaking anxiety shortly before and during presentations, as well as during Q&A sessions.

HOW DO YOU FEEL ABOUT GIVING PRESENTATIONS?

Do you enjoy giving presentations? Do you know many people who do? Do you know anyone who does? Is it humanly possible to enjoy giving presentations? Believe it or not, some people actually do. Many others who may not necessarily use the word *enjoy* to describe their feelings about giving presentations still embrace the task wholeheartedly when necessary.

- Understanding the purpose
- Determining the audience's information expectations and needs
- Selecting the right information
- Organizing the information effectively
- Choosing the right type(s) and number of visual aids
- Staying on schedule
- Determining appropriate appearance
- Making a professional presentation

If you do not enjoy giving presentations, challenge yourself. When you become skilled, experienced, and confident enough, then you will enjoy making dynamic, effective presentations and gain the satisfaction of knowing that you have mastered a challenging skill set.

PRESENTATION ANXIETY: WILL YOU CONTROL IT OR WILL IT CONTROL YOU?

Let's cut to the chase and put the bad news out there. Most people do not like to give presentations. Are you surprised? Are you like most people? Given the choice, most people would rather have someone else speak. When asked why they do not like to give presentations, most people are quick to cite presentation anxiety as the reason. Some call it *presentation anxiety*, while others call it *speaking anxiety* or *stage fright*. No matter what they call it, they are all talking about the same uncomfortable feelings. In general terms, **presentation anxiety** (*glossophobia*) is a tense emotional state resulting from one's apprehension of speaking before groups. The degree of anxiety varies from person to person, with typical symptoms ranging from heightened nervousness, poor sleep patterns, and sweaty palms to overwhelming feelings of fear and self-doubt.

presentation anxiety
A tense, emotional state resulting from one's attitude and feelings about speaking in front of a group. Also known as *glossophobia*.

© benchart/Shutterstock.com

Even though we understand on a logical level that others also experience presentation anxiety, most of us convince ourselves that other speakers are either not nervous or far less nervous than we are. Take solace in knowing that you are not alone when it comes to presentation anxiety. While this awareness alone will not resolve your nervousness, it will help you keep your feelings in perspective. You are faced with the same challenges as everyone else—the challenges to face up to your presentation anxiety and to learn to manage and use it productively.

WHY DO MOST OF US EXPERIENCE PRESENTATION ANXIETY?

What makes us anxious about public speaking? There are a number of reasons, and not surprisingly, the reason or reasons that plague one person do not necessarily plague others. So, each of us is faced with the challenge of determining specifically what makes us anxious. Knowing the reasons behind our speaking anxieties is a good starting point. We may even discover that some of the reasons are unwarranted. For those that are not, however, we are then in a better position to identify relaxation techniques and presentation anxiety control techniques that will help us control our fears.

Now, let's look at the typical reasons behind presentation anxiety. Self-pride is the main reason most of us experience presentation anxiety. We simply do not want to embarrass ourselves before a group of people. Most of us want our audience to think we are knowledgeable, competent people who have our act together. We certainly do not want people to laugh at us or pity us when we say or do something embarrassing. Even comedians and clowns want people to laugh with them, not at them. Most speakers want to do a good job.

Self-pride is not the only reason most people experience speaking anxiety. Here are some other reasons.

- Insufficient planning
- Insufficient preparation
- Insufficient practice
- Lack of familiarity with the presentation topic
- Lack of confidence in the presentation topic
- Tension associated with knowing that big stakes are riding on the outcome of the presentation
- Tension associated with knowing the boss or other influential people will be in the audience
- Fear of certain sizes of audiences
- Realization that you have been ill or tired leading up to the presentation
- Realization that you have been stressed about other matters leading up to the presentation
- Fear that you will not finish in the allotted time or that you will finish too early
- Fear that the microphone or visual aid equipment or software will not work properly or that you are not familiar enough with it to fix it on the fly
- Fear of audience apathy
- Fear of not having a response for an audience member's question
- Fear of having to deal with aggressive audience members

Hopefully, your presentation anxiety level was not heightened as you read the above list. Good speakers come to grips with their fears and learn to control them. They appreciate the importance of understanding the reasons behind the fears. Understand that most of the reasons for presentation anxiety can be controlled through careful planning and preparation.

BENEFITS OF MANAGING AND USING SPEAKING ANXIETY WHILE PLANNING AND PREPARING PRESENTATIONS

The trick is to learn to manage and use your presentation anxieties, instead of struggling to eliminate them. Most of us naturally seek to eliminate our anxieties and fears as quickly as possible, which is understandable because they make us uncomfortable and appear to threaten our perceived sense of control. However, good speakers know they can derive benefits from presentation anxiety experienced during the planning and preparation stages. For example, presentation anxiety can motivate you to:

- Start planning and preparing early
- Gain a clear understanding of your objective
- Learn about your audience
- Learn your presentation topic thoroughly
- Gain confidence in your presentation topic
- Derive your information from reliable sources
- Determine the right amount of information to include in your presentation
- Check out the presentation site and equipment well in advance of the presentation date
- Develop backup plans for equipment and software malfunctions
- Practice extensively
- Prepare for question-and-answer sessions

MANAGING AND USING SPEAKING ANXIETY WHILE PLANNING AND PREPARING PRESENTATIONS

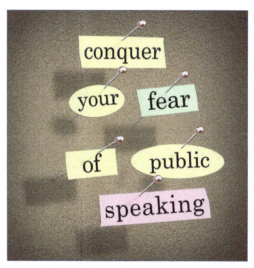

© iQoncept/Shutterstock.com

Although presentation anxiety is typically most noticeable shortly before and during presentations, most speakers experience some anxiety while planning and preparing their presentations. Fortunately, you can do several things to manage and use presentation anxiety during the planning and preparation stages. Some relaxation strategies and strategies for managing and using presentation anxiety while planning and preparing presentations follow.

RELAXATION STRATEGIES WHILE PLANNING AND PREPARING PRESENTATIONS

Relaxation helps us keep a reasonable perspective on our presentation anxiety. It also allows us to be more objective and thorough as we plan and prepare presentations. Finally, relaxation helps us look to the presentation day with optimism, not dread.[3] Consider the following suggestions.

- **Exercise**. Choose a type of exercise you enjoy, then have fun while working off some of that speaking anxiety.
- **Listen to relaxing music**. Listen to relaxing music while you plan and prepare your presentation or take a break, sit back, close your eyes, and take it in.

- **Meditate**. Use meditation to calm down, give your mind a rest, and place yourself in a positive frame of mind.
- **Visualize your presentation**. Visualize yourself giving a dynamic, effective presentation. Build self-confidence by visualizing yourself moving successfully through the presentation, from your introduction to your closing.
- **Watch movies, read, and play computer games**. Give your mind a break from your fears by getting lost in a good movie, book, or computer game.
- **Volunteer**. Step away from your presentation anxiety for a few hours and do some volunteer work for a charitable organization. This will take your mind off your fears for a while and put your presentation anxiety in perspective.
- **Treat yourself**. Be especially kind to yourself. This may mean treating yourself to that dessert you might not normally eat or buying a special item of clothing that makes you feel good.

Lists of strategies for relaxation and for managing and using presentation anxiety shortly before and during presentations, as well as during Q&A sessions, are presented in Chapter 14.

PRESENTATION ANXIETY CONTROL STRATEGIES TO CONTROL SPEAKING ANXIETY WHILE PLANNING AND PREPARING PRESENTATIONS

Use one or more of the following suggestions to reduce anxiety while planning and preparing your presentation.

- **Identify and embrace the reasons you are anxious**. Write them down on paper, rank them, then decide how you will manage and use them as you plan and prepare your presentation.
- **Begin planning and preparation early**. Waiting until the last minute to do these things simply adds to your anxiety.
- **Gain a clear understanding of your presentation objective**. Remove any doubt regarding your objective.
- **Familiarize yourself with your audience**. Remove unknown elements that might otherwise feed your fears.
- **Learn your presentation topic well**. Gain confidence in knowing that you are secure in your understanding of your presentation topic. The audience looks to you as the expert!
- **Determine the appropriate information to include**. Take comfort in knowing you are choosing information that your audience needs to know.
- **Select information you will share from authoritative sources**. Remove concerns that you will either not be sharing good-quality information or that your audience will question your sources.
- **Determine the right amount of information to include**. Remove fears that you will share too much or too little information, which will result in your presentation running over or falling short of the allotted time.

- **Check out the presentation site and equipment well in advance of the presentation**. Familiarize yourself with the presentation setting, hardware, and software to remove unknown elements about which you might otherwise worry.
- **Develop backup plans for potential equipment or software malfunction**. Reduce your fears by knowing how you can proceed if your equipment or software does not work properly.
- **Get extremely comfortable with the first couple minutes of the presentation**. Knowing that your presentation will get off to a good start reduces your fears and builds your self-confidence.
- **Practice extensively**. Practice often using good practice techniques. If you can, practice in a room similar in size and shape to the room in which you will give your presentation. In addition, practice your speech in front of people with whom you are comfortable, such as family or friends. They can provide you with priceless feedback regarding your presentation. If necessary, public speaking coaches are available to help you with your presentation and anxiety.[4]
- **Prepare thoroughly for question-and-answer sessions**. Anticipate questions and prepare your responses and reactions in advance to reduce your fear of intimidation by audience questions.
- **Prepare yourself physically**. Eat right, get enough sleep, and exercise some. This makes you alert and objective while planning and preparing, as well as during your presentation.

SUMMARY: SECTION 3— PRESENTATION ANXIETY

- Presentation anxiety refers to a tense emotional state resulting from one's attitude toward and feelings about speaking in front of groups.
- The main reason for presentation anxiety is self-pride. Other causes of anxiety range from insufficient planning and preparation to fear of equipment failure to audience apathy.
- The trick to benefiting from presentation anxiety is to manage it instead of struggling to eliminate it.
- Relaxation techniques include exercising, listening to relaxing music, meditating, visualizing your presentation, watching movies, reading, playing computer games, doing volunteer work, and treating yourself.
- Anxiety control techniques range from thoroughly planning and preparing your talk to preparing yourself physically.

PLANNING BUSINESS PRESENTATIONS

Planning is the foundation on which effective presentations are built. Good planning contributes to presentations in which speakers meet their objectives and their audience's needs. The following website contains information about all presentation skills components: www.abacon.com/pubspeak/histsit.html.

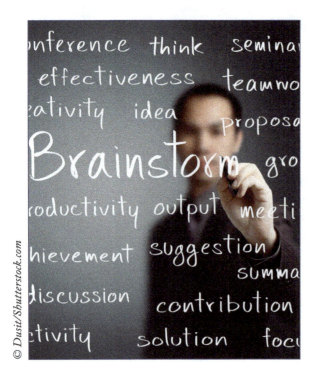

© Dusit/Shutterstock.com

Planning a presentation involves determining what it is you need to accomplish and how you will do it. Think of the planning process as being one of answering a series of questions. The questions and answers discussed here provide a sense of the activities involved in planning presentations.

WHAT IS MY PRESENTATION OBJECTIVE?

At the heart of this question is determining if your task is to share routine information, provide instruction, persuade audience members toward a specific objective, or make an official position statement. Write out the specific purpose so that it remains clear in your mind as you plan and prepare.

WHAT DO I NEED TO KNOW ABOUT MY AUDIENCE?

Familiarizing yourself with your audience and its needs is critical to planning and preparing effective presentations. The idea here is to analyze your audience so you will be able to achieve a good fit between your objectives and your audience's needs and expectations.

For example, determine your audience's information needs and expectations. This involves determining what information they already know, what information they expect, and what information they need. While making such determinations, do your best to identify their level of understanding and anticipate their probable reaction to your presentation—both content and presentation style.

It is useful to determine audience size for a variety of reasons. Such information makes it possible for you to select appropriate types of visual aids and font sizes. While flip charts and whiteboards may work for small audiences, to get the job done properly with large audiences, computer-generated visual aids are the more appropriate choice. Determining audience size in advance also makes it possible to decide whether you will need to use a microphone. When your audience size exceeds 100 people, expect to use a microphone.

Determining audience type is a crucial step in organizing your presentation. For example, if you have a friendly audience you want to be warm in your presentation and include a little humor. If your audience is neutral, you might want to present both sides of an issue using a pro-con pattern and employ more facts, statistics, and expert opinions. And if your audience is hostile, you might use a noncontroversial, chronological pattern, objective data, and expert opinions that are more appropriate than anecdotes and humor.[5]

FIGURE 13–3: ¡PRESENTING TO DIFFERENT LEARNING STYLES

- Visual: Photos, videos, charts
- Auditory: Stories/anecdotes, metaphors, dynamic delivery
- Tactile/kinesthetic: Provide hands-on learning exercises, e.g. activities¡

© snapgalleria/Shutterstock.com

© Graphicworld/Shutterstock.com

© Batshevs/Shutterstock.com

FIGURE 13-4: PLANNING AND PREPARING PRESENTATIONS FOR INTERNATIONAL AUDIENCES

Here are some general suggestions for planning and preparing presentations to be given to international audiences.

- Learn about your audience's culture, especially its business customs.
- Gain a clear understanding of your audience's expectations.
- Determine the level of formality that your audience expects. (Most expect a high level of formality and professionalism.)
- Determine if your status and age are important to the audience.
- Practice speaking more slowly than you would if you were giving a presentation in the United States.
- Identify your accent characteristics (e.g., drawl, speed) and practice controlling them so they do not interfere with clarity.
- Avoid slang and profanity. You do not want to confuse or offend your audience.
- Use technical jargon sparingly. If you have to use jargon, explain it.
- Use humor sparingly. Humor translates poorly into other languages and cultures.
- If you will not be speaking in your audience's native language, plan to sprinkle a few words and phrases in their language into your presentation, but first test these words with a native speaker before the presentation.
- As you practice, be aware of your nonverbal communication habits and how they will be interpreted by your international audience (e.g., eye contact, gestures, etc.).
- Determine the type of visual aids your audience prefers (e.g., computer-generated, handouts) and whether they should be prepared in advance (e.g., PowerPoint slides) or they can be developed during the presentation (e.g., whiteboards, flip charts).
- Be extremely clear and specific with your host regarding your equipment needs. Test your equipment ahead of time to ensure it works properly and meshes with any hardware or software you plan to use. Plan for a worst-case scenario.
- Determine your audience's appearance expectations. (Most foreign audiences expect the speaker's appearance to be professional and conservative.)

Finally, determine the composition of your audience. Are the members similar or diverse in terms of job title, education, age, gender, cultural backgrounds, etc.? Given their composition and expectations, what level of formality will your audience expect? Should you give your entire talk and then entertain questions? Or, should you encourage discussion throughout your presentation? Should you dress formally and remain behind the podium during the presentation? Or, should you dress casually and move around before your audience?[6] Additional information pertaining to understanding your audience is available at this website www.abacon.com/pubspeak/histsit.html.

WHAT INFORMATION DO I NEED TO SHARE?

This question really pertains to two separate issues. You should be concerned about sharing the right information, and you should be concerned about doing it within the suggested time frame.

First, identify the information needs of your audience. This suggests that you will determine who your audience is and what information your audience expects and needs. Your audience may know what information they expect, but they may not realize they need additional information. This is where you plan the information needs accordingly and fill in the gaps.

Having identified your audience and its information expectations and needs, you are now faced with the challenge of determining how to organize and present the information in a way that is consistent with the amount of time allotted for the presentation.

Selecting too little information often results in ineffective presentations. The problem is further compounded when a presenter speaks more rapidly during the presentation than he or she does during the practice sessions. The result is an ineffective presentation that falls noticeably short of its recommended time frame.

Selecting too much information also contributes to ineffective presentations. When you include too much information in your presentation, one of the following four problems typically occurs. (1) You speak at a recommended rate, but disrupt audience members' schedules when your presentation runs long. (2) You speak at a recommended rate, but must skip important points in your quest to finish on time. (3) You speak at a recommended rate, but skip or rush through the summary. (4) You speak too fast and rush through visuals in your quest to include all your information and still finish on time.

WHAT INFORMATION SHOULD I PRESENT VISUALLY?

To answer this question, ask yourself how your audience will benefit from your visual aids. For example, is the purpose of your visual aids to help your audience understand and retain information presented? Is the purpose to simplify complex or detailed information? Is the purpose to emphasize specific information or show a trend? Is the purpose to introduce your presentation or is it to highlight key points in the summary? Assign a purpose to each visual aid you consider including. If you see no clear, driving purpose to a proposed visual aid, drop it. Visual aids should be developed in conjunction with development of the talk. They should not be developed as an afterthought or included for show.

WHAT TYPES OF VISUAL AIDS SHOULD BE INCLUDED?

The answer is: those that best support your presentation. The good news here is that you have several visual aid types to choose from. The bad news is that you have more types of visual aids to become familiar with and consider when planning presentations. Here are several examples.

- **Handouts.** Are a good choice when you have more information to share with your audience than you are able to include. Handouts are most frequently used with small, informal audiences.
- **A flip chart or whiteboard**. Is a practical choice if your intention is to develop lists during presentations. Flip charts and whiteboards are most frequently used with informal audiences. They do not provide a practical alternative for large audiences,

due to the obvious lack of visibility and because formal audiences expect professionally prepared visual aids.

- **Items**. Refers to tangible things a speaker would hold up before an audience, for example, a prosecuting attorney might show a murder weapon to a jury in a criminal trial. Items are an appropriate type of visual aid for both informal and formal audiences. In either case, the audience must be small or some will not be able to see the item.
- **Demonstrations**. Provide a practical way to communicate visually when you want to walk your audience through a particular action. For example, a speaker could invite a colleague or friend to the front of the room and the two could demonstrate the proper way to shake hands at a job interview. Demonstrations are also limited to small audiences due to the restricted visibility factor.

bar charts
Graphs that show numerical comparisons.

- **Bar charts**. Are used to show numerical comparisons. **Bar charts** are typically computer-generated and displayed digitally. Keep them simple. For example, 3D bar charts are often confusing. There is too much going on, and the 3D angles often distort clear comparisons. Use distinctly different colors for each comparative bar in multiple-bar charts. They are equally effective for informal and formal audiences, as well as small and large audiences. (See Figure 13-5.)

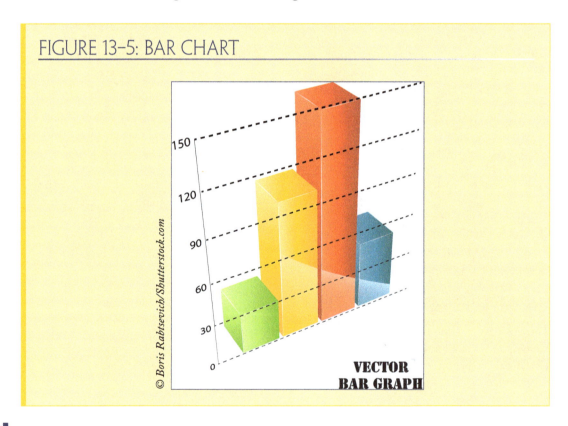

FIGURE 13–5: BAR CHART

line charts
Graphs that show trends.

- **Line charts** are is used to show trends. **Line charts** are typically computer-generated and displayed digitally. Use different color lines in multiple-line charts. They are equally effective for both informal and formal audiences, as well as small and large audiences. (See Figure 13-6.)

FIGURE 13–6: LINE CHART

© M88/Shutterstock.com

- **Pie charts** are used to show comparisons of a whole (100 percent), such as budgets. **Pie charts** are typically computer-generated and displayed digitally. Use distinctly different colors for each slice of the pie. They are equally effective for both informal and formal audiences, as well as for small and large audiences. (See Figure 13-7.)

pie charts
Graphs that show comparisons of parts of a whole.

FIGURE 13–7: PIE CHART

© ra2studio/Shutterstock.com

- **PowerPoint.** The main idea with regard to PowerPoint slides is to keep them simple. Avoid including too much information on a PowerPoint slide. Select a font style and a type size that are legible and easy to read from a distance. Document cameras, also known as digital overheads, provide a good alternative to overhead transparencies.

How familiar are you with developing effective PowerPoint slides? The following questions will help you answer the question if you are unsure.

A. Is it better to select a relatively simple background design and then use it across all of your presentation PowerPoint slides <u>or</u> is it better to select a background design that has a lot of components (very busy) as a means of holding your audience's attention?

B. Is it better to use a legible font (e.g., *Arial, Times New Roman, Calibri*) <u>or</u> is it better to use a scripted font (e.g., *Freestyle Script, Segoe Script*) as a means of adding additional interest to your PowerPoint slides?

C. Is it better to use a 13-point type size for PowerPoint slide titles and 9-point type size for PowerPoint body information <u>or</u> is it better to use 40- and 26-point type sizes instead?

D. Is it better to use six or more colors on a PowerPoint slide <u>or</u> is it better to use five or fewer?

E. Is it better to include one emphasis technique (e.g., *italicizing*) in each PowerPoint slide <u>or</u> is it better to use emphasis techniques on PowerPoint slides sparingly so their emphasis is not compromised?

<u>Key:</u> A - question #1, B - question #1, C - question #2, D - question #2, E - question #2

---

document cameras
magnify images of two-and three-dimensional objects, documents, photographs, etc.

guidance reminders
Reminders that speakers include in their presentation notes.

- **Document cameras.** Magnify images of two-and three-dimensional objects, documents, photographs, etc.
- **Guidance Reminders.** Reminders that speakers include in their presentation notes.
- **Transparencies.** Provide an alternative to PowerPoint slides and not long ago were a common way to present information visually prior to the advent of computer-displayed visuals. Transparencies work best with small, informal audiences.
- **Drawings and illustrations.** Sometimes that adage, "A picture is worth a thousand words," is spot on when making visual aid decisions. For example, if you want to display all or a portion of an architectural drawing or schematic, a drawing or illustration would be a practical choice. They are equally effective with informal and formal audiences, but need to be used with small audiences due to limited visibility.
- **Spreadsheets.** Portions of spreadsheets are often used when the speaker wants to display specific numbers or groups of numbers. Spreadsheets are equally effective with informal and formal audiences, but work best with small audiences due to limited visibility.
- **Photos.** Like drawings and illustrations, photos are at times the most effective way to say what you want to say. They are equally effective for informal and formal audiences, as well as for small and large audiences.

- **YouTube videos.** At times a short video clip is the right visual aid choice. For example, you could show a short YouTube video that displays the proper way two businesspeople would greet each other in a given country or culture. If possible, use YouTube video clips in the 1–3-minute range. Short video clips are equally effective for informal and formal audiences, as well as for small and large audiences.
- **Wordles.** Wordles are word clouds. If you want to display several terms at once, including them in a wordle is an interesting and colorful way to do so, since the terms are displayed at different angles and in different type sizes and colors. Wordles are equally effective for informal and formal audiences, as well as for small and large audiences. (See Figure 13-9.)

FIGURE 13-9: WORDLE

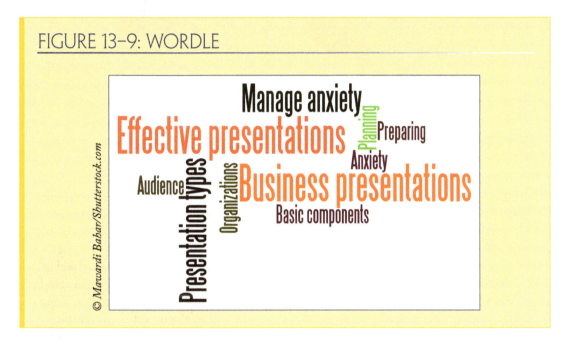

© Mawardi Bahar/Shutterstock.com

- **Mindmaps.** Mindmaps are created using diagramming software used for planning and organizing. *Mindomo* is a popular online mindmap program. From a presentation perspective, mindmaps provide a visual aid alternative if you want to display an entire process. You can focus your audience's attention on portions of mindmaps by enlarging and bringing forward those portions. Mindmaps are equally effective for informal and formal audiences, as well as for small and large audiences. (See Figure 13-10.)

FIGURE 13–10: MINDMAP

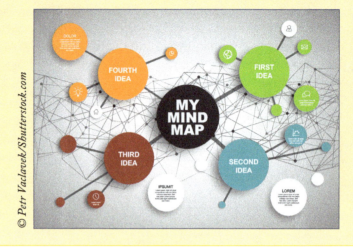

© Petr Vaclavek/Shutterstock.com

- **Prezi.** Prezi is an open canvas that allows users to navigate between a number of different media forms (e.g., text, video, images, etc.). Essentially users can zoom in and out of various media. To really liven up some of your visual aids, include some Prezi slides. However, do not include too many because they can be busy and distracting. Prezi slides are equally effective for informal and formal audiences, as well as for small and large audiences.
- **GoAnimate.** GoAnimate helps you make animated video clips using pre-made or user-designed animated characters (e.g., people, animals). You can even develop animated characters that look like you in animated form. You can have them standing still or moving around and they can be silent, talking, or making sounds. You can even give animated characters your voice via audio-/video capture programs like Camtasia Studio. You can even take photos of scenes and use animated forms of them as your backdrops. GoAnimate provides interesting and colorful ways to capture and keep your audience's attention. GoAnimate clips are equally effective for informal and formal audiences, as well as for small and large audiences. (See Figure 13-11.)

HOW MANY VISUAL AIDS SHOULD BE INCLUDED?

Audiences expect to see visual aids in business presentations. They are not optional. Fortunately, today's affordable technology and presentation software make it possible for us to create professional-quality visual aids in a matter of minutes at little cost. The challenge, however, is to produce simple, clear visual aids in a quantity you can present effectively and professionally in your allotted time.

Do not develop too many visual aids. Sharing, displaying, and discussing visual aids during presentations is time consuming if done correctly. In addition, audiences need sufficient time to take in, comprehend, and retain the information on each visual aid. The general rule is that it is better to do a good job of presenting too few visual aids, than a poor job of rushing through too many.

FIGURE 13-11: GOANIMATE

© YummyBuum/Shutterstock.com

Determining which visual aids to use typically depends on one or more of the following three characteristics.

1. **Audience and Room Size**. If the audience is small (25 or fewer), visuals aids presented on flip charts, whiteboards, and overhead transparencies are typically visible to all audience members. As the audience size increases, computer-generated visual aids, films, and slides are more readily visible to the entire audience.
2. **Expected Formality Level**. If your audience expects a formal presentation, prepare professional-quality visual aids (e.g., PowerPoint slides, video clips) in advance. If it is an informal presentation, then handouts and pre-prepared and unprepared flips charts are sufficient.
3. **Purpose of Your Presentation**. If your purpose is to make an official declaration before your employees, investors, etc., prepare high-quality, computer-generated visual aids and other multimedia. If your presentation is instructional, whiteboards and unprepared flip charts provide you with the flexibility to accomplish your goals.

WHAT ARE MY EQUIPMENT AND SOFTWARE NEEDS?

A number of factors govern your equipment and software needs. They include audience and room size, expected level of formality, and presentation purpose.

By planning equipment and software needs early, you position yourself to assure your needs will be met. Your host may supply some or all of your equipment requirements. In this case, you must clearly communicate your specific needs to him or her in advance. Do so in writing so he or she will have a checklist to work from and so there can be no doubt about what you need. Or, you can take responsibility for arranging all or some of your equipment and software needs. This is often the preferred approach, simply because it eliminates (often unjustified) concerns that the host will not have the requested equipment or forget to make the requested arrangements. Even if you arrange for your equipment and software needs, it is still a good idea to create a checklist.

FIGURE 13-12: PLANNING AND PREPARING FOR EQUIPMENT AND SOFTWARE PROBLEMS

Good speakers anticipate problems and take measures to avoid them or deal with them effectively when they arise. When planning, try to think of every conceivable equipment and software problem that could occur. The purpose of doing so is not to worry you, but to remind you to plan for less-than-perfect equipment and software.

Some equipment and software problems can be planned for and avoided. For example, plan to take along backup copies of computer-generated visual aid files, a laptop and portable projector, spare bulbs for the projector, dry-erase markers, a dry erase eraser, a short extension cord, a power strip, and a couple of three-prong adaptors.

Other potential problems require a backup plan. For example, plan to produce a handout containing a duplicate set of what you intend to show on the screen. This way if the computer, software, and/or projector decide not to cooperate, you have a plan B.

WHAT APPEARANCE DOES MY AUDIENCE EXPECT?

Appearance as it relates to business presentations is interesting. If your appearance is consistent with your audience's expectations, it typically goes unnoticed. However, if your appearance is inconsistent with their expectations, it will typically be judged unfavorably. Some will even form a less-than-favorable impression of you and your presentation before you get started. They will assume that since you did not adhere to appropriate appearance guidelines, your professional stature and presentation information are suspect. At minimum, inappropriate appearance will distract some of your audience members from the information you are sharing.

What is appropriate appearance for a business presentation? Well, it varies based on the presentation situation. Some business presentations warrant conventional, conservative (formal) appearance (e.g., dark suit, white blouse or shirt, conservative necktie or scarf, well-polished shoes, well-kept hair and fingernails, moderate make-up and jewelry). In some presentation settings, however,

less-conventional (casual) appearance (e.g., casual business attire, well-kept hair and fingernails, moderate make-up and jewelry) is preferred by audiences. Then, there are those occasional presentation settings where either a formal or a casual appearance is acceptable. Unless you know differently, when speaking to upper-level executives in your organization or to external and international audiences, the general rule is to go with formal appearance as described above.

© Peter Bernik/Shutterstock.com

Figure 13-13 contains four presentation scenarios that remind us that preferred presentation appearance does, indeed, vary from setting to setting.

FIGURE 13–13: PRESENTATION APPEARANCE SCENARIOS

1. **Presentation to Management**
   Imagine a scenario in which you are a distribution center employee for a package delivery company. You have figured out a way to do your job more efficiently, thus saving the company money. You have been asked to give a presentation to some of the company's upper-level managers describing your new approach to doing your job. Would you dress in formal business attire (e.g., suit, dress shoes, etc.) or business casual attire?

2. **Professional Conference Presentation**
   Imagine you have been asked to give a presentation at a professional conference. Would you dress in formal business attire (e.g., *suit, dress shoes*, etc.) or business casual attire or would either formal business or business casual attire be equally acceptable?

3. **Presentation Outside of the United States**
   Imagine you have been invited to give a presentation on behalf of your company in a business setting outside of the United States. Would you dress in formal business attire (e.g., *suit, dress shoes*, etc.) or business casual attire?

4. **Presentation to United Auto Workers (UAW)**
   Imagine you have been invited to give a presentation to a group of UAW members at a large automobile assembly plant in the greater Detroit, Michigan area. Would you dress in formal business attire (e.g., *suit, dress shoes*, etc.) or business casual attire or would either formal business or business casual attire be equally acceptable?

   Key: Scenario #1 - formal business attire, Scenario #2 - either formal business attire or casual business attire, Scenario #3 - formal business attire, Scenario #4 - business casual

It is always best to identify in advance your audience's appearance expectations. In some instances, this is fairly easy to do. However, with today's trend toward casual dress in the business place, it can be unclear just how "dressed up" you should be. If you cannot identify your audience's expectations, lean toward dressing more conservatively. If you are still confused as to what is meant by conventional, conservative appearance, read some of John Malloy's thoughts on the matter. He has published a number of "dress for success" books for women and men. Or, you could visit your campus career center for additional advice.

FIGURE 13–14: FORMAL BUSINESS APPEARANCE SUGGESTIONS

Appearance Suggestions for Women
- Moderate jewelry: earrings (one per ear), bracelets, necklaces, rings, and watches are acceptable
- Moderate makeup, moderate perfume if you choose to wear any (none is better)
- No visible tattoos
- No visible piercings in eyebrows, nose, and/or tongue
- Manicured nails
- Non-distracting hair style
- Natural hair color
- Dark-colored suit or pants suit
- Dress shoes with lower heels, polished
- Briefcase, portfolio, or purse of good-quality leather

Appearance Suggestions for Men
- Moderate jewelry: rings and watches are acceptable; no earrings, bracelets, or necklaces
- No makeup
- Moderate cologne or aftershave if you choose to wear any (none is better)
- No visible tattoos
- No visible piercings in eyebrows, nose, and/or tongue
- Clean, well-trimmed fingernails
- Conservative hair style
- Natural hair color
- Conservative-style, dark-colored suit (not a sports coat and slacks)
- Solid color shirt, preferably white
- Necktie, conservative pattern
- Socks same color as suit
- Dress shoes, polished
- Briefcase or portfolio of good-quality leather

In summary, the time and effort invested in planning presentations are not wasted. Careful planning provides a strong foundation on which to prepare and ultimately give effective presentations.

PREPARING BUSINESS PRESENTATIONS

Once you have devoted adequate time to planning your presentation, the next steps involve preparing and practicing. Before moving on, however, consider visiting speeches.com/index.shtml. This website contains information on how to prepare presentations.

Preparing presentations involves several steps. If done right, each step takes time—some more than others. Build quite a bit of time into your schedule for these activities. You do not want to be rushed as you approach the day of the presentation. This only fuels your presentation anxieties, resulting in a less-effective presentation. Follow these preparation steps.

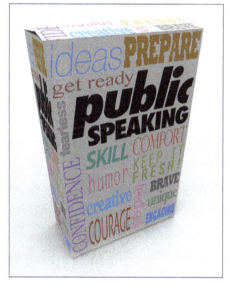

© iQoncept/Shutterstock.com

VISIT YOUR PRESENTATION SITE

If possible, visit your presentation site well in advance of the day of your presentation. If you cannot visit your presentation site physically, try to visit it virtually. This involves asking your host to send you a video of the room or, at minimum, photos. If this is not possible, ask your host to send you information such as room dimensions, whether you will need a microphone, audience size, and number and location of electrical outlets. Visiting your presentation site prior to the presentation, in person or otherwise, is the smart thing to do. Here are some sample benefits of doing so.

- You remove one unknown element from the process, which should reduce some of your presentation anxiety.
- You become familiar with the seating arrangement. Make sure to ask if the seating arrangement will be different on the day you are scheduled to speak and if so, how so.
- You gain an appreciation for how loudly you need to speak and whether you need to use a microphone. Then you can practice accordingly.
- You can determine the extent to which you can move around based on the room size and design and the location of the podium and equipment.

© razihusin/Shutterstock.com

- You can determine appropriate font size for your visual aids.
- You become familiar with the location of the podium, equipment, and electrical outlets. For example, you might decide that you need to take along a laptop, a portable projector, a power strip, some three-prong adapters, or an extension cord.
- You become familiar with the light and dimmer switches and how they operate.
- You become familiar with how the screen is raised and lowered.
- You can determine the distance between you and your audience and how to best deliver eye contact based on the room dimensions and design.

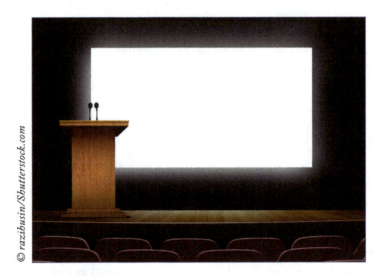

By removing so many unknown elements, you greatly enhance the effectiveness and efficiency of the preparation process, conduct more realistic practice sessions, and reduce some of your speaking anxiety.

If you are able to visit your presentation site in person, then practice your presentation there. It's a great wonderful opportunity to become familiar with the surroundings, while getting somewhat comfortable at the same time.

GATHER THE PRESENTATION INFORMATION

During the planning stage, you determined your audience's information expectations and needs. Now, it is time to gather the necessary information.

The information may come from a variety of sources ranging from company records and interviews to the Internet. Remember to gather valid information from reliable sources. Be especially careful about information you locate on the Internet. It is difficult to confirm the reliability of some Internet sources. It is equally difficult to confirm the validity of the information from those sources. For obvious reasons, you do not want to create a situation where audience members question the validity of your information and the reliability of your sources during your presentation or during the question-and-answer session.

ORGANIZE THE INFORMATION

Once you have gathered the information, structure it so it is clear and flows logically.[7] Do not make your audiences struggle to keep up or figure out your logic. Remember, they are hearing the information for the first time and do not have the opportunity to hear it a second and third time to aid in understanding and retention. Your efforts to logically organize the information may go unnoticed, but audiences will notice a presentation that is illogical or unorganized.

Organize your information into the following three presentation components.

1. **Introduction**. Introduce yourself (name, job title, affiliation, etc.), mention the purpose of your presentation, tell your audience when you will entertain questions, and share a brief overview of your talk so your audience has a framework to follow.
2. **Body**. Present the information in detail, with special emphasis on key points.
3. **Closing**. Announce the close, briefly recap the key points, extend a call for action if the purpose is to persuade, and close with a memorable statement. Finally, extend an invitation for questions.

As you organize the information, give some thought to where visual aids will logically support your goal. Determine specific visual aid types and contents after you have organized the information.

FIGURE 13-15: PLANNING AND PREPARING TEAM PRESENTATIONS

Here are some general suggestions for planning and preparing team presentations.
- Plan together by defining clear objectives, audience characteristics, appropriate information.
- Divide the work fairly, based on each team member's strengths and interests. Determine who will speak, who will handle equipment and visual aids, etc.
- Assign a leader to coordinate each member's segment and make sure everyone stays on schedule.
- Agree on the approximate number of visual aids to include in each segment and the type that all team members will use. Consider using a single visual aid template for all members.
- Determine appropriate dress and appearance. Then, agree that all team members will adhere to the same standard.
- Visit the presentation site and, among other things, decide where members will stand during the introduction and where they will sit or stand while other members are speaking.
- Determine how each speaker will introduce the next speaker and segment.
- Prepare for the question-and-answer session together. Encourage each member to be prepared to respond to all audience questions so no one is caught flat footed without an answer.
- Practice together. Be especially alert to inconsistencies among speakers (e.g., speaking style, level of formality, vocabulary level, degree of eye contact, visual aids, transition between speakers).
- Teach and coach each other. Help teammates improve their presentation skills and learn to manage and use presentation anxiety.
- Determine who will step in and give another team member's portion of the presentation if that team member is ill on the presentation day.

DEVELOP AN OUTLINE

Business audiences typically prefer that speakers present their information naturally in what some describe as a conversational tone. Therefore, you are discouraged from reading from a written or memorized script. Presenters who read their script typically sound stilted and even rigid. Furthermore, with a script you run the risk of losing your place and not finding it again if you are interrupted or otherwise distracted (which happens). This is especially true if you work from a memorized script.

Write your outline on 5x7-inch notecards.[8] As you write your outline, keep the following suggestions in mind:

- Write words and phrases, not sentences and paragraphs.
- Use a large enough print or font size so you can read them clearly and not lose your place.
- Write on one side of each notecard only to eliminate concerns about whether you covered the material on the reverse side.
- Write a page number on each card in case you drop your cards and need to quickly reorder them.
- Write personal guidance reminders on your note cards. **Guidance reminders** refer to presentation techniques you suspect you will perform inadequately. For example, if you are concerned that you will not give your audience enough eye contact, draw an eye here and there on your notecards as a reminder. If you worry that you will speak too fast, write *slow down* occasionally in a different ink color.

Some speakers find it helpful to start by writing a script, then converting it to an outline. Doing so helps them avoid overlooking information they want to include and also helps them get comfortable with the information to be presented.

DEVELOP YOUR VISUAL AIDS

KISS Principle
Keep It Short and Simple, which reminds speakers to design and develop visual aids that are short and simple.

Your goal is to develop visual aids that can be quickly and easily understood by your audience. The **KISS Principle** (Keep It Short and Simple) applies to developing visual aids for business presentations. Avoid developing "busy" visual aids that have too much going on. Be careful not to overuse visual aids such as clip art, animations, and YouTube clips. Ask yourself, Does the visual aid serve a purpose? Is it appropriate? Will it distract my audience? Does it compromise the amount and quality of information presented on a visual aid? Avoid distracting your audience by using more than one font style on a visual aid. In addition, be sensitive to how you use colors. For example:

- Limit the number of colors used on a visual aid to no more than five.
- Use bright colors such as yellow to emphasize key information.
- Understand color and mood associations. For example, red is associated with operating at a loss, yellow is associated with positive themes, blue and green are neutral, red and yellow combinations raise people's blood pressure, and color blind people are affected by the red-green combination. Note that not all cultures make the same color associations.
- Avoid placing similar colors next to each other.
- Ensure effective contrasts. Use light-colored text on dark backgrounds in darkened rooms, dark-colored text on light backgrounds in rooms where the amount of light filtering in cannot be controlled. Avoid dark colors on dark backgrounds and light colors on light backgrounds.

Business audiences react positively to colors in visual aids. Just be careful to reap the benefits by following the basic color selection rules. In addition to the suggestions presented above, consider the following when developing visual aids:

- Make the print or font size large enough to be seen by everyone in your audience. The size and dimensions of the presentation room will determine the appropriate size. A 24-point type size works well in most settings.
- Use legible font styles (e.g., Times New Roman, Arial). Avoid flamboyant fonts (e.g., English Gothic).
- Do not use fill patterns (diagonal lines, dots, etc.) with colors to distinguish between slices in pie charts and bars in bar charts. Colors are preferred over fill patterns.
- Use three-dimensional, multiple bar charts cautiously. They are susceptible to mis-reading. The three-dimensional feature works best with pie charts.

Develop back-up visual aids for those unwanted times when the equipment or software malfunctions. For example, make one or more soft copies of your PowerPoint slides to use just in case your main copy does not work properly. Make a hardcopy set of your PowerPoint slides to display on a document camera. Make handouts containing your slides. None of us want the equipment or software to fail us; however, it does at times. Backup visual aids help us move past these unwelcomed, uncomfortable moments without getting overly frustrated.

PREPARE FOR EQUIPMENT AND SOFTWARE PROBLEMS

Anticipate and take measures to effectively contend with equipment and software problems. Equipment and software do not always work as planned; however, such unwanted situations do not have to doom your presentation. Do some pre-planning to work through such situations. Here are some troubleshooting suggestions:

- If you are using electrical equipment, collect one or more extension cords, power strips, and three-prong adapters.
- If you are using battery-operated electrical equipment, purchase spare batteries.
- If you are going to use a portable projector, get some spare light bulbs.
- If you are using a computer, arrange for a backup computer (e.g., notebook, tablet, etc.).
- If you are using a projection system, arrange for a backup portable projector.
- If you are using an overhead project, get a portable projector and some spare light bulbs.
- If you are using software, make backup copies to take to the presentation.
- If you are using a whiteboard, assemble some extra dry-erase pens and an eraser.
- If you are using a flip chart, take along extra marker pens, an extra flip chart, and a portable tripod stand.

Like it or not, equipment and software will fail at the least opportune times. Your preparations will pay big dividends when these times occur.

PREPARE FOR THE QUESTION-AND-ANSWER SESSION

The two best approaches to prepare you for the "Q&A" session are learning your presentation topic thoroughly and anticipating questions.

1. Become very knowledgeable of the facts in your presentation and comfortable with your topic so you will be relaxed as you respond to audience questions. Of course, this means you must learn more about the topic than you plan to share in the presentation.

2. To the extent that your intuition and experience allow, anticipate the questions most likely to be asked. Next, determine your responses. Finally, write out the questions and answers and take them with you to the presentation.

As you prepare, remind yourself not to take audience questions personally and, in turn, get defensive. There is no need to be overly anxious about Q&A sessions. Remind yourself that you are the expert on the topic; otherwise, you would not have been asked to speak. Furthermore, as you prepare, remind yourself that if you are asked a question for which you do not have an immediate answer, it is acceptable to pause and reflect on it before responding. If you are unable to give an adequate answer, offer to contact the audience members later with an answer. Finally, you may be concerned about the possibility of aggressive audience members. Like it or not, they come with the territory. You will not necessarily enjoy the experience, but you will survive and live to speak another day. If you have aggressive audience members, plan to keep your responses brief, but complete. Also plan to use a courteous tone and maintain pleasant facial expressions. However, avoid prolonged eye contact with such individuals; it is viewed as aggressive. In addition, have a plan so you do not let aggressive individuals dominate your Q&A.[9, 10] For example, it is acceptable to remind the individual that, since time is limited, you would be happy to discuss his or her concerns following the session. Alternatively, do not call on the individual if he or she continues to try to dominate the session.

Finally, conduct some Q&A practice sessions. Practice in front of some of your colleagues, friends, or family members. Ask them to play an active role, asking you some questions you cannot immediately answer. Also, instruct someone to get aggressive in their questioning, so you get some practice dealing with that type of situation. It is far too common for speakers to overlook preparing and practicing for Q&A sessions and quietly worry about their outcome instead.

Notes

1. M. Munter and L. Russell. *Guide to Presentations.* (Upper Saddle River, NJ: Prentice Hall, 2002), 8–9.

2. S. H. Gale and M. Garrison. *Strategies for Managerial Writing.* (Mason, OH: Thomson/South-Western, 2006), 279.

3. Tim Hindle. *Making Presentations.* (New York, NY: DK Publishing, 1998), 47–48.

4. S. Xavier. "Effective Presentations Take More Than Skill." *U.S. Business Review* 7, no. 8 (2006): 6–7.

5. M. E. Guffey. *Essentials of Business Communication*, 6th ed. (Mason, OH: South-Western, 2004), 336.

6. Andrew D. Wolvin, Roy M. Berko, and Darlyn R. Wolvin, *The Public Speaker/The Public Listener* (Boston: Houghton Mifflin, 1993), 71–78.

7. Hindle, 26–27.

8. Ibid., 29.

9. Wolvin et al. 218–219.

10. Hindle, 60–61.

14

DELIVERING BUSINESS PRESENTATIONS

LEARNING OUTCOMES

After reading this chapter, you should be able to:

1. Discuss how to manage presentation anxiety immediately before and during business presentations as well as during question-and-answer (Q&A) sessions.

2. Explain the importance of starting and ending business presentations on time.

3. Describe recommended business presentation techniques.

4. Describe webcasting and how it is used in the business place.

5. Describe podcasting and how it is used in the business place.

6. Explain how to conduct effective Q&A sessions.

7. Describe ways to evaluate your presentations and Q&A sessions.

© Rawpixel.com

SELECT KEY TERMS

INTRODUCTION

The closer you get to the presentation, the more likely your speaking anxiety will increase. Several practical techniques for managing speaking anxiety shortly before and during presentations as well as during Q&A sessions are presented in this chapter. It is important to respect your audience members' schedules by starting and finishing your business presentations on time.

Wear a pleasant facial expression and smile occasionally. In addition, make sure your posture is good, gesture frequently, and make occasional eye contact with audience members. Use your voice qualities to the fullest. For example, use a conversational tone, change your volume intermittently, and vary your speaking rate. Furthermore, your visual aids should be of professional quality and left before your audience long enough for them to grasp. Finally, expect a Q&A session will occur immediately following your business presentation. Here are some sample suggestions for conducting effective Q&A sessions: relax and maintain a positive attitude, know how you will handle questions you are unable to answer, repeat or paraphrase each audience member's question before responding, do not embarrass anyone, and do not get defensive.

The intent of this chapter is to provide you with information on how to deliver effective business presentations and conduct effective question-and-answers sessions following those presentations. The goal of this chapter is realized through discussions of the following topics: the final hours leading up to the presentation, presentation anxiety, delivering business presentations, conducting effective question-and-answer sessions, and evaluating your presentations.

THE FINAL HOURS LEADING UP TO THE PRESENTATION

As your presentation date grows closer, it becomes increasingly important for you to do those things that keep you healthy and alert. Eat right, get an appropriate amount of rest and sleep, relax some, and exercise. You know the drill! This is especially true the day and night preceding the presentation.

Most speakers find it helpful not to be rushed the morning of the presentation. They understand that being rushed that day contributes to speaking anxiety as well as increases the chance that they might forget something essential. Seasoned speakers build enough time into their schedules to dress appropriately, eat a good breakfast, gather and organize their presentation materials, and find a quiet place to collect their thoughts and relax.[1]

If you must travel a distance to reach your presentation site, learn the route ahead of time and leave early so you have a cushion of time to offset delays. It is even a good idea to travel the route at least once before the presentation date, so you are familiar with it. You will likely be a bit anxious as it is, so you do not want to add to these feelings by misjudging travel time and conditions.

While the following suggestion applies to some speakers more than others, it is not a good idea to arrive at your presentation site immediately before you are scheduled to begin. As a general rule, arriving 15 minutes early should get the job done. Arriving much later hardly gives you enough time to get set up, visit the restroom if needed, and relax before the presentation begins. Furthermore, it is unprofessional and discourteous to start the presentation late. On the flip side, arriving more than 15 minutes early may work against you. If you have too much extra time, you may become nervous.

Once in the room, busy yourself with those activities necessary to giving your presentation. For example, go ahead and open computer files if using presentation software and check your microphone if you intend to use one. In addition, get out the pointing device you plan to use. If you are using a laser pointer, make sure the batteries are strong. If not, replace them before you start your presentation. This is also a good time to get out your notecards and make sure they are in order. If you still have a few minutes to spare before the presentation is scheduled to begin, visit with some of the audience members who arrived early. You should find that calming.

> ## SUMMARY: SECTION 1—
> ## THE FINAL HOURS LEADING UP TO THE PRESENTATION
> - Eat right, get enough rest and sleep, and relax.
> - Build enough time into your schedule the morning/day of the presentation so you can achieve the expected appearance, eat a proper meal, gather your materials, and relax.
> - If you are traveling to your presentation site, leave early enough to offset traffic delays, to locate parking, etc.
> - Arrive at the presentation site approximately 15 minutes early.
> - Set up your equipment and software—both preferred and backup.
> - Walk around the room and visit with some of the audience members.

PRESENTATION ANXIETY: BEFORE AND DURING PRESENTATIONS

The discussion concerning presentation anxiety continues here with the focus directed toward four distinct time periods near and including the presentation: the night before the presentation, the day of the presentation, the few minutes on site before the presentation begins, and the presentation.

PRESENTATION ANXIETY—THE NIGHT BEFORE THE PRESENTATION

People who are nervous about giving presentations often notice an increase in their apprehension level beginning the night before they are to speak. If this describes you, do what you can to avoid adding to your speaking apprehension. For example, do not spend the entire evening practicing the presentation and fretting about the event. Instead, plan a relaxing evening! Have a nice dinner, then spend the evening with friends or family or lost in a good book or movie. The idea is to replace your feelings of apprehension with enjoyable, relaxing thoughts. This approach reduces, not adds to, your speaking anxieties. It can also leave you more rested for the presentation. Of course, get a good night's sleep.[2]

PRESENTATION ANXIETY—THE DAY OF THE PRESENTATION

No matter what time your presentation is scheduled, it is good technique to start the day positively. Following a good night's rest, go out for a morning walk or run and make it a point to enjoy your surroundings. Follow up your walk or run with a long, refreshing shower, then treat yourself to a good, healthy breakfast. The result will be that you feel better about yourself and more positive about your presentation. There is nothing to be gained from starting your day worrying about the presentation. Activities like those recommended above truly help you manage your presentation anxiety and redirect anxious feelings and thoughts in positive ways. Keep the same positive theme going if your presentation is later in the afternoon or evening.

Making sure that you have gathered all the materials on your checklist that you need to take to the presentation helps you control nervous feelings. Knowing that you have what you need (e.g., notecards, visual aids, backup software, handouts) has a calming effect.

Be careful not to overuse medication as a way to control your nervousness. Some speakers suggest that taking a couple of aspirin 15 minutes before they speak has a calming effect. This may be worth a try. However, drinking alcohol and taking other drugs shortly before giving a presentation could spell disaster for the presentation and may also turn into a destructive habit that you repeat before every presentation.[3]

Get an early start, so you do not worry about arriving on time. This is especially true if you have to travel to your presentation site. As you know, roads, streets, and highways are often crowded, and commercial airline flight delays and cancellations are common. There is a lot of stress and nervousness associated with any form of travel. So, control it instead of letting it work against you. It is a good technique, when feasible, to travel the route in advance of the presentation date to eliminate some of the unknowns. It is not uncommon for many of us to be challenged by locating the correct parking garage and then navigating our way through it and onto the elevator that will deliver us to our destination.

FIGURE 14-1: RELAXATION EXERCISES FOR MANAGING ANXIETY

Patricia Fripp, a San Francisco-based executive speech coach and former president of the National Speakers Association (http://www.nsaspeaker.org/), suggests that when dealing with speaking anxiety, seek out a secluded area and go through the following relaxation exercises:

- Stand on one leg and shake the other. Upon putting your foot back down, it should feel lighter. Switch, and do the other leg.
- Shake your hands quickly. Hold your arms above your head, bend them at the wrist and elbow, and then lower them. This will help your hand gestures feel more natural.
- Relax your face muscles by chewing in a highly exaggerated way.
- Do neck and shoulder rolls.

Source: Patricia Fripp. "Presenting Your Talk." Women in Business, 58, no. 5 (2006): 43–45.

PRESENTATION ANXIETY—THE FEW MINUTES BEFORE THE PRESENTATION

Imagine you are scheduled to give a presentation, and you are about to arrive at the presentation site. You are anxious and hope to control these nervous feelings during the final few minutes before the presentation begins. The following paragraphs contain some good suggestions for controlling anxiety.

Arrive Early Doing so will provide you with a few minutes to calm down and settle in before the presentation begins. This way you will not feel rushed as you set up for the presentation. Do not just stand still or sit down. Move around as you set up and, if time allows, walk around the room and visit with some of your audience members. These activities should reduce your anxiety level as you near the start of the presentation.

Make the Right First Impression As you enter the presentation room, audience members will form **first impressions** of you. You want these first impressions to have a positive effect on your presentation anxiety. First impressions really center on your audience's perceptions of how confident you are, how you are dressed, and how willing you are to connect with them. So, walk confidently into the room with normal strides, as opposed to shuffling in. Maintain good posture; do not slouch. Wear a warm, pleasant expression on your face; do not show doubt or apprehension. You might even smile occasionally as you make eye contact with audience members who are already there. Extend the same courtesies to those who enter later. Such actions help your self-confidence and warm up your audience to you. When you share pleasant facial expressions and smiles, audience members typically do the same. This relaxes you.

Make Sure Your Appearance Meets Audience Expectations If you have studied your audience, you will arrive at the presentation site confident that your appearance is appropriate. In essence, you will have eliminated one more thing that might contribute to presentation anxiety. Appearance refers to several characteristics, ranging from dress and hair style to the amount, type, and location of make-up, jewelry, tattoos, and body piercings.

Check Out Your Equipment and Adjust the Curtains/Blinds and Lighting Make sure the equipment works properly, load up software, close the curtains or blinds, and adjust the lights. If necessary, switch to backup equipment or backup approaches without making a fuss about it in front of the audience. You control the situation. Do not let them see you sweat! The combination of the physical movements involved in performing the above-mentioned activities and the knowledge that the equipment and lighting are ready will reduce your presentation anxiety.

Visit with Audience Members Before the Presentation Allow enough lead time that you can move away from the front of the room and visit with some of the audience. This may sound like an unnerving suggestion; however, making relaxed contact with audience members prior to a presentation typically makes us less anxious about them. You may choose to visit with a small group of two or three or sit down and visit with one individual followed by another. Simply have a casual visit, small talk about topics such as the weather, an upcoming holiday, current news or sporting events, and the like. You might consider learning some of their names so you can call on them by name during the **Q&A session.**

Use Silence Immediately Before You Start Both you and your audience need time to settle down immediately before you start your presentation. Tell them that you are about to start your presentation, then allow 5–10 seconds of silence before you begin. During these few seconds do not shuffle papers like newscasters often do immediately before going off camera. Instead, make eye contact with several members of your audience while maintaining a pleasant facial expression.

Acknowledge Your Presentation Anxiety Accept the fact that you are nervous. Most speakers admit to experiencing some degree of presentation anxiety. The trick is to manage and use it properly, which can result in your giving a more dynamic, persuasive presentation than you would otherwise. Recognize that your feelings of nervousness are normal; then take a drink of water followed by a deep breath, relax, and move ahead.

PRESENTATION ANXIETY—DURING THE PRESENTATION

© Sam72/Shutterstock.com

Now it's time to start. The following suggestions will help you manage anxiety during your presentation.

Start on Time Assume your audience members are on a tight schedule and must be elsewhere immediately following your presentation. Avoid giving them a reason to think poorly of you and feel anxious about their own schedules simply because you did not start on time. They know that if you start late, you are likely to end late.

Introduce Yourself, Your Topic, and the Purpose and Structure First This is painless information to share, especially during those first few awkward seconds.

Be Familiar with the Information You Will Share During the First Few Seconds after Introductions This helps move you through the beginning of the presentation—the time when many of us are the most nervous.

Use Humor Throughout the Presentation Only If Appropriate Appropriate humor has the potential of warming up your audiences. When you see them smile or laugh, you relax and become less apprehensive. Keep in mind that the best humor in business presentations is humor related to your topic.

Remember, too, that humor backfires easily. If one or more audience members find the humor offensive or in bad taste, you might find yourself facing a cold audience during the remainder of the presentation. Of course, in settings where the topic is serious or controversial, avoid humor altogether.

Make Eye Contact with Supportive People As you begin speaking, use eye contact to establish rapport with audience members. Locate some friendly faces. They could be people you visited before the presentation or others with whom you feel you are connecting. When you feel nervous, return to those faces for a moment's moral support.

Present from Notecards or a Tablet Outline but not from a Memorized Script Presenting from memorized scripts often contributes to presentation anxiety, because speakers worry—subconsciously or consciously—about forgetting what they want to say or losing their place. You are actually relaxed presenting from notecards or a tablet since you have something to refer to that helps keep you on track.

Know What Information to Omit or Summarize If You are Running Out of Time The realization that we must complete our presentation by a given time contributes to presentation anxiety. If you go into a presentation knowing what information is expendable, you will be more relaxed. As you move through presentations, be sensitive to the time and whether you are falling behind schedule. If you do fall behind, either omit or summarize predetermined information so you can end on time. Do not be unnerved by this technique. After all, the audience does not know you have cut off part of your presentation.

Insert Pauses Throughout Your Presentation As you move through your presentation, pause when you feel you need a moment to collect yourself. This also provides a good opportunity to take a drink of water. Do not view pauses (silence) as scary interludes. Instead, think about how they are beneficial to you and your audience.

Move Around During Your Presentation Some speakers appear to anchor themselves to the floor and hold their bodies rigid. This adds to their presentation anxiety. Most speakers find that moving around while speaking reduces nervousness. Some of this movement occurs naturally in the course of handling visual aids and pointing at information displayed on screens, whiteboards, and flip charts. Consider moving away from the podium and taking a couple steps periodically.

Use Visual Aids Using visual aids reduces presentation anxiety. On one hand, they give you an opportunity to move away from your notecards, which often relaxes you. In addition, the physical movement associated with presenting visual aids tends to relax you.

Be Enthusiastic Enthusiastic speakers are dynamic, effective speakers. They have learned to harness their nervous energy and reroute it in a productive direction (e.g., voice qualities, gesturing, facial expressions, movement).

© g-stockstudio/Shutterstock.com

Avoid Digressions You made an outline and notecards for a reason, so use them. When stories and anecdotes occur to you during the presentation, avoid telling them. Digressions throw off your timing and rhythm, so you may lose the point you were trying to make.[4]

Slow Down! When speakers have little experience or are nervous, they tend to talk too rapidly, which causes difficulties for audience members in following and understanding the presentation. Make a conscious effort to slow down and listen to what you are saying.[5]

Maintain a Positive Mental Image See yourself giving a successful presentation.

DELIVERING BUSINESS PRESENTATIONS

Well, it is finally time to start the presentation! All of the effort, energy, and time you invested in planning, preparing, and practicing are about to pay off. All you have to do is either turn on the microphone or raise your voice and say, "Let's begin." Suggestions pertaining to delivering your presentation follow.

START AND FINISH YOUR PRESENTATION ON TIME

It is safe to assume that your audience will appreciate it if you start and finish your presentation on time. After all, they probably have other activities scheduled following the presentation and do not want to have to leave late because you did not start or finish on time.

As a general rule, you should be able to stick to your presentation time frames if you plan, prepare, and practice. Your actions during the final few hours leading up to the presentation, including arriving at the presentation site early, increase the probability that you will meet your objective.

Even so, you can take steps to avoid being knocked off schedule. Even the best-laid plans can go awry, so consider the following suggestions:

© Karramba Production/Shutterstock.com

- Start on time even if all of your audience members have not arrived. You want to avoid the hassle and nervousness associated with "playing catch-up" that comes with starting late.
- Start on time using your backup visual aids if necessary. All equipment and software issues should be dealt with beforehand. Do not delay the start of a presentation because your visual aid equipment or software is not functioning properly. Also keep in mind that if your preferred visual aid equipment or software does not function properly, it is not professional to mutter a profanity. This point is stressed in Figure 14-2.

- Ask audience members to hold all their questions and comments for a Q&A session that will be held after the presentation. Entertaining questions and comments during the presentation can throw your schedule way off, resulting in finishing late, rushing through, and/or leaving out large amounts of information you had hoped to share.

Keep in mind that both you and your audiences will have a more positive and relaxing experience if you make it your business to start and finish your presentations on time.

MAKE SPEAKER INTRODUCTIONS

Once you have announced to your audience that it is time to begin, pause for a few seconds so they can finish their side conversations, sit down, and settle in. Then, make some brief introductory remarks.

This is the point in the presentation when you mention your name and job title, the organization you represent, and your topic. This sounds simple enough! However, do not do like some nervous speakers and omit the speaker introductions or rush through them. Consider presenting this information on a PowerPoint slide. You could even display it for a few minutes before the presentation begins.

In the case of team presentations, the person scheduled to speak first should begin by introducing him- or herself, his or her job title, organizational affiliation, and presentation topic. Next, this speaker should introduce each of the other team members, having each stand or step forward one step when introduced. Then, repeat the presentation topic and mention specific portions he or she will address. After each team member speaks, he or she should reintroduce the next speaker and mention their specific contribution.

As was recommended with individual presentations, with team presentations, present speakers' names and job titles, organizational affiliation, and the presentation topic on a Power Point slide. It is also a good idea to display it a few minutes before the presentation begins, listing the team members' names in the order they will speak.

GIVE A PRESENTATION OVERVIEW

Before sharing detailed information, outline your presentation for your audience. Doing so sets the stage for the audience to know what to expect. If done properly, it also increases audience attention, understanding, and information retention.

It is at this point that you should clarify the presentation's purpose or objective, as well as describe the presentation's structure. Tell your audience that you will begin with an introduction in which you will share an outline of your talk. Then, tell them that in the body of your presentation, you will give a detailed talk based on the outline, followed by a summary of the key points you made.

Finally, clarify how questions will be handled. You may choose to entertain questions and comments during your presentation or handle all of them during a Q&A session following the presentation. You might even do both. No matter which approach you choose, communicate it to your audience before going farther.

USE NOTECARDS AND TABLETS EFFECTIVELY

As a rule, business audiences prefer speakers present from notecards or small tablets as opposed to presenting from memorized or written scripts. Working from outlines on notecards or tablets results in a conversational tone. Audiences greatly prefer this because they find such presentations to be more interesting than those read from scripts. Giving presentations from outlines on notecards and small tablets forces speakers to become very familiar with their topics and practice more than they might have otherwise.

Most speakers find it most practical to write their presentation outlines on notecards or tablets rather than 8½x11-inch paper which is clumsy to handle and distracting for audience members.

Here are some suggestions pertaining to presenting from outlines on notecards.

© Adam Tinney/Shutterstock.com

- Most speakers prefer 5x7-inch notecards, instead of 3x5-inch cards. The latter are too small to hold much information, and speakers tend to write so small or reduce the font size to the point that they are difficult to read.
- If your notecards are keyboarded, use a minimum font size of 14 points to improve ease of reading.
- Use a dark ink and boldface so it is easier to read at a glance.
- Double space the lines on the notecards so you are less likely to lose your place.
- If your notecards are handwritten, print so the material is clearer.
- If your notecards are keyboarded, select a legible font. Fonts such as *Times New Roman* and *Calibri* are easy to read, whereas scripted fonts are not necessarily readable at a glance.
- Write or keyboard on only one side of each card. This way you do not have to worry about whether you have already covered the material on the flip side.

- Write a page number on each notecard to help you keep them in order.
- Include presentation guidance reminders in your notecards. You do not share these reminders with the audience; they are there to help you. First, acknowledge to yourself your presentation shortcomings. Then, remind yourself of them in your notecards. For example, if you know that you do not give your audiences the degree of eye contact they expect, draw an eyeball on every notecard. Seeing these during the presentation will remind you to look up and make eye contact. Whether you use symbols or words as reminders, produce them in a color other than the color of your presentation outline. This way you will not accidentally mix them up with the outline material. Furthermore, by writing them in another color, you increase the chance that you will notice them.

Here are some suggestions pertaining to presenting from outlines on tablets.

© Stuart Jenner/Shutterstock.com

- For obvious reasons, make sure your tablet is fully charged before your presentation.
- If possible, use a smaller tablet such as the 6x3-inch Galaxy Note tablet or smartphone with a good-size screen instead of one of the many larger tablets on the market. Doing so will be less distracting for your audience.
- If your tablet has a cover, make sure the color or pattern will not be a potential distraction.
- Type your outline using a minimum font size of 14 points to improve ease of reading.
- Boldface your entire outline so it is easier to read at a glance.
- Double space the lines on your outline so you are less likely to lose your place.
- Keyboard your outline using a legible font. Fonts such as *Times New Roman* and *Calibri* are easy to read, whereas scripted fonts are not necessarily readable at a glance.
- Include presentation guidance reminders in your outline. You do not share these reminders with the audience; they are there to help you. First, acknowledge to yourself your presentation shortcomings. Then, remind yourself of them in your outline. For example, if you know that you do not give your audiences the degree of eye contact they expect, draw an eyeball on every notecard. Seeing these during the presentation will remind you to look up and make eye contact. Whether you use symbols or words as reminders, produce them in a color other than the color of your presentation outline. This way you will not accidentally mix them up with the outline material. Furthermore, by writing them in another color, you increase the chance that you will notice them.

- Familiarize yourself with public speaking apps that you can use to create and use tablet-based presentation outlines.

Finally, presenting from notecards and small tablets typically reduces presentation anxiety. As they move through their presentation, speakers do not have to worry about losing their place, which can so easily occur when we present from memorized or written scripts!

DISPLAY APPROPRIATE BODY LANGUAGE

Apps for Public Speakers
http://appadvice.com/
applists/show/apps-for-
public-speakers

Body language (nonverbal language) is an important component of audiences' first impressions of business speakers—the way they walk, their posture, their facial expressions, and the amount of eye contact they share. Body language is also very important during presentations! Specifically, presentation body language includes facial expressions, eye contact, posture, gestures, and moving around, which are discussed next.

Facial Expressions Speakers should wear a pleasant facial expression. In addition, they should smile and laugh when appropriate. Such expressions help capture and hold audiences' attention and, in general, warm them up to speakers. Audiences perceive the speaker as being friendly, approachable, knowledgeable, and sincere.

Audiences are more likely to be persuaded by friendly looking speakers than by speakers who wear a blank expression or an expression of anger or annoyance. However, be careful not to wear a fixed smile throughout presentations. Most people find this distracting and even annoying. In addition, do not wear a forced smile. You've seen that smile on the faces of adolescents who are asked to smile for photographs. That smile looks unnatural and phony.

© Karramba Production/Shutterstock.com

Eye Contact Eye contact is important to American business audiences. They expect business speakers to share the same degree of eye contact with them that we share with each other in daily lives—not too much, but not too little. Good speakers do not stare at individuals during their presentations, nor do they avoid making eye contact by focusing on their notecards or the ceiling, floor, or back wall. Speakers who make too little or no eye contact are often perceived as manipulative, unnecessarily nervous, unprepared, or unsure of what they are saying. None of these interpretations may be accurate, but it is what the audience perceives that counts. If your audience is small (30 people or fewer), you are encouraged to make eye contact with each person several times during your presentation. The larger the audience, the more unlikely it becomes that you can make eye contact with every audience member.

How should you make eye contact with large audiences? Two practical suggestions come to mind. One approach is to mentally divide your audience into sections and make eye contact with one or two friendly faces in each section. This way your entire audience will feel as though you are making eye contact with them. Another approach involves locating a friendly face or two in the left-most section, the center section, and the right-most section of your audience about one-third of the way back from the front. Sweep your eye contact back and forth across the room from friendly face to friendly face, which gives your entire audience the impression that you are making eye contact with them. Just be careful not to favor a certain section of the room with your eye contact. For example, some speakers will make all of their eye contact with those in the center section of their audience, whereas others focus solely on audience members seated near the front of the room. The name of the game when it comes to eye contact is to make sure it is balanced.

As can be expected, audience expectations regarding eye contact vary among cultures. Be sure you learn about these differing cultural expectations before presenting in other countries. For example, in most Middle Eastern countries male speakers should make little or no direct eye contact with female audience members.

Posture Audience members form perceptions based on speakers' posture. Speakers who exhibit good posture are thought to be confident, knowledgeable, and interested in their topic. They are also viewed as individuals who know how to carry themselves professionally. On the other hand, speakers who do not square off their shoulders, do not stand up straight and slouch, stand on one foot, or lean on the podium are perceived as uninterested, lacking confidence, and generally not knowing how to carry themselves professionally.

Mary Munter and Lynn Russell, business communication experts, offer the following advice regarding your formal "opening stance": (1) Place your feet shoulder-width apart, rather than close together or far apart. (2) Distribute your weight evenly, using both legs equally for support. (3) Divide your weight between your heels and the balls of your feet, rather than leaning back on your heels or up on your toes. (4) Position your feet straight out, avoiding a "duck" stance by making sure your toes are not farther apart than your heels. (5) Do not lock your knees.[5]

While good posture is necessary, keep in mind that we refer to a "relaxed" good posture. This means you should avoid being physically rigid. Rigid posture is awkward for the speaker as he or she attempts to move and gesture and is often noticeable to the audience.

Gestures Much like appropriate facial expressions, gesturing holds the potential of capturing and holding your audiences' attention. Gestures, like appropriate facial expressions, contribute to dynamic presentations that persuade audiences to action. Imagine how much more interested you are in observing a speaker who captures your attention with gestures and uses them to stress information he or she is sharing than one who does not gesture at all.

Gesturing occurs when speakers raise their forearms, moving them slightly from the left or right, much like a conductor directs an orchestra or concert band. In addition, gesturing involves speakers opening up their hands and fingers. Gesturing is done for the purpose of emphasizing points. It has also been suggested that "complex thinkers use complex gestures" during presentations, meaning two handed gesturing above the waist.[7] But do not overdo the gestures in an attempt to look like a complex thinker because you might just end up looking funny. Remember to keep it as natural as possible. Several helpful suggestions regarding gesturing during presentations are listed here:

Gesture with a purpose in mind. American audiences find constant gesturing distracting and annoying. As was mentioned above, gestures are used for emphasis; thus they should be used sparingly. To do otherwise greatly reduces their attention-getting, persuasive qualities.

Gesture with both hands. When you do so, you give more balanced attention to your audience. Speakers who gesture with only one hand tend to favor the portion of the audience closest to that hand. Speakers actually turn their body and head slightly in that direction. Their eye contact and attention fixes on that portion of the audience, leaving the remainder of the audience wondering where they fit in. In addition, there is a tendency for speakers who gesture with only one hand to place their other hand in their coat, skirt, or pants pocket, which is distracting.

Keep all fingers open to the audience. What this means is avoid pointing one of your index fingers at the audience. This is more likely to happen if you are gesturing with one hand only. Many of us conjure negative feelings or memories when another person points an index finger at us. Such an action is associated with being lectured to, scolded, etc.

Avoid quick, jerky gestures. Speakers who make abrupt movements are perceived as being nervous. In turn, they make audience members apprehensive, all of which distracts from the presentation.

Gesturing is critical to effective presentations. Keeping in mind that many speakers do not gesture, gesture too little, gesture too much, or gesture inappropriately, you are reminded to practice gesturing. Make it as much a part of your practice sessions as practicing your talk, displaying your visual aids, eye contact, etc. Appropriate gesturing is not as simple as it sounds but can be achieved if you are willing to make it part of your practice sessions.

Moving Around Speakers are encouraged to move around during their presentations. This is helpful in capturing and recapturing audiences' attention.[8] It is similar to what happens when a speaker raises or lowers his or her voice or pauses before making a point. Audiences pay attention. Moving around also helps speakers manage presentation anxiety. The physical movement is relaxing.

Be careful not to wander aimlessly, dance back and forth, bounce up and down, or pace back and forth predictably like a dog in a backyard dog run. Such movements distract your audience from your message. In addition, be sensitive about moving too close to audience members and running the risk of invading their spatial comfort zones. For example, most Americans feel uneasy when another person moves closer than an arm's length from them. Others prefer an even greater distance. For example, most Japanese prefer a greater distance than Americans.

Of course, there are situations where you may not be able to move around. If you are speaking to a large audience and must use a microphone attached to the podium, you have no choice. Even then, you may be able to take a step in either direction, assuming the microphone is powerful enough to still pick up your voice. At minimum, move your head periodically and gesture as a way to capture and recapture your audience's attention.

AVOID DISTRACTING NONVERBAL BEHAVIORS

While nonverbal elements such as facial expressions, eye contact, posture, gestures, and moving around enhance the quality of presentations, several nonverbal behaviors are counterproductive (e.g., leaning on the podium, fiddling with a rubber band, tugging on jewelry) because they distract the audience's attention from the speaker's message.

Speakers are typically unaware that they are exhibiting these distracting behaviors. When speakers put their hands in their pockets, they probably do not realize they are distracting their audience. In turn, when speakers continuously tap pencils or pens on the podium, they are equally unaware of their actions.

So what can speakers do to eliminate such distracting behaviors? First, they must identify them. Suggestions for identifying distracting nonverbal presentation behaviors are presented in Figure 14-3.

FIGURE 14-3: IDENTIFYING DISTRACTING NONVERBAL PRESENTATION BEHAVIORS

- **Videotape your presentation.** Watch the videotape to identify your distracting, nonverbal behaviors.
- **Have a colleague or a friend sit in on one or more of your presentations.** Ask this person to note your distracting, nonverbal behaviors. You may even give him or her a list of the more common distracting behaviors before the presentation, so he or she is better prepared.
- **Following presentations, ask one or two audience members if they observed any distracting, nonverbal behaviors.** If you were exhibiting the behaviors, they should be fresh in the minds of these individuals.

Notice that none of these suggestions pertain to practice sessions. Speakers rarely exhibit these behaviors when practicing. Instead, they typically exhibit them during presentations. Such behaviors are the byproduct of speaking anxiety not being channeled in more-productive directions.

Once you have identified your specific counterproductive behaviors, commit them to writing so you do not forget them the next time you prepare for a presentation. This is a good time to prioritize them if two or more have been identified. This way you can get a start first on those behaviors that are most damaging.

Some distracting nonverbal behaviors, such as fiddling with a rubber band or paper clip, can be easily eliminated. Other behaviors, such as rocking from foot to foot, require ongoing effort to conquer.

Those that are not as easily eliminated include tugging on one of your ears, crossing your arms, resting your chin in your hand, leaning on the podium, rocking back and forth from one foot to the other, clasping your hands as if praying, placing your hands on your hips, fiddling with your pointer, holding your hands behind your back, and crossing your hands in front of your body in what is typically referred to as the "fig leaf" position. These are the types of nonverbal behaviors we must eliminate. An effective technique is to periodically remind yourself of such behaviors via "guidance" (reminder) notes or symbols included in your notecards. This "guidance" approach helps you recognize and immediately deal with these behaviors as you move through your presentations.

Then there are those nonverbal behaviors that can easily be prevented. For example, putting your hands in your pockets, playing with keys or change in your pockets, fiddling with rubber bands and paper clips, tapping pencils and pens, fiddling with jewelry and neckties, and twisting your hair. What makes these behaviors easier to avoid is that they can be dealt with (prevented) before the presentation. You can sew your pockets shut; put your keys and change in your purse or briefcase; place rubber bands, paper clips, pencils, and pens out of sight; leave dangling jewelry at home; wear a tie pin and button your coat to restrict access to your necktie; and tie your hair back if it is long enough to twist.

USE YOUR VOICE EFFECTIVELY

How a speaker uses his or her voice holds incredible potential. Used effectively, it can capture audience attention, gain their interest, excite them, thrill them, and persuade them to accept and act on the speaker's message. How you use your voice plays a major role in whether your presentations are viewed as dynamic and effective or monotonous and ineffective. Here are several suggestions on using your voice effectively.

Use a Conversational Tone U.S. audiences prefer speakers who use a conversational tone because they find it more interesting than the rigid tone and monotone voice of a speaker who reads from a written script.

Speak Clearly Use good diction. Pronounce words clearly. Speakers are unclear because they do not know how to pronounce some words properly, have too little practice, speak too fast, mumble, slur words, fade away near the end of sentences, or have strong regional or foreign accents.

Speak Loud Enough so Everyone in the Audience Can Hear Ask your audience shortly after you begin if everyone can hear you. Also ask them if you are speaking too loudly. Invite them to tell you during the presentation if the volume of your voice needs adjusting. Ask these questions even if you are using a microphone.

Change Your Volume Intermittently Changing your volume periodically during presentations serves several productive purposes. If you want to really capture your audience's attention or emphasize a point, raise or lower your volume. Varying your volume helps you avoid sounding monotonous.

Use Pitch Effectively Switch your voice back and forth periodically from high to low. This helps you avoid sounding monotonous.

Vary Your Speaking Rate Switch your voice back and forth periodically between faster and slower. This also helps you avoid sounding monotonous.

Avoid Speaking Too Fast When speakers speak too fast, audience members have trouble processing and retaining the information. For one, information is presented too quickly. For another, the fast speaker is more likely to slur and mispronounce words. Speaking too fast rarely occurs during practice sessions. Instead, it rears its ugly head at presentations, where we are more likely to be nervous.

Make Sure Your Voice is Sincere Doing so can go a long way in winning your audience's trust and support. Be aware that nonverbal cues (e.g., facial expressions) that communicate insincerity are damaging. Even if your words and tone of voice promote sincerity, your nonverbal cues are judged as the most honest form of communication.

Project Friendliness and Enthusiasm in Your Voice Audiences prefer friendly, enthusiastic speakers. Your enthusiasm makes you a more dynamic, persuasive speaker.

Insert Pauses Throughout Your Presentations Pauses provide you with an occasional breather and a chance to take a drink of water. Furthermore, they give you an opportunity to collect your thoughts before moving to a new topic or point.[9] They also provide your audience with a chance to catch up or take a quick mental break. Pauses help presenters who have a tendency to speak too fast because pauses force the speaker to stop. Finally, pauses are effective emphasis tools. Some speakers pause immediately before making an important point as a way to capture their audience's attention. Other speakers pause immediately after an important point so the audience can reflect on what was just said.

Eliminate Verbal Fillers and Junk Words **Verbal fillers**, also referred to as *verbal tics*, are verbal sounds that serve no purpose. The most common among these "filler sounds" are *um* and *ah*. **Junk words** refer to words or phrases that, like verbal fillers, serve no purpose. The most common among these filler words are *ok*, *like*, and *you know*.

Speakers use verbal fillers and junk words when they are struggling to come up with their next words or are in the midst of switching to their next topic or point. Verbal fillers and junk words are rooted in presentation anxiety, but can be controlled. The simplest suggestion is to replace them with pauses. Slowing down your speaking rate can also help. Remind yourself of this problem via reminder notes or symbols on notecards. Of course, the trick is to first become aware of your verbal fillers and junk words. Like distracting nonverbal behaviors, we are rarely conscious of these habits. Have others tune into yours and then work on eliminating them from your presentations.

Getting Tongue Tied If you stumble over your words, pause to collect your thoughts, and move forward. There is no need to apologize.

verbal fillers
Sounds that serve no purpose; speakers often include them while searching for their next words or switching to their next topic or point. Same as *junk words*.

junk words
Words and phrases such as *ok*, *like*, and *you know* that serve no purpose; speakers often include them while searching for their next words or switching to their next topic or point. Same as *verbal fillers*.

FIGURE 14-4: GIVING TEAM PRESENTATIONS

Here are some general suggestions for giving team presentations.

©Janos Levente/Shutterstock.com

- The first speaker should greet the audience, introduce him- or herself, and state the presentation topic.
- Next, the first speaker should introduce his or her teammates (names and job titles). Do not rush this.
- Before sharing information on his or her specific portion of the presentation topic, the first speaker should give an overview (outline) of the entire presentation.
- When handing off the talk to a teammate, the speaker should mention the next speaker's name and tell the audience briefly what the next speaker will present.

BE PREPARED, SKILLED, SINCERE, AND ENTHUSIASTIC

Dynamic speakers share the information their audiences need, do so skillfully, and are sincere and enthusiastic. They capture their audiences' attention, persuade them, and move them to action. Such speakers bring vitality and genuine believability to their presentations. They understand that the goal of most business presentations is to convince and persuade their audiences. Effective business speakers know they can do so not only by sharing the right information, but also by being prepared, skilled, sincere, and enthusiastic. For example, they know the value of moving around, maintaining normal eye contact, gesturing, emitting friendly facial expressions, and projecting genuine sincerity and enthusiasm through their voices. An effective business speaker also knows how to choose the right medium for her or his needs and audience. Recent choices in those mediums include both webcasting and podcasting.

Webcasting is the term used to describe audio or video presentations broadcast over the Internet that are either downloaded or streamed live.

There are several versions of webcasts, including presentations. For example, executives located around the world can all log on to view the same presentation. Or, professors can upload video lectures so that online students can view them. The other side of webcasts includes full-fledged TV shows that are viewable online and newscasts that are available online rather than on TV. No matter what the purpose, Figure 14-5 lists some tips for presenting webcasts.

webcast
Audio or video broadcast over the Internet, either downloaded or streamed live.

© fotoscool/Shutterstock.com

A major challenge when making webcast presentations is holding onto your audiences' attention. Webcasts are similar to conference calls in that others know they cannot be seen. Thus, they are tempted to do other things (multi-task) during your presentation like they often do during conference calls. However, you would prefer that they give your presentation their full, undivided attention. Figure 14-6 contains a number of tips for overcoming the webcast distraction factor.

© Andrey_Popov/Shutterstock.com

Podcast refers to a series of audio and video files that are downloaded or streamed to computer or mobile devices such as smartphones and tablets. The users' convenience is really the advantage of the podcast. One of the biggest advantages to podcasts is their mobility. For example, you could listen to a presentation in your car, on an airplane, or while riding the subway home from work.

Podcasts vary in length, as could be expected, and do not have to be listened to at the time they are recorded. If you cannot listen to a presentation in its entirety, you can easily come back to the remainder of it later.

© marekuliasz/Shutterstock.com

FIGURE 14-7: PRESENTING TO INTERNATIONAL AUDIENCES

© Kheng Guan Toh/Shutterstock.com

Here are some general suggestions to keep in mind when delivering presentations to foreign audiences.

- Match your appearance to your audience's expectations (e.g., dress, jewelry, etc.).
- Provide audience members with a written, detailed outline before you begin.
- Be aware of your nonverbal communication and how it will be interpreted.
- Smile periodically! Smiles are well received by people around the globe.
- Avoid slang and profanity. Doing so may confuse or offend your audience.
- Minimize technical jargon. If you must use jargon, explain it.
- Slow your speaking rate.
- Enunciate clearly.
- Control your accent so it does not interfere with clarity.
- If you are presenting in English and it is not your audience's native language, sprinkle a few words and phrases in their native language into your presentation, but first test these words with a native speaker before the presentation.
- Use professional-quality visual aids developed in advance of the presentation.
- To focus your audience's attention on what you are explaining, use a pointer with your visual aids.
- If you use an interpreter, be sure he or she is communicating your intended message.
- Use humor cautiously! Humor is usually lost in translation.
- Maintain a high level of formality and professionalism throughout presentations to foreign audiences.

If you want to expand your knowledge of presentation skills as well as work on improving your delivery skills, contact Toastmasters or Toastmasters International at www.toastmasters.org and arrange to attend some meetings and training sessions. The purpose of these organizations is to help people become effective speakers.

SUMMARY: SECTION 3— DELIVERING PRESENTATIONS

- Start and finish on time—respect your audience members' schedules.
- Make speaker introductions—your name, job title, organization, and topic.
- Give a presentation overview with an outline so the audience knows what to expect. Mention when questions and comments will be entertained.
- Use notecards effectively—present from an outline on notecards instead of a written or memorized script.
- Display appropriate body language, using pleasant facial expressions, normal eye contact, good posture, gestures that serve a purpose, and moving around.
- Avoid distracting nonverbal behaviors. Do not fiddle with pens, rubber bands, and jewelry or put your hands in your pockets.
- Use your voice effectively: Use a conversational tone; speak clearly; speak loudly enough; vary volume, pitch, and speaking rate; avoid speaking too fast; put sincerity, friendliness, and enthusiasm in your voice; insert pauses; and eliminate verbal fillers and junk words.
- Use visual aids effectively: Make them visible to all; introduce and explain each visual aid; leave each up on view long enough; talk to the audience, not the visual aid; and paraphrase the contents. Focus your audience's attention and remove each visual aid after discussing it.
- Be prepared, skilled, sincere, and enthusiastic. This captures the audience's attention, persuades them, and helps you control presentation anxiety.
- Adjust to the needs of foreign audiences. Be sensitive to their expectations and level of understanding.

CONDUCTING EFFECTIVE QUESTION-AND-ANSWER SESSIONS

Q&A sessions are an inevitable component of most business presentations. Do not allow the unpredictable nature of them to unnerve or frustrate you. We all know that, unlike the presentation itself, you do not have complete control over what the audience will say. However, there are many things you can do to ensure the success of your Q&A sessions as well as build your confidence. Focus your energies and attention on what you can control.

If you find the thought of conducting Q&A sessions to be unnerving, you are in good company. Most speakers feel the same way. Unlike the presentation itself, you do not have much control over what happens. However, there are some things you can do to reduce your apprehension about Q&A sessions. Several suggestions are presented in Figure 14-8.

FIGURE 14-8: TIPS FOR CONTROLLING ANXIETY DURING Q&A SESSIONS

- **Maintain a Positive Attitude.** Remind yourself that they invited you to speak because you have information they want. The likelihood that you are about to face a hostile audience is slim. Even if one or two audience members are a bit aggressive, most of your audience will be supportive.
- **Remind Yourself That You are the Expert.** Give yourself a confidence boost by reminding yourself that you are the expert. In other words, you should be able to answer most questions. Of course, it is to your advantage to anticipate and prepare for audience questions.
- **Do Not be Alarmed by Questions You are Unable to Answer.** Be realistic. You will probably be asked a couple of questions for which you do not have an adequate response. Avoid the urge to guess or base an answer on insufficient information. Instead, say that you need to look into the topic further and that you will get back to him or her with a response shortly. Ask the questioner to stop by after the Q&A session to share contact information with you, such as a business card. It is a good idea at that time to write the question on the back of the business card.
- **Be Prepared to Control Difficult Audience Members.** The two types of people most speakers least like to have in their audiences during Q&A sessions are those who want to dominate the conversation and those who are aggressive in their questioning and reactions to your responses. As for the dominator, remind yourself that you are in control. Respond to others' questions, but do not feel obligated to respond to all of the dominator's questions or comments. As for the aggressive person, keep your responses brief and do not become defensive. If he or she asks you a question you are unable to answer adequately, follow the suggestions mentioned above. If the individual continues to be rude, ignore him or her. Refuse to be intimidated by such a person and do not acknowledge his or her presence.

As with presentations, Q&A sessions should be planned, prepared, and practiced. Chapter 13 covered suggestions on how to do these things. There are techniques you can use to manage nervousness while conducting these sessions, several of which were discussed earlier in this chapter. What follows are suggestions on how to conduct Q&A sessions to ensure success.

Inform the Audience of the Time Frame At the start of the Q&A session, tell your audience exactly how many minutes it will last and what time it will end. Since you do not want anyone to leave the session feeling short changed, make it easy for audience members to contact you later. Tell your audience at the start of the session that you may not get to answer all their questions and that they should contact you if they have unanswered questions. Of course, you need to share your contact information (e-mail address, phone number, fax number, etc.) on a handout or by distributing business cards. In addition, you might invite them to write down unanswered questions and their contact information. You can collect this information immediately following the Q&A session and get back with your responses on a later date.

Control Smartphone and Cell Phone Distractions It is safe to assume that most audience members have a smartphone or cell phone. These devices may ring during your Q&A session, distracting you and your audience. To forestall those interruptions, ask the audience at the start of your presentation to switch these devices to vibrate. If they feel the need to respond to an incoming call, encourage them to leave the room quietly.

Relax and Maintain a Positive Attitude Remind yourself that they invited you to speak because you have information they want. It is safe to assume that most of your audience, if not the entire audience, will be friendly and supportive.

Also remember that your audience views you as the expert on your topic. If you have planned, prepared, and practiced for your presentation and the Q&A session as recommended, you should be able to answer most questions adequately.

Have a List of Anticipated Questions and Answers You can Turn To It is a good idea to go into Q&A session already familiar with questions you anticipate will be asked and the responses you will share if asked. Take a written list of these anticipated questions and answers to the presentation. If you get nervous or feel especially rushed for time, you have the written list to fall back on. You can simply say, "I know I have the information you want here in my notes."

Be Ready for Questions You are Unable to Answer or to Answer Thoroughly Do not be alarmed if you are asked a question you are unable to answer at all or at least thoroughly. It happens to the best of speakers, so why should you be spared the thrill?

When you find yourself in this situation, avoid the urge to say something for the sake of taking a jab at a response. Instead, tell the person who asked the question that you need to look into it further or reflect on it a little longer, and you will get back to him or her with a response as soon as possible. Of course, you want to ask that individual to see you immediately following the Q&A session so the two of you can share contact information. It is a good idea at that time to write down the question so you do not forget it.

Be a Good Listener Good listeners communicate to others that they respect them and what they have to say. You can win audience members over to your side and enjoy a more successful, relaxed Q&A session by showing such respect. Give each speaker your full, undivided attention, being careful not to interrupt or finish his or her sentences in your haste to respond.

Ask Audience Members to Repeat or Restate Questions When Necessary Sometimes you simply did not hear the full question. Other times an audience member asks a several-part question that needs to be broken down and clarified. Still other times, you may want to "buy a little more time" to reflect on your response before giving it. Asking the questioner to repeat or restate the question buys you those extra seconds.

Repeat or Paraphrase Each Audience Member's Question Before Responding This serves two major purposes. (1) The person who asked the question knows you heard exactly what he or she asked, and (2) you know your audience members have also heard the question.[10]

Keep Discussions on Track In addition to responding to questions and even asking the audience an occasional question, speakers are responsible for facilitating Q&A sessions. That means starting and finishing the sessions on time, as well as keeping discussions on track. Speakers need to intercede when they see the conversation is drifting too far off topic. How do you intercede tactfully and move the conversation back on track? Probably the single best approach is to wait until the person speaking comes up for a breath of air or ends one thought. At this juncture, jump in and politely compliment the speaker on his or her response. This leaves the speaker feeling good and not necessarily cut off. Then, immediately redirect the conversation back on track or ask if there are other questions.

Do Not Embarrass Anyone Most people do not like being embarrassed, especially in public. If they are, they will typically not say anything more or will get up and leave the Q&A session. Others in the audience may react similarly. They see they are at risk of having the speaker publicly humiliate them also.

Most speakers do not intentionally set out to humiliate audience members. However, it can occur unintentionally. For example, an audience member asks a question about something you spoke about at length during your presentation. You are surprised by the question and respond in an abrupt, condescending tone: "I believe I covered that topic thoroughly during my presentation!" Now, visualize the audience member sliding down in his or her seat, feeling humiliated and possibly even angry.

Do Not Get Defensive Snapping back and even arguing with audience members serves no useful purpose. You will get upset and likely discourage other audience members from asking questions. After all, they just saw you snap back at one of them, and they do not want to be on the receiving end of that behavior.

Control Difficult Audience Members The two types of difficult audience members most speakers least prefer to interact with during Q&A sessions are: (1) those who want to *dominate the conversation* and (2) those who *get aggressive* when asking questions and hearing the responses.

Those who dominate. It is likely you will have at least one person in your audience who, if allowed to do so, will dominate the conversation. This individual will ask far more questions and share far more responses than anyone else, if not controlled. Your job is to control him or her, thus allowing and encouraging others to get involved. The best thing to do is control these individuals before they control you. For example, at the start of the session tell the audience that due to time limitations each person can ask one question and then, if time allows, each can ask more. Or, at the start of the session ask audience members to raise their hand when they wish to ask a question or get in on a conversation. This way you can control who you call on and, in turn, how much each person is involved.

Those who get aggressive. As much as you may want to, you cannot ignore aggressive audience members. However, you can choose not to call on them frequently. If they are not controlled, they typically try to dominate the session. They are not only aggressive, they are typically aggressive dominators!

Your best bet is to try to calm them down. How? Practice good listening techniques. Maintain a pleasant facial expression. Maintain normal eye contact, instead of glaring at them. Use a courteous tone when speaking to them even though you would rather use a defensive or aggressive tone. Avoid raising your voice even though your aggressive audience member is probably doing so. Keep your responses to them brief, while complete. Finally, if the person continues to be a jerk, ignore him or her. Do not be intimidated by such a person. Simply do not acknowledge his or her presence in the room! Remind yourself that, as a speaker, it is your responsibility to maintain control.[11]

Conduct Effective Team Q&A Sessions If you just completed a team presentation, all members of your team should participate in the Q&A session. As a rule, all members should be prepared and willing to jump in to respond to all questions asked, not only those directed to him or her or those pertaining to his or her portion of the presentation. For example, each member should also be able and willing to speak up when an audience member directs a question at the entire team as opposed to an individual. The same holds true when he or she sees a teammate struggling with providing a clear and thorough response.

SUMMARY: SECTION 4— QUESTION-AND-ANSWER SESSIONS

- Control your apprehensions about Q&A sessions.
- Inform your audience of the time frame.
- Control smartphone and cell phone distractions.
- Relax and maintain a positive attitude.
- Take along a list of anticipated questions and responses.
- Anticipate being asked questions you will be unable to answer or to answer thoroughly.
- Be a good listener.
- Ask audience members to repeat or restate questions when necessary.
- Keep discussions on track.
- Be careful not to embarrass anyone.
- Do not get defensive.
- Control difficult audience members.
- Conduct effective team Q&A sessions.

EVALUATING YOUR PRESENTATIONS

If your goal is to either become or remain a good speaker, you must work at it continuously. Otherwise, your presentation skills and confidence will grow rusty. Working at speaking skills continuously is only part of what it takes. The other part involves identifying your strengths and weaknesses so you know what to work on. As the old saying goes, "You can't fix it unless you know it's broken." Good speakers understand the value of evaluating each presentation they give as a way of identifying and better understanding their strengths and weaknesses. While recognizing our presentation strengths brings each of us a sense of satisfaction and boosts our confidence, it is important that we also recognize and accept our shortcomings.

© Rawpixel.com/Shutterstock.com

Speakers use several approaches to evaluate their presentations. Keep in mind that the suggestions here also pertain to evaluating question-and-answer sessions, which should be viewed as a component of the presentation.

Evaluate Your Presentation Skills While Speaking You do not have to wait until a presentation ends to evaluate your efforts. Do so as you work your way through each talk. Awareness of speaking strengths boosts your confidence. Acknowledging weaknesses helps you avoid repeating them later in the presentation.

Ask a Friend or Colleague to Sit in on Your Presentations and Evaluate Them Provide this person with an evaluation form that will make his or her job easier and more thorough. Prior to your talk, brief your volunteer about your most consistent weaknesses so he or she can look for them. Shortly after the presentation, sit down with your friend or colleague and discuss his or her observations.

Ask a Friend or Colleague to Videotape Your Presentations Ask a friend or colleague to set up a video camera on a tripod in the back of the room and record your presentation and Q&A session. Shortly after the presentation, view the video alone and reflect on your observations. Or, view it with others and discuss your observations as you work your way through the video or after you watch it in its entirety. Whether you watch it alone or with others, use an evaluation form. If you view it with others, compare evaluations as a way to identify both consistent and inconsistent perceptions regarding your presentation strengths and weaknesses.

Ask Your Audiences to Evaluate Your Presentation Another way to identify your presentation strengths and weaknesses is to ask willing audience members to complete an anonymous evaluation form immediately following your presentation. The challenge is to develop an evaluation form that is short and easy to complete. Check-off items (questions) and those requiring numerical ratings or rankings work well. The first and fifth sample presentation evaluation forms presented at the URL in the side margin provide good options. Avoid asking general questions such as, "How was my presentation?" and "Were my visual aids helpful?" The evaluators are likely to leave such questions blank, respond in such general terms that you learn little of any value, or simply answer yes or no, which does little for you.

Sample Presentation Evaluation Templates http://www. sampletemplates.com/ business-templates/ presentation-evaluation. html

Sit Down Shortly After Each Presentation and Evaluate It You could conduct a self-evaluation shortly after each presentation. Find a quiet spot where you can sit down and relax. Once you are settled in, develop a written list of strengths and weaknesses while the presentation is still fresh in your mind. Like presentation videotapes and evaluation forms gathered through other evaluation approaches, your written list will be helpful when you plan and prepare for future talks.

Evaluate Your Presentation Skills While Watching Others Present You have an opportunity to evaluate your own skills each time you watch another person give a presentation. During and immediately after these presentations, contrast your own approach and skills with their performances. Every speaker exhibits some strengths and some weaknesses against which you can contrast your own. There is usually much to learn about our own skills by observing others.

In summary, what is important is that you conduct some form of evaluation of your presentations to help you grow your speaking skills and confidence so you can become an effective speaker. You will not use all of the above-mentioned approaches. None of us do. It is important; however, for you to choose one or more from the list and take charge of your presentation destiny!

Notes

1. Tim Hindle. *Making Presentations.* (New York, NY: DK Publishing, 1998), 47.

2. Ibid.

3. L. Todd Thomas. *Public Speaking Anxiety: How to Face the Fear.* (Fort Worth, TX: Harcourt Brace College Publishers, 1997), 29–30.

4. Mary Ellen Guffey. *Essentials of Business Communication*, 6th ed. (Mason, OH: Thomson/South-Western, 2004), 353.

5. Ibid.

6. James V. Connor. *Cuss Control: The Complete Book on How to Curb Your Cussing.* (New York, NY: iUniverse, 2006).

7. Carmine Gallo. "The Camera Doesn't Lie." *Business Week Online http://www. businessweek. com/stories/2007-01-03/the-camera-doesnt-liebusinessweek-business-news-stock-market-and-financial-advice.*

8. Andrew D. Wolvin, Roy M. Berko, and Darlyn R. Wolvin. *The Public Speaker/The Public Listener.* (Boston: Houghton Mifflin Company, 1993), 195.

9. Rich Sorenson, Grace DeBord, and Ida Ramirez, *Business and Management Communication*, 4th ed. (Upper Saddle River, NJ: Prentice Hall, 2001), 222.

10. Michael Osborn and Suzanne Osborn. *Public Speaking*, 3rd ed. (Boston: Houghton Mifflin), 354.

11. Hindle, 61.

USING VISUAL AIDS TO ENHANCE PRESENTATIONS

15

LEARNING OUTCOMES

After reading this chapter, you should be able to:

1. ⌐Understand the purpose of visual aids.

2. Understand how to prepare visual aids.

3. Demonstrate effective use of visual aids.⌐

© ESB Professional/Shutterstock.com

SELECT KEY TERMS

Pointers

USE VISUAL AIDS EFFECTIVELY

Audiences have come to expect visual aids in presentations. In a world of visual images (e.g., TV, Internet, movies, presentation software, video games), people have grown to expect visual aids in presentations.

Each visual aid should serve a purpose beyond meeting audience desires.[1] Presenting a point visually may be the clearest way to communicate it. Visuals also simplify large amounts of information or numbers. Other times, visual aids display comparisons (bar charts and pie charts) and show trends (line charts). Visual aids reinforce, emphasize, or clarify information. They are also used to preview and summarize presentations. Visual aids are integral presentation components, not afterthoughts tossed in for visual effect. Purposes such as these are introduced in Chapter 13, along with suggestions regarding colors, fonts, three-dimensional features, fill patterns, length, simplicity, and backups. Here are several recommendations for using visual aids.

Number Your Charts, Figures, Tables, Graphs, Diagrams, and Illustrations This comes in especially handy during the Q&A portion of your presentation. Numbering makes it easier for audience members to refer to specific visuals and for you to return to a specific visual, rather than wasting time trying to figure out which visual about financial aid, for example, the audience member is referencing.[2]

Make Sure Your Visual Aids are Visible If you follow the guidelines suggested in Chapter 13, this should not be an issue. However, ask your audience to tell you if there is a visibility problem. Some speakers try to cram too much information onto a single visual aid, which results in readability and clarity problems. Similar problems occur when speakers misjudge the color combinations they use in graphics and visual aid backgrounds. For example, using yellow text on a white background does not work. Neither the slide with too much text nor the slide with a poor color combination appears as if it would cause a readability problem for the audience when we look at it on our computer screens. However, such problems are noticeable on large screens.

Do not block your audience's view with your body, the podium, or the equipment. Project information higher on screens and stand to the side of screens, whiteboards, and flip charts.

Introduce Each Visual Aid Do this so your audience members know how that information fits into the presentation.

Explain Each Visual Aid Explain and discuss each visual aid. Do not merely display the visual aids and expect your audience members to figure them out on their own.

Display Visual Aids Long Enough Leave each visual aid up long enough so audience members can comprehend the content. Do not be in a rush to move onto the next visual aid. Be especially careful if you project several visuals through a computer and have them set on a timer whereby one disappears and the next appears automatically every few seconds. Having the technology available to do this is impressive; however, it takes a very skilled speaker to use it effectively.

Talk to Your Audience; Do Not Talk to Your Visual Aids Some speakers talk with their backs to their audiences while explaining visual aids. They literally talk to their screens, whiteboards, or flip charts. Stand to the side so your body is turned slightly sideways in the direction of the screen, whiteboard, or flip chart. Use a pointer to focus your audience's attention.

Paraphrase the Contents of Each Visual Aid Do not read the contents of each screen word for word. To do so is redundant and monotonous.

Focus Audiences' Attention on the Point You are Making You can use laser and extension **pointers**, fade-in and fade-out features on presentation software, and cover up information not being discussed on overhead transparencies. Figure 15-1 suggests several ways to use pointers properly.

© Andresr/Shutterstock.com

FIGURE 15–1: USING POINTERS EFFECTIVELY

- Extension pointers (radio antenna pointers) work well in settings where the screen is low, and the room and audience are small.
- Laser pointers and pointers built into presentation software work well in settings where the screen is high, and the room and audience are large.
- Presentation software features such as fading in and fading out serve the function of more traditional pointing devices.
- Laser pointers, while inexpensive and popular, require some practice and a steady hand. If used improperly, audience members are easily distracted by the somewhat erratic dot jumping around the screen.
- Be careful not to aim laser pointers at people's eyes and be careful to keep them away from children who would view them as toys. Lasers can injure eyes if pointed directly at them.
- If you give presentations in a variety of settings, purchase a combination extension/laser pointer. This lets you can adapt to any setting.

Remove Visual Aids after Discussing Them You do not want to distract your audience with old information after you have moved on to new information. Erase the previous information from the whiteboard, turn the flip chart page to a blank page, advance the PowerPoint to a blank slide, or turn off the overhead projector. You get the idea. It is easy to plan ahead for this.

Figure 15-2 contains a number of tips for presenting visual aids effectively.